In the Path of God

IN THE PATH
OF GOD

ISLAM AND
POLITICAL POWER

Daniel Pipes

Basic Books, Inc., Publishers

NEW YORK

The author gratefully acknowledges the National Committee to Honor the Fourteenth Centennial of Islam for the map (© 1980) on page 19; and Olivier Carré, Presses Universitaires de France for the map (© 1982) on page 20.

Library of Congress Cataloging in Publication Data

Pipes, Daniel, 1949–
  In the path of God.

  Includes bibliographical references and index.
  1. Islam and politics. 2. Islam—20th century.
3. Islamic countries—Relations—Europe. 4. Europe—
Relations—Islamic countries. I. Title.
BP173.7.P56 1983   297′.1977   83–70764
ISBN 0-465-03451-9

138885

To my parents, Irene and Richard

Contents

PART III
ISLAM IN CURRENT AFFAIRS

Acknowledgments

I HAVE many people to thank for their help. Margaret Sears suggested the idea for this book in November 1979. Arthur Waldron asked the questions that made me draw the connections between Islam and oil. Maureen Gallery and Daniel Brumberg helped research those connections. Michelle Wallace guided me through aspects of the Jewish law. Robert Kolson gave me the benefit of his critical reading. Paula Roberts provided fresh perspectives and fine editorial counsel. Joseph E. Fletcher, Jr., amended the sections I sent him for review. Duran Khalid, William H. McNeill, and John Obert Voll graciously read the entire manuscript in draft and offered helpful suggestions. Any mistakes that may remain, however, are my responsibility alone.

Of many stimulating discussions on the topic of Islam and politics, particularly helpful were those with Imtiaz Ahmed, Ahmad Hasan al-Baquri, Barbara Croken, Leila Fawaz, Ulrich Haarmann, Albert Hourani, Stephen Humphreys, the late Taha Hussein, Shah Murad Ilham, Halil İnalcık, Nikki Keddie, Martin Kramer, Nurcholis Madjid, Ross Monroe, Fazlur Rahman, Wilfred Cantwell Smith, Moshe Yegar, and Marvin Zonis.

The Department of History and the Division of the Social Sciences at the University of Chicago generously provided me with affiliation and the use of their facilities during the two years that I had a grant to write this book, October 1980–September 1982.

Several publishers have kindly permitted me to use materials that I wrote first in their pages: Praeger Publishers, publisher of *Islamic Resurgence in the Arab World* (New York, 1982, edited by Ali E. Hillal Dessouki); the National Strategy Information Center and Crane, Russak, publishers of *The Fulcrum of Power: The Third World Between Moscow and Washington* (New York, 1984, W. Scott Thompson and Andrew Walworth, principal authors); the Foreign Policy Research Institute, publisher of *Orbis: A Journal of World Affairs;* Falconwood Publications Limited, publisher of *8 Days: Middle East Business;* and the Dow Jones Company, publisher of the *Wall Street Journal.*

Acknowledgments

I use accepted spellings where these exist; where they do not, I render foreign words and names into English according to accepted scholarly methods. Diacritical marks, however, are omitted. For simplicity's sake, regions and countries are referred to by their current names, even where this is anachronistic. With few exceptions, references are supplied only for quotations.

D.P.
Chicago and Washington
April 1983

In the Path of God

Do battle in the path of God
against those who battle you.
—*The Qur'an*

Religion without power is only
philosophy.
—*Sir Muhammad Iqbal*

This world is political!
—*Imam Ruhollah Khomeini*

1

Understanding Islam in Politics

Much of the conventional wisdom
about Islam and politics needs to be
examined with skepticism.
—*Michael C. Hudson*

EVENTS in recent years have made clear the extraordinary role of Islam in world politics. As fundamentalist Muslims took power and achieved international importance in such states as Pakistan and Iran, understanding Islam became necessary to interpret their goals and ideology. Islam also gave direction to governments in Saudi Arabia and Libya, influenced electoral politics in democracies such as Turkey, India, Malaysia, and Indonesia, and posed important challenges to Communist regimes in Yugoslavia and Afghanistan. Islam heightened domestic tensions in Nigeria, the Sudan, Egypt, Syria, Iraq, and Burma, and it defined rebellions against the central government in Chad, Ethiopia, Cyprus, Lebanon, Thailand, and the Philippines. It fueled international conflicts between Turks and Greeks, Arabs and Israelis, Pakistanis and Indians, and Somalis and Ethiopians. In the Arab-Israeli dispute, for example, Islam helped account for the nature of Arab resistance to Israel's existence, the intense involvement of such distant countries as Iraq and Libya, and the meaning of the call in the Palestine National Covenant for the establishment of a "secular and democratic" state in Palestine.

There has been an increasing need to understand the political impact of Islam. Proposals for solving the Arab-Israeli conflict must consider the special Islamic concern for the control of territory. American or Soviet negotiators

3

seeking military bases in the Middle East must take into account vehement Islamic sensibilities against the presence of non-Muslim troops. NATO strategists must keep abreast of Islamic sentiments among Turkey's population if they want to gauge the likelihood of the alliance's southeast flank holding firm. As Muslims of the Soviet Union increase in number and grow out of their isolation, the Islamic drive for self-rule will probably shape their aspirations; in all likelihood, they will use religious institutions to organize against the regime and they will look to foreign Muslims for support. Even business interests need to watch Islam, for many key oil-exporting states entertain "powerful sentiments of grievance and resentment against the Christian West"[1] which could seriously upset the oil market in coming years.

How Muslims feel and act has enormous international repercussions: they number about 832 million strong and make up roughly one-fifth of mankind; substantial groups of Muslims live in ninety-one countries and in them constitute a population of about 3.6 billion. Muslims control most of the oil available for export and they inhabit many of the globe's most strategic areas. Yet the question of Islam in politics has been given little serious thought until recently and remains a largely obscure topic in the Western world. In my view, this is not so much because of the subject matter's complexity but because of the many blinders that obstruct the vision of observers. For Westerners, the main problems have to do primarily with an historic animosity toward Islam and a disinclination to acknowledge the political force of religion. In the hope of clearing up some of these problems, this initial chapter discusses some obstacles that face a Westerner interested in understanding Islam and politics.

Impediments to a Westerner's Understanding

RECOGNIZING RELIGION'S IMPACT ON POLITICS

For Westerners of the late twentieth century the notion that Islam—or any religion—acts as an autonomous political force may be a somewhat novel thesis. The influence of religion in the West has diminished so much during the past five hundred years that many persons, especially intellectuals, find it difficult to appreciate the political import of religion in other times and places. Developments such as the Iranian Revolution, the central role of the Catholic church in Poland, and the rise of fundamentalist pressure groups in the United States provoke much discussion, but the deeper, ongoing influence of religion tends to be ignored. Three obstacles are especially important in this: secularism, materialism, and modernization theory.

Secularization is a "process whereby religious thinking, practice and institutions lose social significance" and are increasingly restricted to the domain of private faith.[2] Since the early Renaissance the West has experienced a steady contraction of religion away from politics, ethics, education, and the arts; this process has gone so far that faith retains hardly any importance in the lives of many people. But secularization has not been universal, for some people in the West and many in other regions of the world, especially Muslims, are still deeply swayed by religious concerns. Secularized observers often disbelieve that the faith that they disdain can retain such force. For someone who views religion as a sign of ignorance and backwardness, the passions it arouses can be baffling. "To the modern Western mind, it is not conceivable that men would fight and die . . . over mere differences in religion; there have to be some other 'genuine' reasons underneath the religious veil."[3] For someone whose daily life is not touched by faith, understanding the power of religion in politics is difficult and requires an open mind and a willingness to see things from a different vantage point. There is a tendency to discount the power of religion. Khomeini's rise to power is viewed as a result of economic discontent, of social tensions, political disenfranchisement, repression, charismatic leadership —anything but the fact that millions of Iranians believed this man could create a new order which, in fulfilling God's commands, would solve Iran's problems. More generally, "many commentators . . . believe that present Islamic activism is primarily nationalist or socialist or economically motivated movements dressed in the garb of religion." Yet, "to ignore religious desires and to concentrate only on the economic drives or secularized political motives is to limit unnecessarily the scope of our understanding."[4]

The philosophical doctrine of materialism impedes comprehension of religion in politics even more than secularism. This doctrine originated in the nineteenth century, when European intellectuals, expressing unlimited confidence in rationality and science, formulated elaborate theories to demonstrate how predictably mankind responds to its environment. One of these theories was Karl Marx's historical materialism which emphasized the importance of changes in economic conditions. According to Marx, the system of labor (slave, serf, capitalist, or socialist) determines all other aspects of society, including its politics, social relations, and culture. Neo-Marxists later modified this theory to allow more flexibility, but Marxist thought continues to emphasize the role of economic relations, while discounting the importance of ideas (scornfully dismissed as "ideology"). Individuals may believe they are motivated by ideals—patriotism, religious fervor, justice, and humanitarianism—but materialists invariably discern hidden economic motives. They believe that a calculus of cost and benefit, often unconscious, determines most actions. For example, abolitionists in the United States thought they were motivated by morality to fight the slave trade, but the materialists would argue that slavery hurt their economic interests. So, too, material concerns spurred American rebels in 1776, French revolutionaries in 1789, and Nazi supporters in the 1930s.

The trouble with this is that the theory of materialism reduces humans to one-dimensional beings, and the truth is not so simple. Economic factors indisputably have a major role (and they had been quite neglected before Marx), but they do not singly determine behavior. One cannot ignore the wide range of emotions that are not tied to material self-interest: loyalties to family, tribe, ethnic group, language group, neighbors, nation, race, class, or religion sometimes overlap with material interests and sometimes run contrary to them. Material factors alone fail to account for the actions of a George III or a Hitler. They cannot explain the endurance of Communist rule so long after its economic deficiencies have become manifest. Nor can they explain why Japan, an island almost barren of natural resources, is so much better off than mineral-rich Zaire. Much less do material factors show why so many people willingly give up their lives for political causes they believe in.

Similar problems arise when economic motives are assigned to actions taken in the name of religion. Materialists dismiss faith as a camouflage for self-interested drives, and they consider it naïve to accept religious impulses at face value. But how do material interests explain the wars of the Reformation that split communities and made family members into one another's enemies? What possible gains could the early Mormons have expected as they left their homes and trekked to Utah? Though the Crusades, the long conflict in Ireland, and the recent proliferation of religious sects in South Korea all had economic dimensions, it is surely mistaken to view them primarily as economic phenomena. The Crusades, for example, were far more than an imaginative method of making work for the unemployed or a way to gain new markets; material factors alone could never have inspired such enormous undertakings, with such risks. And how would material factors explain the suicide massacre at the People's Temple in Guyana?

Islam too must be understood as a potent force. Popular views in the West ascribe almost everything Islamic to "fanaticism," as though this were an independent cause,[5] but serious discussions usually discount the role of Islam in favor of material factors. For example, a collection of essays, published in 1978 under the title *Muslim-Christian Conflicts: Economic, Political and Social Origins,*[6] covers five countries (Lebanon, Egypt, the Sudan, Yugoslavia, and Cyprus), but not once in 245 pages do the authors ascribe clashes between Christians and Muslims to emotions arising from religious allegiance! As the book's subtitle indicates, they interpret every conflict as a symptom of material griev-ances. But how would such grievances explain, for instance, what happened during one week in May 1982 in Lebanon: the explosion of a car bomb outside a mosque under construction, injuring four persons; the bombing of a West Beirut mosque near the house of a former Muslim prime minister; the assassi-nation of a senior Islamic figure; the killing of a Maronite priest; and the sui-cide mission conducted in a Maronite church in Tripoli, killing three and injur-ing five? Whatever the economic relations between Muslims and Christians, these acts could have been inspired only by religious sentiments; similar exam-ples can be found in all the other conflicts too. The mere fact of adherence to Islam has profound political consequences. If one-quarter of India's people had not converted to Islam, the subcontinent would not have been split as it was; further, the millions of Muslims who abandoned their homes in India to move to Pakistan neither expected nor received material benefits for this transfer. Islam, like other religions, inspires impractical acts which cannot be ascribed to economic self-interest.

Modernization theory, an explanation of how nations develop, was articu-lated in the two decades following World War II, during a unique period of prosperity and self-confidence in the West, when science seemed invincible and progress irresistible. Modernization theory postulates that all nations must fol-low the lines laid down by the first countries to become modern, especially Britain and the United States. In the political sphere, this means rationaliza-tion, the civic society, and secularization. Religion is seen as an obstacle to modernization and its hold is expected to weaken as nations advance.

These ideas were already discredited before 1979, but the Iranian Revolu-tion delivered a final blow. Modernization theorists could not account for the emergence of Ayatollah Ruhollah Khomeini as the Iranians' leader against the shah, whose revolt represented the first major political movement *away* from Western political ideals in the twentieth century. Until Khomeini, the leaders of all great social upheavals in modern times espoused objectives deriv-ing at least in part from European thought, whether liberal, Marxist, fascist, or other. Prominent non-Western leaders such as Kemal Atatürk, Gamal Abdul Nasser, Ahmed Ben Bella, Kwame Nkruma, Robert Mugabe, Ma-hatma Gandhi, Pol Pot, Ho Chi Minh, Mao Tse-tung, Sukarno, and Fidel Cas-tro espoused goals familiar to the West, notwithstanding their local flavor. They conceived of all aspects of public affairs—sovereignty, economics, justice, welfare, and culture—in ways that could be traced to European origins, and this encouraged many observers to assume that peoples everywhere in the world must emulate the West politically.

But Khomeini was different. Although unconsciously influenced by Western notions, he rejected them; his lack of interest in the West was symbolized by his spending four months in the tiny village of Neauphle-le-Chateau and never visiting Paris, a mere twenty miles away. Khomeini's goals existed entirely within an Islamic context; further, he had no Western constituency and was indifferent to his image in Stockholm or Berkeley. Satisfied to live as his ancestors had, unfamiliar with the Western concepts of progress, he wished for nothing more than to return to the Islamic ways he supposed had once prevailed in Iran. Khomeini showed that the force of religion need not wane with the building of an industrial society, that secularism need not accompany modernization. Yet the discrediting of modernization theory did not signal its disappearance; the notion that religion is on the way out has been so widely disseminated that it may take decades before it loses force. Perhaps the time has come to suggest that secularization is a transient process peculiar to the West; not only will it not affect the rest of the world, but it is likely to be reversed even in the Occident: "An historian of the non-Western world can hardly fail to see Western secularism as a sub-facet of specifically Christian history; indeed, of specifically Western Christian history."[7]

Together, secularization, materialism, and modernization theory cause the press and scholarship too often to ignore Islam's role in politics. In recent times, Islam came to the attention of Western analysts in the mid-1950s, as the Soviet Union, threatening Western interests, built up links to Abdul Nasser's government in Egypt and other countries of the Middle East. In response, European and American writers debated the relationship of Islam to communism. One school of thought saw Islam as a "bulwark against communism," on the grounds that its emphatic monotheism precluded Muslims from accepting any ideology based on atheism; the other (and more subtle) view was that structural similarities made the transition from Islam to communism an easy one. As fears that the Middle East would accept Marxism-Leninism abated, however, interest in Islam among political observers subsided, and nationalism became the focus of attention. Discussion of Islam as a political factor then went into dormancy for about twenty years. Views expressed in a 1965 book, *Islam and International Relations,* summed up the attitudes of those times. One writer, Fayez A. Sayegh, stated that "at least with respect to 'neutralism,' . . . Islam has had little, if any noticeable influence upon the reasoning, planning, decision-making, or expression of Muslim policy makers." The volume's editor noted that most of the authors "maintained that Islam is actually of quite limited significance in shaping the attitudes and behavior of Muslim states in international relations today."[8] For years, politics in Muslim countries was discussed almost without reference to Islam.

Attention to Islam increased after the 1967 Arab-Israeli war, and even more after the 1973 conflict. In 1976, Bernard Lewis urged in "The Return of Islam" that more attention be paid to the phenomenon of Islam, criticizing "the present inability, political, journalistic, and scholarly alike, to recognize the importance of the factor of religion in the current affairs of the Muslim world."[9] Westerners were increasingly receptive to the role of Islam by the time Khomeini appeared. As he gained power, the Western world watched with amazement; Islam seemed capable of unleashing the most extraordinary forces. Then, overreacting to events in Iran, many in the Occident suddenly thought Islam capable of anything; "in a remarkably brief span of time, Islam has been elevated from a negligible coincidence of human geography, to a political force of global import."[10] Indeed, interest in Islam became excessive, leading one journalist to complain in 1981 that "where before Islam was largely ignored, now it is seen everywhere, even where it has no particular relevance."[11] The war between Iraq and Iran which broke out in September 1980 was almost universally understood in terms of Shi'i-Sunni* differences and the threat of Shi'i revolt in Iraq, though the cause of fighting had much more to do with a straightforward dispute over territory.[12]

But if Islam received too much attention in Iran, it remained underestimated elsewhere. In May 1981, the press portrayed disturbances in the Yugoslav province of Kosovo in purely nationalist terms, as Albanians versus Serbs, and stressed the Albanians' economic plight, without making any mention of the underlying Muslim-Christian tension. In other cases, the impulse toward materialistic interpretations prevailed: increased emphasis on religious law in Pakistan was portrayed as a function of economic travails, and the upsurge of the Muslim Brethren in Egypt was seen as a symptom of poverty.[13] Economic factors did have great importance—I shall argue that changes in the oil market accounted for much of Islam's new force—but they fitted within a cultural context molded by religion. Were Iranians Buddhist, a religious leader would not have vanquished the shah; were Lebanon entirely Christian, the civil war would not have occurred; were Israel Muslim, its neighbors would have accepted its establishment.[14]

Western discussions of the Islamic revival of the 1970s consistently de-emphasized the importance of religious feelings; indeed, some analysts even disputed the significance of Islam in the Iranian Revolution.[15] Others denigrated the role of Islam more generally. In 1977, Michael C. Hudson referred to "the growing irrelevance of Islamic standards and criteria" to Arab politics.[16] Two studies of Islam and politics which appeared in 1982 made even more sweeping and more surprising statements. Thomas W. Lippman asserts that "religion as such had nothing to do, for example with Somalia's decision to end its partnership with the Soviet Union" or the Libyan invasion of Chad,

---

*The turned comma in the word Shi'i is the Arabic consonant 'ayn, a voiced pharyngeal fricative. Although unrelated to any sound in Indo-European languages, it is integral to Arabic and is retained throughout this book.

or Arab opposition to the Baghdad Pact, and so forth; Edward Mortimer concludes a book on "the politics of Islam" with the observation that "it is more useful, in politics at any rate, to think about Muslims than to think about Islam."[17] (Why then, one wonders, did he write a book about Islam?)

FALSE PARALLELS WITH CHRISTIANITY

Approaching Islam in politics with the Christian experience in mind is misleading. Because the community of Christians shares almost no political traits, there is a mistaken predisposition to assume that Muslims also do not.

Superficially, there is much in common between the two faiths. Just as devout Christians disagree on their proper role in public life, so do observant Muslims. At one extreme, medieval popes and Imam Khomeini* claimed supreme political authority for the religious leaders; at the other, some Protestant sects and Sufi (mystical) orders encouraged their adherents to total political quiescence. The role of Christianity varied enormously in the Roman Empire, medieval Scandinavia, fifteenth-century Ethiopia, Calvinist Geneva, Spanish Mexico, Mormon Utah, and Soviet Russia; so too did Islam in Muhammad's Medina, Abbasid Baghdad, Almoravid Spain, Mongol Iran, Mataram Java, the Murids' Senegal, the Turkish Republic, and Saudi Arabia.

Catholic, Orthodox, and Protestant Christians spanned the entire ideological spectrum, advocating every form of political authority and economic system, working toward mutually exclusive goals—all in the name of the same religion. The Catholic church served as a bulwark against communism in Poland, yet priests led leftist causes in South America. New Protestant movements in South Korea and the United States were identified with conservative causes, while the Zimbabwean clergy had a key role in rebelling against White rule in their country. It is difficult to imagine what a book on "Christianity and political power" could say that would apply to Christians generally; any search for common themes would surely fail.

"Islam and political power" might appear to have as little validity, for pious Muslims had political objectives as diverse as those of their Christian counterparts. In recent years, the three most prominent and self-conscious Islamic states were neatly spread across the political spectrum, Saudi Arabia being aligned with the United States, Libya with the Soviet Union, and Iran rejecting ties to either super-power for as long as it could. Some Islamic movements opposed pro-Western governments (as in Egypt and Turkey) and others conflicted with Soviet-backed regimes (as in Syria and Afghanistan). In the Sudan,

---

*I use the title "imam" rather than "ayatollah" because this was the accepted title for Khomeini after his return to Iran in February 1979.

10

Islamic sentiment favored greater state control, in Thailand it inspired a revolt against the central government. Islam had a populist quality in Tunisia but served as an instrument of state in Pakistan. Identification with the religion indicated defiance of the regime in the USSR and solidarity with it in Malaysia. Islam stood behind conservatism and revolution, peace and war, tolerance and bigotry; how does Islam and politics lend itself better to generalizations than Christianity and politics?

The answer is that Islam, unlike Christianity, contains a complete program for ordering society. Whereas Christianity provides grand moral instructions but leaves practical details to the discretion of each community, Islam specifies exact goals for all Muslims to follow as well as the rules by which to enforce them. If Christians eager to act on behalf of their faith have no script for political action, Muslims have one so detailed, so nuanced, it requires a lifetime of study to master. Along with faith in Allah comes a sacred law to guide Muslims in all times and places. That law, called the Shari'a, establishes the context for Islam as a political force. However diverse Muslim public life may be, it always takes place in the framework of Shar'i ideals. Adjusting realities to the Shari'a is the key to Islam's role in human relations. Hence, this analysis emphasizes the role of sacred law, the motor force of Islam in politics.

Emphasis on the law implies slight treatment of other aspects of Islam. In general, what does not touch on the Shari'a receives little attention here. Topics nearly omitted include: (1) Theology. Whatever its spiritual significance, theology has little bearing on public life. To the extent that disputes about the nature of God, faith, the Qur'an, and the day of judgment do affect politics, it is through their impact on the Shari'a. (2) Sufism. The mystical orientation of Sufi groups often implies a lack of interest in details of the law or in public affairs; those Sufis who do become engaged in politics have concerns which fit into the same Shar'i context as everyone else. (3) Differences in sect and *madhhab*. Mainstream Muslims (that is, Muslims whose faith is acknowledged as valid by a majority of other Muslims) follow legal tenets so similar to each other that their differences can be ignored. Practices of the Sunni, Shi'i, and Khariji sects do vary, but only in minor ways; for example, Shi'i laws differ most dramatically from those of the Sunnis in that they permit temporary marriage. Sunni Islam contains four *madhhab*s, or rites of law, whose rulings differ enough to affect crucially a defendant in a courtroom but not so much as to concern us. (4) Fringe groups. Such non-mainstream groups as the Assassins, Druze, 'Alawis, Ahl-i Haqq, Baha'is, and Ahmadis venture far from the Shari'a, and in doing so they step beyond the pale of Islam. Small in numbers and eccentric of doctrine, these minor sects will not be covered here. (5) Intellectual discourse. Thinkers affect Islam's role in politics only to the extent that they deal with the Shari'a. Philosophical, historical, and moral discussions are ignored here except where they touch on the problems of living in accordance with the sacred law. (6) Personal faith. Islam in politics concerns the implementation of laws more than individual faith. A believer is more likely to try to live by Islamic precepts, but not always. Non-Muslims or Marxists from a Muslim background occasionally find it useful to apply some of the Islamic laws (this happened in the European colonies and in Soviet-dominated Afghanistan), while devout believers who are mystics or secularists may resist implementing the Shari'a.

ISLAM AS AN IDENTITY

There are other sources of confusion between religion as a personal faith and as a factor in social relations. The topic in this book is Islam as a source of laws, affiliations, customs, attitudes, and traditions, with an emphasis on its influence over behavior in the public sphere. In contrast, the faith of the individual Muslim will not be discussed at length; this is in part because, from a political viewpoint, it eludes analysis, and in part because it usually has little direct bearing on matters of power. Private feelings need not be related to political actions.

Examples may help to demonstrate this point. Muhammad Ali Jinnah, the founder of Pakistan, and most of his strongest supporters were Western-educated and not notably pious Muslims, yet it was they who fought to establish a state defined along religious lines. In contrast, the Islamic leaders opposed the creation of Pakistan and preferred to remain citizens of India. (This parallels the Israeli case: Zionism appealed mostly to assimilated Jews.) By all accounts, Muhammad Anwar as-Sadat was a pious man, yet he strenuously resisted the efforts of Islamic fundamentalists in Egypt, he made the country's family law more European, and he was assassinated by Islamic extremists. In contrast, some of the leaders of the Iranian Revolution, notably Abolhassan Bani-Sadr, were suspected of indifference to the Almighty; this did not prevent them, however, from taking an active part in the most rigorous re-assertion of political Islam in the twentieth century. Throughout the 1970s, as Mu'ammar al-Qadhdhafi developed his own ideology and moved further away from Islam, he placed increased emphasis on Islam as a political bond and identity. In secularizing societies, the notion of a "non-believing Muslim" is widespread; in the Soviet Union, for example, Communists of Muslim origin routinely avow that while they are atheists, they are also Muslims and proud to be so. Perhaps the sharpest distinction comes from Lebanon: a driver, the story goes, was stopped at a checkpoint sometime during the civil war and asked to tell his religion. "Atheist," came the answer. But in the midst of a war fought along religious lines, the guard needed to know the driver's confessional affiliation, not his personal beliefs, so he asked, "Are you a Christian atheist or a Muslim atheist?"

MUSLIM AND CHRISTIAN RELATIONS

Iranian occupation of the United States Embassy in Tehran in November 1979 did more than prompt a diplomatic crisis between two governments; it also unleashed a flood of passions among Iranians and Americans. Iranians took to the streets by the thousands to blame America for every conceivable ill in Iranian life, "from assassinations and ethnic unrest to traffic jams [and] drug addiction."[18] Imam Khomeini called America the "Great Satan," vilified its culture, and insulted its leaders. Americans responded with uncommon rancor, harassing Iranian students and painting Khomeini's dour features on dart boards and toilet bowls. Iranians provoked more American venom than any other foreign people since World War II; Koreans and Vietnamese, for example, never inspired a fraction of this abuse. The passions on both sides hinted at something more than the usual political difference; they suggested the pinching of a nerve.

Previous tensions between Iran and the United States could hardly explain this outpouring of feeling, for the two states had enjoyed consistently good relations from W. Morgan Shuster's trusty service as Iran's financial advisor in 1911 to Jimmy Carter's exuberant New Year's Eve toast to the shah in 1977, when he described Iran as "an island of stability in one of the more troubled areas of the world" and termed this achievement "a great tribute to you, Your Majesty, and to your leadership and to the respect, admiration and love which your people give to you."[19] The two governments enjoyed a broad cooperation, especially in the two vital areas of oil production and staving off the Soviet Union. Tens of thousands of Iranians studied in the United States and similar numbers of American technicians worked in Iran without arousing special problems.

If previous relations between Iranians and Americans cannot account for the strength of feeling in 1979, the explanation lies further back, in the long history of hostility between Muslims and Christians. Details follow in chapter 4; suffice it here to note that since A.D. 634, when, only two years after the death of Muhammad, Arabians and Byzantines first went to battle, Muslims and Christians have experienced a uniquely bellicose relationship. Arabians, Turks, Moors, Moros, and Somalis earlier filled the role now taken by the Iranians, while Greeks, Spaniards, Franks, Russians, and Ethiopians had the American part. Even today, Muslims and Christians carry on the long tradition of conflict in such places as Chad, the Sudan, Uganda, Cyprus, Lebanon, and the Philippines. As a diplomat recently observed in reference to the Muslim-Christian rivalry in the Malaysian province of Sabah: "What is happening in Sabah today is only a small reflection of what happened in the Crusades 1,000 years ago."[20]

This hostile legacy still lives, influencing Muslim and Occidental perceptions of each other. On the Muslim side, resentment and envy of the West have seriously impaired attempts to come to terms with the modern world. On the Christian side, biases inherited from medieval times concerning the corruption of the Islamic faith, the licentiousness and violence of its adherents, and the fanaticism of its appeal continue still to shape attitudes. "People who melt at the plight of Asians and Africans are unaffected by that of Arabs and Moslems."[21] Of course, any attempt to see Islam and the Muslims as they really are requires that these prejudices be recognized and set aside. Common images of fatalism, fundamentalism, and fanaticism are simplistic and mean; they do injustice to a full and rich faith which satisfies the spiritual and emotional needs of hundreds of millions of adherents. The old biases are false and gratuitous.

If uncritical hostility has been the historic obstacle to understanding Islam, a new tendency toward uncritical adulation is almost equally unhelpful. In recent years, Islam has won the self-serving support of two types of Westerners. The first group uses it as a vehicle to attack its own society; for people who feel ill at ease in the West, embracing Islam serves as a way to change allegiance and to reject the world they grew up in. Conversion to Islam by the British foreign service officer Harry St. John Philby[22] or the American boxer Cassius Clay symbolized a radical rejection of Western ways precisely because Islam is so widely considered antithetical to the West. Although few go so far as to convert, other people—Jews, anti-Semites, and disaffected intellectuals especially—take up Islamic causes as a way to express their own discontent. Radicals such as Voltaire, Napoleon, and Marx, all known for their antagonism toward religion, had a soft spot for Islam, precisely because it stood for the negation of religion as practiced in the West.

The second group of apologists, more recent but far more influential today, promotes Islam for profit. Praise for Islam and the Muslims often translates into better access to research materials for professors, funds for administrators, visas for journalists, votes at the United Nations for diplomats, and trade opportunities for businessmen. Incentives for Islamphilia have multiplied many times with the coming of the oil boom and the huge increase in disposable income available to some Muslims.

With the exception of the Black Muslim movements in the United States, pro-Islamic sentiments tend to be restricted to the elite in the West, for it is they alone who have enough contact with Islam to become familiar with it or gain from it. Sufi disciples come from the ranks of the affluent no less than do the sponsors of the National Committee to Honor the Fourteenth Centennial of Islam, an American group organized in the late 1970s to promote goodwill toward Islam and funded primarily by businesses with interests in the Arab oil-exporting states. Thus, a dichotomy results: while a few Westerners at the top praise Islam for personal reasons (be it alienation or profit), the masses, still swayed by the old hostility, despise and fear Islam.

IDEAL AND REALITY

Islam calls forth intense reactions. It inspires a powerful loyalty among Muslims which no other faith can rival. Muslims almost never apostacize and they feel particularly strong bonds to their fellow believers. At the same time, Islam provokes an unparalleled animosity from non-believers, thanks to its reputation as an aggressive faith. These contrary opinions of Islam are roughly equal in scope; just as Muslim solidarity has a strong emotional appeal from Morocco to Java, so too does a suspicious, even hostile, reaction prevail among non-Muslims from Spain to Bali.

Accordingly, polarized attitudes dominate almost every discussion of Islam as a social and political force. Muslims and those sympathetic to Islam emphasize the idealism of the faith, while its detractors concentrate on the failings of Muslims. "There is a tendency . . . for believing Muslims to use the term [Islam] as an ideal, and for outside observers to use it [to mean] an historical-sociological actuality."[23] Believers speak of Islam's concern with justice, its high moral and political standards, and its cultivation of learning; opponents respond by noting the corruption, political instability, and illiteracy in Muslim countries. Muslims see their society as spiritually superior to the materialistic West; critics call this an excuse for continued poverty. Supporters recall Islam's medieval splendor, denigrators point to its contemporary woes. What Muslims call communal solidarity, foes call facelessness; warm relations for one appear as a lack of privacy for the other. Muslims decry open sexuality in the West and claim that the veil protects the honor of women; for outsiders, Islamic mores are hypocritical, the veil demeans females, and honor merely justifies the double standard for men and women. Promiscuity appalls Muslims, polygamy scandalizes Westerners.

But it is Islam's attitudes toward non-Muslims that provoke the most arguments: Muslims proudly point to their record of tolerance and contrast it with the attacks on their lands by the Crusaders, modern European imperialists, and Zionists. Islam's critics emphasize the lack of equal rights for

15

non-Muslims under Muslim rule and the persecution, insecurity, and humiliation they must endure. They claim also that the Muslim conquests in the Middle East, Europe, Africa, and India were as aggressive as those of the West.

But these polemics do not elucidate the impact of Islam. When one side selects the most attractive ideals of a religion, and when the other chooses only the worst aspects of its history, a disengaged observer lacks balanced information to reach his own conclusion. A lack of non-partisanship severely impedes intelligent discourse about Islam in politics.

A related problem concerns the tendency of Westerners to take Islamic ideals at face value. While those ideals do profoundly influence Muslims—which is a premise underlying this study—conclusions cannot be drawn directly from them to explain political patterns. For example, one might take the Muslim record in war, and the Western tendency to invoke Islam to explain both success and failure. When Muslims do well, it is explained by their belief that houris in heaven will reward them eternally for death in battle against infidels. This explanation, first heard in early medieval times, still surfaces; as recently as 20 July 1980, a *New York Times* correspondent wrote that the Afghan insurgents do so well against the Soviet Union because they believe that "dying in the name of Islam is a glorious death, one that will insure their place in paradise." When Muslims lose, Islam can be used to explain that too: the Qur'an imbues the Arabs with a love of words, they get caught up in the mists of their own rhetoric, and so their military efforts against Israel are undermined. Thus does Islam spur fanatical resistance in one place and inefficacy in another. Islam is called on to explain other opposites too—fatalism in Malaysia and endemic instability in Syria. Such simplistic characterizations should be discarded.

The real force of Islam in politics lies not in the sparse injunctions of the Qur'an or in the hypothetical unity between religion and politics, but in the complex interaction between Islam's ideals, Muslim historical experience, Western civilization, and current events. To understand these, it is necessary to know something about Islamic law and Muslim history, not just in recent times nor exclusively in the Middle East, but also in previous eras and other regions. In particular, the importance of looking outside the Middle East needs emphasis.

CONCENTRATION ON THE MIDDLE EAST

"Islam" so vividly conjures up the Middle East that the 612 million Muslims living outside the Middle East receive far less attention than the 220 million within it.[24] Mention of Islam brings to mind Arabs, Persians, and Turks, deserts and camels, baklava and strong coffee, men in flowing robes and veiled women—not Fulanis, Bosnians, and Malays, nor the lush plains of Bangladesh, the gruels of Mali, or the sarongs of Indonesia. Muslims receive attention in rough proportion to their proximity to the eastern Mediterranean. Thus is it easy to miss many facts: that Indonesia has the largest Muslim population of any country; that the Indian subcontinent has more Muslims than does the entire Middle East; that more Muslims are citizens of the Soviet Union than of any Middle Eastern country save Turkey; and that China has a larger Muslim population than the entire Arabian peninsula. Perhaps most surprising, six of the nine countries with the largest Muslim populations are outside the Middle East (Indonesia, Pakistan, Bangladesh, India, the Soviet Union, and Nigeria).

Several reasons account for the prominence of the Middle East. First, it has a special importance and visibility in Islam, being the region where the religion was born, developed, and elaborated; now, as in the past, nearly all the key events take place there. As the core of Muslim life, the Middle East is the location of the most important sites of Islamic pilgrimages (Mecca and Medina as well as others in Israel and Iraq), the key educational institutions (such as Al-Azhar University in Cairo), publishing houses dealing with Islamic topics (Cairo first, followed by Beirut), and leading Islamic movements (the Muslim Brethren, reformist thought, the Iranian Revolution). Arabic and Persian, the two international languages of Islam, are read, spoken, and cherished wherever Muslims live. Languages spoken by Muslims outside the Middle East are unknown inside it, their thinkers unheard of, their political movements without general impact. For these reasons, Muslims in the remoter regions look to the Middle East for spiritual direction, and this situation is seldom reversed. A Syrian would as soon look to Yugoslavia or Indonesia for guidance in Islam as a Frenchman would look to Latvia or New Zealand to learn about European philosophy.

Second, the Middle East is the Muslim area most in contact with Europe. This made it the focal point of Western concern throughout history and the region at the forefront of the Muslim response to modern Europe. Other factors making the Middle East prominent include its location in the heart of the eastern hemisphere (increasing its cultural centrality), the antiquity of its civilization, the presence of Israel, and the oil boom.

Outside the Middle East, only Pakistan can aspire to a role of international importance in an Islamic context, yet even its claim is relatively weak. Pakistan has a very large Muslim population, a sophisticated culture, and strong lines of fundamentalist and reformist thought. It underwent the unique experience of coming into existence as an Islamic state (through the partition from India in 1947). But Pakistanis use primarily Urdu and English, neither of which is widely known by men of religion in the Middle East, so their works remain largely unknown in the core area. Language, however, is not the main obstacle: such writers as Abul Ala Maududi and Abul Hasan Nadwi published in Arabic too, yet even they could not win an influence on Muslims as great as that of Middle Easterners.

The prominence of the Middle East means that most studies of Islam stay within this small portion of the Muslim world and do not touch the full range of Muslim life. Focusing exclusively on the Middle East, however, misses the richness of Muslim experience and the complete picture of Islam's influence. One may legitimately study the Muslims of only the Middle East (or any other region) but it is improper to portray this as a study of Islam in general or as valid for Muslims everywhere, which is so often done. The Muslims of the Middle East are not typical: they have fewer non-Islamic cultural elements to contend with and they fall most thoroughly under the influence of Islam's civilization. No doubt the Middle East is the key Muslim region, but it is far from the only one. Hausas in West Africa are no less inspired than Kurds in Iraq by Islamic goals, and Malays are part of Islamic history as much as Yemenis; an assessment of Islam in politics (or Sufism or the arts) requires that the gamut of Muslim peoples be taken into account.

Muslims live in places rarely associated with Islam. One European country, Albania, has a majority Muslim population, and significant minorities live in Yugoslavia and Bulgaria. Ethiopia, famous as the Christian enclave in Africa, is nearly half Muslim, as is Nigeria. Fiji in the mid-Pacific has an 8 percent Muslim element, and three nations of the Caribbean basin, Trinidad and Tobago, Guyana, and Surinam, have Muslim minorities of, respectively, 6, 9, and 20 percent. Sizeable Muslim communities exist as far north as the Volga River and as far south as South Africa. In the past generation, Islam has acquired a formidable new presence in countries such as the United States, Britain, France, Germany, and South Korea.

POOR TERMINOLOGY

The study of Islam is complicated by confused and imprecise terms. A brief discussion of usages here may help to reduce these ambiguities.[25]

"Islam" is the faith in one God and in the Qur'an as the literal word of God. A "Muslim" is one who accepts the Islamic faith. These terms derive from the Arabic, closely reproducing its pronunciation, and are acceptable to everyone. "Moslem" and "Mussalman" are older pronunciations of Muslim, reflecting Persian and Turkish influences; while not incorrect, they have an archaic ring and have fallen out of current usage. The term "Muhammadan" (or "Mo-

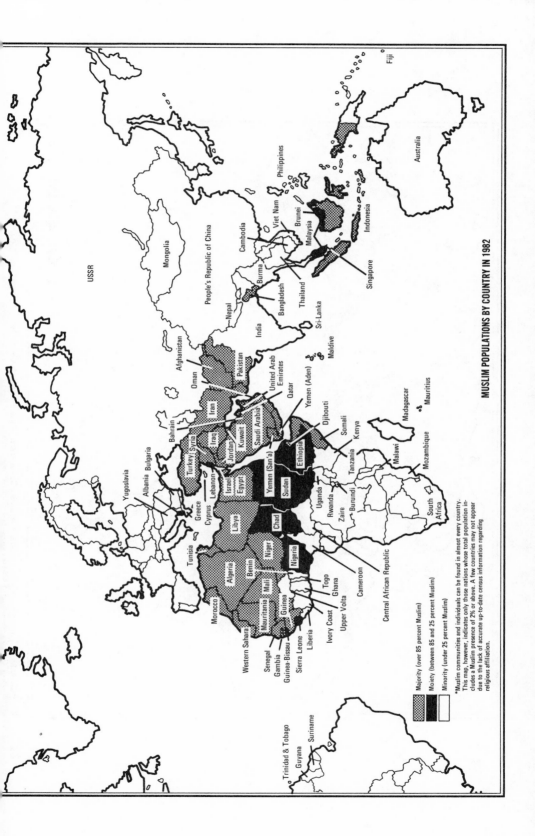

MUSLIM POPULATIONS BY COUNTRY IN 1982

Majority (over 85 percent Muslim)

Moiety (between 85 and 25 percent Muslim)

Minority (under 25 percent Muslim)

*Muslim communities and individuals can be found in almost every country. This map, however, indicates only those nations whose total population includes a Muslim presence of 2% or above. A few countries may not appear due to the lack of accurate up-to-date census information regarding religious affiliation.

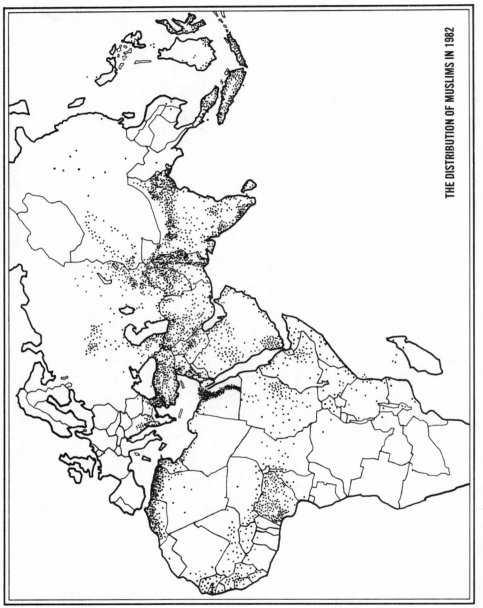

THE DISTRIBUTION OF MUSLIMS IN 1982

SOURCE: Olivier Carré, *L'Islam et l'etat dans le monde d'aujourd'hui* (Paris: Presses Universitaires de France, 1982), pp.-10-11.
NOTE: One dot represents about 100,000 people.

hammedan" or "Mahometan") also means Muslim, but this is a Western neologism dating from the sixteenth century, which imitates the formation of the word "Christian" by taking the religion's central figure and naming his followers after him. But this term is inaccurate and gratuitously offensive to Muslims, for Muhammad's significance in Islam does not compare to that of Jesus Christ in Christianity (indeed, in Muslim eyes, his stature is hardly greater than that of Jesus; one might as well call them Christians). "Muhammadanism" as a synonym for Islam compounds this error and is even more insulting to Muslims. The confusion that surrounds these terms can be illustrated by the farcical adjective synonyms provided in *The New Roget's Thesaurus* for Mohammedan: "Moslem, Moslemic, Moslemite, Mussulmanic, Islam, Islamic, Islamistic, Islamitic."[26] Ethnic terms have also been used to designate Muslims, including: Saracen, Moor, Arab, Turk, and Tatar. Even today, "Arab" and "Muslim" are often used interchangeably, although five-sixths of the Muslims do not speak Arabic and about five million Arabic-speakers are Christian.

Islam is variously used in English to refer to a place, a people, a faith, and a civilization: "in Islam," "the Islamic community," "the Islamic religion," and "the Islamic world." But this overtaxes a single word and invariably leads to confusion. Marshall G. S. Hodgson suggests referring to the place as Islamdom (patterned on Christendom), to the people as Muslims, to the faith as Islamic, and to the civilization as Islamicate (patterned on Italianate).[27] The distinction between Islamic and Islamicate is subtle and will be discussed at some length in the conclusion to Part I.

"Islamdom" encompasses all Muslims, wherever they form communities (that is, wherever they are more than isolated individuals). It differs from *Dar al-Islam,* which refers to territories under Muslim control, and from *Dar al-Harb,* lands not under Muslim control. Islamdom includes all Muslims, whether living in Dar al-Islam or Dar al-Harb. Like Islamdom, *umma* ("the community of Islam") also refers to the whole body of Muslims, but Islamdom has a geographic quality and the umma has spiritual and emotional connotations. The umma also includes isolated individuals.

I employ Arabic words where translations into English conjure up wrong images (such as "holy war" for *jihad*) or cumbersome ones ("the Abode of War" for Dar al-Harb). Although the use of Arabic words may make this book more of a challenge to read, it is necessary if exact meanings are to be conveyed. In one special case, however, a well-known Arabic word is translated regularly into English: Allah. Calling the Lord of Islam Allah seems to imply that Muslims direct their prayers to a divinity who differs from that of the Jews and Christians, whereas, in fact, Muslims worship the same Lord; Allah is merely the Arabic translation of God. To emphasize this, Allah is normally referred to as God in this book. Note how profoundly this changes our understanding of the Islamic statement of faith, from the bellicose-sounding "There is no God but Allah," to the unthreatening "There is no diety but God."[28]

For an understanding of Islam's role in politics, an outsider must consciously push aside some familiar concepts and tools of analysis. For Westerners, the conventional division of politics into right- and left-wing has little value when categorizing Islamic movements. Nationalism in Islamdom is transformed into something quite distinct from its Western prototype, while law and territory have wholly different meanings. Unless the reader makes efforts to think along new lines, he will probably find comprehension of Islam elusive. When dealing with Islam, first impressions are usually faulty. To take one prominent nonpolitical example: assuming that human relations have the same implications in Islamdom as in the West, Europeans and Americans naturally interpret the harem in light of what it would mean to them—something akin to the Victorian ideal of frail females staying at home, out of harm's way. In fact, harems reflect a vision of women as sexually insatiable beings who must be kept away from men, lest they seduce the men from devotion to God and so foment anarchy.

Ironically, it is more difficult to distance oneself from Western notions when dealing with Westernized Muslims; whereas understanding of the Ottoman Empire or Khomeini's Iran obviously requires adjustment of the standard Western tools of political science, Turkey or Tunisia can be seen in more narrowly Western ways, for so much of the tone and style of their politics resembles public life in Europe and America. But this is superficial; despite speaking French fluently or wearing a tie to work, nearly all Muslims live culturally more in a context formed by Islam than in one formed by the West.

This Book

Fi sabil illah is Arabic for "in the path of God" or "to the glory of God." Most of the many occurrences of this expression in the Qur'an are associated with warfare against infidels. The Qur'an exhorts Muslims to fight (2.190), it assures them that dying for this purpose is only apparent (3.169), and tells them that the deeds of those slain in the path of God will not be forgotten (47.4). Many verses encourage Muslims to spend money freely on righteous warfare and assert that those who believe in God must fight for Him.

In time, however, the expression came to mean all duties incumbent upon Muslims. It was connected to pious action broadly defined, especially to whatever contributed to the public good. Thus do beggars cry out for donations *fi sabil illah* and scholarly work is undertaken "in the path of God." The verbal form of *sabil,* "path," acquired the meaning "to spend on good works" and one of those works, water fountains for public use, came to be know as *sabil*s. For parallel reasons, *fi sabil illah* became associated with political activities, which were also to be pursued in the service of God. A devout Muslim perceived participation in public affairs as essential to progress along the path of God.

But the umma did not agree on a single path. The Muslim efforts to fulfill God's demands varied according to era. This book divides Muslim history into three periods: the premodern (to 1800), modern (1800–1970), and contemporary (1970–83). Part I explains the two ways by which Islam affected public life in the centuries when it was an integral civilization, before the European impact. First, Islam, alone of all the major religions, prescribes specific and detailed laws covering politics, war, economics, and justice, so that devout Muslims had an exact idea of how they should act. To the extent that they did live according to the laws, Islam had a direct bearing on political life.

Second, Islam had an even greater indirect influence. Patterns evolved that were not inherent to the religion but resulted from the experiences of Muslims. The legal precepts are so demanding that they were never fully implemented. To reconcile Islamic laws with reality, Muslims developed compromises. For example, Muslim peoples, disillusioned with politics, withdrew from public life. This and many other political characteristics were shared by most Muslims, despite their innumerable spatial and temporal differences. Historical experience also generated patterns. By any standard, premodern Muslims were on the whole wealthier and more powerful than their neighbors. Their history of superiority over non-Muslims created expectations of worldly success and disdain for non-Muslims. Although Islam does not inculcate an opinion about Europe, Muslims from West Africa to Southeast Asia did in fact respond to it in similar ways. These indirect features were no less important than those directly required by Islam. Together, they made up a distinct political culture.

Part II demonstrates how, from the late eighteenth century onward, an Islamic background obstructed efforts to come to terms with the challenge of modernity. Muslim relations with Europe were bad and political customs clashed on almost every major point. Muslims felt especially humiliated by European conquest. Everything went wrong; although desirous of what the West had, Muslims were unable to adopt the necessary methods. A paralyzing ambivalence resulted. While the civilization of Islam was not sufficient, that of the West was not accepted; old ways were discredited and new ones were indigestible. Because the umma was immobile, poverty, weakness, and cultural stagnancy followed. This was Islam's modern dilemma, a trauma that increased with the decades.

Then, around 1970, many Muslims stopped trying to adopt Western ways and once again sought solutions in Islam. Part III considers the factors contributing to this change, among which the OPEC boom was the most important. By making some Muslims wealthy and powerful, oil income transformed the psychology of the Muslim world as a whole and reversed the two-centuries-old sense of failure. New money gave Saudi Arabia and Libya the means to further Islamic causes around the globe. Wealth from oil also lay behind the disruptions that brought the Imam Khomeini to power in Iran and galvanized Muslim sentiments everywhere.

But just as the OPEC boom was a fluke of commodity pricing, so was the Islamic revival weakly based. It did not solve the problems of modernity but only temporarily finessed them. As the oil market changes and Middle East prosperity diminishes, chances are that the recent enthusiasm for Islam as a guide to political action will wane. Then Muslims will again turn to Western models in search of answers to their most pressing problems.

I approach the subject of Islam and politics from within the Orientalist tradition of European and American scholarship. This tradition has often been attacked recently, notably by Edward Said, on two grounds: the limitations of its method, which relies heavily on language skills, philology, and the study of texts; and the supposed bias of its approach, which reflects an imperialistic mentality. Both criticisms contain elements of truth, but the fact remains that the Western academic study of Islam provides the only basis for an analysis of the religion in relation to political life. Certainly, the Orientalist tradition cannot be replaced by the recent profusion of writings by social scientists and journalists, few of which have the vision or profundity of the works by observers such as the Dutch scholar, traveller, and colonial administrator, Christiaan Snouck Hurgronje; the Austrian humanist Gustave E. von Grunebaum; the British Arabist Sir Hamilton A. R. Gibb; the French social and economic historian Claude Cahen; the Canadian religious historian Wilfred Cantwell Smith; and the American historians of Islam Marshall G. S. Hodgson and John Obert Voll. An exceptional analysis of Islam in politics, written by someone outside the Orientalist tradition, is V. S. Naipaul's account of his travels in 1979–80 in several Muslim countries.

Unfortunately, Muslims themselves have added relatively little to the study of Islam as a force in public life. There are notable exceptions—the writings of M. Jamil Hanifi, Fatima Mernissi, Abbas Kelidar, and Detlev Khalid have all vitally contributed to this book—but Muslims usually view the faith from a perspective not helpful to someone seeking critical analysis. As H. A. R. Gibb observed in 1942: "I have not yet seen a single book written by an Arab of any branch in any Western language that has made it possible for the Western student to understand the roots of Arab culture. More than that, I have not

seen any book written in Arabic for Arabs themselves which has clearly analyzed what Arabic culture means to the Arabs."[29] Five years later, Gustave
E. von Grunebaum noted that "this statement could be extended to include
the non-Arab Muslim and his failure to interpret his culture to both himself
and the West. It holds good today as it did when it was written, and it is likely
to hold good for some time to come."[30] Another thirty-six years later, the situation has not fundamentally changed; the reasons for this problem will be discussed in chapter 8.

This study touches on extremely sensitive topics; it may help to defuse controversy over my opinions if I state explicitly and in advance my own vantage
point. I write from outside the Islamic faith, having studied Islam all my adult
life and spent years living among Muslims. Writings by others and my own
observations have given me materials for assessing Islam as a persuasion, its
appeal, and its practical consequences. I respect the Islamic way of life, admire
much about it, and sympathize with efforts to live in accordance with its precepts. Muslims struggling to bridge the gulf between Islam and modernity have
my admiration, for their task is arduous.

This book grew out of an interest in the political role of Islam, a topic I
have pursued since first taking up the study of Middle East history as an under-
graduate. Initially, I wrote on the premodern period; then, in 1979, the Islamic
revival sparked a widespread interest in Islam and politics that encouraged
me to write on contemporary issues. It is my belief that the historical dimension is too often missing from discussions about Islam in public life and it is
this that I especially hope to provide.

I aspire, as objectively as possible, to analyze the condition of modern Muslims; my intent is not to suggest solutions to their problems but to explain their
circumstances to others. By the definition of their faith, Muslims must disagree
with some views expressed here (especially the key notion that many Islamic
goals are humanly unattainable), for they see Islam from within and I do so
from without.

PART I

The Premodern Legacy

2

Islamic Sacred Law and Politics

Islamic government is rule by
sacred law.
—*Imam Ruhollah Khomeini*

ERNEST GELLNER, a leading sociologist of Muslim life, recently noted the
similarity that exists between Muslim societies, then expressed his bafflement
how these similarities came to be:

For all the indisputable diversity, the remarkable thing is the extent to which Muslim
societies resemble each other. Their traditional political systems, for instance, are much
more of one kind than were those of pre-modern Christendom. At least in the bulk
of Muslim societies, in the main Islamic block between Central Asia and the Atlantic
shores of Africa, one has the feeling that the same and limited pack of cards has been
dealt. The hands vary, but the pack is the same. This homogeneity, in as far as it obtains,
is all the more puzzling in the theoretical absence of a Church, and hence of a central
authority on Faith and Morals. There is no obvious agency which could have enforced
this homogeneity.[1]

This chapter suggests that the sacred law of Islam, the Shari'a, is the "obvious
agency" that Gellner seeks. Sacred law is the key to Islam in politics, the critical
instrument by which Islam affects the mundane lives of its adherents. In the
words of Gotthelf Bergsträsser, the author of a basic study on the subject, "Islamic law in its fullest sense regulates the cult, . . . it is the embodiment of the
true Islamic spirit, the most decisive expression of Islamic thought, and the essential kernel of Islam generally"; or, in Christiaan Snouck Hurgronje's concise
assessment, "Islam is a religion of law in the full meaning of the word."[2]

Sacred Law in Three Monotheisms

Having developed out of a long tradition of Middle Eastern religion, many of Islam's characteristic features are best understood in the context of its two major predecessors, Judaism and Christianity. This is especially the case with the sacred law; here, Islam resembles Judaism as closely as it differs from Christianity.

For Jews, fulfilling the sacred law is the primary means of serving the Lord. Although Judaism does not neglect feeling and faith, it has long placed special emphasis on the importance of correct actions. Over the centuries, Jews developed a highly elaborated and detailed body of regulations, known as the Halakha, to help them act correctly. The Halakha covers nearly every aspect of life, including matters such as food, clothing, family relations, economic activities, and justice. ("Law" in English comprises a much smaller scope than the Halakha; this must be kept in mind when speaking of the Jewish law.)

Jewish sacred law originated with the Ten Commandments received by Moses on Mt. Sinai in about 1230 B.C. and was further elaborated in the Pentateuch (the Five Books of Moses). According to traditional rabbinic calculations, the Pentateuch includes 613 precepts, of which 248 are positive (for instance, in Deut. 23:19, "When you are encamped against an enemy, you shall be careful to avoid any foulness") and 365 negative (in Lev. 19:35, "You shall not pervert justice in measurement of length, weight, or quantity").[3] They deal with sacrifices, vows, ritual purity, temple donations, dietary restrictions, idolatry, war, slaves, torts, agriculture, justice, sex, the monarchy, as well as other matters. Numerous as these are, the biblical injunctions are only the fundaments of Jewish law; they required much elaboration and extension before they could serve as a legal system for the Jews.

According to Jewish tradition, Moses received two messages on Mt. Sinai, the Written Law (the Pentateuch) and the Oral Law. The latter elucidates the Written Law and provides the methods for interpreting it. In keeping with its oral nature, Jews worked on the Oral Law for centuries without writing down their views. Scruples against writing were overcome only after the Jewish dispersal from Palestine in 586 B.C., when it became apparent that portions of the Oral Law would be lost if not committed to writing. Discussions about the laws were compiled during a millennium, until the sixth century A.D.; the full body of these writings are known as the Talmud, a vast compendium which applies the Oral Law to Jewish life. But it does not contain laws as such; rather, it is a jurisprudent's guide to the laws. Unwieldy and unsystematic, the Talmud is a scholar's resource rather than a legal book. To make the laws accessible, various handbooks were written, counseling Jews on the specifics of the Halakha. Although the main principles of Jewish practice were set in place by the sixth century, refinements and amendments continued to be made in the form of commentaries, codifications, and *responsa* (decisions rendered by rabbis in answer to specific problems).

Consistent with the emphasis on law, the bulk of Jewish intellectual effort has gone into studying the Talmud. Ideally, each male should be able to apply it to his life and thus know exactly how to act; in fact, many Jewish communities have achieved something remarkably close to this goal. In contrast, theology (the study of God) usually has received little attention.

A detailed code of law such as the Halakha amounts to more than a legal system; it creates a whole way of life. Observant Jews share practices that distinguish them from others and encourage strong communal ties. Kosher rules, liturgy, Sabbath restrictions, and living separately from Gentiles have had special importance in assuring the survival of the Jewish people. By requiring Jews to withdraw from the mainstream of most societies they have lived among and to create their own environment, the Halakha has greatly helped Jews maintain their religion through the centuries of persecution and pressures to abandon their faith.

These pressures began in a serious fashion about the time of Jesus, when Jews had to contend with the distressing and novel realities of life under Roman rule. The Jewish monarchy had come to an end, Roman gods were forced upon them, and Hellenistic culture attracted many of them away from their faith. Jews responded to these changed circumstances by establishing new sects with varying solutions, including the Pharisees, Sadducees, Theraputae, Zealots, Sicarii, Essenes, and the Qumran community. Initially, Jesus and his followers were viewed as yet another Jewish sect, for they lived by the Halakha and considered themselves Jews. Jesus proclaimed in the Sermon on the Mount: "Do not suppose that I have come to abolish the Law and the prophets; I did not come to abolish, but to complete. I tell you this: so long as heaven and earth endure, not a letter, not a stroke, will disappear from the Law until all that must happen has happened. If any man therefore sets aside even the least of the Law's demands, and teaches others to do the same, he will have the lowest place in the kingdom of Heaven, whereas anyone who keeps the Law, and teaches others so, will stand high in the kingdom of Heaven (Matt. 5:17–19). Elsewhere, Jesus states that "If you wish to enter into life, keep the commandments" of Moses (Matt. 19:17). Nor did Jesus' message create problems for Jews: miracles, sacraments, the emphasis on love, the separation of politics from religion, and the ascription of divine qualities to a human all had Jewish antecedents and could be accommodated within the faith. Even believing in Jesus as the Messiah did not take his followers beyond the pale of Judaism. For these reasons, Jesus' first followers are called Jewish Christians; they had faith in Jesus while continuing to live by the Halakha. During Jesus' lifetime, Gentiles were not seen as possible followers.

Even while Jesus kept the Halakha, he modified it in important ways, deriding petty attention to legal detail and exalting the spiritual qualities of observance. For example, he broke the Sabbath by condoning the plucking of corn by his hungry disciples and by healing a man with a withered arm; he then derided the Pharisees for objecting to these humane actions (Matt. 12:1–13). Similarly, he modified several of the other most stringent Halakhic regulations, including those concerning the washing of hands, murder, adultery, divorce, oaths, retribution, fasting, and prayer (Matt. 15:2–11; 5:21–22, 27–28, 31–32, 33–37, 38–42; Luke 5:33–35).

Jesus scorned experts in the Halakha and the group of Jews who most stressed application of the law, the Pharisees, because they "load men with intolerable burdens, and will not put a single finger to the load" (Luke 11:46). He advised listening to them but not following their example: "Do what they tell you; pay attention to their words. But do not follow their practice; for they say one thing and do another" (Matt. 23:3). Elsewhere he admonishes his followers, "Beware of the doctors of the law, who love to walk up and down in long robes, receiving respectful greetings in the street; and to have the chief seats in synagogues, and places of honour at feasts. These are the men who eat up the property of widows, while they say long prayers for appearance' sake, and they will receive the severest sentence" (Mark 12:38–40).

When asked the greatest commandment of the Halakha, Jesus answered: " 'Love the Lord your God with all your heart, with all your soul, with all your mind.' That is the greatest commandment. It comes first. The second is like it: 'Love your neighbour as yourself.' Everything in the Law and the prophets hangs on these two commandments" (Matt. 22:37–40). While not exactly doing away with the Halakha, Jesus transformed it out of existence by conflating thousands of precepts into two. Also, in John's account, Jesus distanced himself from the Halakha by referring to it as "your own Law" (John 7:19, 8:17, 10:34). But at no time did he reject that law.

It was the apostle Peter who, after Jesus' death, began moving away from Jewish practices. In a bizarre dream, he received permission from the Lord to ignore the kosher laws of the Halakha and to eat any food:

Peter went up on the roof to pray. He grew hungry and wanted something to eat. While they were getting it ready, he fell into a trance. He saw a rift in the sky, and a thing coming down that looked like a great sheet of sail-cloth. It was slung by the four corners, and was being lowered to the ground. In it he saw creatures of every kind, whatever walks or crawls or flies. Then there was a voice which said to him, "Up, Peter, kill and eat." But Peter said, "No, Lord, no: I have never eaten anything profane or unclean." The voice came again a second time: "It is not for you to call profane what God counts clean" (Acts 10:10–15).[4]

The annulment of Jewish food laws instantly eradicated a central distinction between Jew and Gentile; with this, Peter began the momentous process of releasing Christians from the duty of obeying the Halakha, calling it "a yoke which neither we nor our fathers were able to bear" (Acts 15:10). Gentiles need not follow the Halakha when they convert to Christianity: "We should impose no irksome restrictions on those of the Gentiles who are turning to God [that is, converting to Christianity], but instruct them by letter to abstain from things polluted by contact with idols, from fornication, from anything that has been strangled, and from blood" (Acts 15:19–20). Making the Halakha voluntary increased the attraction of Christ by eliminating the daunting prospect of having to live by the Jewish law.

Saint Paul then went a step further and turned Christianity into a distinct religion by making it no longer possible to be Jewish and Christian at the same time. Paul argued as follows: He noted that Abraham, the first Jew, lived before there was such a thing as Halakha; specifically, he was not circumcised. As Genesis states: "Abram put his faith in the Lord, and the Lord counted that faith to him as righteousness" (Gen. 15:6). To Paul, this meant that "it was not through law that Abraham, or his posterity, was given the promise that the world should be his inheritance, but through the righteousness that came from faith" (Rom. 4:13). Paul suggested that this promise remains valid, that righteousness through faith is God's most lasting covenant with man.

The Halakha was added "to make wrongdoing a legal offence," helping to keep order in society and showing mankind how to serve the Lord (Gal. 3:19). But it was meant only as a temporary aid, a crutch: "The law was a kind of tutor in charge of us until Christ should come, when we should be justified through faith; and now that faith has come, the tutor's charge is at an end" (Gal. 3:24–25). Faith sufficed from Abraham to Moses, the law regulated affairs from Moses to Jesus, and now faith reappears with the coming of Jesus. Jews served God by fulfilling His law, an onerous duty and an indirect way to pay tribute to him; Jesus provides an easier, more direct way to approach God, that of love and faith. Thus, according to Paul, the Halakha lost validity with the coming of Christ.

Faith replaced the law: "A man is justified by faith quite apart from success in keeping the law" (Rom. 3:28). All this was made possible by Jesus, "for Christ ends the law and brings righteousness for everyone who has faith" (Rom. 10:4). Although Paul called the law "holy and just and good," and he himself sometimes maintained it for missionary purposes, he was adamant on the separation of Christians from the law and the impossibility of becoming a Christian while keeping it (Rom. 7:12; 1 Cor. 9:20–2). "Those who rely on obedience to the law are under a curse," or, worse: "When you seek to be justified by way of law, your relation with Christ is completely severed" (Gal. 3:10; 5:4). Observance of the Halakha was not only unnecessary, it was positively harmful, for it interfered with progress to faith. Anyone who insisted on living by the sacred law of Judaism could not be a follower of Jesus. "If righteousness comes by law, then Christ died for nothing" (Gal. 2:21). Thus, the followers of Jesus formed a religion distinct from Judaism: Jews obeyed the law and Christians ignored it. Jewish Christians (observant Jews believing in Jesus' ministry) survived until the second century but their numbers dwindled rapidly after that; Gentile Christians (who did not keep the Halakha) henceforth prevailed.[5]

The Pauline approach did not make action irrelevant, but it changed the understanding of what constitutes proper behavior. Jews must exactly adhere to a myriad of detailed regulations, some with ethical content (such as the Ten Commandments), others without (such as the prohibition on wearing clothes "woven with two kinds of yarn, wool and flax together" Deut. 22:11). Christians must live justly, loving their Lord and their neighbors; the many regulations are gone. Faith must inspire Christians to ethical living or it has no value; as the Letter of James puts it, "if [faith] does not lead to action, it is in itself a lifeless thing" (James 2:17).

Casting off the Halakha meant abandoning the Jewish way of life that grew out of it. Nor did a Christian way of life develop in its stead, for Christianity has no program analogous to the Jewish one; there is only one way to live by the Halakha but there are many ways to live ethically. Christians have some universal regulations, food prohibitions and sexual injunctions especially (1 Cor. 5–8), but these lack the detailed, far-ranging quality of the Jewish laws. A pious Christian does not constantly encounter the minutiae of his faith as does an observant Jew. Christian communities wishing to live in constant touch with their religion must draw up their own precepts, for their holy books contain none. Each of the highly regulated Christian societies that has appeared, such as the medieval monasteries, Calvinist Geneva, and the Anabaptist communities, has chosen its own rules. Some Christian groups, such as the Puritans, even revived selected Jewish laws. But all Christian laws are limited in time and space; the most widespread of them, the canon law, was applied only during some centuries and only to Roman Catholics.

With time, customary practices often acquired the force of law. In many cases, this slipping away from the Pauline spirit was followed by a reform re-emphasizing faith. When the Catholic church became legalistic and burdened with innumerable regulations, the Protestant Reformation of the sixteenth century dramatically reasserted the doctrine of faith over works. Protestant movements had such success, they eventually influenced Catholic and Orthodox Christians too. The Pauline doctrines have never been better entrenched than today; indeed, as I shall argue in a later chapter,[6] they have also deeply influenced Jews and Muslims. In contrast to the Jewish concentration on studying the sacred law, Christians characteristically have dwelt on theology, on questions about the nature of God, his relations to man, and on matters of right belief.

"In blasphemy indeed are those who say that God is Christ the son of Mary" (Qur'an 5.18). With this assertion, the Qur'an rejects the divinity of Jesus and with it, the central premise of Christian faith. In an effort to achieve an uncompromising monotheism, the Qur'an condemns the Christian trinity as tritheism (worship of three gods) and, in effect, it returns to the Jewish approach to God.

Islam in the Qur'an honors and respects Jesus as prophet, it accepts his virgin birth, his miracles, and the holy spirit within him; but it denies his crucifixion, "They killed him not nor crucified him" (4.157) and it scorns the notion of his being the son of God. According to the Qur'an, he was a human being, "no more than a servant [of God]" (43.59). Reducing Jesus merely to a prophet undermines the whole religious edifice Saint Paul built. If, like the other prophets, Jesus was but a human "who ate food and walked through the streets . . . not exempt from death," (25.20, 21.8), how could he lead others to salvation? As a mortal, how is it that "Christ ends the law" (Rom. 10:4), as Paul claims? From the Islamic viewpoint, Jesus' mission was valid but misunderstood by his disciples. Paul and the others distorted his message, worshipping the man instead of heeding his revelation. In Muslim eyes, Paul's entire teaching is nonsense.

Rejecting Paul means discarding righteousness through faith and returning to sacred law. Islam not only shares Judaism's emphasis on absolute monotheism, but it also stresses the importance of correct action. "Law is the core of the faith, the terrestrial expression of its divine message to . . . society."[7] In many ways, Islam seems to follow directly on Judaism, as though Christianity did not exist. Whereas Paul transformed the Jewish faith into something structurally and spiritually new, Islam kept many of the key features of Judaism. "In the Islamic case, as in the Jewish, the word of God is, fundamentally, an imperative."[8] If Christianity changed the Jewish message, Islam universalized it, changing details but keeping the same approach to God. "It is this crucial insistence on the centrality of law that clearly separates Judaism and Islam from Christianity."[9] Parallel concern with sacred law creates similarities in Jewish and Muslim ways of life; further, while Judaism hardly influenced Christianity from Paul's time onward, it continued directly to affect the development of Islam; "much of the spirit that formed Muslim expectations of what a religion should be was inspired by Jewish example."[10] As a result, Jews and Muslims have a strikingly wide range of characteristics in common; the description of these and the survey of Christian-Muslim contrasts which follow help to understand the repercussions of living by a sacred law.

To begin with, the Qur'an, like the Hebrew Bible and contrary to Christian scriptures, contains a great many regulations; about one-tenth of the 6,238 verses of the Qur'an instruct Muslims in actions, though only eighty or so of them provide specific injunctions. Some define strictly religious matters such as fasting and pilgrimage; whatever concerns women (marriage, adultery, divorce, and seclusion from men) has great prominence, as do other aspects of family life: orphanage, adoption, inheritance, and so forth. There are prohibitions on usury and gambling as well as dietary and sumptuary restrictions. The Qur'an instructs Muslims about slaves, non-Muslims, warfare, contracts, judicial procedure, almsgiving, and criminal punishments.

Just as Moses gave his people a Written and an Oral Law, so did Muhammad. The Qur'an came as divine revelation to Muhammad; transcribed, it became the written text of Islam and the most authoritative source of its laws. Islamic tradition has it that accounts of Muhammad's own personal statements (in contrast to the divine words which passed through him) and actions were orally transmitted for many generations before being written down. Known as *Hadith* Reports, these anecdotes and quotes about Muhammad are the *Sunna,* the "path" incumbent on Muslims to follow; combined with the Qur'an and elaborated through reasoning by analogy and established by a consensus of scholars, they form the Shari'a, Islam's sacred law.

In the same way that the Halakha regulates far more than does the Bible, so does the Shari'a go far beyond Qur'anic precepts. The Qur'an may be seen as the constitution of Islam and the Shari'a as the corpus of laws that explicate it. Where the Qur'an is restricted to prohibitions and commands, the Shari'a specifies details and prescribes penalties for transactions. Theft, for example, is mentioned only once in the Qur'an: "Cut off the hand of the male or female thief as punishment for his or her crime" (5.41). This terse pronouncement does not suffice for a court of law; leavened with *Hadith* Reports and reasoning by analogy, however, the 'ulama were able to elaborate a full code from this one sentence, deciding such matters as: what constitutes theft, what evidence is required for conviction, how to carry out an amputation, and what punishments to inflict on repeated offenders. None of these matters is self-evident and all required several centuries of debate until a final resolution was reached.

Because the Halakha and the Shari'a were seen as divinely inspired, all parts of them had equal importance. For Muslims, "no question was too minute to receive a ruling from God," and it was for this reason that "the most important ritual acts, great problems of civil and criminal law, details of the toilet, formulas of greeting, table-manners and sick-room conversation were all on the same level."[11]

The Muslim construction of a legal system out of the Written and Oral Laws closely resembled that of the Jews. "The logical reasoning applied to the development of the religious law is largely identical in Islam and Judaism. This is not a mere coincidence inherent in the nature of things; but, as some of the terms used show, must be based on direct connections."[12] Such influences are hardly surprising; the compilation of the Talmud was drawing to a close in Iraq just as the *Hadith* Reports were being collected in the same region. Surely some Muslim scholars were aware of their Jewish predecessors, especially as more than a few of them were converts from Judaism. By the time of its full elaboration in about A.D. 1000, the Shari'a resembled the Halakha in many of its details, in its spirit, and in the range of its jurisdiction; thus was Islam "indebted to Judaism, be it by way of complete or partial acceptance, modification or outright rejection and opposition."[13]

Although in theory both the Jewish and Islamic codes remained mutable, in fact all the major rules became fixed and, with time, legal experts increasingly concerned themselves with minor, even trivial matters of the law. While Jewish scholars debated ceremonies for a Temple which had disappeared many centuries earlier, Muslim jurists pondered such unedifying problems as who inherits what when a child dies leaving as his only survivors eight great-grandparents. When novel situations arose, prominent religious authorities of both faiths gave *ad hoc* decisions (called *responsa* in Judaism, *fatwa*s in Islam) which, if generally accepted, became law. Neither tradition had any notion of the law evolving over time to meet changing circumstances, a fact of very great importance in the modern era.

To assure compliance with the law, Muslims demanded more of themselves than the Shari'a strictly required. "In the same way as the Rabbinical commentators of the Pentateuch placed 'a fence about the Law' by requiring a precautionary margin in order to ensure the entire fulfilment of its dictates, so the interpreters of the Koran demanded more than their original."[14] In both religions, such fences were particularly prevalent in what concerned diet and sex. The prohibition on pork led, for example, to the virtual elimination of pigs from Islamdom; veils and harems were developed to reduce physical temptation. These cautionary rules then became integral to the religion and its way of life.

Religious authorities in the two traditions shared much too; as for Jews, so for Muslims, learning about even the driest legal matters was considered a form of worship, making scholars of the sacred law men of religion, rabbis and 'ulama. They had no sacerdotal or liturgical function, for individual Jews and Muslims both pray directly to God, but they helped their followers live properly according to the many and complex demands of the law by interpreting it on a daily basis: Do two drops of milk in a pot of meat make it unkosher? How far must a traveler go to be excused from the Ramadan fast? Expertise in the law led to other roles for both rabbis and ʿulama, who acted as judges, educators, community leaders, and intermediaries with government authorities. These diverse functions meant that the place of worship, the synagogue or mosque, also served as law court, place of study, community center, and hospice. Sons of rabbis and ʿulama often inherited their fathers' positions. The absence of priestly duties implied that neither kind of leader fit into a hierarchical structure. Instead, rabbis and ʿulama gained stature through an informal process of deference and prestige. Maimonides, the outstanding Jewish thinker of the medieval period, rose to prominence in a manner similar to that of an Iranian ayatollah today.[15]

If sacred law makes Islam structurally akin to Judaism, it also accounts for Islam's crucial differences from Christianity. The contrast between ethics and law pervades the two religions. Whereas Christian scholarship concentrates on theology, Muslim learning centers on *fiqh,* the study of Islamic jurisprudence. A simple Christian learns correct beliefs, boiled down to the catechism; his Muslim counterpart learns a simplified list of duties sometimes known as the "pillars of the religion" *(arkan ad-din).* These include reciting "There is no deity but God and Muhammad is his Prophet," praying, fasting during the month of Ramadan, almsgiving, and the pilgrimage to Mecca (in Arabic: *shihada, salat, sawm, zakat,* and *hajj).* (Some also include "righteous war," *jihad,* in this list.) The most heinous Christian act is heresy, or false belief; its Islamic equivalent is *bidʿa,* deviation or wrong action. Christians conflicted over theology and Muslims over power. Catholics, Orthodox, and Protestants differed initially over the best approach to God and then acquired the features of political movements, while the Sunni, Shiʿi, and Khariji sects began by disputing the leadership of the Muslim community and only later acquired theological overtones. Also, Islam's four legal rites *(madhhabs)* at times took on social and political functions.

Christian priests, who serve as intermediaries between mankind and God, derive their authority from their sacramental functions; in contrast, the ʿulama have no such role but use their knowledge of the law to serve as exemplars, teachers, judges, and community leaders. (For this reason, translating ʿulama into English as "clerics" leads to misunderstandings; better to call them "Muslim rabbis.") The pope guides his community in faith and stirs controversy when he strays too far into politics; the caliph is a political leader who provokes opposition when he makes religious pronouncements.

The Shariʿa is more than a set of rules; it entails a whole mentality and a way of life which, when fully adhered to, permeate the minds, actions, and feelings of Muslims. It is "the most typical manifestation of the Islamic way of life, the core and kernel of Islam itself."[16] Observant Muslims live in touch with the law at all times. G. E. von Grunebaum notes that "Islam affected the believer's life at every hour," and V. S. Naipaul characterizes it this way: "To be a devout Muslim was always to have distinctive things to do; it was to be guided constantly by rules; it was to live in a fever of the faith and always to be aware of the distinctiveness of the faith."[17] Someone not familiar with Muslim (or Jewish) tradition may have difficulty comprehending how thoroughly religion can pervade daily life. Every custom, institution, relationship, and attitude has some connection to the faith; even the most minor and private matters (defecating, bathing, tooth cleaning, and sleeping) are subject to sacred regulations. Very few acts are neutral and, in particular, anything bearing on sex or politics provokes strong Islamic responses. As traditionally lived, Islam concerns itself with laughing, singing, crying, eating, loving, and working. W. C. Smith sums it up: "Islam for Muslims is not an abstract idea but an idea in operative practice."[18]

By influencing so much, sacred law served as the vital bond of unity for both Jews and Muslims. Although neither the Halakha nor the Shari'a are unitary—they vary according to rite, sect, location, and era—the grand outlines of both are very much the same in all places and times. Detailed sacred law provided two geographically dispersed peoples with the means for each to build a shared common identity.

As a result, the Islamic mentality is characterized by dichotomies; things either conform to Islam or they oppose it. Persons are believers (Muslims) or not (kafirs); territory is ruled by Muslims (Dar al-Islam) or not (Dar al-Harb); non-Muslims are under Muslim control (dhimmis) or not (harbis); warfare is righteous (jihad) or not (fitna); taxes meet Shar'i conditions (zakat) or not (maks); and meat comes from properly slaughtered animals (dhabiha) or not (mayta). Fervent Muslims encourage "a love of Islam and abhorrence of un-Islam."[19] The more extreme their feelings, the more simplistic and dogmatic this dichotomy becomes.

The dualistic mentality is not aberrant, but fundamental to Islam, with roots going back to the Qur'an: "No student of Islam can but be struck by the violent contrast the Quran presents between the believers and their opponents. . . . Perhaps in no other religious system has the power of antagonism toward adversaries been so successfully harnessed in the cause of communal solidarity as in Islam."[20] The deep dichotomy between Muslim and kafir goes back to observance of the Shari'a, for "affiliation with the community is expressed primarily in action," by carrying out God's commands to the letter.[21] In the end, it is a determination to belong to the community of Islam which is perhaps "the most important single factor accounting for the amazingly strong emotional cohesiveness of the Muslim community.''[22] One critic describes it this way: "The Islamic idea of unity or union [always consisted of] men abased together before the creator and bound by rigid rules. There was an unspoken corollary: everything outside that community was shut out, everything outside was impious, impure, infidel.''[23]

Muslims hardly ever apostacize from their religion; with the rarest of exceptions, once a Muslim, always a Muslim. Islamic regulations emphatically prohibit conversion by condemning renegades to death, but even in Dar al-Harb, where non-Muslim rulers usually protect an apostate from this fate, he still meets rejection by his family and community, which is pressure enough. Penalties alone, however, cannot account for the extraordinary hold of Islam on its adherents; no less critical are the strong bonds of loyalty it inspires, imbuing Muslims with a special pride and a sense of confidence in their faith. The Muslims' phenomenal early success in worldly affairs (more on which is in chapter 4) may also have influenced this feeling. As a result, the very notion of leaving Islam for another religion normally strikes Muslims as preposterous.

In its moderate form, this Islamic mentality creates a gulf between believer and non-believer typically not breached in social or intellectual intercourse. In its extreme form, it leads to violence and lasting resentments. Kafirs are acutely aware of the superior and antagonistic attitudes held by Muslims; they respond by fearing Islam and regarding Muslims as unceasingly aggressive. This holds for Christians in Greece, Mossi animists in West Africa, Jews in Yemen, Hindus in Gujarat, Zoroastrians in Iran, Buddhists in Thailand, and Confucians in Yunnan. Non-Muslim responses fit a clear pattern: dislike of Muslims and an irreducible feeling of dissimilarity.

Public Ideals in Islamic Sacred Law

The huge body of injunctions in the Shari'a that guides the actions of believers may be, for analytical purposes, divided into two categories, public and private, according to the role of the state.[24] Private regulations are defined here as those in which the state mainly intervenes to punish offenses, while public regulations involve state participation at all stages. For example, in economic affairs, prohibition on interest is private because individuals arrange loans and the state acts only to prevent abuses; but taxation is public because it involves the state from the first. Dietary restrictions, family relations, and prayer rituals are all clearly in the private domain, just as warfare and political authority are in the public. The two overlap in the judicial realm, where courts backed by the state's authority hear cases dealing with private affairs. So long as private acts do not threaten the public order, the ruling authorities stay away; for related reasons, private Shar'i precepts can be maintained in Dar al-Harb, but not so the public ones. Although fundamental to understanding the Muslim way of life, the private sphere will be largely omitted from the following discussion because it rarely touches on Islam as a political force.

Just as Jewish and Christian practices provide the necessary background to understanding the role of sacred law in Islam, so too do they clarify the connection between religion and politics. The fact that Christianity has no political program is due largely to Saint Paul's elimination of the law; righteousness through faith means Christians can, for the most part, ignore the state. Politicians inspired by Christ's teachings are of course a boon, but government behavior does not normally impinge on the spiritual life of believers and can therefore be ignored by pious Christians. In addition, it is significant that Christianity developed in the context of Roman rule; the Empire provided a state authority in so powerful and seemingly permanent a fashion that Jesus, Paul, and other early Christian leaders had no reason to be concerned with establishing a state structure. Because an authority already existed, Christians could afford to ignore politics and concentrate on matters of piety and ethics. So long as the faith is not persecuted, devout Christians can tolerate most political structures and nearly any laws. The Christian faith demands great efforts from individuals but almost nothing of governments. Thus could Jesus call for the separation of the secular and spiritual domains: "Pay Caesar what is due to Caesar and pay God what is due to God" (Matt. 22:21). The division of private and public life encourages Christian believers to concentrate on their own concerns and, to a practical extent, to eschew politics.

But not all have done so. While most churches (notably the Eastern Orthodox and those based outside Europe) remained circumspect about power, the Catholic church of Western Europe and some of its Protestant offshoots became extremely involved in politics. Their role in public affairs, however, was always a delicate one, for church power is anomalous and ill fits the Christian spirit. While the clergy has frequently wielded great influence over public affairs, from Saint Ambrose in the fourth century to Archbishop Makarios of Cyprus in the 1970s, their activities have repeatedly prompted intense opposition. Christianity's lack of a mundane agenda means that the religious authorities have no mandate to acquire political power; when they do so anyway, it is on their own initiative and at their own risk.

If Christianity never had a political program, Judaism had one which withered away. That this could happen indicates how much less central politics is to the Halakha than it is to the Shari'a—Islam's imperatives could have never lost importance to premodern Muslims. The critical difference lies in

41

historical circumstances: existing as a people before they became a religious community, the Hebrews depended politically less on their religion than did the Muslims, who had come together only on account of religion. By the time of Moses, the Jews had already long been a people; the fact that they shared powerful bonds of kinship, a common language, and a long heritage meant that they did not depend on faith to hold them together.

Judaism did subsequently become a religion of state; accordingly, the Bible includes a few precepts regulating the monarchy, military service, warfare, and taxation.[25] Had the Jews retained their political independence, these regulations no doubt would have grown in number and importance; but from the fall of Jerusalem in 586 B.C. until the creation of the modern state of Israel in 1948, Jews lived almost always under non-Jewish rule, exceptions to this being either transient (the Hasmoneaen dynasty, 164–65 B.C.) or remote (Ethiopia, the Yemen, and among the Khazars). Provisions dealing with public life became increasingly irrelevant as Jews adapted themselves to rule by authorities either indifferent or hostile to the Halakha. Meanwhile, regulations about private life acquired greater importance and became the foremost mechanism for the survival of Judaism. In other words, Jews grew accustomed to living under alien rule. They learned to accommodate virtually any regime by insulating themselves from the affairs of state and creating islands of Halakhic piety. As part of this effort, from the third century A.D. forward, they acknowledged the civil law of a country in which they lived as religiously binding on themselves, so long as it did not conflict with the Halakha. Judaism thus developed into a faith with minimal connections to politics. Today, the public aspects of the Halakha are as defunct as those regulating animal sacrifices; modern Israelis have made no serious effort to conduct public life along its lines.

Such an abandonment of public ideals would be unthinkable in Islam, where, in Max Weber's view, "an essentially political character marked all the chief ordinances."[26] The connection to politics has been immutably deep from the very inception of the religion. Muhammad founded a religious community *ex nihilo.* He lived in western Arabia, a stateless region where tribal affiliations dominated all of public life. A tribe protected its members (by threatening to take revenge for them), and it provided social bonds, economic opportunities, as well as political enfranchisement. An individual lacking tribal ties had no standing; he could be robbed, raped, and killed with impunity. If Muhammad was to attract tribesmen to join his religious movement, he had to provide them with an affiliation no less powerful than the tribe they had left behind. Thus did Muslim leaders offer a range of services resembling those of tribal chiefs, protecting their followers, organizing them for wars of booty, dispensing justice, and so forth. The key point is this: because Muhammad created a new community, the religion that was its raison d'être had to meet the political needs of its adherents. Unlike the Christians, who lived within a massive and enduring empire, or the Hebrews, who had ethnic bonds before becoming Jews, the Muslims depended on their religion to provide them with an authority and an identity.

Once instituted, Shar'i public ideals took on a life of their own and became the basis of Shar'i doctrines which permanently mold the life of Muslim communities. "The central position of the *Shari'a* in state and society as understood in classical Islam cannot be overemphasised."[27] Its precepts cover politics, war, social relations, economics, and justice.

Unity among Muslims is the paramount political goal of Islam. Ideally, a single state should extend the breadth of Dar al-Islam; failing this, Muslim governments should be at peace with each other. The many differences between believers—geographic, cultural, linguistic, ethnic, racial, tribal, class, and ideological—must not prevent them from viewing each other as brethren in faith, nor should it get in the way of friendly, cooperative, and peaceable relations. Islam acknowledges the variety of its adherents but ascribes them no political significance; the chasm separating Muslims from non-Muslims alone matters—and it affects all politics.

A single man, the caliph, or imam, is to rule all Dar al-Islam. Members of the three branches of Islam disagree about the way to select him,[28] but they all affirm that he has a mandate to rule Dar al-Islam as the temporal successor of Muhammad. Although frequently compared to the papacy, the caliphate fundamentally differs from it. As successor to Saint Peter, the pope inherits priestly and apostolic functions, not governmental duties; in contrast, the caliph rules Dar al-Islam but has no authority over decisions bearing on the faith. (In practice, however, in both cases their authority did overlap.) The caliph has two principal duties, applying the Shari'a and extending its domain (or, if times are bad, defending it from attacks by non-Muslims). From an Islamic viewpoint, whence a ruler comes, what language he speaks, or where he keeps his capital hardly matters; what counts is that he be an active Muslim who enforces Shar'i regulations and protects Muslims.

As the ruler's second duty implies, the division between Muslim and non-Muslim has dominated the military sphere too. While the Shari'a prohibits fighting between observant Muslims, it permits (and on some occasions even requires) Muslims to make war on non-Muslims. War on behalf of Islam is known as *jihad* and is usually translated into English as "holy war."[29] But "holy war" brings to mind warriors going off to battle with God in their hearts intent on spreading the faith—something like medieval European crusaders or soldiers of the Reformation. Jihad is less a holy war than a "righteous war," fighting carried out in accordance with the Shari'a. Of course, jihad must be on behalf of Islam, but the emphasis of its definition is on legality, not on holiness. A Muslim may go to battle with thoughts of Allah or he may dream of booty; the key is that his behavior should conform to the Shari'a and thereby increase the scope of its application. Not every attack on non-Muslims qualifies as jihad; there are elaborate restrictions which, if transgressed, make the fighting non-Shar'i and therefore not jihad. For instance, if an attack breaks an oath, it is not righteous war. Conversely, jihad can be directed against Muslims who flout the Shari'a, including apostates and brigands—hardly what "holy war" brings to mind.

More important yet, jihad is not holy war because its purpose is not to spread the faith. Non-Muslims commonly assume that jihad calls for the militant expansion of the Islamic *religion;* in fact, its purpose is to spread the rule of Islamic *law.* The logic behind law being the central concern of jihad has special importance for the topic of Islam and political power: to approach God properly, man must live by the Shari'a; because the Shari'a contains provisions which can only be executed by a government, the state has to be in the hands of Muslims; Muslims must therefore control territory; to do this, they need to wage war—and thus, the provision for jihad. If Muslims do not rule, kafirs do; by definition, the latter do not see the Shari'a as a sacred law. For expediency's sake, to minimize Muslim antagonism toward their rule, non-Muslims may enforce some Islamic precepts, especially private ones, but they would never go to the effort of implementing Shar'i public regulations. For these reasons, Islam requires the expulsion of non-Muslims from power and their replacement by believers, by force, if necessary.

Jihad, offensive in Dar al-Harb, defensive in Dar al-Islam, takes many forms: insurrection, invasion, aid to neighbors, self-defense, or guerrilla action. In addition to polities, tribes and individual warriors can launch a jihad on their own. Muslim power should be extended both to areas where Muslims already live and to where they do not, for Shar'i rule (in the Islamic view) brings advantages even to non-Muslims by preventing them from engaging in practices forbidden by God. Jihad, Muslims believe, should continue until they take control of the entire planet and all mankind becomes subject to Islam's law.

This goal has little in common with the widespread image of jihad as "Islam or the sword." Jihad impels Muslim conquests, not Islamic conversions, leading to the political subjugation of non-Muslims, not their religious coercion. "The primary aim of the jihad is not, as it was often supposed in the older European literature, the conversion by force of unbelievers, but the expansion—and also the defence—of the Islamic state."[30] In no case may the vanquished be compelled to embrace Islam; as the Qur'an puts it, "There is no compulsion in religion" (2.256). Conversion to Islam is not the purpose of righteous war, only its sweet by-product.

Islam makes no distinction among non-Muslims who resist Muslim political control; known as *harbis* (deriving from the Arabic *harb*, "war"), they must all be subjugated. Once defeated, however, their faith takes on crucial importance; for while the Shari'a allows some religions to continue to be practiced in Dar al-Islam, it proscribes others. Polytheists *(mushrikun)*, whose beliefs Islam considers wholly repugnant to God, may not practice their faith under Muslim rule. When conquered, they must convert to a monotheism or flee Dar al-Islam; otherwise, they face enslavement or even execution.

More fortunate are the Jews, Christians, Sabaens, and Zoroastrians, those peoples who believe in a single God and possess a holy scripture. Islam considers the faiths of these, known as People of the Book *(Ahl al-Kitab)*, faulty but nonetheless acceptable to God. Peoples of the Book who submit to Muslim political dominion are *dhimmis* (protected peoples). In return for the right to practice their ancestral religions, dhimmis pay extra taxes and must accept civil constraints and disabilities. They may not proselytize or build new places of worship; they may be subjected to petty and humiliating sumptuary regulations (such as prohibitions on certain clothes, the riding of horses, or living in multistoried dwellings). In court, dhimmis resemble slaves and Muslim women; the testimony of each of these counts about half that of a free Muslim man. Dhimmis also may not serve in the government or the military, for the public domain is a Muslim preserve. They may not make policy, administer, judge, or fight; these activities have direct implications for implementation of the Shari'a and are thus unsuitable for non-believers.

The Shari'a also legislates a system of taxation, which is based on the requirement to give charity. *Zakat,* or almsgiving, is a spiritual obligation connected with prayer, a way for a Muslim to purify himself from sin, to thank God for his well-being, and to demonstrate his concern for the brotherhood of Muslims. Although theoretically voluntary, zakat contributions already were obligatory in Muhammad's lifetime; and it was the first caliph, Abu Bakr, who made the zakat a tax collectible by the state. After that, the terms of zakat hardly changed; despite great economic and legal development, the original precepts from the time of Muhammad have remained "the only levy for Muslims ever sanctioned by religious law."[31]

The exact terms of zakat collections derive from the *Hadith* Reports. Zakat regulations distinguish between five forms of wealth: crops, fruit, livestock, precious metals, and merchandise. On annual crop and fruit yields Muslims pay one-tenth. Provisions concerning cattle are more complex: the herder must own a minimum number of head before he pays zakat; animals have different values; work animals are a special case; domestic beasts differ from wild ones;

and so forth. Finally, precious metals and merchandise are taxed at a rate of 2.5 percent. Zakat regulations allow very little scope for either taxpayer or government to modify these rates of assessment.

Islamic law provides for the disposal of property to a corporate body for perpetual ownership, *waqf* ("mortmain"). Liberal provisions made it possible for families to enjoy the benefits of the waqf, although this was not their original intent.

Finally, the Shariʻa requires that the government sponsor a judicial system to apply the civil, criminal, and commercial laws of Islam. Judges should be picked from among the legal scholars, the *faqih*s. The ruler personally must live by the Shariʻa and in particular by its prohibitions against drinking, gambling, dancing girls, unregulated sexual activity, and punishments that lack Shariʻi sanction. The Shariʻa bestows a unique importance on the behavior of political leaders. Governments monopolize the right to declare war, set tax rates, or punish crimes; for the implementation of these and other regulations, individual Muslims depend on their leaders to act in accordance with the Shariʻa. The government falling into improper hands—those of lax Muslims or non-Muslims—jeopardizes the standing of its citizens before God. For this reason, Muslim rulers have a far greater *religious* significance than do ordinary citizens. The individual who neglects the fast of Ramadan harms only himself, whereas the king who wages unrighteous war injures the entire community.

These observations lead to two general conclusions about Islam and politics. First, Islam and government are interdependent. Islam needs the state to effect public Shariʻi precepts, while the premodern Muslim government derives most of its legitimacy from maintaining the law. Thus, Shariʻi precepts connect the divine will to government policy, combining the two so thoroughly that devout Muslims (with the exception of some mystics) cannot disengage from being concerned with public life. A Muslim intent on fulfilling all Islam's requirements must live under Shariʻi rule; to assure this, he must involve himself in politics. "To be a Muslim is not simply a matter of individual belief; it means participating in the effort to implement God's will on earth."[32] The Shariʻa involves Islam so intimately in state affairs that no boundary can be drawn between religion and politics. Religious imperatives have political implications, political actions have religious significance.

Second, action on behalf of the Shariʻa takes two forms, depending on political conditions. Where Muslims rule and non-Muslims do not threaten, implementing the Shariʻa is a matter of getting the leaders to act in accordance with its precepts by pressuring them to apply the law or by replacing them with other leaders who will; borrowing a term from Christianity, I call the spirit behind such efforts "legalism."[33] But where kafirs rule or threaten Dar al-Islam, the first priority is to establish Muslims securely in power; only after that is achieved can devout Muslims work for legalist goals. Muslims under attack in Dar al-Islam have to repulse their enemies, while Muslims living in Dar al-Harb can either break away from their rulers or overthrow them. I call the impetus behind any of these efforts against non-Muslims "autonomism."

Legalism and autonomism together define the entire range of mainstream Islamic political action. In Islamic terminology, legalism corresponds to the goal of *al-amr bi'l-ma'ruf wa'n-nahi 'an al-munkar* ("the promotion of virtue and the punishment of vice"), while autonomism is the urge behind jihad.[34] Legalism is concerned with the status of Islam, autonomism with the power of Muslims. Legalism aims to apply the Shari'a, autonomism to establish its prerequisite conditions. In the end, both movements have the same goal: to create a government conducive to a fully Shar'i way of life, unimpeded by unwanted alien influences. These are the timeless imperatives of Islam, defining the goals of all movements on its behalf, whether premodern or modern, West African or Southeast Asian, governmental or oppositional, conservative or revolutionary, defensive or offensive, practical or visionary, peaceful or militant, minoritarian or majoritarian, and regardless of temperament or motives.

3

The Medieval Synthesis

> The sacred law could not be disregarded; nor could it, despite many adaptations, be really carried out in practice.
> —*Max Weber*

> The gap between what ought to be and what is, is strong in any religion, but it seems to be particularly strong in Islam.
> —*Gustave E. von Grunebaum*

ISLAM'S IDEALS are manifold and they are clear; but how do they work in practice, how fully have adherents implemented them? Again, a distinction must be drawn between private and public precepts. Premodern Muslims generally considered themselves successful at living in accordance with regulations concerning private life. Vastly disparate peoples around the world adopted stringent Shar'i restrictions, even where these conflicted with their own inherited customs. Polytheists became monotheists, monogamists became polygamists, matrilocals became patrilocals, matrilineals became patrilineals, cow-worshippers became beefeaters, bride prices replaced dowries, and fruit juices replaced alcohol. Local customs rarely gave way entirely, but Muslim peoples did come widely to share Islamic practices such as marriage customs, holiday celebrations, and butchering techniques. Shar'i customs fulfilled less well were usually the less personal, for example, the ban on interest fees or the dividing of inheritance shares. The success of precepts regulating the private sphere added greatly to Islam's hold over individual believers. As a result, the appeal of Islam lay largely in "the world of men in their families";[1] by satisfying personal needs, the sacred law became closely identified with a whole way of life.

Muslim experience with the public precepts was another matter, however. The study of any period or region of premodern history shows that Muslims persistently failed to live up to the public regulations to their own satisfaction. From the seventh-century caliphate to the fundamentalist movements of the eighteenth century, the Islamic state proved elusive. If premodern Muslims were able rigorously to implement the Shari'a here and there for brief periods, their overall experience was one of frustration; in general, Shar'i public ideals remained beyond the umma's reach. Dramatic contrasts between the implementation of private precepts and the non-implementation of public ones led Joseph Schacht, foremost historian of the Shari'a, to write:

> We can distinguish three different kinds of legal subject-matter . . . according to the degree to which the ideal theory of the *shari'a* succeeded in imposing itself on the practice. Its hold was strongest on the law of family (marriage, divorce, maintenance, &c.), of inheritance, and of pious foundations *(wakf)*; it was weakest, and in some respects even non-existent, on penal law, taxation, constitutional law, and the law of war; and the law of contracts and obligations stands in the middle.[2]

This chapter ignores those laws applying to the private sphere or to contracts and obligations; the concern here is with penal law, taxation, constitutional law, and the law of war—that is, with the public domain, where ideals and realities were at greatest variance. Before analyzing the reasons for this disparity and assessing its importance, one point must be emphasized: the observation that premodern Muslims did not implement the Shari'a is not my personal judgment but my understanding of Muslim perceptions. Just as Muslims in recent times unanimously believe that no government carries out the sacred law in its entirety, so too did their ancestors believe this in previous ages. To the best of my knowledge, Muslims nowhere at any time considered the Shari'a's public provisions completely implemented, at least not on a regular basis. This attitude had the greatest significance for Islam in politics.

Non-Implementation of the Law's Public Ideals

POLITICAL

A single state for all Muslims existed only about 130 years, from A.D. 622 to 753; after that, Muslim polities proliferated, emerging at a rate of about one every five years for the next century and at a slower rate after that. As Dar al-Islam expanded across the eastern hemisphere, new peoples with their own political traditions joined the umma. Whereas this expansion indicated vitality, it also destroyed any possibility of attaining Muslim unity. The Shar'i ideal of a single Muslim state receded into the background, irreparably broken despite the avid wishes of most Muslims. Muslim polities kept multiplying to the point that all but the very most idealistic abandoned hope of union. No state possessed the force necessary to bring all Muslims under a single rule and the competing leaders were hardly inclined to give up their own power for the sake of union.

In the view of most Sunni 'ulama, only the first four caliphs (the successors to Muhammad as leader of Dar al-Islam) were fully legitimate, for they alone applied the Shari'a conscientiously; their successors were only grudgingly recognized. In the Shi'i view, genuine Islamic government lasted an even briefer period, for they recognize as valid only the third of those first four caliphs, 'Ali ibn Abi Talib. The caliphs then lost their standing, beginning in 756, when the first rival Muslim ruler came to power in Spain. One century later, in 861, a group of palace soldiers took control of the caliphate in Baghdad. In 909 and 929 rival caliphates were established in Tunis and Cordova. And in 945 the original caliphate fell under the control of Shi'i tribesmen and permanently lost almost all its temporal power outside Iraq. The Mongols eliminated Abbasid rule in 1258, though a shadow line continued in Egypt for two and a half more centuries and the Ottoman ruler claimed to be "Caliph of all Muslims" in 1727.[3] Kemal Atatürk abolished the Ottoman caliphate in 1924 and, with the exception of a few unsuccessful claimants in the following years, there has not even been an attempt to revive the caliphate, Islam's central political institution, since that time.

MILITARY

In the initial years of Islam, when Muslims won almost every battle they fought and their borders kept expanding, jihad dominated their relations with Dar al-Harb, as the Shari'a demanded. But with time, as it became clear that the Muslims would not conquer all, as jihad petered out, Muslims entered into mutually tolerant, and sometimes even friendly, relations with the states of Dar al-Harb. Peace became a standard condition, in direct contradiction to the Shari'a, and in some cases lasted for centuries. In Nubia the Muslims made a treaty with the local peoples in 652 which stayed in force for over six centuries. With time, "the masses of Muslims lost interest in what was happening on the frontiers: they had enough to do in establishing themselves in the conquered countries and arranging their internal quarrels."[4]

Those internal quarrels, known in Arabic as *fitna*s, occurred with alarming frequency after the first decades and quickly consumed more energies than did jihad. Muslims first fought among themselves in 656 when a dispute over the caliphate pitted 'Uthman, the third caliph, against his successor 'Ali ibn Abi Talib. A civil war began one year later and the first major anti-government revolt took place in 681. Regional rebellions started in eastern Iran during the 720s. *Fitna* increasingly turned into conflict between states in the latter eighth century, as independent kingdoms split from the caliphate, beginning with remote regions such as Oman and Spain, then in such key provinces as Khurasan, Kurdistan, and Egypt.

With time, as Dar al-Islam expanded, most Muslim states acquired Muslim neighbors, against whom they inevitably made war on occasion. Between the Arab conquest and the French expedition of 1798, Egypt's rulers had the Crusaders to fight—otherwise, virtually all their enemies were Muslims. Despite the fact that Muslims were a minority in India, the many Muslim dynasties of the subcontinent probably fought each other more than the Hindus. It is impossible to quantify the ratio of jihad to *fitna,* but a reasonable estimate might be one to two or one to three. Some of the greatest Muslim conquerors made their mark by attacking other Muslims. Tamerlane (r. 1370–1405) invaded Anatolia, the Fertile Crescent, Iran, Central Asia, and India; Selim the Grim (r. 1512–20) nearly doubled the size of the Ottoman Empire by conquering Iraq, Syria, and Egypt; Babur (d. 1530) founded the Mughal Dynasty by defeating the other Muslim rulers of northwestern India. More recently, 'Abd al-'Aziz ibn Sa'ud built today's Saudi Arabia from scratch through thirty-two years of warfare (1902–34) against Muslim foes.

As soon as Dar al-Islam was ruled by more than a single government, two premier ideals of Islam became irreconcilable, the call for Muslim unity and the ban on war between believers. Unless Muslim states combined peacefully, which they never did, any attempt to establish greater Muslim unity required spilling Muslim blood. Therefore, a devout ruler could not try to bring Muslims under his aegis; yet, if he lacked pan-Islamic aspirations, he forfeited a principal source of political legitimacy.

Sentiments in favor of Muslim cooperation remained strong, but they had little practical effect. Thus arose what Claude Cahen terms "the contrast between the incontestable solidarity of feeling and the almost total absence of collaboration among states."[5] Failure to eliminate war between believers disturbed Muslims more than any other failure to implement Shar'i goals, for it acutely symbolized the inability of Islam's laws to create a new political order.

SOCIAL

Rulers sought dhimmi subjects because the Shari'a sanctioned more taxes from them than from Muslims. As presently will be seen, Islamic taxes hardly ever covered government needs, so additional sources of legal revenues were prized. This had the curious consequence that the more pious a ruler was and the more concerned to follow Shari'i regulations, the greater his incentive was to encourage dhimmi subjects not to convert. Quite contrary to the Muslims' reputation for imposing their religion on others, rulers in Dar al-Islam sometimes prevented dhimmi subjects from becoming Muslim; as early as the seventh century, the governor of Iraq, Hajjaj ibn Yusuf, refused to recognize the conversion of some of his subjects and called out the troops to return them to their villages. A ruler who encouraged conversion despite its economic penalty to himself was either so pious that he ignored fiscal needs or (more likely) so hopelessly dependent on non-Shar'i taxes that the prospect of a few more illegal revenues hardly mattered.

The expansion of Muslim power far beyond the lands of Jews, Christians, and other monotheists created unexpected problems. In India, for example, where Muslims ruled over huge numbers of Hindus, it was out of the question to compel them to choose between conversion, eviction, enslavement, and execution. In practice, therefore, peoples not "of the Book" had to be treated like dhimmis. The Muslim authorities came to recognize Hinduism as a monotheism possessing sacred scriptures. Thus, Hindus living under Muslim rule were eligible to enjoy the privileges of dhimmis—especially the right to continue to practice their own religion. Similar accommodations were reached with Buddhists and Confucians; and at times even animists in Africa, Inner Asia, and Southeast Asia came to be treated as dhimmis.

From an Islamic viewpoint, far worse than this was the reliance by Muslim rulers on dhimmis to fill public offices. From the very first years of Islam, kafirs staffed key political and military positions. Few in number and poorly skilled, tribesmen from Arabia could not on their own rule the immense empire created by the initial Islamic expansion. Until converts to Islam enlarged the community of Muslims, the caliphs depended on dhimmis to administer such advanced areas as Egypt and Iran. Subsequently, as the pool of Arabian soldiers dried up, dhimmis acquired a large role in the armed forces. Early use of dhimmis in these capacities established an important precedent which was henceforth imitated to such an extent that some dhimmi groups became identified with certain functions. Copts became the mainstay of the Egyptian bureaucracy while Hindus filled government positions at virtually all levels in India. French mercenaries provided the heavy cavalry in medieval Andalusia and Greeks became sailors on Ottoman ships.

Ironically, the ways in which Muslim rulers failed to apply Shar'i regulations with regard to the dhimmis status benefited non-Muslims; but these harmed the rulers' reputations as pious Islamic leaders.

FINANCIAL

Although most economic provisions of the Shari'a proved untenable, two in particular had importance for public life: restrictions on taxes and the inviolability of waqfs. The first Muslim rulers found the zakat sufficient, for the conquests provided them with a massive inflow of booty and their subjects were predominantly non-Muslims who paid higher taxes. The first need for additional duties to cover government expenditures may have been in 764 when Caliph al-Mansur was building a capital city at Baghdad. He attempted to embue the new taxes with an Islamic image by appointing Muslim religious authorities to collect them, thus causing considerable unhappiness among the 'ulama. Yet Muslim rulers, even the most pious ones, found that Shar'i taxes could not pay for normal government expenses (mostly related to the army and royal court) and they persistently supplemented their revenues by assessing taxes not mentioned in the Shari'a (known in Arabic as a *maks,* in the plural, *mukus*), but in many cases rents, tolls, customs, tariffs, imposts, levies, assessments, excises, and capitations were called zakat to give them a semblance of legality—fooling no one, of course. Before long, *maks* became standard practice, as "the fiscal needs of the Muslim states after the ninth and tenth centuries simply no longer allowed for permanent renunciation of the noncanonical [namely, non-Shar'i] resources." A state which forewent the revenues brought in by non-legal taxes found that these "could never be made up for by the enforcement of the canonical, yet obsolete zakat with its insufficient tax yield."[6]

As non-Shar'i taxes proliferated, their elimination became a vital goal for devout Muslims. Restricting taxes to only the zakat "became the paragon of the lost order of primordial Islam, of the divine state on earth, which worldly tyrants have destroyed and adulterated. Return to the zakat, implying the abolition of the illegal extra levies, became the watchword of radical Muslim reformers."[7] The attempt was made most notably by the Almoravids in Spain after 1090, followed shortly by the Ayyubids in Syria and Egypt. Even when the founder of a dynasty held strictly to the zakat, his successors invariably returned to *maks.* For Saladin, founder of the Ayyubid dynasty, applying the Shari'a "in the lands under his direct control was an issue of the highest priority. Whenever people approached him complaining about illegal taxes and imposts, he hastened to order their abolition. Saladin's son promptly reenacted, and even increased, the former mukus."[8] The persistent inability of Muslim rulers to live within the financial constraints established by the Shari'a undermined the legitimacy of their governments and alienated their subjects.

*Waqf*s supposed to last in perpetuity never did. Just as in Europe, these mortmain properties were eventually expropriated because they created an intolerable imbalance of wealth. Beneficiaries of waqfs found themselves an irresistible target to aging regimes desperate for new sources of income or new conquerors unconcerned to preserve prior agreements. As a consequence, few mortmain properties lasted much beyond the duration of a dynasty.

JUDICIAL

The Shar'i legal system entails the most remarkably narrow rules of procedure, allowing hardly any discretion to the presiding judge, the qadi. Shar'i laws are administered in only one forum, a court with a single judge: there are no lawyers, no juries, no multiple-judge courts, no appeals courts. The rules of evidence are as simple as they are difficult to fulfill: in most cases, the plaintiff must produce two adult Muslim men of good character and established position to give identical oral testimony in which they claim firsthand knowledge of wrongdoing. Some variation is allowed, but not much: one man and two women can take the place of two male witnesses or the plaintiff himself may sometimes serve as witness; four male witnesses are required in adultery cases. Circumstantial evidence is not accepted, no matter how convincing: an unmarried girl giving birth is not proof of fornication. Rather, reputable witnesses must see the sexual act *in flagrante delicto.* The fact that "criminal offences are not normally committed in the presence of two male adult witnesses of high moral probity" means that conviction is often impossible to get, even when the evidence is overwhelming.[9] Herein lies the basic impracticality of the Shari'a: "the emphasis of the Islamic law of procedure lies not so much on arriving at the truth as on applying certain formal rules."[10]

Judges have but two functions before reaching a verdict: "to determine, first, which party carries the burden of proof and, second, whether the witnesses that are to be called are qualified, on grounds of integrity of character and so forth, to testify or not. Once these two issues have been decided and the legal process set in motion, the judge merely presides to see that the process follows its prescribed course. The testimony is given, the oath [giving the defendant an opportunity to swear his innocence] is administered or refused and the verdict follows automatically." Where testimony conflicts and no verdict is evident, the judge may abstain from making a judgment and the case is dismissed.[11]

Historians have suggested that these extreme limitations on the qadis were designed to protect them from pressure by the political authorities; the less control judges had over procedure, the less susceptible they were to outside interference. Perhaps more important, judges wanted protection from the sacred law itself. Many of the leading qadis were recruited from the ranks of jurists, scholars who preferred studying the law in the isolation of their libraries to applying it in courts of law. Although jurists stayed far from the courts, happy to let government officials do the business of judging, they were frequently called to serve on the bench. Some strenuously resisted (one man accepted an appointment only after being threatened with getting thrown off a roof if he refused), but many did agree. Weighed down by the immensity of their responsibility, they protected themselves from possibly miscarrying the law by developing a procedure so strict that it absolved them of almost all individual decisions.

As a result, Shar'i justice did not work; it was too cumbersome, inflexible and irrational; "Shar'i criminal law was so mild that most pre-Modern Muslim rulers felt bound to save their subjects from the results of applying it intact."[12] Noel Coulson writes that Shar'i courts "as a whole considered themselves bound by the doctrine as expounded in the Shari'a manuals; and because this doctrine proved insupportable in practice, jurisdiction in matters of general civil law, contracts and commercial transactions, was assumed by other tribunals."[13] Those tribunals included courts that applied customary laws; market inspectors who enforced Islamic morals and behavioral standards; police chiefs who applied their own brand of justice; and *mazalim* (complaint) courts which first heard grievances against the government, then expanded to hear property cases and many other matters more properly falling under Shar'i jurisdiction. All these courts used simple means of procedure to arrive at reliable decisions, unhampered by the cumbersome and unrealistic restrictions imposed by the Shari'a. In some regions, these alternate courts so expanded that qadis eventually handled only family law (marriages, divorces, and inheritance in particular). Even rulers devoted to implementing the Shari'a took recourse to alternate courts, always for the same practical reasons. "As a result of all this, a double administration of justice, one religious and exercised by the *kadi* on the basis of the *shari'a,* the other secular and exercised by the political authorities on the basis of custom, of equity and fairness, sometimes of arbitrariness, of governmental regulations, . . . has prevailed in practically the whole of the Islamic world."[14]

Shar'i justice rarely penetrated the government itself; rulers ignored its provisions at will, taking women as they pleased, executing viziers on whim, and dispensing a *One Thousand and One Nights* style justice. Only the most devout kings allowed themselves to be restricted by the Shari'a; and lower ranks of the government also rarely concerned themselves with the niceties of Shar'i justice. The divide grew deep: "orthodox Islam refused to be drawn into too close a connexion with the state. . . . The result was that Islamic law became more and more removed from practice, but in the long run gained more in power over the minds than it lost in control over the bodies of Muslims."[15] In other words, Muslim peoples became ever more devoted to the Shar'i principles which eluded them.

The Shari'a calls for peace among Muslims, but how can many millions of believers never conflict? How can a single ruler control the vast expanse of Dar al-Islam? Governments and armies needed dhimmis, and polytheists had to be considered no different from dhimmis. Shar'i taxes were inadequate for agrarian countries, mortmain regulations ignored the effects of accumulated wealth, and the judicial system failed to meet the needs of litigants. Islamic theory assigned government the task of carrying out important aspects of the Shari'a, but in reality, "few Muslim rulers in history have made it the main business of state, as the Koran had intended, to enforce Allah's eternal laws."[16]

In the end, most of the Shari'a was not implemented. As H. A. R. Gibb writes, "The political and administrative institutions, a large part of penal jurisdiction, and most large-scale commerce lay outside its range of effective action, even if their procedures might sometimes be accommodated within its framework by means of legal fictions."[17] Christiaan Snouck Hurgronje saw the situation similarly: "All the departments of life which should be controlled by [the Shari'a] were from the beginning actually controlled by custom or by the caprice of the rulers. The whole political part of the Canon Law [that is, the Shari'a] is a disapproving criticism of the actual situation in all Moslim states. . . . The main body of this Canonical Law has never been put in practice."[18]

In this way, Muslims differed from the adherents of other religions; although no body of faithful entirely satisfied the moral and ethical requirements of its religion, Muslims alone had a public sphere in which to fail as well. Clive S. Kessler notes: "All religions collide with social reality, and Islam more than others because of its problematic social theory. It is precisely because, unlike the other major religions, Islam is believed to be sociologically equipped that it occasions in its followers the most poignant and testing experience of those more general dilemmas."[19] If governments in Christian countries transgressed Christ's message, their evil actions had no direct bearing on the faith of their citizens; but because the Shari'a makes demands on the rulers, political failings had direct repercussions. "In spite of [Islam's] political incapacity, no religion keeps men's eyes more fixed on the way the world is run."[20]

The Shari'a stands in a unique relationship to the state: on the one hand, it bestows legitimacy on a government and sets policies; on the other hand, it was created by private scholars remote from political office and it may be amended only by them, not by the government. The fact that the Shari'a imposes conditions on governments that cannot be implemented to the satisfaction of Muslims is undoubtedly the result of its being drawn up by jurists not answerable to public officials. The Shari'a is as much an intellectual's vision of politics as Marxism, and just as impractical.

Withdrawal from Power

Non-implementation of the Shari'a confronted Muslim peoples with a choice of two responses, one conservative, the other radical: they could acknowledge human foibles, resign themselves to the imperfect circumstances in which they lived, and accept the status quo; or they could struggle relentlessly to suppress these failings, align Muslim society with Islamic ideals, and create a Shar'i utopia. Because the latter option meant rising up against existing governments and violently overthrowing them, bringing massive unrest and possibly destroying the Islamic way of life, Muslims rarely took this route, more often preferring to accept things as they were. Through most of Muslim history, the urge to rebel against unrighteous governments was rejected in the interests of avoiding *fitna.* "So long as the secular governments did not interfere with the social institutions of Islam and formally recognized the Shari'a, the conscience of believers was not outraged and the task of building up a stable and universal Muslim society could go on."[21]

A balance between Shar'i goals and human realities emerged; this is what I call the *medieval synthesis,* an immensely stable and attractive combination of ideal goals and pragmatic actions which held in several continents and over many centuries. This willingness to accept imperfect conditions will be referred to as *traditionalist* Islam. Traditionalists were Muslims who, finding the medieval synthesis satisfactory, did not attempt to implement the sacred law in its entirety. For them, the preservation of Muslim society took precedence over complete implementation of the law. They did pressure for improvements, but in careful, gradual ways, making sure not to ruin a tolerable situation in the pursuit of a better one.

At the heart of the traditionalist attitude lay the willingness of the 'ulama, keepers of the sacred law, to abide by partial implementation. They made the gap between ideal and reality more tolerable by condoning minimalist interpretations of the Muslim duties and bending the law when it was not applicable. The ban on interest between Muslims was clearly impractical; with the approval of the 'ulama, Muslims circumvented it by resorting to legal tricks which permitted interest payments while fulfilling the letter of the law.

On the public level too, no serious attempt was made to effect the Qur'anic or *Hadith* doctrines in their entirety. Muslims came to terms with the fact that many kings ruled, not one caliph; that the umma was irrevocably split; that Shar'i-sanctioned taxes did not suffice; and so forth. The scriptures may have "a strong tendency to put the collectivity above the individual and to treat individual believers as equals," but "these tendencies have not usually had political or economic consequences in traditional Islam." Specifically with regard to wealth, "no serious, sustained attempt was made to translate the Brotherhood of Believers into economic terms."[22]

In politics, the 'ulama came to accept almost any ruler:

Successive jurists made [sundry] accommodations with a deteriorating reality, until finally the whole system of juristic constitutional theory was tacitly abandoned, and a new approach devised, based on the principle that any effective authority, however obtained and however exercised, was better than unrestrained private violence. "Tyranny is better than anarchy," became a favourite theme of the jurists.[23]

This eventually became the prevailing attitude of Muslim subjects toward their governments. Among Muslims living in Dar al-Harb, similar realistic attitudes developed and they endured kafir rule far more often than they rebelled.

Non-implementation became so universal that the more a Muslim appreciated the sacred law per se, the less he expected it to be applied. According to Snouck Hurgronje, "all classes of the Muslim community have exhibited in practice an indifference to the sacred law in all its fulness, quite equal to the reverence with which they regard it in theory."[24] Knowledgeable about the law as they were, the 'ulama were "the last to contradict" the general awareness that the Shari'a had "never been put in practice"; instead, they emphasized "the fact that the laws expounded by them are only fitted for a better society than that of their contemporaries" and relegated the fully Shar'i society to the remote future. Discussions about the law "are full of sighs of despair over the ever-wider cleavage between ideal and reality," yet the Muslim legal experts accepted this condition as normal and natural.[25]

Acceptance of the medieval synthesis meant that Muslim peoples, whether in Dar al-Islam or Dar al-Harb, usually submitted to the control of existing governments, however deficient these might be from a Shar'i viewpoint. As Shar'i goals were subordinated to the need for stability, obedience to the political authorities became the norm and preservation of the status quo became an end in itself, creating an overwhelmingly conservative political environment.

Toleration of the status quo did not imply, however, a willingness to asso-

ciate with the authorities who maintained it. Working closely with the government implied becoming party to violating the Shari'a, so Muslims of all stra-
ta—landowners, merchants, artisans, intellectuals, and farmers—removed
themselves from public administration and the armed forces.[26] As rulers carved
up Dar al-Islam, warred against fellow believers, relied on dhimmis, extracted
illegal taxes, expropriated waqfs, and imposed their own notions of justice,
subjects responded by staying away from state affairs. "The spiritual health
of the community could be safeguarded only by avoiding all personal commitment to and contamination by the agencies and the hirelings of political
power."[27] Islam's lofty public ideals made Muslim subjects view the world of
power as polluted and purposeless, and retreat from it.

Egypt provides a striking illustration of withdrawal from public life: for
two-and-a-half thousand years, not a single ruler of Egypt considered himself
a native of the country, a "son of the Nile." These rulers were from all points
of the compass—Tunisia, Libya, Nubia, Ethiopia, Arabia, Syria, Iraq, Iran,
Turkestan, Kurdistan, the Caucasus, Anatolia, Greece, Albania, Italy, France,
and Britain. In 525 B.C. the Persians conquered Egypt, and they were followed
by Alexander the Great, the Romans, the Arabians, and a long sequence of
Muslim dynasties, all of which originated outside Egypt—the Umayyads, Abbasids, Tulunids, Ikhshidids, Fatimids, Mamluks, Ottomans, and Muhammad
'Ali's line—and then by the French and British. Not until the overthrow of
King Faruq by the Free Officers in 1952 did native Egyptians again control
their own country.

Egyptians excluded themselves almost completely from military affairs as
well. In contrast to their considerable role before the coming of Islam in 642,
they opted out during the Islamic period—except for some Bedouin units. It
was only in the nineteenth century, with suitable foreign soldiers in short supply and the ruler of Egypt, Muhammad 'Ali, aware of the power of the French
citizen army, that Egyptians were recruited for the armed forces. Even so, descendants of foreign soldiers, known as Turko-Egyptians, controlled the army
until the beginning of this century. Native Egyptians did play a larger role
in the bureaucracy, rising sometimes to positions of high responsibility, but
these tended to be Copts rather than Muslims.

Because Muslim governments everywhere failed to implement the Shari'a
in roughly parallel ways, a similar pattern of withdrawal occurred throughout
Dar al-Islam; indeed, this was the single most distinctive aspect of public life
in premodern Islamdom. Muslims living in the tenth or the eighteenth century
agonized equally over the inflexibility of Shar'i court procedures, Malays and
Hausas equally regretted Islamic disunity, and all believers grieved when Muslim rulers made war on each other. Not attaining Islamic ideals affected Muslims no less than achieving them; Shar'i injunctions in the breach lost none

of their significance. This accounts for some of the most important features of Muslim politics, including: the dependence on outsiders as administrators and soldiers, the wide gap between rulers and ruled, apolitical behavior of the masses, weak allegiances to governments, and the instability of governments.

The unwillingness of the Muslim subject to fill government positions forced rulers to look elsewhere for manpower. "The Muslim would require of his political organization a certain perfection; if this was lost, the principle of obedience which he owed it was also lost."[28] Foreigners, non-Muslims, slaves, and other outsiders replaced him, and in the process created a nearly insurmountable barrier between the governors and the governed. This in turn further alienated Muslim subjects from the state. Changes in rulers were "mere dynastic conflicts, irrelevant to the welfare of the community as a whole."[29] Kings, shahs, padishahs, sultans, emirs, sheikhs, and beys inhabited a world of their own, surrounded by a military elite, speaking their own languages, casually indifferent to the welfare of the masses. "For most of his subjects, the sultan's power was . . . absolute but almost irrelevant."[30] In the end, two societies emerged, a ruling class of outsiders and the rest of the population.

In a supreme irony, the public ideals of Islam had an impact exactly contrary to their intent. Although Shar'i precepts imply that observant Muslims should involve themselves closely with government, in fact they caused believers to draw away from public life. The failure to implement the Shari'a prompted Muslim subjects to turn inward and reduce their contact with the authorities. They paid taxes, fulfilled their obligations, and hoped to be left in peace. While leaders butchered, rebelled, invaded, and plundered, the subjects did their best to stay out of the way, devoting themselves instead to private affairs which offered surer and more acceptable rewards. Family life, social intercourse, cultural and religious activities, and business took the place of politics.

The Shari'a called for the subordination of public affairs to the sacred law but instead separated the two. The cliché that Islam makes no distinction between religious and political affairs is true in theory; in reality, the effort to merge them caused a massive disjuncture. Instead of incorporating the world of politics into that of religion, Shar'i precepts broke the ties, preventing all but a few Muslims from taking part in public life. Claude Cahen sums up the situation in this fashion:

In a society where the law, given by God, is safeguarded by the community, where the sovereign is neither its source or guardian, the state cannot be conceived of except as a superstructure with which the populace does not feel solidarity, a superstructure all the more remote because the princes took measures contrary to the law and, in the Middle Ages, were in addition often aliens themselves. This made the search for structures of solidarity (and protection too) all the more oriented toward the private domain. These structures did not need to derive from Islam itself, but could predate it; other societies, starting with Europe's, had them as well. All the same, Islam offered them the fullest scope.[31]

This disjuncture accounts for the weak sense of loyalty to the state in premodern Islamdom. What mattered to a Muslim were small-scale affiliations, such as the tribe village, or city quarter—a myriad of minuscule but enduring associations. He also felt an attachment to the umma as a whole. But he lacked allegiance to the political unit; the domain that rulers controlled appeared arbitrary and almost meaningless. It made little difference that he happened to be the subject of this or that state, for the government neither touched his daily life nor did it rouse him at times of war. Even when Muslim kingdoms did correspond to cultural units (such as Morocco, Egypt, or Iran), they still had little claim to their subjects' loyalties. Just as an American is merely resident in his state but a citizen of the United States, or a Frenchman is resident in a *département* but a citizen of France, so Egyptians were residents in a kingdom but citizens of the umma. "Egypt in Islam was not so much a nation or even a country as simply a place"; more generally, "there were no geographically defined communities in the Muslim world."[32]

Wars between Muslim ruling elites looked like pointless jousts to the masses, who stayed aside. Going to war for the kingdom appealed to Muslims about as much as going to war for a state government might appeal to an American; he would do so only to save his life. For a believer, the king in Cairo at war with the king in Damascus was like the governor of Illinois at war with the governor of Indiana. Even jihad did not help bring rulers and subjects closer, for warfare against non-Muslims enhanced the Islamic spirit, not allegiance to a king.

Muslim political loyalty was directed to a notion that had no structure. The umma, unlike the United States government or the French republic, was not a political reality. Muslims gave their support to an abstraction—as though Americans saved their warmest feelings not for their nation but for North America or the Occident. "Loyalty thus went more to the ideal than to the real state."[33] As a result, most Muslim peoples inhabited "a cosmopolitan social order that was not state oriented."[34]

Indeed, existing political structures were often despised: the Muslim's "first loyalty was to the ideals and institutions of Islam, and this might involve a negative attitude, or even demand a hostile attitude, to the secular rulers."[35] Kingdoms came and went, leaving little impress on their subjects. Muslims expected little of their governments and took refuge in ideals. Wilfred Cantwell Smith observes:

As armies marched back and forth, and principalities abruptly rose and fell, the so-cial order and especially the moral order existed insofar as they did exist for most of the population not . . . because of the ruler and the state structure but almost despite them. . . . Only a few of the norms could actually be implemented, but the whole disem-bodied pattern of them could be and was to be reverenced.[36]

Muslim subjects drew "a sharp *de facto* line of demarcation between political and religious authority," relegating the former to as distant and unimportant a role in their lives as they could.[37]

Muslim withdrawal from power was a major cause for the endemic instabil-ity of Muslim states; unable to call on their subjects, the rulers lacked legiti-macy and maintained their grasp on power only by force of arms. For this reason, as Georg Hegel observed, Muslim kingdoms and dynasties were a "boundless sea" on which "there is a continual onward movement; nothing abides firm."[38]

As a result of these conditions, according to G. E. von Grunebaum,

the state becomes a superstructure with which the population does not identify itself and whose territorial boundaries and other forms of structure are basically ir-relevant so long as it guarantees the preservation and, if possible, the expansion of religion. . . .[39]

[The medieval Muslim concerns himself with politics] only when faith is at war with unbelief. He assumes no responsibility for social or civic betterment beyond defraying his canonical [that is, Shar'i] obligations to the authorities and to his fellowmen. He is frequently impatient with his rulers and thinks little of rioting, but on the whole he is content to let the princes play their game. . . . No Muslim government ever tried to develop civic sentiment. Accordingly, there was little attachment to the political body to which one happened to belong or to any particular regime (except on sectarian grounds). But there was an overwhelming feeling for the oneness of the Muslim com-munity.[40]

Devotion to that oneness of the community often increased as a result of disappointment with local rulers. The Shari'a as a whole benefited in some ways from the inadequacy of real conditions, becoming "an inner reality much more persistent and vital than the transient political existence of the Islamic empire. For this law held the *umma* together and provided through its univer-sality a bond much stronger and more enduring than any other loyalty."[41] Put another way: the fact that Islam's social and political theory "was never in classical times applied served only to enhance (through years of turmoil and oppression) popular commitment to it, and the fact that it was dreamed and debated rather than applied served only to exempt it from ever being tested, for its weaknesses, by practice."[42] The vision of a single Muslim government applying the Shari'a helped believers endure their disappointment with actual political conditions. In the detached world of Muslim political aspirations, religious bonds counted infinitely more than proximity, language, or ethnic affiliation; and a vague, dreamy quality became characteristic of Muslim attitudes toward legitimate power.

Withdrawal from power meant that personal piety emerged as a satisfactory way for devout Muslims to fulfill their religious obligations. In the medieval synthesis, private life became distinct from politics.

Occasions for Action

If the inability of the rulers to implement Shar'i precepts drove premodern Muslim peoples from public life, sporadic attempts to apply the law attracted wide support. The opportunity to further Islamic goals prompted powerful responses and inspired great political and military efforts. For a movement in Islamdom to gain popular support, it had to aspire to bring Muslims more fully under Shar'i rule. Although Muslim subjects were often referred to by the Arabic term ra'iya ("tended flock"), indicating their passivity, it would be more apt to see them as cattle which, normally placid and compliant, sometimes turned against authorities and stampeded them. Rejection of the medieval synthesis happened rarely, usually at moments of acute crisis, but often enough to keep Muslim rulers apprehensive.

The contempt Muslims felt for their actual rulers did not extend to the state itself, which was always seen as the agency that could one day put the ideals of Islam into effect. "Despite all the imperfections of the governors," writes H. A. R. Gibb, "government as such retained something of a moral aura as the defender of the interests and religious values of the community." Muslims continued to hope that a state would eventually fulfill their expectations; they looked beyond the men, institutions, and policies in power at the moment and concerned themselves with the "preservation of the system of religious and moral duties elaborated in the law." Muslims pulled back from political affairs, which seemed tawdry and useless, while keeping faith in the possibility of Shar'i government; they gave up on their rulers but not on the ideals of Islam. "This distinction between authority and power is fundamental for an understanding of the Muslim attitude toward government."[43] As opportunities arose to bring politics in line with the Shari'a, Muslims were galvanized, in sharp contrast to their usual somnolence in public matters.

When Muslims did act politically, they almost invariably followed the legalist or autonomist drives delineated at the end of chapter 2. Muslim peoples living in Dar al-Islam either rejected the medieval synthesis and took up arms against their own rulers (legalism) or they fought non-Muslims (autonomism).

LEGALIST MOVEMENTS

However strong the traditionalist approach, Muslim peoples at some level never forgot the precepts of Islam in their entirety and in some fashion were concerned to abide by them. Efforts to portray *fitna* as jihad and *maks* as zakat were not convincing; obedience to the law being the foremost way for a Muslim to submit to God's wishes, efforts to implement the Shari'a recurred occasionally and had great force. Radical legalist movements could take either of two forms: some prepared for the end of the world, others looked back to a mythic golden age. The first type of movement, which anticipated an imminent day of resurrection, took on a messianic form. The Islamic messiah, known as the *mahdi* ("the rightly-guided one") begins the process that leads to the end of history and ushers in the day of judgment. Shi'is believe the mahdi will bring a law more perfect than the Shari'a (which helps explain why so many Shi'i messianic movements, including the Assassins, Druze, 'Alawis, Ahl-i Haqq, and Baha'is, easily slip beyond the bounds of mainstream Islam). Sunnis, however, believe that the mahdi will initiate an age of perfect adherence to the Shari'a; to them he is thus an ideal vehicle for legalist movements. Of many Sunni movements devoted to eradicating non-Shar'i practices, perhaps the most significant was that of the Almohads which rose to power in North Africa under Ibn Tumart in the early twelfth century.

Most Muslims expressed their devotion to the Shari'a in non-apocalyptic ways, however, concerning themselves more with recalling the faith and actions of the Prophet Muhammad and his companions than preparing for the day of judgment. By minutely interpreting every act of the early Muslims and viewing them as paragons of Islamic believers, Muslims used them as models of conduct. In its moderate form, this impulse served as the rationale for basing the Shari'a on *Hadith* Reports; in its extreme form, it inspired radical attempts to live exactly as did the early Muslims. In recognition of their stress on the fundamental features of Islam, these radical legalists will be called *fundamentalists*.[44] Fundamentalism developed as the main alternative to the medieval synthesis. Whereas traditionalists accepted the non-implementation of the Shari'a, fundamentalists demanded its full application, as they imagined had been done in the first years of Islam.

It may help to clarify the distinction between legalism and fundamentalism: the former is an impulse, the latter a specific program. Legalism includes any drive to apply the Shari'a, be it traditionalist, mahdist, fundamentalist, or other. Fundamentalism refers specifically to a rejection of compromise and an attempt to implement the sacred law in its entirety. Because fundamentalist movements are spectacular and on occasion powerfully important, the mention of Islam and politics usually brings them first to mind. Their premodern history is briefly discussed here; their modern role is analyzed at greater length in chapter 6; and their impact on politics in recent years is documented in chapter 9.

The origins of the fundamentalist spirit go back to the earliest period; the Kharijis, Islam's third major branch (the others being the Sunnis and the Shi'is), emerged in the 650s, fervent to follow Shar'i precepts in every detail, ready to denounce as non-Muslims whoever disagreed with their extreme views. Within Sunni Islam itself, four *madhhab*s, or rites of law, emerged by the tenth century, each with slightly different rules and emphases. One of them, the Hanbali, demanded the strictest adherence to the law, and its doctrines at times inspired radical legalism; indeed, it was a Hanbali thinker, Ahmad ibn Taymiya (1263–1328), whose writings laid much of the groundwork for the subsequent development of fundamentalist thought.

Until the eighteenth century, however, radical legalists only occasionally succeeded in disrupting the conservative consensus of traditionalist Islam, before disappearing again. It was only in the eighteenth century—in large part as a result of the tensions attendant on the expansion of Islam and Muslim rule to new regions in Europe, Africa, India, and Southeast Asia in late medieval times—that fundamentalism developed institutional supports. As many new peoples converted to Islam, they introduced non-Islamic influences which Muslims responded to in latitudinarian or legalist ways. In some cases, diverse cultural elements were allowed expression and even institutionalized: in the Ottoman empire, society was organized along confessional lines, known as the *millet* system, giving non-Muslims unusual freedom; Akbar, the Mughal king, disestablished Islam and attempted to found a new court cult acceptable to both his Hindu and Muslim officers; the Sikh religion made an appeal to Hindus and Muslims alike; and so forth. But other Muslims had the contrary response, and this resulted in the intellectual and organizational growth of legalism, which then peaked in the eighteenth century. This era, once dismissed as the dark age of Islam, has special importance for modern times, for it was then that many of the radical programs of religious purification developed which did so much to determine the shape of fundamentalist movements in the following centuries. Of these, probably the most important were the Neo-Sufi brotherhoods and the fundamentalist thinkers in western Arabia.

Sufi brotherhoods had mobilized legalist movements before the eighteenth century—for example, in the establishment of the Almoravid, Almohad, and Safavid dynasties—but they had in general been less interested in Shar'i precepts than in making spiritual connections to God. The Sufi urge tended to be mystical, antinomian, and very little concerned with dry laws; not until the eighteenth century did Sufi brotherhoods become an important vehicle of legalist opposition to latitudinarianism. The dedication that these brotherhoods showed to bring society into conformity with Shar'i requirements made them fundamentally different from their predecessors; to distinguish them, the new brotherhoods are sometimes called Neo-Sufi.

Most notable of these was the Naqshbandiya, which had originated in Central Asia and took on a strongly fundamentalist character in India (where it led the opposition to the type of reform attempted by the emperor Akbar). Naqshbandi brotherhoods spread rapidly through most of Islamdom, including Egypt, Turkey, the Levant, the Hijaz, Yemen, the Caucasus, Turkestan, and Sumatra. Some of the most renowned Muslim fighters against imperial European expansion, including Shamil in the Caucasus and leading figures of the Sepoy revolt in India were closely associated with the Naqshbandiya. Other Neo-Sufi brotherhoods had a more regional impact. The Khalwatiya spread to most of Muslim Africa, where it split into suborders, such as the Tijaniya in Morocco and West Africa and the Rahmaniya in Algeria and Tunisia. Brotherhoods with special regional impact included the Tayyibiya in Morocco, the Darqawiya in Algeria, the Sanusiya in Libya, the Khatmiya in the Sudan, the Salihiya in Somalia and the Sammaniya in Indonesia. Many persons, including religious leaders, belonged to more than one brotherhood, intertwining them in ways that have yet to be unravelled.

The second, often related, development began with the activities of religious scholars in the two holy cities of Arabia, Mecca and Medina. Both had long been sites of religious thinking, but it was only in the seventeenth century that their efforts to reconsider the *Hadith* Reports made them intellectually prominent. The scholars reviewed basic Shari'a documents with an eye to purifying society of non-Islamic practices. As in the Protestant Reformation, the assertion of the right to reconsider old decisions was in ways even more important than the specific content of that review. Even though these scholars (like Martin Luther) had a profoundly conservative intent, their activities had a radical effect, clearing the way for others too to re-examine the Islamic record and draw new conclusions. The efforts of scholars in Mecca and Medina became known throughout Islamdom via the hajj, as pilgrims each year returned from the Hijaz bearing new ideas.

Some of the more prominent disciples of the scholars included: (1) Jabril ibn Umar, who studied in Cairo and taught the new ideas to Uthman dan Fodio; in 1804, the latter launched the Fulani jihads in the northern Nigeria area which convulsed the region for decades. (2) Muhammad ibn 'Abd al-Wahhab studied for many years in Mecca and founded a movement that came to be named after him, the Wahhabiya, probably the most extreme fundamentalist movement ever to succeed politically. In 1744, he formed an alliance with a tribal leader, Muhammad ibn Sa'ud which assured the Wahhabis a lasting voice in Arabian politics. In turn, the Wahhabis influenced other fundamentalists; for instance, a Moroccan sultan sent a delegation to Mecca in 1812 to learn about Wahhabi practices. (3) A Moroccan scholar, Ahmad ibn Idris, studied in Mecca and later established an independent state, run by religious leaders, in Asir province, to the south of Mecca. (4) Shah Wali Ullah, the outstanding Islamic thinker of India, studied in the Hijaz in the early eighteenth century. (5) Shariat Allah, the founder of the Fara'idiya, a fundamentalist movement in Bengal, studied in Mecca for twenty years before returning home and agitating for fundamentalist goals. (6) Abd ar-Ra'uf as-Sinkili studied for nineteen years in Arabia before going back to Indonesia and spreading a Neo-Sufi order. (7) Abd as-Samad al-Palimbani studied and taught in Mecca before he too returned to Indonesia to propagate a brotherhood. (8) Three scholars returning from Mecca called for stricter legalism and founded the Padri movement of Sumatra. (9) Ma Ming-hsin of Kansu province in China studied on the Arabian peninsula before establishing the New Teaching which later fomented a revolt against the Chinese authorities.

A host of other fundamentalist figures emerged in all parts of Islamdom, pushing for a purification of Islamic practice and stricter adherence to the Shari'a. Prominent among these were Sulayman Bal of Senegal, Ibrahim Musa of Guinea, al-Mukhtar al-Kunti of Timbuctoo, the Aydarus family of Yemen, and the Akhbari faction in Iran. After centuries of accommodation and conservatism, new networks and ideas shook established practices and set precedents; Neo-Sufi brotherhoods and novel intellectual trends gave a new tone to politics and a fresh impetus to legalism from one end of Islamdom to the other. Neither before the eighteenth century nor since have fundamentalist Muslim intellectual and organizational forces been so powerful. Were it not for these developments, the program of fundamentalist Islam would have been far less well developed for application in modern times.

Fundamentalist movements followed a regular pattern of flaring up and burning out; regardless how fervent the founder and his followers, their momentum could not be sustained against the force of realities. Thus, fundamentalist states eventually turned into traditionalist ones as calls for exact application of the laws subsided and the medieval synthesis once again prevailed. This pattern applied equally to Kharijis of the eighth century, Naqshbandis of the eighteenth century, and Wahhabis of the twentieth, all of whom tended toward a balance of Islamic idealism and Muslim needs.

AUTONOMIST MOVEMENTS

Rule by aliens strikes a raw nerve, engaging passions and stimulating Muslims to action; jihad mobilizes Muslims far more often than legalism. The urge to place Muslims in charge is so deeply imbued that even the smallest Muslim minorities in Dar al-Harb hope someday to break away from control by kafirs. This longing at times seems to disappear from the political landscape, only to re-emerge with great suddenness and force whenever an opportunity arises. Subjugation by non-believers—or even a mere threat of this—overturns the normal pattern of quiescence and engages Muslim peoples in public affairs. Withdrawal from power may become so ingrained that it acquires the force of tradition, but it can be shattered by the prospect of jihad. In general, premodern Muslims believed that "the civil duty of the subject was obedience; . . . only when the Faith itself was in danger had he the right, under proper leadership, to resort to force."[45]

In the early centuries, jihad was usually offensive. The great Arabian conquests took the first generations of Muslims from the hinterlands of Arabia to West Europe and Central Asia. A Byzantine march came into existence right after Muhammad's death and lasted until the last trace of Byzantium was eradicated in 1461. Muslim warriors crossed the Straits of Gibraltar in 711 and opened the Spanish frontier, which closed only with the defeat of Granada in 1492. An Indian zone was initiated just a few years later, in 715, and climaxed with Akbar's control over nearly the entire subcontinent in the sixteenth century. Less enduring and more sporadic fronts took shape along the Nile River, in Central Asia, and in East Africa.

Occasionally too, premodern Muslims came under attack, in which case they responded in force. Most devastating were the waves of invaders from Inner Asia, the worst of which were the Mongols. Time and again, as Muslim armies proved unable to stop the steppe invaders, Muslim subjects took up arms to defend themselves. Crusader attacks lasted two centuries and provoked what historians have dubbed the "counter-crusade," in which Muslim populaces got involved militarily against the Europeans. In general, Muslims got involved without reluctance when Kafirs threatened.

In theory, Muslims must live in Dar al-Islam: "either Islamic law and institutions are given full expression and dominate state life or, failing that, if the state is non-Islamic, Muslims should try to reverse the situation or leave."[46] In a few cases, this strict dichotomy was actually enforced. In Europe, the Islamic urge to live in Dar al-Islam and the Christian antipathy toward Islam led to the evacuation of Muslims from several regions when they fell under Christian control. More often, however, Muslims remained in Dar al-Harb and adapted to rule by Kafirs.

From the standpoint of Muslim governments, the two Islamic urges had contrary implications: legalism pitted subjects against their own rulers, autonomism induced cooperation with their rulers against the unbelievers. Ruler and ruled clashed when the issue was the authorities' inadequate application of the Shari'a; but subjects sometimes contributed valuable help when non-Muslims threatened the state. Although premodern rulers rarely exploited autonomism for this purpose, jihad could serve as a way to deflect legalist sentiments. Autonomism had another virtue too; whereas legalist efforts were never implemented to the satisfaction of subjects, autonomist movements often succeeded, thereby increasing the prestige of the state. Jihad offered a unique avenue for Muslim leaders to associate themselves with Islam; leaders who did this could win the backing of their own peoples and even win support by foreign Muslims. It was for this reason that about 20,000 volunteers traveled 1,000 miles in 965, from eastern Iran to Syria, for the opportunity to fight Byzantium. Similarly, the early Ottoman polity attracted warriors from far beyond its own borders to do battle with Christians in the Balkans.[47]

Legalism and autonomism did not mean that Muslims opposed everything non-Islamic. Foreign cultural elements vetted and judged innocuous entered the civilization of Islam; the Qur'an itself contains foreign words and the early Muslims of Arabia took on many traits from the peoples they conquered. Non-Muslims were tolerated so long as they did not challenge Muslim dominion; the Shari'a itself guarantees dhimmi rights. In both cases, cultural and political, the key factor was control. So long as Muslims ruled, they chose which foreign traits to incorporate and they decided on political terms for the dhimmis. Trouble developed when non-Muslim power and non-Islamic cultural elements got out of control, leading to military conquest of Dar al-Islam and the dominance of non-Shar'i ideals. The nineteenth century brought exactly this, an Islamic nightmare, in the form of West European imperialism.

4

Relations with
Non-Muslims

Disbelief is one religion.
—*A* Hadith *Report*

JUDGED AGAINST the record of kafirs, the premodern umma enjoyed a record of remarkable success. It boasted victorious armies, economic well being, an expanding religion, and cultural brilliance. Its success was perhaps greatest in relation to the Christians of West Europe, the "Franks" of Muslim parlance. The legacy of Muslim strength and Christian weakness led the umma to become overly confident and wrongly scornful of the Franks, while Christendom developed an exorbitant hatred of Islam. For the Muslims, both these attitudes turned out to be costly in the modern period, when they had to contend with Europe and its civilization. In this way, relations between Muslims and Franks long before the nineteenth century colored Muslim responses to the challenge of modernity.

Believers Ascendant

From Muhammad's lifetime and for the next thousand years, to the great days of the Ottoman, Safavid, and Mughal empires, Muslim achievements consistently outshone those of their neighbors in Europe, Central Asia, India, and Africa. It may be difficult to imagine in the late twentieth century, but Islamdom long predominated over its rivals in power, in wealth, and in culture. Attain the Shar'i way of life Muslims did not, but they could reasonably see themselves singled out as the recipients of God's special favor; how else might they interpret their extraordinary record of worldly achievement?

The notion that God rewards the faithful is not peculiar to Muslims but arises in all religions when circumstances permit. Nineteenth-century West Europeans, stunned by *their* military and cultural supremacy, often saw God's hand in their success, much as Muslims had earlier; some Jews, elated by the creation of the modern state of Israel, drew cosmic conclusions from it. The difference is, this interpretation occurs only occasionally among Jews and Christians, disappearing with the first winds of adversity, while it characterizes and pervades Islamdom. Jews and Christians expect tribulation, Muslims expect triumph. These attitudes do not inhere in the religions but developed as a result of dissimilar historical experiences. Jews and Christians had to insulate their faith from failure and persecution, while Muslims enjoyed the very best of fortune.

It is probable that in all primitive religions, gods are judged according to their efficacy. In the minds of polytheists such as the ancient Greeks, the best god is that one who brings success in battle, protection from famine, and safety from the elements. He is judged comparatively; even if buffeted by earthquakes, polytheists feel justified by their god if others are more harmed; also wealth and power are also judged against the record of non-believers. When disaster strikes, faith in one's own god diminishes, however, and defeat in battle commonly results in the losers accepting the victor's deity. So too with the primitive monotheists; the Hebrews originally approached God expecting Him to protect them and make them prosper. Though often challenged, this attitude survived until 586 B.C., when the Jews lost to the Assyrians and were confronted with the extinction of their kingdom, the destruction of the Temple, and exile to Babylon. How could God let His Chosen People fail so dismally? Assyrian victory seemed to imply that Jews had an inferior God, jeopardizing their faith.

Two prophets, Ezekiel and the man known to biblical scholars as Second Isaiah, proposed answers to this dilemma and in the process permanently changed the nature of Jewish faith. Ezekiel stressed the Jews' evil ways and argued that the Lord abandoned the Temple as a punishment to them; the Assyrian victory was intended to impress on Jews the need for repentance. God not only rewards men for correct faith and action (as had always been believed), but He punishes them for wrongdoing. Ezekiel's teachings implied that strict adherence to God's laws could prevent such a catastrophe from recurring. With this simple explanation, defeat became part of the divine plan and Jewish devotion to the Lord was assured through adversity.

Second Isaiah, according to William H. McNeill, interpreted the disaster in a yet more theological way, seeing it as "a sure sign that the day was at hand when the sins of Israel would be forgiven and the glory of God become manifest to all the nations. In his view, the sufferings of the Jews were not simply punishment for their disobedience, but part of a far grander divine plan; for when Israel, purged and repentant, had been restored in glory, true religion and just government would be established everywhere."[1] The more Jews suffered, the more comfort they could take in the imminence of the Kingdom of God. Jews have often in the subsequent two and a half millennia had recourse to these thoughts in times of acute hardship—notably following the destruction of the Second Temple in A.D. 70 and in the Nazi holocaust. By disengaging the role of God from the here and now, these two prophets added a new dimension to Judaism, making it a succor in times of stress as well as a path to success. Suffering and failure lost their sting when integral to faith.

Early Christians inherited this attitude toward adversity and had immediate need for it during three centuries of erratic Roman persecution. From its inception, Christianity included doctrines that protected the faithful from the doubts that might result from their lowly standing and apparent failure. The church portrayed suffering as essential: the execution of Jesus was God's gift to man and martyrdom proved perfect faith. In the memorable words of Tertullian (ca. 160–240), "The blood of the martyrs is the seed of the Church."[2] Even when Christianity became the faith of kings and conquerors, in the early fourth century, it retained the humble flavor of its origins. No matter how politics distorted its message, memories of pain and adversity were never far removed; the cross, its central symbol, permanently commemorated anguish and brutal death. When Christians "become successful on the worldly plane, this has not been regarded as a success for them as Christians, as an achievement of or for their faith. That the course of history should prove favorable is no particular spiritual triumph. Conversely, a disintegration in temporal affairs is not, for Christians, a religious failure."[3]

How different is Islam! Its counterpart to the cross is the crescent, a symbol from the banners carried into battle by Muslim armies. And whereas Christian martyrs sacrificed themselves passively to prove their faith, tortured by pagans or mauled by their lions, Muslim martyrs gave their lives as soldiers on the battlefields that extended the domains of Islam. Christians had to account for the brutal murder of their Messiah and the persecution of his followers; in contrast, Muhammad became ruler of Arabia and the caliphs presided over the most spectacularly successful religious movement in human experience. Because it remains even today vivid in the Muslim consciousness, the story of Islam's rise bears a quick repeating.

Islam dates to A.D. 610, when Muhammad received the first divine revelation; before long, several acquaintances accepted him as Messenger of God. But Mecca's leaders rejected the new religion and in 622 forced Muhammad to flee with his small body of followers to Medina, a nearby city. From this nadir of fortune, Muhammad parlayed a position as tribal arbiter and leader of the Muslims into a base of independent power, quickly winning control over the whole town of Medina. He led Muslim warriors on raids and into battles with such success that by 628 the Meccans signed a treaty with him permitting the Muslims to enter their city for pilgrimage purposes; less than two years later, Muhammad abrogated that treaty and captured Mecca—returning to his hometown as ruler just eight years after fleeing from it under cover of night. Between 630 and 632, Muhammad extended his power to the rest of Arabia, establishing the most powerful indigenous state in the peninsula's history.

After Muhammad's death in 632, the fledgling community took two years to consolidate its position in Arabia, then sent its warriors north to attack the two great empires of the Middle East, Byzantium and Sasanid Iran. In twelve years, 634–46, Muslims conquered most of the territories between Egypt and eastern Iran, achieving victories—Marj as-Saffar, Yarmuk, al-Qadisiya, Heliopolis—that still resonate powerfully among believers. It seemed that, armed with faith in Allah, nothing could stop the soldiers of Islam. Consolidation of the conquests required a couple of generations, from 646 to 697, during which time Muslims mostly fought among themselves over control of the empire. These disputes had permanent repercussions for Islamic history (notably the Sunni-Shi'i-Khariji split) but they did not tarnish the Muslims' sense of invincibility. Conquests resumed in 697, lasting until 715; this second round was yet more astonishing than the first, for while a number of armies expanded spectacularly fast and wide (such as those of Alexander the Great, Tamerlane, and Napoleon), only two (the Arabians and the thirteenth-century Mongols) succeeded in following up the initial burst of victories with a second wave, extending the conquests still farther. Less than a century after Muhammad fled Mecca, Dar al-Islam stretched far beyond the Middle East to North Africa and Spain, Sind and Central Asia.

Victories against non-Muslims soon slowed, but they did continue. Believers reached Sicily in 827, the Indian heartlands in 1001, Anatolia in 1071, the Balkans in 1356. They took Constantinople in 1453, much of Java in 1526, and south India in 1565. Dar al-Islam also expanded peacefully, when kings converted; for example, Paramesvara, the ruler of Malacca, accepted Islam in 1410 and thereafter his city was a major Muslim center of Southeast Asia. In West Africa, kings and chiefs were usually among the first local people to convert to Islam. Islam also had religious attraction for large numbers of ordinary citizens wherever it reached, including such highly civilized regions as Iran, Egypt, Spain, Anatolia, and the north Indian plains. Jews, Christians, Zoroastrians, Manicheans, Hindus, Buddhists, Confucians, polytheists, and animists all forsook their faiths, heritages, and social milieus to join the umma, testifying to Islam's superior appeal. Just as territories brought into Dar al-Islam by force usually stayed there, so peoples converted to Islam remained Muslim, adding to the umma's sense of confidence.

Muslim civilization, independent of the Islamic faith, attracted non-Muslims and influenced them. Islamdom's scientific advances, practical inventions, technical methods, intellectual creations, artistic styles, and literary forms had a major impact on the other civilized peoples. Medieval Europe, for example, took scientific and philosophical knowledge from the Muslims, and these contributed in critical ways to the emergence of modern thought. Muslim culture had special influence on the Jews who lived in Islamdom, for their geographic dispersion and the similarity of their sacred law facilitated assimilation. The umma also enjoyed wealth, as shown by a profusion of palaces, mosques, and public works on the grand scale, as well as by elegant courts, large armies, and the finest universities.

Power, religious expansion, cultural brilliance, and prosperity combined to imbue Muslims with a sense of shared achievement and confidence. As a community, "uniformly through the ages, but taking different forms, Muslims felt a sense of superiority with regard to non-Muslims."[4] As an individual, a person might be indigent or downtrodden, but as a Muslim he could bask in the glory of his religion and civilization, strong and creative, fulfilling God's mandate better than any kafirs. "The Muslim achievement was seen as intrinsic to their faith."[5] Although Islam's culture began to stagnate in the thirteenth century, its military and religious expansion continued until about 1700. Even in the fifteenth century, as the Portuguese and Spanish explorers took to the seas, "Islam, and not European Christendom, was the most obviously expanding community."[6] As a result, "an intelligent and informed observer [at that time] could hardly have avoided the conclusion that Islam, rather than the remote and still comparatively crude society of the European Far West, was destined to dominate the world in the following centuries."[7]

The Muslims' explosive beginning and subsequent success had many consequences, several of which have great importance for modern politics. First, memories of the early invincibility created extravagant expectations of eventual dominion, making losses appear transient and victory permanent, allowing Muslims almost to discount the setbacks they encountered. Second, success meant that Muslims were unfamiliar with the tolerant interplay of customs and gods. As heirs to Middle Eastern universalist monotheism, they scorned alternate ways; as Muslims, their power shielded them from the culture of others. Premodern Muslims were uniquely insular, able to ignore the innovations, ways, and beliefs of unbelievers.

When Muslims did listen to others, it was on their own terms. In the first century of Islam, the umma came under many influences: Greek, Jewish, and Iranian especially, also Egyptian, Roman, and Indian. Other cultures deeply affected the new religion and shaped its civilization, but Muslims accepted foreign ways only when these suited them. Greek philosophical thought challenged Islam especially, forcing the Muslims to answer such questions as, Was the Qur'an created? and Why does evil exist? Incorporating foreign influences took several centuries, during which time the Muslims debated which foreign elements were compatible and which were not. In the realm of philosophy, for instance, they decided by the twelfth century that most of Greek speculation harmed faith and ought not to be cultivated by a pious believer.

The umma had never met an enemy capable of defeating it on the battlefield *and* surpassing it culturally. Premodern conquerors offered no direct challenge to Islam's civilization, being either too primitive (such as the steppe invaders who quickly converted to Islam) or too marginal (Byzantines, Crusaders, or Chinese). No single force facing the Muslims combined physical and cultural power. Consequently, the umma became accustomed to ignoring other peoples' practices or beliefs.

Third, Islam's rapid rise from obscurity to international empire had a touch of the miraculous for Muslims; how could they have attained all this without God's approval and support? The record of early success conveyed a message with religious implications, demonstrating God's pleasure with the umma. Such startling achievements vis-à-vis non-Muslims meant that Muslims had no need to protect themselves with the ideas developed by Ezekiel and Second Isaiah; instead, they could blithely indulge in the notion that accepting the Qur'an translated into worldly well-being and could allow themselves to see success as a reward for correct faith and righteous action. The high degree of correlation between faith in Allah and prosperity convinced many believers that Islam brought mundane happiness; Wilfred Cantwell Smith writes that "in some ways, at least for the community, [Islam] has been characteristically a religion of triumph in success, of salvation through victory and achievement and power."[8] This static, essentialist vision of history posed no problems so long as favorable material conditions confirmed the expectations of Muslims. "They could look out upon the society that they had constructed with the gratifying sense that it led the world. God had told men how to live; those who accepted this and set out to live so were visibly receiving His blessing."[9] But when history no longer lived up to expectations in the nineteenth century, this vision proved to be one of the umma's heaviest burdens.

Premodern Muslims had a dual historical experience. They failed the sacred law but they achieved great human success. Unable to attain God's way, they still came nearer to it and prospered more than non-Muslims. Along with the frustrations came deep satisfactions; the venture of Islam brought outstanding benefits from any comparative viewpoint, yet it never allowed Muslims to feel self-satisfied. The spirit of premodern Islam is characterized by concurrent failure and success: they were bad Muslims but the best of men.

Disdain for West Europe

Muslim worldly success colored relations with most unbelievers, giving the umma a relaxed self-confidence. Dar al-Islam was growing, ever more distant regions were converting to the faith, and use of Arabic and Persian was spreading. Secure in their well-being, Muslims knew little and cared less what infidels did. For many centuries, Muslim perceptions of the kafirs fit well with the superior attitudes encouraged by the Qur'an; indeed, they jibed so well that even when one group of non-Muslim peoples, the Christians of West Europe, developed instruments that lifted their mundane status far above the umma's, Muslims hardly noticed. This blindness took on a critical importance in modern times, when Muslims were forced to come to terms with European supremacy.

In addition to diffuse feelings of superiority over all kafirs, premodern Muslims also enjoyed a special sense of advantage in relation to the Christians of West Europe, the Franks. In part, this had to do with the Qur'anic vision of Christianity, in part with the umma's historical experience with the Europeans.

Perforce, the following account of Muslim-Christian relations emphasizes the negative, for memories of conflict, such as the Crusades and the battle for Spain, endure more powerfully than do those of trade, cultural exchange, and acts of tolerance. Who, after all, remembers Roger II, the Norman king of Sicily in whose court Muslim scholarship flourished in the twelfth century? Because Europeans and their descendants around the world recall Muslim threats the most vividly, and because Muslims associate West Europeans with the conquest of virtually the whole of Islamdom, an interpretation of their attitudes must stress their mutual difficulties.

THE QUR'AN

In the Islamic vision, all true religion is Islam, everything else is distortion. As such, Islam has existed since the beginning of time, not just since Muhammad's mission in the early seventh century. Islam is inherent to the human psyche; a child is born Muslim but then converted to another faith by his parents. Even nonhuman creatures accept Islam. Appearances to the contrary, Muhammad was not the first Muslim; according to the Qur'an, this honor belonged to Abraham, the first monotheist, who "was not a Jew nor a Christian but a true Muslim" (3.67).

If Islam existed in the abstract since the creation, humans had no access to it until Muhammad made the Qur'an known. He was not the first prophet sent by God to inform mankind, but the first to convey the Lord's message fully and accurately. The Qur'an mentions by name twenty-eight prophets, including Adam, Abraham, Noah, Moses, Jesus, and several non-biblical figures from the Arabian tradition, and it indicates that there had been yet more. Each people had a prophet to teach them about God; yet every prophet either distorted the divine message or it was wrongly understood by his followers. As a result, no one exactly knew Islam, but various religions, especially Judaism and Christianity, had access to a substantial portion of its message. Then God chose Muhammad for a final revelation and this time it was conveyed faultlessly. Other prophets proved their divine inspiration by such supernatural feats as parting the seas or healing the sick; Muhammad's miracle was the Qur'an itself, a perfect recitation of God's word and an inimitable piece of literature. The faultless Qur'an renders obsolete earlier holy books, all of which mix divine truth with human error.

To the Muslim, Jewish monotheism appears nearly correct, yet Jewish exclusivity strikes him as improper; God's message must be shared with all the world. Christianity appears to him to have an opposite plan; he applauds its universal nature while deploring those elements of tritheism (belief in three gods) which he detects in the doctrine of the Trinity. Muslims take notions such as the "chosen people" or the Trinity at face value and have no interest in Jewish or Christian attempts to explain their rather more subtle meanings. Muslims believe that Islam alone combines strict monotheism with universal appeal.

Just as Christians long viewed Islam as a heretical movement stemming from their own faith, Muslims see Christianity as an earlier and faulty version of Islam. For non-believers Islam began with Muhammad; for Muslims, it has always existed as the Word of God. Although Muhammad lived centuries after Moses and Jesus, Islam long antedated them all and Muhammad merely made it known to mankind. From this vantage point, Islam is able to deal with its predecessors with an easy confidence. Jews and Christians should accept Islam, of course, but if they cling to their ancestral religions, this hardly bothers Muslims, who see the earlier monotheisms as flawed and therefore unthreatening.[10] Muslims dismiss most of what preceded Islam, saving some bits, discarding the rest. For example, they never read the Hebrew or Christian scriptures, except for scholarly purposes, and even then rarely; why confuse matters when the Qur'an says it all? For these reasons, Muslims "have religious convictions for genuinely imagining that they know real Christianity better than Christians do themselves. And in what then appears to them as the 'pseudo-Christianity' of historical and personal existence, the faith by which Christians actually live, they have not been intellectually interested."[11]

The Qur'an includes numerous biblical stories, changed to fit the new context. For example, Mecca replaces Jerusalem as the central religious city; Abraham lived in western Arabia and built the Ka'ba of Mecca with Ishmael's help. Jesus takes on a wholly different role in the Qur'an. Some of the Christian doctrines about him remain intact, such as the virgin birth, the presence of the Holy Spirit, the divine revelations, and the miracles. But the Qur'an flatly rejects Jesus' death by crucifixion: "They killed him not nor crucified him."[12] It scorns the notion of his divinity and condemns with special vehemence the notion of Jesus as the Son of God. "He was no more than a servant [of God]," a man like all men.[13] When "the Christians call Christ the Son of God . . . they but imitate what the unbelievers of old used to say."[14] Christians take Jesus as their Lord despite the fact that "they were commanded to worship but One God: there is no God but He."[15] The very notion of a Son of God is wrong because God "does not beget, nor is he begotten."[16]

The Qur'an also revises other key aspects of Christianity, implying for example that the Trinity consists not of the Father, the Son, and the Holy Spirit but of the Father, the Son, and Mary. Christian remonstrances fall on deaf ears; the Qur'an is God's perfect Word and bringing any aspect of doubt into it would bring the whole faith of Islam into question. These theological differences create intractable problems for discourse between Muslims and Christians. While Islam honors and respects Jesus, it consigns him to a role Christians cannot accept. Jesus in the Qur'an is just one of a string of prophets who attempted to bring Islam but spread a garbled message instead. Invariably, in the words of one Protestant scholar, "disagreement centers on the role of Jesus in relation to God and on the divinity of the son of Mary."[17]

The Qur'an encourages relaxed attitudes toward its monotheistic predecessors, offering them a fair measure of tolerance while according them little respect. So long as they accept the rule of the Shari'a, the followers of obsolete religions are tolerated but not esteemed.

HISTORY

The Qur'an predisposed Muslims to pay scant attention to Christians; then the actual behavior of West Europeans repulsed the umma even further. To a premodern Muslim, Europe stood out for its tenacious resistance to the Muslim armies, its unique aversion to the call of Islam, and its reputation for barbarism. In response, Muslims felt disdain toward Europeans, the last people on earth they expected to have to emulate.

Europeans resisted incorporation into Dar al-Islam by holding three lines of defense: Iberia in the west, the Balkans in the center, and the Ukraine in the east. Although Muslims did reach deep into Europe on occasion, all of their major thrusts ended in failure. They lost Sicily in 1091, Spain in 1492, the Crimea in 1783, and the entire Balkans except for part of Thrace by World War I. Such defiance of Muslim rule made Europe the outstanding realm of Dar al-Harb and the umma's most persevering antagonist.

Not only did Europeans defend themselves well, but they counterattacked from the eleventh century onward. The Byzantines won back part of northern Syria; Genoa and Pisa cooperated to take Sardinia in 1016 and Corsica a few years later; Leon and Castille conquered Toledo in 1085, the first major step toward Christian rule in Spain; the Normans took Sicily and Malta in 1091; the Georgians expanded their kingdom; and the Armenians captured Edessa. In a sense, the Crusades were a logical outgrowth of this fighting elsewhere in the Mediterranean basin. The first wave of knights crossed into Dar al-Islam in 1097; Christians conquered Jerusalem in 1099 and established four Latin states (Jerusalem, Edessa, Antioch, and Tripoli). Saladin's capture of Jerusalem in 1187 meant that for the next centuries Christian efforts were largely devoted to its reconquest, using ever-more circuitous approaches. The Crusaders launched attacks on Constantinople, Egypt, and Tunisia but did not even get close to Jerusalem again. (Ironically, the only exception was the Holy Roman Emperor who won the city through peaceful negotiation in 1229 and held it for fifteen years.) Although the Crusaders lost their last toehold in Palestine when Acre fell in 1291, the crusading spirit carried on for another century and a half, with the final efforts directed against the Ottomans. The attempt to win Jerusalem for Christ brought warfare to various parts of Dar al-Islam, including the Balkans, Anatolia, Egypt, Tunisia, and Morocco.

European Christians took advantage of almost every opportunity to harm the umma. Most notably, European kings and the pope attempted to cooperate with the Mongols as these soldiers from the steppe nearly vanquished the entire Middle East. The Armenians entered into alliance with the Mongols, Christian leaders in Dar al-Islam sent out feelers, and the Vatican sought a formal treaty. Muslims, who considered the Mongols as an especially evil scourge, long resented this Christian perfidy.

Besides resisting militarily, the Europeans also did not convert to Islam. Islam spread from the west coast of Arabia in all directions, but hardly to Europe; Christians of North Africa, East Africa, the Fertile Crescent, Arabia, Anatolia, and Iran accepted Islam in large numbers, but not those to the north. Of the few who did, most had to hide their religion or leave their homelands and seek refuge in the Middle East when they fell under Christian control; this happened in Spain, Sicily, Hungary, Greece and (after a long interim) the Crimea. Christian rulers did not want Muslim subjects, Muslims did not want to live in Christendom; by tacit agreement, the umma contracted along with Dar al-Islam when the Franks won territory. The only lasting conversions in Europe were made among remote peoples such as the Albanians, Bosnians, and Volga Tatars. Europe today has a Muslim population of about eleven million, as well as some six million migrant workers; Islam has been Europe's second largest religion since World War II. From the Muslim point of view, however, this is an insignificant body of adherents compared with the Muslim populations found elsewhere in the eastern hemisphere. Nearly all of Africa north of the equator accepted the call of Islam, more than one-quarter of South Asia, and about two-thirds of the peoples living on the islands of Southeast Asia. Even in distant China, where Muslims hardly ever enjoyed political power, the Han peoples converted to Islam as often as the Franks.

Muslims saw West Europe as a cold and inhospitable region, inhabited by barbarians—a northern counterpart to sub-Saharan Africa. In part, this impression was a result of the circumstances which prevailed when the two civilizations first came into contact in the eighth century. The Franks had but a crude culture, an intolerant religion, and little to export other than slaves. The disparity between two famous contemporaries, Charlemagne (r. 768–814) and Harun ar-Rashid (r. 784–809), exemplified the contrast: while Charlemagne maintained an impoverished court which had to keep moving because no single region could afford to keep him and his entourage for long, Harun ar-Rashid lived in the splendid Round City of Baghdad. Carolingian political institutions and intellectual culture were primitive compared with those of the Abbasids, as were their arts, laws, and social life.

In the 940s, al-Mas'udi characterized the Franks:

> Their humors have little warmth, their bodies are extended, their characters are dried out, their morals rough, their comprehension weak, and their tongues heavy. Their pallor is so extreme that they appear bluish. Their skin is delicate, their hair thick. Their eyes are also blue, matching their complexions. Humid vapors make their hair lank and reddish-brown. Their religions lack substance due to the nature of the cold and the lack of warmth. Those who live in the far north are the most stupid, useless and bestial; and these characteristics increase yet more the further one goes north.[18]

A little over a century later, the Franks' reputation had sunk even lower, at least in the eyes of the Spaniard, Ibn Sa'id, who referred to the Franks as resembling animals more than men. . . . The cold air and cloudy skies [cause] their temperaments to become frozen and their humors to become crude; their bellies are extended, their coloring pale, and their hair too long. They lack keenness of understanding and acuteness of mind, they are dominated by ignorance and stupidity, and blindness of purpose is widespread.[19]

Once formulated, this picture of the north Europeans lasted for many centuries, and was hardly affected by developments taking place in Christendom.

The umma took little interest in the Franks before the late eighteenth century. "The Muslim world had its own internal lines of communication by land and sea, and was thus independent of Western routes and services. Muslim civilization, proud and confident of its superiority, could afford to despise the barbarous infidel in the cold and miserable lands of the north."[20] Even the Crusades failed to awaken interest in Europe. Muslims made no serious effort to understand the reasons behind these unprovoked invasions of the eastern Mediterranean, nor did they study Frankish languages, customs, or history. The assurance of Usama ibn Munqidh, a Syrian aristocrat who lived from 1095 to 1188, indicates the Muslim attitude toward these intruders: "Those who have recently arrived from the land of the Franks are coarser in manners than those who have acclimatized and lived longer among Muslims."[21] Such scorn had already become dangerously anachronistic by 1400, when the renowned Muslim thinker Ibn Khaldun concluded a survey of cultures with this uninterested appraisal of the Franks:

We are told that philosophical learning is flourishing in the land of the Franks of Ruma [here, Italy] and what lies beyond it along the northern shore [of the Mediterranean]. Philosophical thought is said to be revived, its instruction widespread, its books comprehensive, its scholars numerous, and its students many. But God alone knows what goes on over there![22]

The twelfth-century renascence, "the Renaissance, the Reformation, the scientific revolution, and the Enlightenment had passed without effect in the Islamic world, without even being noticed."[23] Muslims ignored these developments—as well as those taking place in Sung China or Vijayanagar India— because they felt no need for new answers. The umma had achieved so complete a cultural balance by the thirteenth century that it turned inward, abandoning earlier interests in the natural world, philosophical inquiry, and non-Muslims. It resolved its own contrary influences, achieved satisfaction in private life, and established a consensus on the basis of the medieval synthesis. Few Muslims felt an urge to search for stimulus outside their environment, which was highly patterned and remarkably stable. Creativity and originality became very scarce (the aspect European observers commented on most often—rather than on the successful synthesis). "A triumph of the conservative spirit"[24] encouraged the study of ancient texts, their commentaries, glosses, and super-glosses. Besides affecting religious studies and the rest of intellectual life, this spirit also restricted the Muslim view of Europe. The Franks' place had been decided long ago and was no longer open to change, even among the Ottomans and Moroccans, the Muslims most aware of developments to the north.

It was not just a matter of ignorance; Muslims acquainted with European innovations were also left unconvinced. Jews brought a printing press to Istanbul in 1488, but Muslims did not publish books until nearly two hundred and fifty years later, in 1729 (and even then only under the influence of a Hungarian convert and only for thirteen years). Industrial and mechanical advances impressed Muslims who visited Europe but no efforts were made to learn about them. By the time Europe was worth listening to, the Muslims had so insulated themselves from outside influences that nothing short of a cataclysm could shake them. Even as it fell behind, the umma retained a supercilious attitude toward the Franks: "An eighteenth-century Ottoman knew as much of the states and nations of Europe as a nineteenth-century European about the tribes and peoples of Africa—and regarded them with the same slightly amused disdain."[25] For example, having only a misty notion of European geography, in 1770 the Ottoman government formally protested to Venice when Russian ships appeared in the Mediterranean. It had lost knowledge of the Atlantic Ocean and the Straits of Gibraltar, and Turkish officials assumed the Russian ships had sailed from the Baltic to the Adriatic via a channel under Venetian control, a mythic passageway that was shown on their maps.

Muslim relations with Europe were twice out of step. In the early centuries, when the umma was at its most expansive and most open to other influences, north Europe had nothing to offer, so a condescending attitude toward the Franks developed, which remained essentially unchanged for centuries. Then, by the time Europe had become culturally dynamic, Muslims were dead to the outside world. Muslim introversion came at the worst possible moment, occurring just as Europe embarked on a venture of unique creativity which was soon to affect every other civilization. "Relative to what was happening in Christian Europe, the Muslim decline was of no transient import; it determined the posture of Islamdom at the most fateful point in the career of the Islamicate, as of all other, societies: at the advent of Modernity."[26]

Christian Hostility

The easy superiority and disdain felt by premodern Muslims for Europe was met by a dislike that approached hatred on the Christian side. If Muslims could ignore Christendom, the reverse was hardly possible. The umma threatened Europe militarily and religiously and isolated it from the rest of the world. Like the Muslim view of the Franks, so the Christian impression of Islamdom was developed early and lasted, with only minor modifications, until the eighteenth century.

European feelings about the Muslims were far more hostile than those directed toward any other non-Western people. This difference became clear as European explorers made their way around the globe, beginning in the early 1400s, and had favorable experiences with the Chinese and the Japanese, the Buddhists and the Hindus, the pagan Africans and the American Indians. The Muslims stood out as *the* great antagonists.

In part, this was because Islam first made itself known to the Christians with devastating effect. Two years after Muhammad died in 632, Muslim warriors began raiding Byzantine territory to the north of Arabia; a mere eighty-two years later, they had conquered lands stretching from the Pyrénées to Central Asia. In many of these regions, Christians made up a majority of the population. Without warning and in less than a century, nearly all of Christendom outside Europe and Anatolia became incorporated in Dar al-Islam. The few regions outside Europe that did survive the initial Muslim onslaught fell thereafter, including Byzantium, Armenia, Georgia, Lebanon, Dongola, and 'Alwa. Only the Christian kingdom of Ethiopia withstood the Muslim autonomist drive, and it too would have succumbed to jihad in the 1540s but for the "not far short of miraculous" intervention by 400 Portuguese bombardiers and riflemen on its behalf.[27]

These lands were lost at a time when much of Europe was a backwater and the Levant and North Africa constituted the heartlands of Christianity, with most of its population, key institutions, and cultural centers. Muslim rule destroyed the primacy of eastern Christianity and decimated the power of their churches. Three out of four patriarchates (Constantinople, Antioch, and Alexandria) virtually disappeared when incorporated into Dar al-Islam, leaving the pope in Rome with a vastly enhanced status.

Even if Muslim rule could sometimes be reversed, conversions could not; Christians living in Dar al-Islam accepted the dominant faith, though at varying rates. Armenians and Lebanese retained the Gospel over centuries, due to a combination of political solidarity and inaccessible terrain, but few other Christian communities did as well. The premodern era saw massive defections to Islam: Christianity disappeared from Arabia, North Africa, and most of Anatolia, while holding on as a small minority elsewhere in the Middle East. Despite bitter theological differences between the Roman Catholics of West Europe and the Eastern sects, the subjugation of co-religionists by the Muslims spurred alarm and anger in the West. They saw Christendom as "a single nation which in the rise of Islam had been robbed of a third of its best provinces," and more thereafter.[28] Memories of this robbery had a marked impact in the nineteenth century, when the Franks reconquered most of the lands that had once been Christian.

Closer to Europe, every major island in the Mediterranean Sea came under Muslim domination, though the duration of Muslim rule varied from several months in the case of Sardinia to over six centuries in Cyprus. On the European mainland, Christians succumbed to Muslim attacks that came in two principal waves, an Arabian version from the west in the eighth to tenth centuries and a Turkish one from the east in the fourteenth to the seventeenth centuries. Although the Arabs could not establish a firm base outside of Iberia, their raids became an unhappy fact of life in much of ninth- and tenth-century Europe. One notable expedition took Muslim invaders to the suburbs of Rome, where they attacked the papal church of St. Peter's; a wall built after this incursion to protect the pope's enclave—with labor provided by Muslim prisoners—eventually led to the establishment of an independent Vatican state. On another occasion, in 954, Muslims sacked the monastery of St. Gallen by Lake Constance on today's Swiss-German border. Italy at one time even hosted an independent Muslim emirate, brief (853–71) and small (at Bari, near the heel of Italy) that it was.

Although frightening to local residents and powerfully etched in their memories, these raids had little staying power; indeed, for many centuries after taking Spain, the Muslims made no lasting advances in Europe. A second wave of conquests began in 1356, when the Ottoman Turks crossed the Bosphorus and captured Gallipoli from the Byzantines. During the next centuries, the Ottomans captured nearly the entire Balkan peninsula, climaxing with their two unsuccessful sieges of Vienna, in 1529 and 1683. Turkish power also reached beyond the Balkans to Poland, Italy, and the Crimea.

Muslims at some time controlled most or all of the modern states of Portugal, Spain, Hungary, Yugoslavia, Albania, Greece, Bulgaria, and Rumania; in addition, they ruled parts of France, Germany, Switzerland, Italy, Austria, Poland, Czechoslovakia, and the Soviet Union. But it was not just the extent of the Muslim assault that gave it such an impact—it was also the Muslims' long endurance and religious intent. Wave after wave of invaders attacked continental Europe from Inner Asia and Scandinavia in the early medieval period, then tapered off. Invasions by such peoples as the Celts, Vikings, and Magyars ended in 955 and never resumed, with the one exception of the Mongol eruption into East Europe in 1240–41. In contrast, the Muslims kept attacking well into the modern era. Thus, other than the Mongols (many of whom converted to Islam, so they too nearly fitted the pattern), *all attacks on Europe after 955 came from Dar al-Islam.* In all, Europe felt endangered by Muslims for over a thousand years, from the attack on Spain in 711 to the second attack on

Vienna in 1683; even later, fear of Muslims continued until the Ottomans lost control of the Balkans in the nineteenth century. This millennial threat made Muslims a special class of foreigner in European eyes.

Also, unlike the Inner Asians and Vikings, who were simple tribesmen with few ambitions beyond plunder, Muslims were civilized peoples who brought a rival faith and an appealing culture. The Muslims not only destroyed property, they also challenged the dominance of the Christian civilization in Europe. Europeans under Muslim rule adopted the Islamic religion, the Arabic or Turkish language, and Muslim cultural forms. More than just a military threat, Islam offered an alternate way of life. Thus was Islam "the only undisguised and formidable antagonist of Christianity" for many centuries.[29] Wilfred Cantwell Smith observes that "until Karl Marx and the rise of communism, the Prophet organized and launched the only serious challenge to Western civilization that it has faced in the whole course of its history. . . . Islam is the only positive force that has won converts away from Christianity—by the tens of millions. It is the only force that has proclaimed that Christian doctrine is not only false but repulsive."[30]

Challenged by Muslims for power and for souls, Europeans responded by viewing Islam as the epitome of evil, a fiendishly clever amalgam of doctrines designed to exploit human weakness. Initial Christian reactions to Muslims set the tone. In a conversation that apparently took place in July 634, two years after Muhammad's death, an old Byzantine scribe was asked was he made of "the prophet who has appeared among the Saracens?" He replied that Muhammad "is deceiving. For do prophets come with swords and chariots?" The questioner, in agreement, said that one would "discover nothing true from the said prophet except human bloodshed."[31] Several months later, in a sermon on Christmas Eve in 634, the patriarch of Jerusalem referred to the Muslims as "the slime of the godless Saracens [which] threatens slaughter and destruction."[32]

From the very first, Christians saw deceit and violence in Muhammad's message; then, when they learned about Muhammad's many wives and the Islamic sanction of polygamy and concubinage, sexual license became their third criticism. Much of their abuse was directed against the person of Muhammad, who was assailed for "the violence and force with which he imposed his religion; the salacity and laxness with which he bribed his followers whom he did not compel; and finally his evident humanity, which it was consistently considered necessary to prove, although no Muslim denied, or even wished to deny, it."[33] Symptomatic of this, "Mahomet" meant an idol in sixteenth-century English and "Mahometry" came to signify idolatry.[34] Muhammad had to be more than human, for how could a mere mortal devise such clever ways to win followers and make them believe such evident falsehoods?

Three themes surfaced again and again in Christendom: the Islamic manipulation of religion, power, and sex. In the concise words of Norman Daniel, Islam stood for "a sexually corrupt tyranny based on false teaching." This triad of deceit, violence, and lasciviousness showed an "astonishing tenacity," appearing again and again in various forms and endless variety through the Middle Ages and even surviving today.[35]

When added to the fear of Muslim military strength, these attitudes transformed the umma into the enemy par excellence. From the *Chanson de Roland* to the Rolando trilogy, from *El Cid* to *Don Quixote,* Muslims filled the role of the archenemy in literature. Arabian hordes, terrible Turks, and Barbary pirates became set foils for Christian valor. In real life, Europeans repeatedly won their statehood by expelling the Muslims, from the Spanish *reconquista* beginning in the early eleventh century to the Albanian war of independence ending in 1912. Not surprisingly, Arabs and Turks represent the national villains in most of southern Europe, especially Spain, Sicily, Serbia, Greece, Bulgaria, and Rumania. Farther north, Edward Gibbon knew just how to horrify his readers when he speculated that, if not for the Franks' victory of 732 at Poitiers, "perhaps the interpretation of the Koran would now be taught in the schools of Oxford, and her pulpits might demonstrate to a circumcised people the sanctity and truth of the revelation of Mahomet."[36]

This hatred of things Islamic was further accentuated by the fact that, aside from the ocean, the Arctic ices, and the tundra forests, medieval Europe was utterly surrounded by Islamdom. From Spain across North Africa to the Levant, on to Central Asia and Siberia, a membrane of Muslim peoples separated Europe from the rest of the eastern hemisphere. Encircled by Muslims before the era of exploration, contact with other kafirs was limited to Jews; only a tiny number of travelers reached non-Muslim Africa or Asia and their reports were often—as in the case of Marco Polo—received with skepticism. Encircled by Muslims, "preoccupied with immediate problems brought on by the threat of Islam, Europe almost completely lost sight of the [non-Muslim] East as a land of reality."[37] Christians hardly realized how limited their vision was: "Islam not only obliged the Christians to live in a tiny enclosed world, . . . it also made them feel that such an existence was a normal one."[38] Surrounded, Europeans sometimes felt isolated and hopeless; as Roger Bacon wrote in the late 1260s, "there are few Christians; the whole breadth of the world is occupied by unbelievers, and there is no one to show them the truth."[39]

To medievals, the planet seemed to contain two major parts, one Christian, the other Muslim. To them, these represented self and other, good and evil. It is not inaccurate to compare this polarity with the modern Western tendency to divide the world into free and communist portions; in both cases, a single, universal ideological division splits mankind. Too, political life in both is dominated by "the problem of the juxtaposition of incompatible and largely hostile systems of thought, morals, and belief embodied in political powers of impressive, not to say awe-inspiring size." For these reasons, R. W. Southern calls "the existence of Islam . . . the most far-reaching problem in medieval Christendom. It was a problem at every level of experience"—practical, theological, and historical.[40]

Anti-Muslim sentiments had a critical role in spurring the development of modern European imperialism. When Europeans ventured to leave their continent, they did so for two reasons, to battle Muslims or to trade; "Christians and spices" was the way Vasco da Gama, the first European to reach India by sea put it, when asked what had brought him so far.[41] To a great extent, the imperialist impulse grew directly out of its crusader precursor. In its first phases, at least, the modern form of European expansion showed as much obsession with combating Muslims as ever did the medieval form, inspiring many of the key figures in the European expansion, such as Prince Henry the Navigator and Christopher Columbus. Although Prince Henry (1394–1460) sponsored the initial Portuguese voyages of discovery that changed the face of the earth, he did so for archaic reasons. He was a devoted Crusader, a man for whom "there was hardly any higher duty or more valued privilege than that of carrying on this secular struggle of the Faith."[42] Anti-Islamic motives also inspired Christopher Columbus (1451–1506), a "single-mindedly consistent" soldier in the cause against Islam. According to Abbas Hamdani, the crusading impulse was "the driving force of his entire active life; . . . the discovery of new lands had no meaning" for him except as steps toward the deliverance of Jerusalem.[43]

Hopes of circumventing Dar al-Islam and making alliances to take Jerusalem played a vital role in nearly all the early travels. "The great voyages of discovery were seen as a religious war" against Dar al-Islam, "a continuation of the Crusades and of the [Spanish] Reconquest, and against the same enemy."[44] The crusading imperative weakened only with the centuries, as the northern European states prevailed over Spain and Portugal on the high seas, and as economic and strategic interests acquired first importance in the formulation of policy.

So profoundly felt was the antagonism toward Muslims that it even influenced "the attitudes with which men of European stock approached the non-Muslim peoples."[45] Pagans appeared to the Portuguese and Spanish much like the nonaligned states do to Americans today, as persons yet uncommitted in the great battle of the age. Then as now, the issues involved were seen to be so vital that everyone had to participate; and, just as the two sides today see neutrals as susceptible to being won over, so Christians then "were prepared to regard all who were not Muslims as potential Christians."[46]

The religious dimension had particularly great prominence in many of the first reports to Europe about newly discovered peoples, for they were written by Jesuits and other clergymen. By reason of their priority and their wide dissemination, these accounts had a powerful and lasting impact on the formation of European attitudes toward the more remote cultures. Pagans in Africa and on the islands of Southeast Asia were seen primarily in the context of their not being Muslim. Because most Hindus lived under Muslim rule, Europeans felt the bonds of common interest with them and viewed them as natural allies. But it was the Japanese and Chinese who most won Europe's favor, due to the attractiveness of their (non-Muslim) civilizations and their receptivity to the Christian faith.[47]

The goodwill toward fellow non-Muslims stood in dramatic contrast to the attitude of Europeans toward the umma. Accommodation with the Muslims rarely went beyond hostile vigilance. These attitudes had many consequences in the modern world, when the force of European armies and civilization offered new scope to an age-old animosity. In time, they became a major obstacle for Muslims attempting to modernize.

Conclusion:
The Civilization
of Islam

ISLAM and the Muslims are so often seen as monoliths that the specialist on these topics finds himself repeatedly called upon to stress their diversity. Islam, he tirelessly points out, varies widely between Sunni and Shi'i, between pre-modern and modern, between the West and the East, between rural and urban, and between the 'ulama and the Sufis; and Muslims vary even more widely than does their faith. So often do the experts have to correct the notion of a single Islamdom that they tend to lose sight of the real issue here. *Of course* Muslims in Morocco and Indonesia differ. Indeed, what is remarkable is not their dissimilarities but that they share so much. To the extent that Muslims do have anything in common across time, place, sect, social background, and political outlook, Islam exerts an extraordinary influence over its adherents. This study approaches Islam in the realm of politics from the perspective of emphasizing and evaluating these similarities.

To do so accurately, a distinction must be drawn between Islam's two forms of influence over the life of its adherents, the Islamic and the Islamicate. To illustrate this dichotomy, we begin with an example from the art of Islam:

Let us imagine an experiment: you have an hour to kill; idly and for the simple pleasure of having beautiful pictures before your eyes, you page through a collection of
art works of all sorts. Greek statues follow Egyptian tomb paintings, embroidered Japanese screens follow bas-reliefs from Indian temples. As you turn the pages, your gaze
falls successively on a panel of sculptured plaster from one of the halls of the Alhambra,
on a page of an Egyptian Qur'an, then on the engraved decorations of a Persian copper
bowl. Rudimentary as your artistic education is, you immediately identify the last three
pictures as belonging to Muslim art. Without being capable of identifying in which
country any of these was made, you are not inclined even for an instant to attribute
them to any place other than the Muslim world.[1]

Even the casual observer senses a bond between Muslim works of art; their
distinct and regularly recurring motifs, such as the arabesque, vegetal and geo-
metric designs, and the Arabic script, make them akin.

What is true of the visual arts holds, if less graphically, in other spheres
of life as well. Muslim entries in a collection of vignettes of family life from
around the world would also stand out: harem scenes from the Alhambra, the
Egyptian man killing his sister because she has been raped, the Iranian groom
seeing his bride's face for the first time after the wedding as they both look
into a mirror. Certain features of Muslim family life—the seclusion of women,
the link between male honor and female chastity, arranged marriages, cousin
marriages, legal prerogatives of men over women, the special relationship between mothers and sons, and so forth—are found throughout Islamdom. Comparable patterns are also found in the realms of literature, education, and justice; and we have seen how much Muslims shared in the public arena.
Wherever one looks, Islam's "flavor is unmistakable."[2]

Yet one hesitates to call this flavor "Islamic," for that would imply that
these patterns are inherent in the religion, which they clearly are not. The
Qur'an and the *Hadith* Reports nowhere prescribe mosque decorations or attitudes toward rulers, yet these did typically resemble each other across Islamdom. Lacking a term for what is characteristic of the Muslim experience but
not required by the Islamic faith or law, Marshall G. S. Hodgson coined the
term "Islamicate." For Hodgson, Islamic means "something that expresses
Islam as a faith," while Islamicate means whatever does not refer "directly
to the religion, Islam, itself, but to the social and cultural complex historically
associated with Islam and the Muslims."[3] "Islamicate" makes it possible to
isolate those features associated with Muslim life but not necessary to religious
practice; for this reason, it will be employed here.

Islamic acts derive from the faith and law of Islam and include beliefs about
God, forms of piety (such as Sufism), and expressions of faith (such as writing
religious poetry, wearing a turban, or going on the pilgrimage to Mecca). Islamicate acts include anything not directly related to Islam as a faith, espe-

cially those inadvertent consequences of the Islamic requirements. Islamicate acts could be abandoned, even reversed, without doing damage to a believer's relations to God; nonetheless, they typify Muslim society. "Islamic literature" is religious writings; "Islamicate literature" is the entire output of Muslim communities, including even anti-religious works. "Islamic art" means art connected to holy subjects and "Islamicate art" encompasses all creations by Muslims. Turkish, which is spoken mostly by Muslims, is an Islamicate language; the arabesque is an Islamicate design; and the harem is an Islamicate institution. None of these follow directly from the faith or law of Islam, but all come with its civilization.[4]

The same distinction holds for public life. Islam makes certain demands on its adherents, such as making war only under specified conditions and paying prescribed taxes; fulfilling these requirements "expresses Islam as a faith" and are therefore Islamic. Other features of public life are not obligatory, do not express Islamic faith, and are thus Islamicate; these include the withdrawal of subjects from political and military affairs, weak loyalties to governments, and disdain for Europe.

The Shari'a lies behind both Islamic and Islamicate patterns. On the Islamic level, the sacred law pulled Muslims in the same direction and created a shared framework which transcended local variations. By establishing goals for all Muslims, it gave them a common outlook and way of life. "The ulema, to the extent in which they have succeeded in imposing Islamic law, succeeded in unifying Islamic society, since the law . . . was the instrument by which the social ethic of Islam was consolidated."[5] Specific circumstances varied, but Islamic parameters stayed nearly the same.

Shar'i regulations were also at the heart of many Islamicate patterns. The Muslim view of kafirs, for example, was shaped by the concepts of Dar al-Islam and Dar al-Harb, jihad, dhimmis and *harbi*s. Simple Shar'i admonitions often had enormous implications for Muslim life. The ban on pork was Islamic but its consequences were Islamicate: it led to the disappearance of pigs in Islamdom, which in turn threw open "the wooded ranges to sheep and goats and thus indirectly brought about a catastrophic deforestation. This is one of the basic reasons for the sparse landscape particularly evident in the Mediterranean districts of Islamic countries."[6] Similarly, the ban on wine meant that the vine retreated "from the plains . . . to the mountains, from the open fields to the gardens."[7] If the pilgrimage to Mecca expressed faith, the ensuing transfer of plants that it occasioned—the importation of rubber to Southeast Asia or that of rice, sugar cane, indigo, saffron, henna, cotton, plums, apricots, artichokes, and spinach to Muslim Spain (and thence to the rest of Europe)—did not.[8]

There has been very little study done of Islamicate acts; most have not even been identified, much less has their connection to Islam been established. Patterns other than those discussed in chapters 3 and 4 include: the establishment of dynasties through conquest from without, not by expansion from within; problems with passing on the rule; power leading to wealth, rather than the reverse; the ubiquity of slaves in and the exclusion of women from public life; the near absence of municipal governments; "irregularity and anarchy" in the building of cities;[9] laws generated by *ad hoc* decisions, not formal legislation; the reliance on cavalry soldiers; an alliance between city-dwellers and nomads; and the "triumph of nomadism."[10]

In contrast to Islamic patterns, which affect individuals, Islamicate patterns affect communities. A person's private faith determines the extent to which he follows Islamic regulations, but it is the whole society that is influenced by Islamicate practices. Devout believers who live in full accordance with Islamic precepts are dispersed throughout Islamdom, differing relatively little in their approaches to God or in their execution of the sacred law. The observant Muslim living in so far an outpost of Islam as Central Africa molds his whole existence to Islam in roughly the same way as the observant Muslim in so strictly Islamic an area as Tunisia. For each of them, the five daily prayers give his life a rhythm, the sumptuary laws give it a tone, Sufism gives it energy, and theology gives it purpose.

But if Muslims in the two places are equally Islamic, they differ in that the Central African is weakly Islamicate while the Tunisian is strongly so. In the outposts, Islam is an individual's creed set among other values; in the heartlands, Islam affects the whole society and determines a large portion of its values. Islamicate influences are cultural traits touching everyone in a society, impious skeptics no less than believers. Pork, for example, is virtually unavailable to Tunisians, regardless of the strength of their beliefs; Islamicate characteristics have little to do with individuals but reflect the extent to which Islam permeates a culture; to a degree they touch all Muslims. Just as every Westerner is in some way affected by the common heritage of Greek thought, Roman institutions, Christian faith, and Enlightenment ideals, every Muslim is heir to a legacy of Arabian conquests, medieval synthesis, worldly superiority vis-à-vis non-Muslims, and the fundamentalist surge of the eighteenth century. Developed during the early centuries, Islamicate patterns became widespread in premodern times and retained a profound influence throughout the modern era.

Islamicate characteristics exist most consistently in North Africa, the Middle East, and the northwest portion of the Indian subcontinent, those regions where Islam spread earliest and won the strongest hold. They exist least in those regions where Islam arrived most recently and has the weakest impact. In Tunisia, where Islam has deep roots, subjects resist military service more than in Central Africa, where the roots are shallow. Egyptians have stronger feelings for the umma and weaker political loyalties than do Somalis. Iranians resent Western civilization more than the Volga Tatars. Pakistanis are more devoted to the Islamic identity than are Bangladeshis. The fact that the Middle East and adjoining regions to the west and east are most intensively Islamicate accounts for their special influence and prestige within Islamdom. As the source and proving grounds for both Islamic and Islamicate developments, they also have special importance in this study.

Although Islamicate patterns are not explicit and their very existence has yet to be established, their impact on the political conduct of Muslim peoples may be even greater than Islamic ones. Islamic influences affect only persons seeking to live by the law; Islamicate influences affect all Muslims. The Shari'a, especially in modern times, inspires only a portion of the umma and it covers only some aspects of public life (saying nothing, for instance, about the way a ruler should be selected); Islamicate influences affect the Weltanschauung of everyone in Islamdom, including even the dhimmis. Between the two, Islamic and Islamicate influences shaped Muslim political culture and constitute the legacy of Islam. These are also the forces that continue to make Islam important today. However much institutions, attitudes, and customs have changed, the Muslim approach to politics derives from the invariant premises of the religion and from fundamental themes established more than a millennium ago.

PART II

Encountering
the West

5

Western Armies
and Civilization

World history since 1500 may be
thought of as a race between the
West's growing power to molest
the rest of the world and the
increasingly desperate efforts of
other peoples to stave Westerners
off.

—William H. McNeill

WERE the Eskimos suddenly to emerge as the world's leading artists and
scholars, were factories in Greenland to outproduce those of Japan, and were
invaders from the far north to conquer the United States and the Soviet Union,
we would hardly be more astonished than were the Muslims two hundred
years ago when they suddenly fell under West European control. The Franks,
long ago dismissed as "resembling animals more than men," turned up in the
later eighteenth century as explorers, soldiers, traders, missionaries, administrators, and Orientalists; within 150 years, nearly the whole of Islamdom had
fallen under their control. In the crisis that followed, Muslims were compelled
to cope with techniques, ideologies, and institutions from the West. Autonomism and legalism never had had to face such powerful challenges, nor had they
ever fared so poorly; Europe's armies almost eliminated Dar al-Islam, and its
civilization came near to destroying the Shari'a. The arrival of the European
imperialists destroyed the medieval synthesis, overturned the high standing
of the umma, and transformed the role of Islam in politics.

Europe's Supremacy

The better to visualize the Western impact, let us begin with the paradigm of France and Egypt. On three occasions, Egypt has been attacked by France and the results of their encounters can serve to symbolize the relations between Europe and Islamdom as a whole. The first assault, which typified the premodern situation, occurred in 1248 when the king of France, Louis IX (better known as Saint Louis) led the last Crusader expedition seriously to try to take Jerusalem from the Muslims. Jerusalem being under the control of the Ayyubids, a dynasty based in Egypt, Louis devised a plan to capture the Egyptian coastal city of Damietta and then return it in exchange for the holy city. French forces did take Damietta in June 1249, but then, buoyed by this success, Louis made the mistake of trying to invade the interior of the country and to destroy the Ayyubid dynasty altogether. The attack went awry, Louis and many French soldiers were captured in April 1250, and, as part of the deal to ransom them, the French forces evacuated Damietta. King Louis and his troops then fled from Egypt to Syria.

Crusaders and Ayyubids faced each other as approximate equals. Their technology, wealth, and cultural levels differed little; they disposed of roughly the same military power; and religious passions motivated both. The French attacked Egypt as Christian believers intent on winning Jerusalem from heathens. The Ayyubids responded in kind, seeing themselves as defenders of Dar al-Islam.

Although the two sides were matched in power and ideology in the thirteenth century, this parity was subsequently broken. West Europeans harnessed their economic potential, scientific capabilities, and social institutions to develop their civilization in unprecedented ways; this process, known as modernization, began in the sixteenth century and proceeds unabated to our time. Two aspects of modernization concern us most: military power and political culture. Military strength did not result just from new weapons and strategies, but from much else as well. European governments gained greater stability as a result of elections and parliaments; they commanded more loyalty from their citizens through political parties and new ideologies; the proliferation of public schools, universities, mass publishing, and the news media endowed Europe with great cultural advantages; the business corporation, limited liability partnership, and stock exchange enhanced the effectiveness of capitalist institutions; paved roads, canal networks, railroads, and the telegraph brought everything together. Europeans were strongest because they were the most civilized, the richest, and the healthiest people in the world.

At about the same time as Europe became so powerful, its culture under-went a process of radical secularization. The eighteenth century saw a re-orientation away from Christianity and toward the development of a nonre-ligious civilization, making what the Franks had to offer non-Christians far more attractive than before. Muslims seeking guidance found answers in the religiously neutral ideas coming from Europe; for the first time, they could learn from Europe without having first to undergo conversion. Their relation-ship to the Franks became totally altered as European culture developed from religious rival to seductive ideology.

The French Revolution epitomized both the military and cultural changes that had taken place: while French armies crushed their opposition, French ideas won a wide following throughout Europe. Muslims too became involved when the French landed in Egypt for the second time, five and a half centuries after Saint Louis. On 1 July 1798 they appeared without warning on the coast near Alexandria. Commanded by Napoleon Bonaparte, who saw this expedi-tion mostly as a way to keep himself and his troops occupied, their mission was to take Egypt and thereby cut the British off from India. French soldiers immediately captured Alexandria, then within three weeks they crushed the Mamluk forces outside Cairo. Napoleon's troops encountered no serious oppo-sition during their blitzkrieg and easily took control of the Nile Valley. Only another European power could have stood up to their overwhelming force—and this indeed happened days later, when British ships destroyed the French fleet waiting outside Alexandria on August first. The French forces, cut off from Europe, stayed on in Egypt for three more years, until compelled to evacuate by the British in October 1801.

The disparity in military power between the French and Egyptian troops was enormous—Napoleon's army enjoyed total supremacy in every respect, including tactics, strategy, weaponry, communications, command hierarchy, discipline, and provisioning. If anything, the disparity in political outlook be-tween the two sides was even greater. Egyptians still viewed their enemy as Christians and as religious foes; the only claim to legitimacy of the Mamluk government in Cairo was its ability to keep kafirs out and to apply the Shari'a. In contrast, the French forces almost ignored the religious dimension of the conflict. Napoleon saw himself not as a Christian conqueror but as a *friend* of Islam and the downtrodden Egyptians. On his arrival in Egypt, he distrib-uted a manifesto in Arabic proclaiming the Mamluk rulers as the real enemies of Egyptians. To win popular support, he established French forms of local government and ruled the country with the Egyptians' welfare in mind. Fur-ther, although Napoleon had little patience with Christianity, he did express sympathy for Islam and showed interest in it. Such tolerance was not confined to Napoleon himself; Baron J. F. Menou, who took over as commander of the French expeditionary forces in June 1800, actually converted to Islam and became known as Abdulla Menou.

The armies of Napoleon represented a new force in politics, a popular army run by leaders claiming to represent their people in the service of a political ideology. Christianity and Islam were irrelevant to the revolutionaries, who fought for the glory of France and for liberty, equality, and fraternity. National interest and ideological fervor counted far more than religion. If Egyptian forces had changed little in military capabilities or world outlook over the centuries, the French army had been transformed in both respects.

⦁ But this power gap could not continue; having seen what Europeans could do, the Egyptians quickly imitated them. Egypt's first Muslim ruler after the French invasion was Muhammad 'Ali, an Ottoman officer of Albanian origin who was garrisoned in Egypt; as a witness to the French occupation, he recognized that modern techniques could enhance his own power. With this in mind, he embarked on a crash program to raise Egypt's military and economic capabilities to the level of Europe's. Recruitment, military training, drill patterns, tactics, and command structures were all copied from the French, as were land surveys, hydraulic planning, disease control, industrialization, and taxation. Muhammad 'Ali assured himself the best and latest techniques by sending Egyptian students to France and employing Europeans in Egypt. He sponsored other innovations too, such as an Arabic printing press, a medical school, and a government newspaper.

⦁ The changes begun by Muhammad 'Ali were continued by his successors, who made concerted efforts to learn methods from Europe to modernize their country. The effects of this could be seen in 1956, when France invaded Egypt for the third and last time. This attack was occasioned by two events: Egypt's president, Gamal Abdul Nasser, nationalized the Suez Canal in July 1956, much to the dismay of its French and British shareholders; then, from 29 October on, Israeli forces overran the Sinai peninsula in an effort to stop the attacks emanating from there. Franco-British paratroopers landed in the coastal city of Port Said on 5 November, ostensibly to protect the canal from the effects of Israeli-Egyptian fighting, but really in cooperation with Israel. By the seventh of November, French and British troops had advanced to Ismailia, thirty miles to the south of Port Said. As in 1798, Egyptian defenses gave way, but this time the government in Cairo mobilized international support, American and Soviet especially, and forced the Europeans to halt. By the end of December 1956, all the foreign troops had been evacuated. Once again, the French had failed.

In 1798, only Britain could stand up to France; in 1956, the two together failed. Egypt had made great progress. Its government in 1956 claimed to represent the nation and it pursued nonreligious ideologies derived from Western sources, including socialism, neutralism, democracy, and social justice. Egypt had acquired leaders intent on forwarding the country's national interests and ceased to be a playfield for foreigners. Overtones of Christian-Muslim hostility still remained in the Suez conflict, but they were not explicit, nor were they critical; on both sides, the issues were those of national rights, economics, and relations with the super-powers.

Three times in seven hundred years, similar events had occurred: France invaded Egypt each time, won initial successes, penetrated the interior, met defeat, beat a hasty retreat, and left the country empty-handed. But beneath the similarities of the expeditions to Damietta, Alexandria, and Port Said, fundamental changes were taking place in the relations between these two countries. Both the French and the Egyptians saw their confrontation in religious terms in 1248; the French evolved a military power and an ideological approach to politics which stunned the Egyptians in 1798; and by 1956, the Egyptians had learned enough about modern ways to outmaneuver the French in international politics. The three invasions symbolized premodern parity, the European surge, and the Muslim catching-up. The crushing defeat of 1798 and others like it elsewhere in Dar al-Islam compelled the Muslims to observe the Franks carefully and to learn from them; one and a half centuries later, they had partially succeeded, for although still inferior in power, they had absorbed European ideas. Part II explains the context in which the changes from 1798 to 1956 took place.

Worldly Failure and Its Effects

The premodern umma, for all its diversity and weaknesses, enjoyed the power of an integral civilization. Defeat or failure seemed transient. Muslims had sufficient confidence in the wisdom of their culture and the strength of their arms that threats from Dar al-Harb prompted few anxieties. Kafirs might conquer a region and local customs might survive every attempt to bring them into line with the Shari'a, but these were manageable intrusions. To a remarkable degree, the umma felt a sense of strength.

This changed with the coming of the Europeans. First indications of what lay ahead appeared in the 1400s when the Indian Ocean trade was disrupted and precious metals brought in from the New World had disastrous economic effects on much of Islamdom; Europeans captured such strategic naval spots as Ceuta, Hormuz, and Malacca; and European techniques began to spread far beyond the Mediterranean. Yet these were only intimations of what was to come. The Europeans made few attempts to conquer Muslims and were not so threatening that Muslims felt compelled to adopt their techniques, much less their political ideas.

The beginning of the real onslaught can be dated to the late eighteenth century, when the British established control over Bengal. (A private corporation, the East India Company, accomplished this, not the British government—but that made little difference to the Bengalis.) Europeans now had power enough to confront Muslims directly. Other blows against Dar al-Islam confirmed Europe's strength: the Russians took Crimea in 1783; the British took Penang, Malaysia, in 1786; and then Napoleon conquered Egypt in 1798. From that point on, the Europeans encroached on a new Muslim territory every few years. By 1919, one and a half centuries later, they controlled nearly all Islamdom. There was no coordinated plan for this assault; well over a dozen nations, including a number of non-European ones, competed in the scramble for Islamdom. The following partial listing gives the dates when many of the regions inhabited by Muslims fell to non-Muslims, from the mid-eighteenth century to the end of World War I; the identity of the non-Muslim conqueror follows in parentheses.

1757	Ili (China)	1841	Sarawak (Sir James Brooke, a
1759	Kashgar (China)		Briton)
1760	Tarim Basin (China)	1843	Sind, India (Britain)
1764	Bengal (Britain)	1849	Kashmir and Punjab, India
1777	Balam-Bangan, Indonesia		(Britain)
	(Holland)		Parts of Guinea (France)
1783	Crimea (Russia)	1849–54	Syr Darya Valley,
1785	Pattani (Thailand)		Kazakhstan (Russia)
	Arakan (Burma)	1856	Oudh, India (Britain)
1786	Penang, Malaysia (Britain)	1858	All India under British crown
1798	Egypt (France)	1859	Daghestan (Russia)
1799	Syria (France)	1859–60	Tetuan, Morocco (Spain)
1800	Parts of Malaysia (Britain)	1864	Cimkent, Kazakhstan (Russia)
1801	Georgia (Russia)	1866	Tashkent, Uzbekistan (Russia)
1803–28	Azerbaijan (Russia)	1868	Bukhara, Uzbekistan (Russia)
1804	Armenia (Russia)	1872	Sinkiang (China)
1808	Western Java (Holland)	1872–1908	Aceh, Indonesia (Holland)
1820	Bahrain; Qatar; United Arab	1873	Khiva, Uzbekistan (Russia)
	Emirates (Britain)	1876	Khokand, Uzbekistan (Russia)
1830	Manchanagara, Indonesia		Socotra, South Yemen
	(Holland)		(Britain)
1830–46	Algerian coast (France)		Quetta, Pakistan (Britain)
1834–59	Caucasus (Russia)		
1839	Central Sumatra, Indonesia		
	(Holland)		
	Aden, South Yemen (Britain)		

1878	Kars and Ardahan, Turkey (Russia)	1891	Oman (Britain)
	Bulgaria (Russia)	1892–93	Lower Niger Basin (France)
	Bosnia and Herzegovina, Yugoslavia (Austria)	1893	Uganda (Britain)
		1896–98	Northern Sudan (Britain)
	Serbia	1898–1903	Northern Nigeria (Britain)
	Montenegro	1898–99	Southern Niger (France)
	Cyprus (Britain)	1899	Kuwait (Britain)
1878–79	Khyber Pass, Pakistan (Britain)	1900–14	Southern Algeria (France)
1881	Ashkhabad, Turkmenistan (Russia)	1903	Macedonia (Russia and Austria)
		1906	Wadai, Chad (France)
1881–83	Tunisia (France)	1908	Crete (Greece)
1882	Egypt (Britain)	1909	Northern Malay Peninsula (Britain)
	Assab, Ethiopia (Italy)	1911–28	Libya (Italy)
1883–88	Upper Niger Basin (France)	1912	Dodecanese (Italy)
1884	Northern Somalia (Britain, France)		Western Sahara (Spain)
	Merv, Turkmenistan (Russia)	1912–34	Morocco (France and Spain)
1885	Eastern Rumelia (Bulgaria)	1913	Southern Philippines (United States)
	Rio de Oro, Mauritania (Spain)		Central Thrace (Bulgaria)
1885–89	Eritrea, Ethiopia (Italy)	1914	All Malaysia (Britain)
1887	Harar (Ethiopia)	1917	Israel; Jordan (Britain)
1887–96	Guinea (France)	1918	Lebanon; Syria (France)
1888	North Borneo, Malaysia (Britain)	1919	Parts of Turkey (Italy, Greece, France)
1889–92	Southern Somalia (Italy)		Iraq
1890	Zanzibar, Tanzania (Britain)		

When the scramble ended, Britain's control in the Indian subcontinent, the Middle East, Africa, and Malaya gave it the most Muslim subjects. Indonesia, with its huge Muslim population, gave Holland the next largest number. Muslims under French rule were more widely dispersed, through Africa and the Levant. Russia had conquered several Muslim regions, including the Crimea, the Caucasus, western Central Asia, and the Upper Volga. Italy, Spain, Portugal, and Belgium all controlled Muslims in their African possessions, as did Germany until World War I. Albania, Yugoslavia, Bulgaria, Greece and Rumania ruled Muslim communities within their national territories. The United States had Muslim subjects in the Philippines and South Africa controlled the Indian Muslims who had emigrated there. Ethiopia, Thailand, and China also ruled substantial numbers of believers. As a result, by 1919, only a handful of Muslim regions retained their political independence: Turkey, Iran, Afghanistan, Arabia, and Yemen. The first three did this by balancing the claims of contending European states (especially Britain and Russia), while the two latter were so remote and barren that they held almost no interest for the imperial powers.

The fact that Muslims long had been accustomed to ruling others heightened the pain of subjugation. The Ottoman Empire had ruled millions of Christians in Southeast Europe for four and a half centuries before it was displaced by the pedestrian regime of republican Turkey (far more interested in imitating Europe than conquering it) and a clutch of independent Balkan states. Parts of India had been part of Dar al-Islam for over a thousand years, making it particularly difficult for Muslims there to face the prospect of permanent rule by kafirs—and to avoid this, the movement for a separate Muslim state, Pakistan, emerged. Britain gave the Jews sanction in 1917 to make Palestine their "national home" at Muslim expense and France carved a large slice out of Syria to create Lebanon, the Levantine Christian state. Muslim states of northern Nigeria lost their political pre-eminence to the Christians and animists of the south. In several colonies, notably Algeria, Russian Central Asia, and Sinkiang (Chinese Central Asia), Muslims watched almost helplessly as kafirs settled their territories and systematically endeavored to eliminate the Islamicate way of life. Dar al-Islam, which once included millions of non-Muslims, had by the early twentieth century shrunk to an area far smaller than Islamdom.

To make matters worse, modern Muslims suffered defeats in other ways too. The existing bases of economic life were upset as cash crops were instituted by the imperial powers, as crafts practiced for generations lost their markets, and as trade routes became unprofitable. Islamicate customs buckled under the pressure of European civilization and the Muslims' fund of knowledge—scientific, technical, mechanical, geographic, and historical—became rapidly obsolete. The fundaments of Islamicate civilization came under question, prompting reactions of shock, despair, doubt, and envy.

To the extent that Muslims had always had to deal with kafir conquests and alien cultural influences, Europe's armies and civilization fitted existing patterns. But prior challenges to the umma had been limited and had not prepared Muslims for unmitigated decline in the nineteenth century. Non-Muslims had previously conquered parts of Islamdom, to be sure, but never much of it; Turkish pagans from Inner Asia, Crusaders, and Spanish *reconquistador*s had torn off no more than fragments of the Muslim patrimony. Non-Islamic cultural elements had never threatened the Shar'i way of life. The worst premodern Muslim experience, that of the Mongol invasion, led to the loss of not much more than parts of the Middle East and involved rude barbarians eventually converted to Islam. Only portions of Islamdom had ever fallen and then not to peoples capable of challenging Islam culturally. In contrast, the modern Europeans conquered most of Islamdom, they enjoyed the highest civilization, and they threatened the Shar'i way of life.

The effect of this assault was to alter the context of Muslim political life. Once active, Islamdom became reactive; once a leader, it became a follower; once an integral civilization, it became ruptured. Military defeat and cultural subjugation resulted in the collapse of the old Muslim complacency and a massive crisis. Traditionalist Islam, the medieval synthesis, compromises, and the spirit of conservatism: none of these sufficed any longer. For the first time in centuries, the umma began rethinking basic questions.

It found three broad options: a turn inward to its own tradition, a turn to the West, or a mix of the two. The Shari'a, key to the umma's premodern political culture, was critical to this choice. Some Muslims relied on it more than ever, others rejected it entirely, and yet others wanted to change it to fit Western ways. The first group, the fundamentalists, tried to exclude European influences by rejuvenating the ways of their ancestors. Secularists took the opposite course and tried to emulate the Europeans. Reformists saw the answer as reconciling Islam and Western civilization. This split over the Shari'a's role has been at the center of the great debate in Islamdom during the past two centuries. Put more abstractly, it represents the conflict between modernization and Westernization.

Modernization and Westernization

Although often used synonymously, these two terms are distinct: the first means becoming powerful and rich, the second means becoming culturally like an Occidental. What constitutes modernization is particularly difficult to specify, however, for this entails summing up all the ways in which the Western world during the past several centuries differs in kind from all other parts of the world, as well as the West in previous centuries. These changes are both wide-ranging and elusive. There is little agreement on the most essential feature of modernity: what was the key event in the process summed up by W. H. Auden as "a change of heart?" Was it the increase of industry, urbanization, mass education, enhanced communications, social planning, complex organizations, rationality, or science? The intricacy of this change makes it difficult to define concisely, or even intelligibly.[1]

Another problem is that we know too little about life in premodern times to understand the chief differences between it and modernity. Definitions based on the study of primitive peoples (who are not a proper contrast) or of contemporary non-Western societies (which are pervasively, if subtly, influenced by modernity) are not accurate; only by looking at the great civilizations of the past, especially the Chinese, Indian, and Islamicate, is it possible to isolate those qualities that constitute modernity; for this reason, defining modernity requires immense knowledge of premodern life as well as a wide historical vision. Few writers have these qualifications. One of them, Marshall G. S. Hodgson, stresses what he calls technicalization, the tendency for "specialized technical considerations . . . to take precedence over all others."[2] This definition is simple, comprehensive, and accurate. A modern society is one in which the institutions that foster technicalization predominate. One aspect of this, but by no means the only, is industrialization, the harnessing of mechanical power to economic activity. Equally critical are changes in the intellectual, social, and administrative spheres. Modernization entails an enormous increase in a people's social power—that is, in the total resources it can muster. Indications of social power include military strength, scientific progress, economic capabilities, and political stability. Specialized technical considerations had been present previously, but it was only in northwestern Europe in the late eighteenth century that, for the first time ever, a critical mass had been attained and the drive toward innovation became institutionalized, prevalent, and permanent.

On the individual level too, becoming modern means arranging ones life so that specialized technical considerations predominate. Or, to put it more concretely, it means becoming good at working in or managing a factory.[3]

In contrast to modernization, Westernization in this book refers to the imitation of European or American customs that are unrelated to economic development. The two processes are so often confused because things Western have become identified with modernity in the eyes of most of the world. It is necessary to distinguish those aspects of Western culture—such as the emphasis on punctuality, the spread of literacy, and the development of capitalist institutions—that played a role in modernization from those—such as the use of the Roman alphabet or racist ideology—that did not. This is not always easy, however, for some features (Christianity, centralized governments) may have been helpful to modernization without being necessary to it.

Identifying all things Western with modernity leads to strange results: thus does listening to the music of Ludwig von Beethoven, who lived two centuries ago, have the aura of a modern activity in countries where everything European is equated with progress. In fact, what is Western need not be modern, nor must everything modern be Western. The zaibatsu, Japan's commercial firms, are modern but not Western. Portugal is Western, but South Korea is more modern. Abandoning the veil is modernizing, adopting the jacket and tie is Westernizing. Learning a European language falls into the first category, studying its poetry into the second. Reducing the number of holidays is one thing, celebrating New Year's on the first of January is the other.

The umma's experience with modernity and the West broadly resembles that of the Jews, for both had to deal with the tensions arising between the sacred law and the new ways. Because Jews encountered this problem in the mid-eighteenth century, about one hundred years before the Muslims did, and because they were even more overwhelmed by it than the Muslims, modern Jewish history provides a helpful commentary on the Muslim experience, suggesting available options and the likely future course. Developments in Judaism will therefore be occasionally referred to for comparative purposes.

Virtually all Muslims agree on the desirability of modernization and appreciate the benefits it brings; becoming strong and wealthy is not an issue.[4] They do not agree, however, on the extent to which this requires Westernization. Must Muslims emulate Western practices to achieve what Europe and America have? Is it really necessary to learn their languages and to accept their political ideologies? Muslims differ in the degree to which Western civilization attracts them or appears necessary to them: some Muslims attempt to maintain the old customs in a technicalized environment, while others abandon the traditional rules and adopt, to a varying extent, Western ways.

On its own, modernization need not diminish adherence to the sacred law except to the extent that the law conflicts with those technical considerations required for modernizing—chiefly in the realm of economics. The prohibition on interest stops investment; inflexible zakat rates almost never meet the tax needs of governments or citizens; the ban on speculative ventures is sometimes understood to exclude insurance and futures markets; mortmain regulations encourage idle use of land and property; inheritance laws deprive the individual of making decisions about bequests, reducing his incentive to earn money or save it; tariff rates that vary according to the religion of the person involved distort incentives; restrictions on female movement and employment diminish the size of the labor force; Ramadan fasting during the daylight hours for twenty-nine days a year reduces productivity; and so forth.

In most other matters, however, Islam and modernization do not clash. Pious Muslims can cultivate the sciences, work efficiently in factories, or utilize advanced weapons. Modernization requires no one political ideology or set of institutions: elections, national boundaries, civic associations, and the other hallmarks of Western life are not necessary to economic growth. As a creed, Islam satisfies management consultants as well as peasants. The Shari'a has nothing to say about the changes that accompany modernization, such as the shift from agriculture to industry, from countryside to city, or from social stability to social flux; nor does it impinge on such matters as mass education, rapid communications, new forms of transportation, or health care.

From the Shar'i point of view, Westernizing is far more problematic than modernizing. Three aspects of Westernization are particularly inimical to the Shar'i way of life: the Christian emphasis on faith, specific differences in custom from Islamicate civilization, and political secularism.

Emphasis on Faith. Although very few Muslims adopted Christianity as a faith, most of them absorbed the Christian approach to God. As Muslims learned about European civilization, they adopted the notion, usually without even realizing it, that ethical behavior matters more than strict observance of the sacred law. Antinomianism, a doctrine associated in modern times most closely with Protestantism, represents a powerful challenge to the Shari'a and even threatens to displace it. The Jewish experience in the last two centuries helps to understand just how serious it is.

Jews lived in Europe for well over a millennium in virtual isolation from the Christian society all around them. They were concentrated in shtetls and ghettoes, spoke their own languages (Yiddish and Ladino), ran their own schools and community organizations, devoted themselves to meticulous observance of the sacred law, and were ready to excommunicate whoever joined the mainstream society. Although physically located in Europe, Jews knew hardly anything about the cultural life of the Christians on all sides of them; most Jews were as removed from Western civilization as their Muslim contemporaries.[5] It was not until the eighteenth-century Enlightenment, when the Christian religion lost its hold over Europe's culture, that Jews were allowed to participate—or that they had any wish to do so. Dazzled by Europe's cultivation of the arts and sciences, Jews then learned German and French, enrolled in the gymnasia and universities, and aspired to full legal, social, and political equality.

Involvement in European life invariably led to a decline in the observance of Talmudic laws. Jews did not so much learn about the Christian emphasis on faith as they unwittingly imbibed it upon joining Christian society and conforming to its way of life. Christian ideas about grace and faith were not consciously adopted but absorbed through daily contact. A child who went to a school that did not enforce Halakhic restrictions on food, clothing, sex, and the Sabbath inevitably felt less attached to the law than one who stayed within a traditional Jewish environment. Debate among Jews over assimilation versus living by the law lasted two full centuries. Indeed, were it not for the destruction of East European Jewry in World War II, the issue might yet be alive. As it is, most Jews came to see their religion in Christian fashion—as a faith and an identity more than a way of life. Since the end of the battle over the Halakha a generation or so ago (though it continues residually in Israel), only a small portion of the Jews continue to uphold the sacred law as of old.

Modern Jews thus repeated the evolution of the first Christians almost two millennia earlier, when faith and ethics replaced the law. In effect, Jews were Protestantized, and became more concerned with ethics, attitude, and intent than with exactness of action. Maintaining the law became an individual decision: a few lived by it completely, some kept the key provisions (Kosher laws, sexual restrictions), others kept just symbolic parts (no pork, fasting on Yom Kippur), while still others ignored it totally. A tolerant attitude developed and some Jews even took pride in the diversity and adaptability of their religious practices—an attitude utterly unthinkable not many generations earlier, when not to keep the law meant not to be a Jew.

As Muslims became familiar with Western customs, they too absorbed Christian notions of faith. These came indirectly and almost imperceptibly with the adoption of European ideas and manners. At no point did Muslims consciously accept the Christian aversion to sacred law; as with the Jews, Christian attitudes penetrated unobserved. The symptoms were clear; Muslims attempted to live ethically and felt no remorse when they neglected sumptuary laws. Any Muslim who consumed alcohol in premodern times realized vividly his sin; but the lines became blurred when some Muslims came to view drinking as irrelevant to faith in God or moral conduct. The notion developed that Shar'i commands could be transgressed without committing sins, and as it spread, Muslims too became Protestantized.

Emphasis on faith rather than on law affected private precepts most because they were traditionally the best implemented. It also reduced adherence to public precepts, for Muslims acquainted with government practices in the West knew how very little Christianity had to do with setting the public agenda. The more Westernized a Muslim, the less he concerned himself with fulfilling public rules of the Shari'a.

Specific Differences. Islamic and Western customs differ in so many details that a Westernized Muslim finds it nearly impossible to maintain the Shar'i commands. Almost every accommodation to Western living patterns reduces one's ability to maintain the law. In this, the Shari'a again resembles the Halakha. As Jews were assimilated in Europe, they found the sacred law an obstacle to assimilation and increasingly ignored it. Halakhic regulations restricted travel, prohibited most social relations with gentiles, and forced Jews to live in their own communities (a solitary Jew could not provide himself with Kosher food). As Jews joined mainstream society, these laws got in the way and so were increasingly abandoned. Regulations concerning food, clothing, Sabbath observance, and the separation of the sexes—customs that had made the Jews of Europe conspicuous and kept them apart for over a millennium—became encumbrances in modern times and were dropped. The Halakha commands distinctive fringed undergarments for Jewish men, full beards, and covered heads; with time, all these disappeared, usually in this order.

Islamic ways differed no less; a Muslim faced innumerable choices in his private life. A man could dress in turban and robe or hat and pants; he could keep his wife in veil and harem or allow her to become visible and mobile; he could furnish his house with cushions or chairs and send his children to a Qur'anic or a European school. The family could remain extended or split into nuclear groupings; on a more subtle level, the family emphasis of old could remain intact or give way to a more individualistic orientation. In general, the notion of applying laws to personal matters (gambling, sex, and drinking) and family relations was increasingly alien to the Western style of living and therefore was subject to erosion as Muslims imitated the West. In public affairs, the chief premodern characteristics differed in nearly every way from those of the modern West; these will be discussed in chapter 7.

The Secular State. The idea of separating religion from politics struck at the very heart of the sacred law. Political secularism first developed in Europe during the Reformation of the sixteenth century. Before that time, virtually all West Europe had been Catholic and the church had played a comprehensive role in public life. The power amassed by men of religion can be symbolized by two incidents: in 1077 the Holy Roman Emperor abjectly pleaded for the Pope's forgiveness while waiting in pilgrim's garb in the snow; and in 1302 another Pope issued a bull that claimed absolute supremacy for his office, both spiritual and temporal, over all kings. With Martin Luther's break from the church in 1517, religious unity in West Europe was broken, leading to vicious fratricidal wars for the next one hundred and thirty years. The violence that accompanied the establishment of the Protestant sects drove some Europeans, exhausted by religious passions, to find a way to contain the bloody disruptions. Thus did political secularism—the agreement to disagree peacefully about religion—emerge, first in the 1570s in the Netherlands and later, with special importance, in North America. The idea of withdrawing religion from politics was not so much a preconceived ideal as a result of historical need: "It was the failure of Europeans to agree upon the truths of religion, within as well as across state boundaries, that opened the door to secularism."[6]

If political secularism developed as a means to keep believers from persecuting one another, it acquired another function by the time of the Enlightenment in the eighteenth century; freethinkers, agnostics, atheists, and others who wished to cut back on the role of religion in public life found secular arguments to be their most effective tool. By the time Muslims were paying close attention to European affairs, in the mid-nineteenth century, keeping faith out of politics had proven to be a forceful means to effect change and increase cultural freedom. For example, in debates between scientists and believers, such as the controversy over biological evolution, scientists relied on secular laws to protect their point of view.

110

For Muslims living in Dar al-Islam and hoping to emulate the West, the separation of religion and politics provided a tool for combatting a sacred law that claimed jurisdiction over the government. Muslims had to disengage religion from politics far more than did Christians, as Islam has had much more to say about public affairs. Political secularism provided progressive Muslims with an argument for disestablishing Islam and promulgating new laws along European lines. Withdrawal of the Shari'a from public life then made it possible for Muslims to write constitutions, set taxes according to need, base judicial processes on human reasoning, establish equal rights for all citizens, and so forth—all of which are contrary to Shar'i precepts. In addition, the separation of religion and politics appealed to some Muslims just because it had been accepted by most of the advanced nations of Europe, and imitating the Europeans was so often seen as the way to become modern. And for Muslims living in Dar al-Harb, the separation of religion and politics provided protection from the state, especially in such countries as Yugoslavia, Russia, Lebanon, and India, where Muslims feared domination by kafir rulers.

In sum, as Muslims made efforts to Westernize, they found the Shari'a "an obstacle to accepting the new European international standards."[7] And conversely, when they tried to maintain the laws of old, Western ways reduced observance of the Shari'a. Protestantization undermined the very notion of sacred law. Imitation of specific Occidental customs prompted Muslims to abandon aspects of the Shari'a that ran contrary to it. Political secularization generated opposition to Shar'i precepts concerning private life. The more Westernized Muslims became, the further they drifted from the Shar'i way of life.

Westernization being inimical to the observance of the Shari'a, Muslim attitudes toward the West became embroiled in the question of fulfilling the sacred law. With Westernization becoming urgent, "the crucial question is whether Islam should serve as a guide and inspiring ideal, or as the rule of life";[8] should Muslims abandon the Shari'a or keep it as always? The very fact that this question could be asked indicates how much things had changed, for the Shari'a had long been the undisputed source of ideals in Muslim life. It entered a wholly new era when challenged by European competition for the allegiance of the umma. European alternatives spawned new attitudes toward the law and transformed its role in politics.

Before 1800, the Shari'a knew no rivals. Though never implemented to the umma's full satisfaction, the law did enjoy an ideological monopoly, for nothing else could lay claim to Muslim aspirations. "The Shari'ah enforced itself by the respect that even its violators perforce paid it; the violations never abrogated the principle."[9] Honored even in the breach, Shar'i ideals faced no competition for its claim as the unique program for Muslim life. Non-Shar'i customs, such as bare-breasted women in Africa or veiled men in the Sahara, were considered transient and local; they were obstacles to the Shariʿa, not alternatives to it. Even Sufis, who often had more pressing concerns than fulfillment of the legal obligations, had no substitute for the Shariʿa—they could only neglect it. Until about 1800, external influences almost always had to fit within a Sharʿi framework.

All this changed with the impingement of Europe's massive power and dynamic culture. For many believers, Christian supremacy cast doubt on the Shariʿa (though not on the Islamic message of faith), whose credibility as the path of God was seriously tarnished when other methods worked demonstrably better. As Muslims began to emulate Europe, they came under the influence of a civilization that frequently ran exactly contrary to the Shariʿa. The monopoly of the sacred law was broken and, for the first time ever, Muslims contemplated replacing Sharʿi ideals with other ones. On the whole, the more a people learned from Europe or America, the more critically it viewed the Shariʿa. The West offered alternatives to the caliphate, jihad, zakat, *hadd,* and the other features of Islamic public life. More disturbing yet, it had a plethora of political ideologies to offer, each of which espoused a distinct world view. As Muslims became acquainted with the full gamut of Western thought, the Shariʿa began to appear as merely one of many possibilities. Believers faced the unfamiliar task of choosing their ideals; how they felt about the Shariʿa when given a choice largely determined how they responded to the challenge of modernity.

In these circumstances, the medieval synthesis no longer sufficed; faced with these new questions, Muslims had to develop new answers. Traditionalist Islam dealt with the problem of Shariʿa non-implementation but could not counsel Muslims on responding to the West. Although the problem of non-implementation did not disappear in recent times, it was often forgotten, overtaken by the more urgent matter of coping with modernity. Muslims living in remote countries (such as Yemen or Afghanistan) or in rural regions had much less contact with the West than did Muslims in more accessible lands and therefore had less need to respond to it. Thus, they found the traditionalist approach satisfactory long after Westernized Muslims had forsaken it.

As the medieval synthesis fell into eclipse, so did its practioners, the ʿulama. Most of them, even in the most Westernized environments, tended to close their eyes to changes and to repeat the worn formulae of their ancestors, unwilling to acknowledge how much circumstances had changed. Thus did ʿulama at the Islamic university of al-Azhar in Cairo go on teaching Ptolemaic astronomical system (in which the sun circles the earth) until compelled to adopt the Copernican system by the Egyptian government in 1961. The men who once served as religious authorities, judges, teachers, and community leaders lost all these roles in the course of modernization. A de-emphasis on *Hadith* Reports had the effect of devaluing the 'ulama's special fund of knowledge. Secularism fostered a view of the 'ulama as the very worst sort of reactionaries. Fundamentalists scorned them as insufficiently fervent and hopelessly compromised. Western legal practices led to the Shari'a being codified, by Muslim and European scholars alike, to facilitate its use in the courtroom; this enabled lawyers and judges not schooled in the Shari'a to practice in Shar'i courts, thus ending a 'ulama monopoly. Western education offered an alternative to the traditional Islamicate curriculum and reduced the value of its teachers, the 'ulama. Western political ideologies induced governments to deal directly with their citizens, eliminating the 'ulama as intermediaries.

Ignored, insulted, and even persecuted, the 'ulama lost their standing whenever modernization rendered the medieval synthesis obsolete. Particularly dramatic incidences occurred in Algeria under French rule, in Libya under Qadhdhafi, in Albania and the Soviet Union under the Communists, in Turkey under Atatürk, and in Iraq under the Ba'thists. The two exceptions to this pattern, Saudi Arabia and Iran, do in fact prove the rule, for these are the only countries wherein the 'ulama adopted fundamentalist doctrines. In Saudi Arabia, they formed an alliance with the Wahhabis which gave them control of the religious domain. In Iran, the 'ulama came to power in 1979 by espousing a unique fundamentalist ideology that stressed the importance of their own role. (Details on both instances follow in chapter 9.) From a long-term perspective, developments in Iran appear to be a final effort by the 'ulama to salvage their position, even at the expense of their traditionalist approach to Islam. Should this fail, the decline of Islam's rabbis may well be henceforth uninterrupted.

For those Muslims having to deal with modern ways, the traditionalist approach exemplified by the 'ulama did not suffice; they needed something stronger, something offering guidance to the main choices of the age: what to take from the West and what to reject. Europe demanded the articulation of new attitudes toward the Shari'a. Of those that emerged, two, reformism and secularism, were entirely novel; the third, fundamentalism, had premodern foundations but acquired a new role in response to the West.

6

New Attitudes toward the Sacred Law

At the present time the Law . . . remains an important, if not the most important, element in the struggle which is being fought in Islam between traditionalism and modernism.

—Joseph Schacht

COMPELLED to choose between Islamicate and Western civilizations, fundamentalists sought to keep what they had and to reject the West; secularists followed the opposite route, abandoning Islamicate ways in favor of Western ones; and reformists tried to combine the two. How Muslims decided this issue depended in large part on their attitude toward the Shari'a. As in premodern times, fundamentalists cherished the Shari'a in its entirety and strove to live by it exactly; they therefore tried to exclude all Western influences. Secularists found the Shari'a irrelevant to development and harmful for adopting Western civilization, therefore they favored withdrawing the Shari'a from public life. Reformists wished both to preserve the Islamic spirit and adopt Western ways; they argued that the two would be reconcilable if Islam were brought up to date. Because the place of the Shari'a "in a modern Muslim state will determine the character of that state,"[1] feelings about the Shari'a determined the political role a Muslim wanted Islam to play.

Two points bear repeating: first, the debate over Westernization concerned ways of life, not faith; only a few of the secularists denied the faith of Islam, and even they hardly dared to make this view public. Thus, when Muslims spoke of their concern about the future of Islam, they were referring to a way of life, not an approach to God. Second, Muslims ascribing to all three points of view agreed on the same ends—the desirability of the riches, power, and culture made possible by modernization—and disputed only the means to achieve them.

Reformism: Westernizing the Sacred Law

Reformist Muslims are committed to bringing the umma into step with modern times by reconciling the Shari'a with Western culture. Their task is hard, perhaps impossible, for the two civilizations are contradictory in many fundamental ways. The reformist goal is to enable Muslims to keep the Shari'a while living Westernized lives. If this succeeds, Muslims can adopt Western techniques and ways of life even while retaining Islamic principles; if it fails, Muslims must choose between secularism and fundamentalism.

By the very definition of their assignment, reformists know something about and admire both Islam and the culture of the West. Although Europe offers many ideologies, most of them agree on a number of ideals that conflict with the Shari'a, such as the need to separate religion and politics, the emphasis on national loyalties, the importance of ethnic divisions, egalitarianism, the rights of women, political representation, and the elimination of slavery. Because reformism arose in the late nineteenth century, in a period dominated by liberal thought, its abiding concern has been "to interpret Islam in terms of liberal humanitarian ideas and values."[2] Within this context, the aims of reformists differ: some, the most modest, see Islam and liberalism as no more than reconcilable; others, more ambitious, claim the two are similar; and yet others go so far as to argue that Islam is the greatest expression of the liberal ideal.

Equating Islam with the ideals of liberalism obviously requires a radical reinterpretation of the faith, and this task the reformists undertake with enthusiasm, developing an argument that permits them to overhaul the Shari'a without discarding it. Projecting Islam as a liberal religion implies abandoning the Shari'a as it was traditionally understood—which was hopelessly illiberal—and changing its precepts. Reformists argue that the traditionalist view of the Shari'a distorted and obscured the real doctrines of Islam; consequently, their principal task is to strip away the false accretions in order to reveal the liberalism of Islam. They do this in two ways: by altering Islam's law out of recognition and by imposing alien values on it.

Of the four sources of the Shari'a (the Qur'an, the *Hadith* Reports, consensus of the 'ulama, and reasoning by analogy), reformists unconditionally accept only the first, the Qur'an. They dispense with the *Hadith* Reports on the grounds that these are not authentic. Drawing (usually indirectly) on the research of such Western scholars as Ignaz Goldziher and Joseph Schacht, reformists argue that the *Hadith* Reports do not, as claimed, date from the time of Muhammad but were devised at least a century later.[3] This means that the *Hadith* are not a necessary aspect of Islamic law.

As for consensus of the 'ulama and reasoning by analogy, they say these are outdated. The 'ulama who developed the Shari'a during the first centuries of Islam were ordinary mortals who propounded laws appropriate to their own circumstances, not for all time. Each generation must reread the Qur'an, reach its own consensus, and use its logical facilities to change the law and make it current. But Muslims failed to do this and instead allowed the law to become stale. In the words of Muhammad Iqbal, "while the people are moving, the law remains stationary."[4] As the laws ossified, they held the umma back and became a source of weakness. Reformists, Erwin I. J. Rosenthal writes,

> insist on formulating new laws appropriate to present needs. For them the *Shari'a* of classical Islam is time-bound and obsolete, if not in principle, then certainly in many of its practical rules and enactments. Their faith no longer includes faith in the divine, immutable, all-inclusive and obligatory character of the law, which to them grew over a long period of time and reflects the ideas and the moral, social and political attitudes of bygone ages, out of touch with contemporary reality.[5]

For reformists, to the extent that the early umma's success was due to the possession of a suitable law, the reassertion of Muslim power today requires adjustments to bring the law into line with current needs. They strip away the entire corpus of Muslim learning; theirs is the Bible without the Talmud.

Confining the Shari'a to the Qur'an has distinct advantages for reformists. First, excluding the other three sources has the effect of eliminating most of the sacred law. On its own the Qur'an legislates relatively little; it says almost nothing, for example, about judicial procedure or the dhimmi status. Second, reducing the Shari'a to the Qur'an allows reformists to interpret the Qur'an however they wish. The *Hadith* Reports, consensus of the 'ulama, and reasoning by analogy came into existence because the Qur'an on its own is often obscure or contradictory. By dropping the other three sources of the Shari'a, reformists free themselves to have the Qur'an endorse such Western ideals as religious tolerance, economic justice, and political participation—not one of which was even conceived of in seventh-century Arabia.

Reformists use the Qur'an in new ways, quarrying it for passages that support their views, and ignoring or suppressing whatever does not accord. Once a source of learning and inspiration, the Qur'an in their hands becomes a collection of disjointed quotes and proof texts. Instead of endeavoring to comprehend God's will, they use it to confirm preconceived notions. The concern to align Islam with Western ways so permeates reformist arguments, it hardly matters how much the Qur'an is distorted in the process. They "invoked such rules of the traditional fiqh [Shar'i] jurisprudence as seemed relevant. But they discarded almost entirely the older discipline of Qur'an interpretation."[6] For example, when discussing the life of Muhammad, the reformist "selects whatever suits his immediate purpose" from an "incredibly vast storehouse of anecdote, . . . sweeping aside the old classical science of [*Hadith* Reports] with its careful controls (however defective they may have been) and substituting no control at all but a purely subjective appreciation."[7] The result is an Islam that accords with liberal notions and a sacred law that does not interfere with living in a Westernized fashion.

Much of the reinterpretation has to do with Qur'anic precepts concerning women, sex, and the family. Christian disgust with polygyny prompted the reformists, ever-sensitive to European opinion, to show how this custom perverts true Islam. For proof, they turn to the Qur'an and emphasize the proviso that immediately follows the verse permitting men to marry up to four wives: "If you fear you will not be equitable with them, then [marry] only one" (4.3). Arguing that no man can possibly treat two, three, or four women with complete equity, reformists conclude that the Qur'an in fact prohibits polygyny. Shar'i permission for men to take more than one wife is deemed a distortion of the Qur'an's intent. Similarly, by rereading those passages that deal with the covering and seclusion of women, reformists find no justification for the veil or the harem. Sometimes they even go on the offensive against the West and point out those ways the Qur'an assures a woman more property rights and family protection than her European counterpart enjoys.[8]

With regard to public affairs, reformists are less certain of themselves and waver between Islamicate and Western ways. They approve of parliamentary liberalism but are disillusioned by its record in Islamdom. They admire the ideal of pan-Islamic solidarity but are not committed to it; national interests are legitimate but Muslim states should not make war against co-religionists. Reformists de-emphasize the traditional understanding of jihad as a call to arms, preferring to interpret it instead as a call to personal redemption. They abolish slavery and untie taxes from the zakat restrictions. Non-Muslims they treat ambiguously, for reformists are caught between the contrary desires to bestow equal status on all citizens and to give Muslims a special place; where non-Muslims constitute a significant proportion of the population, the solution commonly reached is to open all offices to them except for that of head of state.

Properly speaking, governments have no jurisdiction over the Shari'a, only the 'ulama do, and in theory, reformists would allow religious leaders to review new laws to assure their conformity with the Qur'an. But reformists invariably find the 'ulama too traditionalist for their purposes and instead use state power as a way to amend the Shari'a, treating sacred law as though it were, like legal systems in the West, something for the government to alter. Thus have nearly all Muslim governments unilaterally abolished Shar'i regulations concerning the position of women, slaves, and dhimmis.

The reformist assumption that Islam includes or anticipates all that is attractive in Western civilization facilitates the borrowing of new ideas; in a sense, the whole reformist enterprise is designed to disguise the adoption of Western principles. Not acknowledging this source makes them that much more palatable. But dissimulation has a price; by portraying the Qur'an, the Shari'a, and the Islamic heritage as liberal, violence is done to them. The falseness of this argument dooms it to sterility. H. A. R. Gibb severely but justly characterized reformist thinking as mired in "intellectual confusions and paralyzing romanticism."[9]

Reformism begins by assuming the compatibility of Islam with liberalism, then sets out to prove this contention. Not surprisingly, anyone who adapts Islam to liberal ideas (rather than the reverse) finds himself espousing radically new notions about the nature of Islam. The reformist is particularly anxious to discredit the traditionalist view of the Islamic faith, trying as he does "to persuade the 'old-fashioned' Muslims that they, by their social conservatism and their stand upon the letter of the law, are sinning against the light."[10] Bringing Islam surreptitiously into line with Western civilization strikes some observers as a misdirected enterprise; Gibb writes that the reformists err "in assuming as the final objective an ideal determined by considerations external to their own society and in trying to force the two into relation with one another."[11] Without disagreeing with this assessment, it should be noted that insofar as reformist thought allows Muslims to come to terms with Western realities by easing their acceptance, it helps them, even if its logic is faulty and its facts distorted.

Reformism arose in the 1870s, at a time when religious thinkers first knew enough about Europe to try to reconcile its ways with Islam. Jamal ad-Din al-Afghani, a political activist who traveled and lived in many parts of the Middle East, developed the initial ideas; then Muhammad 'Abduh, an Egyptian sheikh who collaborated with al-Afghani, worked them out more fully. 'Abduh quickly won a following throughout Islamdom. His successors in Egypt included the Syrian immigrant Rashid Rida and two outstanding intellectuals, Ahmad Lutfi as-Sayyid and Taha Husayn. His Syrian followers were nearly as distinguished, including Muhammad Kurd 'Ali, 'Abd al-Qadir

al-Maghribi, and Amir Shakib Arslan. Habib Bourguiba, Tunisia's ruler, initiated a reformist policy soon after the country's independence in 1956. 'Abd
al-Hamid Ben Badis founded the Association of Algerian 'Ulama in 1931,
while 'Abdallah ibn Idris as-Sanusi and Abu Shu'ayb ad-Dukkali spread
'Abduh's ideas in Morocco. Students returning from the Middle East founded
the Wahhabi movement of West Africa (unrelated to the Saudi version) after
World War II and influenced many subsequent associations in the region. In
Iran, Ayatollah Abul Qasim Kashani achieved considerable influence in association with the Feda'iyyan-e Islam organization and as speaker of the parliament. Abu'l-Kalam Azad rejected the idea of Muslims in India creating the
new state of Pakistan; he therefore stayed in India, where he became a leader
of the Muslim community there, and later served as president of the Indian
National Congress. 'Abduh's ideas had a key influence on the reformist movements in Indonesia, including the Muhammadijah, Persatuan Islam, and
Sarekat Islam. Some of 'Abduh's impact reached its final destination circu-
itously; for example, reformism arrived in Thailand via an immigrant from
Indonesia.[12]

An independent reformist movement developed in India, beginning with
Sayyid Ahmad Khan (1817–98), the founder of the Muhammadan
Anglo-Oriental College in Aligarh, a center of reformist thought; the Ahl
al-Hadith specialized in scholarship on the *Hadith* Reports; Muhammad
Iqbal, originator of the Pakistan idea, made an ambitious attempt to rethink
Islamic doctrines; and Fazlur Rahman, an independent-minded thinker, had
to leave Pakistan on account of his ideas. Other intellectuals, such as Zia Gö-
kalp of Turkey and Tahir Haddad of Tunisia, also had local impact.

Overall, however, reformist thought became moribund after the 1920s. Since
then, the same sterile, inaccurate claims have been endlessly repeated, decades
after their first articulation. Reformism is a tired movement, locked in place
by the unsoundness of its premises and arguments. Reformists hardly ever
grapple with the difficult issues of Islam and modernity which the vast differences between Islamic and Western ways demand; and those few who do, such
as the Egyptian Hasan al-Hanifi, have little impact.

One indication of their stagnancy is the fact that the reformist with the
greatest practical effect in recent years is Mu'ammar al-Qadhdhafi, a man of
fanatic temperament and unbalanced emotions. He takes reformism to its logical extreme. Qadhdhafi unequivocally rejects any source of Islamic law other
than the Qur'an, which he claims each Muslim has the right to interpret entirely on his own, he disdains traditionalist scholarship, and he persecutes the
'ulama in Libya. Although the Libyan government enacted several Qur'anic
regulations soon after Qadhdhafi came to power in September 1969 (such as
a ban on alcohol and the cutting off of thieves' hands), overall it diminished

state adherence to the Shari'a. Qadhdhafi disputes that such institutions as polygyny, concubinage, and slavery are Islamic; he calls them "backward" (which they certainly are from a Western viewpoint) and threatens that he will personally abandon Islam if they continue to be practiced.[13]

Despite its sterility, reformism has long dominated the religious thinking of the elites in much of Islamdom, for it permits the rulers to press for modernization without challenging Muslim identification with Islam. Reformism enjoyed an almost unchallenged pre-eminence in Islamic circles from the end of the nineteenth century until the 1920s. Those who disagreed with it either held onto the medieval synthesis and refused to pay attention to the West, or they adopted Western ways and abandoned Islam; in either case, they acted spontaneously and without articulated arguments. For fifty or so years, reformism was the only program available.

Then, beginning in the 1920s, several of the most advanced regions of Islamdom (Turkey, Egypt, and northern India) experienced a development that spawned two alternate approaches to the question of Islam and Westernization. This was the era when radical Westernizers, rulers and thinkers alike, gained prominence; these were men who hoped to make the umma rich and powerful by closely imitating the West. Finding that most of the opposition to their programs derived from the goals inspired by the Shari'a, they tried to get around these by adopting political secularism. At the same time, Westernization provoked an opposite response; as the umma had to reconcile old practices with new ones, many Muslims responded by rejecting the foreign influences and turned to their religion for succor and guidance. Thus did fundamentalism emerge along with secularism as the two alternatives to reformism.

Secularism: Withdrawing the Sacred Law from Politics

In the secularist view, modernization requires a wholehearted acceptance of the leading civilization of the age, the Occident's and anything that stands in the way must be brushed aside. For Muslim secularists, nothing impedes development so much as the Shari'a, which they regard as illogical, quirky, and backward; to negate its influence, they seize on the European idea of divorcing religion from public affairs and advocate this for the umma. Unlike fundamentalists, who connect Muslim strength with implementation of the full Shari'a, and reformists, who advocate a Shari'a changed out of recognition, secularists want to eliminate the Shari'a as a force in politics. Whereas fundamentalists stress the connection between bygone Muslim success and implementation of the law, secularists play down the Shari'a's role in history, arguing that it was never critical in the past and need not be now. One secularist, Duran Khalid, observes that

a large part of the Islamic world never knew the Shari'a and despite this developed a rich religious life and identified itself with the transnational community of believers; thus, the assertion of the jurists ['ulama], that without the Shari'a Islam does not exist, is not tenable.[14]

While all secularists concur on the need to separate religion from politics, they disagree on the question of private practices. Three main positions may be identified. Some secularists are pious believers who maintain the daily observances of Islam but withdraw the law from government affairs; they stay away from alcohol and pork, keep the Ramadan fast, and pray regularly, but ignore the Shar'i prescriptions for politics. Combining an open-minded attitude toward Western practices with personal devoutness, they are roughly comparable to the Conservatives of Judaism. Other secularists are antinomians, Protestantized believers who dismiss the whole sacred law as an archaism; in this, they resemble the Reform branch of Judaism. For them, the Shari'a does more than impede modernization; it also distracts from the message of the Qur'an. Finally, non-believers, including Marxists, agnostics, atheists, and other radical thinkers (such as the Ba'thists, a pan-Arabist movement), reject religion in its entirety, both faith and laws. These last are lapsed Muslims, persons who despise the Shari'a and are mortified that their co-religionists retain such an anachronistic and even (from their Westernized viewpoint) barbaric code.

Reformists reduce the sacred law to one source, the Qur'an; political secularists dismiss even that. For the theists among them, the attempt to derive laws from the Qur'an betrays the spirit of Islam, which they see, in High Church fashion, more as a spiritual inspiration than as a guide to specific conduct. And of course, for the atheists, the Qur'an has no role at all for contemporary men.

Secularists view public affairs in ways which are virtually uninfluenced by Islamic values, but instead approximate the common denominator of the Western ideologies that reached them. They open public office to all citizens, subscribe to Western forms of government, permit no role in politics to the 'ulama, and ignore pan-Islamic sentiments. Secularists go to war for reasons of state and national interest, not for religious goals. They advocate equal status for women and non-Muslims and set taxes at whatever level is called for by circumstances. The judicial system should be based on reason and utility; Shar'i precepts may be enforced only when they meet objective criteria of the public good.

The only wide-ranging secular program ever implemented by a Muslim government was that of Mustafa Kemal Atatürk in Turkey. During a fifteen-year period, 1923–38, he promulgated an array of secularist laws that transformed public life. His government abolished the caliphate; adopted a written constitution along European lines; introduced civil, criminal, and commercial codes based, respectively, on Swiss, Italian, and German models; disestablished Islam as the religion of state; gave women the vote; and opened public offices to all citizens. Other Westernizing changes included the suppression of religious orders, the abolition of the fez and robed garments for men, the institution of civil marriages, the replacement of Arabic script with the Roman, the elimination of titles, and the introduction of family surnames. Although this legislation remained on the books after Atatürk's death in 1938, popular pressure forced the government to retreat from strict secularism and Islam gradually re-entered the public arena in subsequent decades.

No other Muslim country followed the Turkish experiment. Indeed, pressure to acknowledge the Shari'a's basic validity remained so strong outside Turkey that secularism hardly could ever be openly discussed. When some brave soul ventured forth, the consequences were usually severe. 'Ali 'Abd ar-Raziq, a sheikh at the Islamic university of al-Azhar in Cairo, wrote a book in 1925, *Islam and the Principles of Government,* which argued that Islam requires the separation of religion and politics.[15] Its publication provoked an uproar and caused the 'ulama of al-Azhar unanimously to find 'Abd ar-Raziq guilty of impious ideas; he was dismissed from the university and banned from holding other religious offices. For a believer to claim Islam has no public role was bad enough; worse yet was for an atheist to deny the truth of the Islamic revelation itself. The official magazine of the Syrian military, *Army of the People,* published an article in 1967 labeling Islam "a mummy in the museum of history," and calling for the building of a "new socialist Arab man."[16] Public reaction flared up with such intense anger—mass demonstrations, strikes, and shootings—that the regime confiscated the offending issue, blamed the article on American and Israeli agents, and directed a military court to sentence the author and his editors to life imprisonment.

Despite the existence of secular regimes throughout the Middle East, in Turkey, Syria, Iraq, and South Yemen, popular opinion in recent years has not permitted public expression of secular views. Indeed, new ideas about Islam and politics came from the less central (and therefore less prominent) countries, although even there, adverse reaction usually overwhelmed the attempt at dialogue. One group, the Republican Brothers of the Sudan, distinguished between those passages of the Qur'an that Muhammad received before he became a political leader (the Meccan verses) and those that followed his ascent to power (the Medinan verses). In this group's view, the former defined the eternally valid principles of Islam whereas the latter were intended only for

Muhammad's own instruction and therefore do not serve as a model for subsequent Muslim life. As nearly all the Qur'an's precepts are contained in the Medinan verses, this reasoning virtually eliminates the Qur'an as a source of commands. Further, if Qur'anic precepts do not apply to Muslims after Muhammad, obviously Muhammad's personal actions and statements, which make up the *Hadith* Reports, also have no wider applicability. The Republican Brothers took the traditional approach head on: whereas the 'ulama used any scrap of evidence pertaining to Muhammad (accepting even fabrications) as the basis for regulating Muslim conduct, the Republican Brothers ignored Muhammad's life and emphasized the spiritual and ethical qualities of the Qur'anic message. For his efforts, the founder and leader of this group, Mahmud Muhammad Taha, was found guilty of apostasy by the High Shari'a Court of Khartoum in 1968.[17]

An even more radical discussion was initiated in Indonesia in 1970 when Nurcholis Madjid, a leader of the Islamic student movement Himpunan Mahasiswa Islam (H.M.I.) suggested that political, social, and economic affairs do not depend on divine revelation but represent human concerns about which men must make up their own minds. Madjid went so far as to call secularization a "liberating process."[18] H.M.I. denied the importance of Shar'i regulations and emphasized instead the faith of Islam shorn of its legal requirements, especially such spiritual aspects as the Friday mosque sermon. When opponents accused this movement of mindlessly copying Western ways, its adherents answered that quibbling over matters of law obscures the transcendent significance of the Islamic revelation. Although Madjid's ideas caused a stir, the Indonesian cultural climate was open enough so that he, at least, did not have to stand before a tribunal.

Traditionalism became increasingly irrelevant as the 'ulama refused to recognize the dilemmas facing Muslims in a modernizing environment. Reformism and secularism did attempt to fill this need, but neither of them offered practical guidelines for daily life; they did not show how to deal with, for example, alcohol or sexual relations. In brief, the inadequacies of traditionalism, reformism, and secularism were such that Muslims were for the most part left to respond to modern challenges on an individual basis. What Gopal Krishna wrote with reference to India applies to all parts of Islamdom: "The mass of Muslims are making their adjustments [to modern life] as best as they can without any satisfactory guidance from a community leadership, traditional or modernist."[19] (It bears noting, however, that this is nothing new in the Muslim experience. In similar fashion did premodern Muslims have to figure out how to blend the demands of Islamic law with local traditions; then, as now, the burden weighed heaviest on individual believers.)

Only fundamentalism provided a program that met the needs of individuals.

It provided specific guidance for daily life and showed Muslims the way to political action in the path of God. Many Muslims found satisfaction in this integral system that swept away old compromises and offered a powerful instrument for resisting concessions to the West.

Before taking leave of the Westernizers, however, it should be noted that their importance is often exaggerated. The reformists and secularists have received a disproportionate share of academic attention; this is in part due to the historian's natural fascination with change, in part due to the abundance of reformists writings (the attempt to reconcile incompatible systems requires extensive argumentation). Also, the European or American scholar studies Westernizers because this allows him to study the effects of his own civilization, while the scholar of Muslim origins dwells on the Westernizers because he probably shares their views. The sheer volume of information on these two groups creates a distorted sense of change in Islamic thinking. Studied more than their influence warrants, the Westernizers crowd out the fundamentalists, who were for many years underestimated and dismissed as hopeless recalcitrants certain to fall into line with Westernization. They probably will eventually, but until now they have had great importance. The Islamic revival of the 1970s showed the power and initiative of fundamentalists; with money, energy, and new ideas, their prestige grew and their influence spread. They deserve close attention.

Fundamentalism: Making the Sacred Law a Political Ideology

Fundamentalists are Muslims who are convinced of the Shari'a's eternal validity and who attempt to live by it to the letter. For them, it is unimportant that the law was developed one thousand years ago: Can the truth become outdated, does God change His mind? Application of the law is the central duty of a Muslim and the chief expression of his faith; anyone who abandons the law or even tampers with it in effect denies the validity of the faith. From this point of view, reformists are as bad as secularists; cutting the Shari'a into disjointed bits and changing it out of recognition is comparable to discarding it altogether. In the fundamentalist view, the law, fully elaborated in the early centuries of Islam, requires updating only to accommodate new circumstances: printing, insurance, tobacco, coffee, and tampons require consideration, to be sure, but what the law does cover remains unchanged. Minor regulations—such as traffic and commercial codes—can be dealt with as the need arises; major ones already exist.

Fundamentalists assume that the umma's strength in premodern times derived from implementing the Shari'a; conversely, they see recent Muslim weakness as a consequence of falling away from the law. Were believers to maintain the Shari'a, it follows, they would flourish as of old. This implies that fundamentalists favor application of the entire body of precepts, even those that run contrary to Western customs. And a long list it is: they urge a ban on alcohol, interest payments, gambling, music, human representations, and the mingling of the sexes. Public displays of sexuality, such as mixed bathing, skimpy or tight clothes, and eroticism in the arts, distress them especially. Fundamentalists call for the strict application of all Islamic laws concerned with family life (including marriage, divorce, and inheritance), mortmain trusts, the Ramadan fast, the alms tax, and criminal justice. They want laws to guarantee employees the right to take time off to pray, the execution of Muslim apostates, the restriction of military and political offices to Muslims, and review boards to assure the harmony of new laws with the Shari'a. Fundamentalists favor the use of Islamicate languages and Arabic script as well as financial support for mosques and Islamic schools, and pan-Islamic solidarity.

In advocating these measures, fundamentalists differ from traditionalists; the distinction between these two types of Muslims is important. Traditionalists accept the medieval synthesis, fundamentalists aspire to implement the Shari'a in its totality. Traditionalists usually stay away from politics, fundamentalists get actively involved. 'Ulama continue the traditionalist legacy, Westernized urbanites lead the fundamentalist movements. Traditionalists control mosques and fill positions in the religious hierarchy, and governments approve of them because they adopt moderate, almost apolitical positions. Fundamentalists are more dangerous to the authorities because they stir passions, lead crowds, and organize sedition.

Iran provides a clear case of the two approaches leading to contrary positions. Traditionalists took part in the movement to restrict the shah's power by means of a constitution in 1905–8; when this failed, they retreated from public life to the accustomed sidelines for precisely the same reasons as traditionalists had in premodern times.

> The disillusionment of the leaders of the Shi'ite hierocracy with the novel experiment of constitutionalism renewed their negative evaluation of political power, which had traditionally manifested itself in pious indifference to worldly politics. With a few exceptions, they withdrew from the political arena after 1911 . . . [holding] piously aloof from the political sphere.[20]

Most Iranian religious leaders, including Mohammed Kazem Shari'atmadari, the most intellectually distinguished ayatollah at the time of the Iranian revolution, remained traditionalist. In contrast, Ruhollah Khomeini adopted a radical legalist position, advocating full implementation of the Shari'a, and brushing aside the medieval synthesis. "While Khomeini considers Islam the only source of law, Shari'atmadari advocates an 'Islamic order' in which the 'principles of Islam are respected,' " but not necessarily followed to the letter.[21] Khomeini went on to take an even more anti-traditionalist stance when he advocated the direct participation of the 'ulama in politics, an idea virtually without precedent in Islam.

Clothing symbolizes the differences of these approaches. Traditionalists wear the clothes indigenous of their region. For them, this is not a political statement; they hardly imagine any alternative. Among the women of Egypt, for example, traditionalists wear long black robes called *milaya*s. Reformists mix styles to preserve something of the old while accepting Western forms; Egyptian women influenced by reformism wear long black dresses. Secularists dispense with the old way completely and accept the new; this means strictly Western apparel, the blouses and skirts worn by women of the West. But fundamentalists reject exactly these Western influences and self-consciously return to the Islamicate forms. They have several choices. In Egypt they devised a new amalgam, the "Islamic uniform" *(zayy Islami)* made up of a dress and pants worn at the same time. In Iran after 1978 they returned to the traditional garb. In Malaysia they adopted the Arabian style of dress of a black piece of cloth draped over the woman's head. Fundamentalists could invent something new, resort to tradition, or borrow from other Muslims.

One final point about traditionalists and fundamentalists. The latter believe, mistakenly, two related notions: that the umma had historically implemented the Shari'a in its entirety and that their own efforts are within the mainstream practice of Islam. In their own eyes, fundamentalists are traditionalists, a subtlety that makes it easy to confuse the two. In fact, while radical legalism does have a long pedigree, it never enjoyed more than momentary success in premodern times. Until pressures generated by the West made fundamentalism one of three responses to modernity, it had always been of far less importance than traditionalism.

Fundamentalism has had so key a role in keeping Islam a political force in the umma's consciousness that it requires much fuller consideration than reformism or secularism. Chapter 9 considers the role of fundamentalism in single countries, while the following account emphasizes four aspects of the fundamentalist program: the transformation of the Shari'a from a legal system to a body of political doctrines, the acceptance of modernization and the rejection of Westernization, the ambition to implement the law in its entirety, and the problematic relations between fundamentalists and governments.

In the traditionalist understanding, Islamic precepts are addressed to individuals, not to the society as a whole. Private strictures apply to all Muslims, public ones only to the rulers. "The Shar'i norms were thought of as a series of particular commands incumbent upon individuals who happened to be in responsible positions."[22] Although the Shari'a involves specific ends, Muslims understood that "there is no 'political theory' in Islam—that is to say, no discussion of the means by which these ideal ends were to be safeguarded."[23] If a political ideology be a body of ideas concerning the proper disposition of power, wealth, and privilege, traditionalist Islam does not have one. Nothing in the Shari'a resembles a theory of "who gets what when and how."[24] Traditionalists call for a state in which the laws are supreme (a nomocracy), not more; the law does not tell how to collect taxes, where to recruit soldiers, or when to declare war. It requires rulers to be adult and male Muslims, without indicating how they should be chosen: popular election, military coup d'etat, theocratic revolution, or almost any other route to power is legitimate. The government may be capitalist or socialist, centralized or anarchic, egalitarian or hierarchic, democratic or autocratic, liberal or totalitarian.

The Shari'a needed almost no justification in premodern times, for no reputable alternatives existed. But other options do very much exist in modern times. Since Western political ideologies first reached Islamdom, they have been seducing Muslims away from the sacred law. As the Shari'a becomes just one of several possible routes, and as many Muslims look outside Islamdom for answers to their critical questions, devotion to the Shari'a requires articulation. To compete with European ideas, pious Muslims can no longer merely assert the correctness of living by the law; they must prove its validity and efficacy.

To prevent the faithful from straying, some Muslims resorted to an emphasis on the Christian character of Europe and an accusation that the Europeans were exporting their customs in order to undermine the Shar'i way of life. This made Western ideologies appear sinister but it did not answer their appeal, especially as most of them owe little to Christianity. Democratic or socialist ideals, for example, can hardly be dispelled by attacking the Christian faith or the Crusaders.

Much more effective was for Muslims to fortify the law by embuing it with the strengths of an ideology. Fundamentalist Muslims took a new look at the law and elicited from it Islamic answers to questions raised by Western ideologies. To keep the Shari'a at the center of Muslim life, they transformed the law into a systematic program of political ideals which could compete with the "isms." They converted "Islamic law as it evolved in the Middle Ages (when it remained largely ideal theory divorced from political reality) into a twentieth-century constitution."[25] Fundamentalists read the Qur'an and the *Hadith* Reports in novel ways and found political instruction where none was originally understood. The Qur'an exhorts Muslims to "conduct their affairs by mutual consultation"; fundamentalists interpreted this as a command to practice democracy; the Qur'anic call for Muslims to "give their due to relatives, the poor, and the wayfarers" they understood as a call for socialism.[26]

Typical of the policies fundamentalists developed are the goals incorporated in the Jama'at-i Islami's "Manifesto: A Pillar of Light for the Muslim World," announced by its leader, Abul Ala Maududi in December 1969. Called "a revolutionary document that aims at bringing about fundamental changes in all spheres of life in Pakistan," its goal is to make Pakistan "a state where the laws of the Quran and the Sunna [that is, the Shari'a] would be in full force."[27] The Manifesto deals with economics, education, justice, and administration. In the name of Islamic law, it prescribes the break-up of monopolies, concentrations of wealth, private ownership of large companies, and real estate holdings of over a specified size. It legislates "healthy working conditions," limited working hours, the "proper price" for agricultural produce, and a reduction in income disparity. And it prohibits "profits beyond a reasonable limit." Wide-ranging as the Shari'a is, it does not cover these economic matters, and certainly nothing so vague as stipulating the "proper price" for farm goods. Maududi translated the sacred law into a detailed system touching aspects of life never envisioned in early times.

This "ideologization of religion"[28] despite its weak underpinnings became standard first among fundamentalists, then among others too. The notion of the Shari'a as an ideology won nearly universal acceptance, as these several examples, taken almost at random, illustrate: in 1950, Muhammad Natsir, leader of the Indonesian fundamentalist political party Masjumi, published a pamphlet entitled "Islam as an Ideology," and seven years later in a meeting of the Indonesian Constituent Assembly, he called Islam "an explicit, unequivocal and complete ideology."[29] In a book entitled *The Economic and Social System of Islam,* Anwar Iqbal Qureshi claims that "the best economic and social system is the one which is provided by the Qur'an," whose teachings he finds more practical than those of any of the "isms" from the West.[30] Another Muslim, Godfrey H. Jansen, writes that "Islam is a polity and a method of governance."[31] The Pakistan government sponsors a body called the Advisory Council on Islamic Ideology. Even a knowledgeable medievalist such as R. Stephen Humphreys writes that "Islam has always been not only a system of belief but an ideology."[32] Fundamentalist Muslims came to see Islam as "almost a blueprint for a social order which could be set off against capitalism or communism as rival social systems."[33] In the words of Anwar Ibrahim, a Malaysian fundamentalist leader, "We are not socialist, we are not capitalist, we are Islamic."[34]

Insisting on the existence of an Islamic system of economics, of politics, of social relations, and so forth, was the way fundamentalists kept Islam in politics. The Shari'a as ideology permitted a forceful and flexible response to Western programs. Fundamentalists can point to the faults of the foreign ideologies—the anarchy of liberalism, the heartlessness of capitalism, the brutality of Marxism, and the poverty of socialism—and argue that Islam has the better solutions. Why go outside the tradition when the answers lie within? Fundamentalists offer the Muslims a vibrant Shari'a they claim can meet all contemporary needs.

They achieve this, as do the reformists, by reading the holy books however it suits them. In fact, nothing in the Qur'an or the *Hadith* Reports implies a preference for capitalism or socialism; Shar'i regulations concerning property, interest, contracts, inheritance, mortmain, alms taxes, and gambling can fit either economic system. But some fundamentalists use the Shari'a to claim that the sanction of private property requires a capitalist system and others argue that the concern for social justice points to socialism. In short, Muslims are made free to draw any conclusions and to call these "Islamic." A vague "Islamic order," unrestrained by objective standards, becomes whatever fundamentalists wish it to be. Such self-definition serves a purpose; in this way, the "political system, of whatever kind, is said to follow Islamic precedent; the economic system, of whatever sort, is said to exemplify Islamic values of social justice."[35] Democrats, strongmen, reactionaries, radicals, and everyone else can credibly cloak their actions with Islam. Islam buttresses hereditary monarchies in Morocco and Saudi Arabia, theocracy under Khomeini in Iran, and military rule under Zia-ul-Haq in Pakistan.

But such malleability also involves dangers. First, whoever seriously seeks moral guidance finds caprice instead. "Without definitive guidelines in Islam, economic policy must be determined on a pragmatic basis; justifications are then drawn from the inexhaustable reservoir of Islamic precedent";[36] the same also applies in the political and social domains. Second, the interpretation of Islam is left to whoever has the power to impose his will. "The enforcement of norms is not left to social consensus but to state coercion. . . . Society is aligned with the state's interpretation of Islamic principles, and the state enforces that interpretation through state institutions."[37] Third, malleability permits anyone to claim that what he favors is Islamic, filling the political domain with imposters and enthusiasts. One outsider observed of Zia-ul-Haq's Pakistan: "The faith was full of rules. In politics there were none. There were no political rules because the faith was meant to create only believers. . . . For everyone in open political life Islam was cause, tool, and absolution. It could lead to this worldly virulence."[38] Similarly, in Indonesia, Islam "offered no political or practical solution. It offered only the faith. It offered only the Prophet, who would settle everything—but who had ceased to exist. This political Islam was rage, anarchy."[39] Fourth, vague, unformulated programs have the consequence that when fundamentalists achieve power, they disagree among themselves about the role of Islam in politics and have no practical vision how to replace Western ways with Islamic ones.

Fifth, when fundamentalists codify the Shari'a, they petrify an evolving rule and make it restrictive. The law had always adapted to time and place in small but key ways, but fundamentalists make it a fixed doctrine, leaving no room for individual responses. They present Islam "as a system, one that long ago provided mankind with set answers to all its problems, rather than as a faith in which God provides mankind anew each morning the riches whereby it may answer them itself."[40] When nothing changes, Islam as such becomes a force in itself; fundamentalists cause "Islam" to be "reified into a fixed and eternal body of ideal doctrine, not subject to human hypothesis or revision. . . . Those who use this phrase ["Islam teaches"] are not calling in the traditional manner on the authority of particular scholars or texts, but on the vague but powerful authority of an entire cultural tradition."[41] As a result, Islam begins to usurp the role of God; Wilfred Cantwell Smith notes that "there are many Muslims throughout the world today who believe in Islam more than they believe in God"; but this is idolatry; a true Muslim "is one who submits not to Islam but to God" and whose faith gives him the freedom to interpret his faith "according to what he honestly believes God's purpose to be in the twentieth century."[42]

Sixth, the vagueness of Islamic ideology allows fundamentalists to indulge in the chimera of absorbing Western patterns within Islam, regardless how much they clash. As Malcolm Yapp puts it, fundamentalists "are strictly traditional in their formulations and modern in their practice and they care little for the resulting contradictions."[43] They want women to be separated from men according to Shar'i rules but also to participate fully in the country's economic development; they call simultaneously for the abolition of non-Shar'i taxes and for increased government spending to aid the poor, for the elimination of interest and for the benefits of belonging to the international financial system, and so forth.

Ironically, in the effort to stave off Western ideologies, fundamentalists radically change their religion and direct it along Western lines. They forsake the traditional understanding of Islamic action in order to respond to the appeal of Western culture. The Shari'a had always been seen as a body of laws defining proper Muslim behavior; in the hands of fundamentalists, it is transformed into a set of political doctrines capable of mobilizing crowds and steering governments. The law remains, of course, but it is no longer an end in itself, only a means to preserving Islam. Thus, in attempting to protect Islam, the fundamentalists Westernize it.

In details too, fundamentalists adopt European notions and institu-

130

tions—which is not surprising when one recalls that their ranks are filled by urbanites living in Westernizing environments, not by remote villagers still thinking and acting in traditional ways. For example, Western influence has caused fundamentalists to understand the meaning of Friday, the Islamic day of religion, in a radically new fashion. In Arabic, Friday is called *yawm al-jum'a,* "the day of congregation," a name dating from pre-Islamic Arabia and referring to the fact that markets were then held on Fridays. Taking advantage of this gathering, Muhammad called on all adult, male, free Muslims to pray in a mosque on Friday at noon. This means suspending normal activities for the duration of the prayer, about an hour, but it does not require taking the day off from work. The fact that Islam does not treat Friday as a sabbath is confirmed by the Arabic name for Saturday, *yawm as-sabt,* "the day of sabbath." Indeed, "the Sabbath institution is foreign to Islam" and Muslims who refrained from working on Friday sometimes even met with the disapproval of the authorities.[44]

Muslims absorbed the idea of a weekly sabbath from the colonial administrators who imposed Sunday as the official day of rest in the parts of Islamdom they controlled. Upon independence, many fundamentalists demanded the sabbath be moved from Sunday to Friday, and such steps were indeed taken in several Muslim countries. While ostensibly a rejection of Western influence, this transfer in fact deepened a Christian practice and made it appear indigenous. In the words of a Muslim correspondent to a Karachi newspaper at about the time the Pakistani government decided to make this switch: "If we think that by observing Sunday we were following Christians and now by observing Friday as holiday we will be not, then we are wrong, because we are still following them by observing a weekly holiday on our religious day, as they do."[45]

A far more significant example of unconscious Westernizing concerns the jurisdiction of the Shari'a. As a religious law, the Shari'a applies only to Muslims; Christians, Jews, and others have their own regulations to the extent that this is practical (the Shari'a takes precedence in litigation between Muslims and non-Muslims). In premodern Islamdom, the law one lived by depended on religion, not location. In contrast, Western legal systems are based on territory; where one lives, not religious affiliation, determines jurisdiction. Many fundamentalists lose sight of this distinction and seek, in the Western fashion, to apply the Shari'a to all citizens of a nation, regardless of their religion.

The effort to extend Shar'i precepts to non-Muslims has had especially great repercussions in Malaysia and the Sudan, two countries where large non-Muslim minorities live under Muslim rule. As part of their legalist campaign, Malay fundamentalists tried to apply to their Chinese and Indian co-nationals the Shar'i law of privacy restricting the time an unrelated man and woman may spend alone together. The platform of Parti Islam, a fundamentalist group, demanded that Islamic laws apply to all citizens regardless of religion.[46] In the Sudan, the Ansar and the Muslim Brethren pressed for application of the Shari'a in the mainly Christian and animist South. For this reason, a committee set up in 1977 to bring existing laws of the Sudan into conformity with the Shari'a frightened the Southerners; when the leader of the Muslim Brethren was appointed attorney-general and made statements like "the intention to apply the *sharia* in Sudan is an authentic expression of what people want,"[47] their fear turned into alarm. Joseph Lagu, former leader of the South's Anya-Nya rebellion noted that "Shari'ah laws cause more fears in the Southern Sudanese and the introduction of Shari'ah laws will make the Southern Sudanese more and more suspicious."[48]

Friday sabbath and the Shari'a as national law became so thoroughly incorporated that all but the most historically-minded lost sight of their foreign origins. Much else also was changed by the fundamentalists without attracting wide notice. The Khomeini government, for example, by allowing women to initiate divorce proceedings and to win separation without their husbands' consent, in effect abrogated the Shari'a in favor of a Western practice. Other features of Western life were also absorbed all through Islamdom—municipal government, the business corporation, the abolition of slavery, the printing press, and photography—and lost their Occidental character.

However much they may wish to reject Western civilization, fundamentalists do accept modernization. They are eager to make use of the factories, the weapons, and whatever else helps to increase their power and wealth,[49] while avoiding anything Western that seems unnecessary for achieving this end. The distinction between modernization and Westernization can be extremely fine. While in exile, Khomeini regularly used cassette tape recorders to spread his message to Iran, and after attaining power he appeared almost daily on television. Because modern means of communication furthered his cause, he adopted them. But the telephone served no such need and Khomeini reportedly spoke into the telephone only once in his life, to speak to his sick brother.[50] He approached all of Western culture in a utilitarian way, as he explained to an Italian journalist:

Khomeini: Music dulls the mind, because it involves pleasure and ecstasy, similar to drugs. Your music I mean. Usually your music has not exalted the spirit, it puts it to sleep. And it destructs [*sic*] our youth who become poisoned by it, and then they no longer care about their country.

Oriana Fallaci: Even the music of Bach, Beethoven, Verdi?

Khomeini: I do not know those names. If their music does not dull the mind, they will not be prohibited. Some of your music is permitted. For example, marches and hymns for marching. . . . Yes, but your marches are permitted.[51]

But can fundamentalists really separate the technology of the West from its culture? It was their effort to do so that attracted the attention of V. S. Naipaul and inspired him to write his masterly inquiry, *Among the Believers.* As a Hindu who grew up in the Caribbean and then became a belletrist in England, he personally bridged the Western/non-Western gap which so troubles fundamentalist Muslims. Naipaul's curiosity was piqued during the Iranian revolution, when he observed the inconsistencies of Iranians living in the United States trying to explain events in their home country. One Iranian pursuing legal studies in the United States spoke effusively on American television about "the beauty of Islamic law" (p. 13); what then, Naipaul wondered, was this man doing in the United States learning American law? As he searched further, other contradictions became apparent. Muslims looked to the West as a source of knowledge and money, as well as a place to go to in times of refuge—yet they resented it and villified it. In a novel by an Iranian, he read about a physician trained in the United States who denounced the "emptiness" of life there. Yet this doctor looked to the West for the methods and tools of his profession; Naipaul observes caustically that "other people in spiritually barren lands will continue to produce the equipment the doctor is proud of possessing and the medical journals he is proud of reading" (p. 15).

What attracted the law student, the doctor, and so many other Muslims "to the United States and the civilization it represented? . . . The attraction existed; it was more than a need for education and skills. But the attraction wasn't admitted; and in that attraction, too humiliating for an old and proud people to admit, there lay disturbance—expressed in dandyism, mimicry, boasting, and rejection" (p. 13). On one level, America inspired hate; on another, need. Muslims found themselves surrounded by a civilization they could not master. That civilization "was to be rejected; at the same time it was to be depended upon" (p. 82).

Hoping to explain this "disturbance," Naipaul undertook a seven-month visit to four Muslim countries, Iran, Pakistan, Malaysia, and Indonesia. Driving through Tehran, he heard Qur'anic readings on the radio and saw mullahs make speeches on television, and he wondered how religious men who delighted in cursing Western culture could allow themselves to depend on two of its most characteristic innovations. The "hanging judge," Sadeq Khalkhali, declared that "during the days of the Prophet swords were used to fight, now they have been replaced by Phantom aircraft" (p. 37); in the same breath he called the country that produced those aircraft the "Great Satan." In smaller ways too, inconsistencies abounded in Iran's new regime: Iran Air stewardesses took their veils off when the plane left the ground, and cakes of sacred Arabian soil were placed in hotel rooms, courtesy of the Hyatt Corporation. An Indian Muslim who moved to Iran and joined the revolution but who sent his sons to school in the United States personified the dilemma. "With one part of his mind he was for the [Islamic] faith, and opposed to all that stood outside it. . . . With another part of his mind he recognized the world outside as paramount, part of the future of his sons."

How did Muslims cope with such "divisions of the mind" (p. 429)? In Pakistan, Naipaul found one way of coping was to exclude the West: "Islam had achieved community and a kind of beauty, had given people a feeling of completeness—if only the world outside could be shut out, and men could be made to forget what they knew" (p. 145). The high hopes of Pakistan's early years were shattered after three decades of difficulties; many Pakistanis turned to Islam for solutions, hoping its strict laws and spiritual dynamism could revitalize their country. Instead, the fundamentalist Islam they took up lobotimizes: "it provides an intellectual thermostat, set low. It equalizes, comforts, shelters, and preserves" (p. 167).

In Malaysia, the split between political power (held by the Muslim Malays) and wealth (held by the non-Muslim Chinese and Indians) created acute problems for Malays; they stressed their Islamic identity to build ethnic pride, yet simultaneously tried to adopt modern ways to advance themselves economically. How could Muslims emphasize Islam while emulating non-Muslims? Xenophobia and false nativism resulted, exemplified by the attempt to re-create Malay village life in modern urban settings.

Even if nearly all Indonesians are Muslim, they too are split rather evenly, with about half upholding traditional culture and the other half identifying closely with Islam. The two are far apart. A father who "lost his daughter" when she converted "to the new Muslim cause" felt not much different from American parents when their children became followers of the Reverend Moon (p. 302). In Indonesia too, the Islamic "disturbance" was evident. "The secular, dying West . . . was taking a long time to die. And more and more people were being drawn into the new world. In this new world, whose centre seemed so far away, so beyond control, newly evolved men . . . felt only their inadequacies." Like fundamentalists elsewhere, they made up for these failings with the "daily severities of their new religious practice," giving them "an illusion of wholeness [and] a promise of imminent triumph" (p. 378).

But, Naipaul concludes, such hopes are false, based on emotionalism and inconsistency of thought. He pays special attention to the benefits of technology. For fundamentalists, cars, radios, and televisions "were considered neutral; they were not associated with any particular faith or civilization; they were thought of as the stock of some great universal bazaar" (p. 33). Likewise, Phantom jets were not thought of as American, "not the products of a foreign science, but as international as swords, part of the stock of the great world bazaar, and rendered Islamic by purchase" (pp. 37–38). Fundamentalists thought modernization to be much narrower than it is. Their attempt to import the fruits of technology but nothing more—the railroads without John Locke, as it is sometimes put—failed; much of the West's civilization, so hated by fundamentalists, is inescapably part of modernization. The products and tech-niques of the West are attached to its culture and customs. Until Muslims re-nounce evasions and squarely confront what Naipaul calls the West's "great new encircling civilization" (p. 82), their psychological, social, and economic travails will continue.

By rejecting the medieval synthesis, fundamentalists commit themselves to apply every facet of the Shari'a; they choose to ignore human foibles and a thousand years of experience. "Being the first to put the idealized Islamic so-cial ethic to the acid test of reality," they, more than other Muslims, directly confronted its "sociological deficiencies."[52] Traditionalists, reformists, and sec-ularists can all, one way or another, defuse the problem of non-implementation, but not so the fundamentalists, whose cause would be under-mined unless they live according to *every* detail of the sacred law. But how can Muslims struggling to contend with Westernization do what premodern Muslims could not? If the umma found Islamic precepts unattainable when they were devised a thousand years earlier, how could they be applied in the twentieth century? The fundamentalist experiment was doomed even before it began.

The historical record shows that every effort in modern times to apply the Shari'a in its entirety—such as those made in Saudi Arabia, the Sudan, Libya, Iran, and Pakistan—ended up disappointing the fundamentalists, for realities eventually had to be accommodated. Every government devoted to full implementation finds this an impossible assignment. For example, the military regime in Mauritania created a commission and gave it four months to propose methods for applying the whole body of the Shari'a. Two years later, little had changed. When asked about this, the Mauritanian minister of justice and Islamic affairs responded with a wonderful example of bureau-cratic obfuscation:

The commission completed its work within the prescribed period, that is, four months. But because implementation is intended to bring us back to a state of normality with regard to Allah, and because it will allow a rehabilitation of the Mauritanian per-sonality—the basic factor of the sovereignty taken from us in the days of colonial occu-pation—we plan to give this happy and important event all the dimensions it merits in terms of contemplation and perfection. We want to implement it for ourselves, not because of any policy for domestic consumption or for the propaganda value it may have. For these reasons, the work of the commission will be studied at the proper time by the pertinent authorities, and the results of this study will be made known shortly, if Allah wills it.[53]

Stripped down, this passage harks back to the argument of the medieval synthesis: we cannot implement the sacred law because it is too demanding and we are unworthy of it.

Confronted with a persistent pattern of Shar'i non-implementation, fundamentalists avoid the obvious conclusion by finding scapegoats. Non-Muslim influence, be it pagan or Western, often takes the blame. Many fundamentalists believe that if they could only reject all of Western culture, the Shari'a would be within reach. Combined with autonomism, such impulses characteristically make the fundamentalists xenophobic, bristling with antagonism toward whatever and whoever is not in Allah's camp.

But the chief scapegoat is the umma itself, the community that never quite fulfills its promise. Fundamentalists routinely blame the practitioners and almost never the system. For them, "Muslim successes are the successes of Islam, while the failures are their own."[54] Naipaul repeatedly came across fundamentalists who held themselves responsible for what they consider to be Islam's poor showing. He asked what went wrong with the experiment of Islam in Pakistan; "Men were bad," came the reply, "they didn't live up to the faith." For the fundamentalist, "failure only led back to faith. . . . If the state failed, it wasn't because the dream was flawed, or the faith flawed; it could only be because men had failed the faith." In Indonesia, reacting to a fundamentalist's dismal portrayal of Islamic history, Naipaul asked, "Aren't you saying Islam has failed?" only to receive the predictable fundamentalist's answer: "No, not Islam. The people. The Muslims." Fundamentalists respond to the inadequacies around them by concluding that no one makes the required effort to live by the Shari'a. Despite nearly fourteen centuries of history, they seek something different, something successful. A Pakistani fundamentalist was asked by Naipaul if it made sense, after all the centuries of Islamic history, to say that Islam had not been tried? "Ahmed became grave. He said, 'No, it has never been tried.' "[55]

(All this resembles closely the predicament of those Marxists who acknowledge the historical failure of Communist states but who, when pushed to account for the reasons, point to personal mistakes by the leaders, such as brutality, the cult of personality, isolation, inflexibility, paranoia. As believing Marxists, they cannot admit that the problem lies deeper than personality, in the very system of Communist rule, for if they found the structure itself flawed, they could not remain Marxist. The fault must lie with Communists, not Communism. Fundamentalist Muslims, like them, must blame the people, never the ideology or the structures.)

Fundamentalists batter themselves against unattainable goals that traditionalist Muslims long ago realized could not be implemented. For example, they are determined to prohibit interest (*riba* in Arabic) on money in accordance with the Qur'anic verse condemning this practice between believers. In attempting this, they defy four thousand years of experience, for since the eighteenth century B.C., when the Code of Hammurabi banned charges on loans, financiers have found ways to elude anti-interest regulations through legal fictions which fulfill the letter of the law while circumventing its spirit. (One common device is the double sale: to borrow $100 from you at 20 percent a year, I sell you an item for $100 in cash which I immediately purchase back from you for $120, payable in twelve monthly installments.) "The 'tricks' used for getting around the ban on interest are just as old as the ban itself."[56]

Widespread use of such legal devices meant that "the prohibition of *riba* had little practical effect" in premodern Islamdom. In the effort to adjust Islam to human needs, traditionalist jurists obligingly closed their eyes to these practices. Radical legalists did occasionally attempt rigorously to enforce the Shar'i ban; "their success, however, was always short-lived, as is shown by the fact that, not long afterward, strict Muslims were to be heard voicing the same complaints, and often yet another reformer would arise."[57] No one could maintain the prohibition on interest for long, no matter how assiduously legalists fought for it.

In modern times, the rise of fundamentalism meant that these efforts became more systematic, as an "abundant literature" emerged detailing "the misdeeds of usurers in all the Muslim countries."[58] Attempts to fulfill the Shar'i injunction took two principal directions. The more ambitious worked from the premise that eliminating *riba* requires an entirely different set of financial institutions; they constructed *de novo* a grand design for a system of "Islamic economics." The less ambitious sought to add interest-free institutions to the already-existing financial system by making them competitive. Shar'i financial practices received increasing attention from the 1920s on, eventually leading to the creation of the "Islamic banks" which proliferated in the 1970s. Occasional efforts to institute interest-free banking were made in previous years, but it was not until the establishment of the Islamic Development Bank (IDB) in October 1975 that this idea took off. Capitalized almost entirely by Saudi Arabia and other newly rich oil states, the IDB was viewed as a model for other banks; its mandate was, by making profits from dividends which matched the profits of Western-style banks, to prove that interest-free banking could work. Others quickly followed, including the Bahrain Islamic Bank, the Faisal Islamic Bank and the Nasser Social Bank of Egypt, the Iran Islamic Bank, the Jordan Islamic Bank for Finance, the Kuwait Finance House, the Muslim Commercial Bank of Pakistan, the Islamic Exchange and Investment Corporation of Qatar, and Dar al-Mal al-Islami based in Geneva. Their practices varied considerably; perhaps the best thought out was the Profit/Loss Sharing Scheme introduced in Pakistan. But Islamic banks did less well than planned; it soon became apparent that, deprived of operating subsidies, they would have to adopt standard financial practices or they would fail. In this and other ways, the fundamentalists were incapable of improving on the medieval synthesis.

Fundamentalists pose special problems to governments because they insist, adamantly and often violently, on an impractical program. Many of them slip into fanaticism, convinced that if they could only implement their vision, all problems would disappear; according to Ali Khamene'i, president of Iran, "an Islamic society, by definition, is one in which there is no disappointment, injustice, or oppression."[59] Such convictions justify almost all political acts, including subversion and coups d'etat when in the opposition and repression when in power. Fundamentalists tend to be totally and unequivocably committed to their program; this both restricts their opportunity for compromise with non-fundamentalists and it encourages cooperation with others of their own opinion. An attempt was made in Turkey in the mid-1970s to include the fundamentalist National Salvation Party in coalition governments, with unsatisfactory results; conversely, the ruling fundamentalists in Iran allowed almost no scope to rival parties. Transnational cooperation between fundamentalists provides moral support and sometimes an important conduit of money, literature, and arms. The Muslim Brethren of Egypt and the Feda'iyyan-e Islami of Iran had contacts during the period 1943–55 and then re-established relations when both were legal again in 1979. The Muslim Brethren of Jordan supplied their colleagues in Syria with crucial support for challenging the government of Hafiz al-Asad. In October 1977, students in Turkey protested against the treatment of Muslims in the Philippines by burning the Philippine flag and taunting the Turkish foreign minister for not doing enough to aid them.

Not every fundamentalist organization becomes active in politics; some stay away due to their utter disapproval of prevailing conditions. The leaders of one extremist group in Malaysia, Jama'at Tabligh, pulled away from public affairs for this reason; others went even further, for example, by boycotting mosques funded by the government because they considered the state to be "in violation of Islamic principles."[60] But such responses are in the minority among fundamentalists, most of whom are intent on changing political conditions.

No matter what a government's orientation, it finds fundamentalists a tribulation. They call for the application of impossible laws, they reject compromise, and they rally the populace against the established order. Every politician in office can be outflanked by an extremist haranguing a mob; even in Iran, the ruling Khomeinists faced radical challenges from such groups as Furqan and the Mujahidin-e Khalq. Authorities respond to this danger in a variety of ways. Frequently they promote those non-fundamentalist forms of Islam—traditionalist, reformist, or secularist, mystical, scholarly, or pietistic—lacking the potential to foment riots and uninclined to plot coups d'etat. Of such state institutions the most elaborate were probably the four regionally-based Spiritual Directorates in the USSR, a loyal agency of the state, charged by the Soviet government to channel the religious activities of Muslim believers. Muslim rulers also keep tame Muslims on the government payroll, in part to serve as a counterweight to the radicals. Thus could Sadat mobilize the 'ulama of Egypt to support war against Israel and then have them sanction the peace treaty six years later. The Malaysian government set up its own missionary movement to compete with the fundamentalists' *dakwah* groups which threatened its popularity.

Muslims in power occasionally sponsor Islamic symbols and ideoiogy to facilitate the acceptance of their policies, without actually letting the Islamic overlay affect the nature of those policies. Even secularist rulers in Syria and Iraq clothed their actions in the mantle of Islam to appeal to the populace, and Sadat suffused his rule with piety. The problem with this is, fundamentalists demand more than show; a government that talks Islam but ignores the legalist and autonomist agenda quickly loses the goodwill of fundamentalists. Because legalism is by far the more difficult to enact, Muslim rulers often deflect fundamentalists by encouraging autonomism. This brings the two parties together at the expense of outsiders; weak rulers frequently bolster their popularity among fundamentalists by relying on a jihad element in their policies. For these reasons, King Hasan initiated the Green March into the Western Sahara, governments in Syria and Iraq stressed the conflict with Israel, and Turkish authorities exploited the war on Cyprus in 1974.

Fundamentalism emerged as a powerful ideology in the eighteenth century and won important political victories as the Wahhabis of Central Arabia took power in the 1740s, the Sanusis of Cyrenaica in the 1840s, and the Sudanese Mahdists in the 1880s. Other fundamentalist movements came close to achieving power but were beaten back. Fundamentalism remained a side-current, however, an attribute of the remote and the laggard, until Muslim peoples came massively into direct contact with the West. City-dwellers in industrializing regions felt the impact most powerfully; and while some Muslims were tempted by Occidental ways, others clutched at their own tradition all the more tightly. Thus, for example, did the Muslim Brethren emerge in Egypt and the Followers of Nur in Turkey during the 1920s, the Jama'at-i Islami in India during the 1940s, and the Khomeini movement in Iran during the 1970s.

In each case, increased contact with Western ways led to an unprecedented

139

involvement of Muslim peoples in politics; this in turn spurred the rise of fundamentalist movements. In premodern times, Muslim subjects had little contact with their governments; rulers were almost always outsiders who held power through coercion and who provided little to their subjects. "Content to let the princes play their game,"[61] subjects devoted themselves to the concerns of private life, especially those of family and faith. Initially, conquest by a Western power left those patterns intact, for these too were outsiders who ruled by force, supplied minimal services, and held the populace at a distance. If the elites were displaced by colonial officials, "the mass of the people of the Muslim world were very little affected, directly, by the Western intrusion and continued to live a life that was little changed."[62]

As colonial rule became entrenched, imperial governments took on more responsibilities with regard to their subjects. By about the 1920s, Muslims became educated in Western ways, they emulated Europe, and they began to work for mass education, the development of industry, and so forth. Post-colonial governments became involved in all these projects; contrary to almost every Muslim precedent, Occidental influences spurred rulers to take direct concern with the affairs of their people. Welfare and education were of central concern, but leaders also became involved in cultural growth, public health, and justice. In turn, the authorities, affected by Western notions of democracy, the civic society, militias, and national identity, made novel demands on the populace, calling on it to participate in public affairs. Modernization mobilized the masses and got them involved in politics, "an unprecedented event in the Islamic world."[63]

If the withdrawal of Muslims from public life in premodern times had a self-perpetuating quality, allowing rulers to skimp on their religious obligations, popular involvement after the 1920s imbued politics with a new legalist spirit. "As political activism changed from an elite phenomenon to mass movements, its character assumed a more religious tone."[64] When citizens took increased interest in government activities, they demanded "that state decisions should reflect the values which had formerly infused the independent [that is, private] institutions," so long the mainstay of Muslim life.[65] They wanted adherence to Shar'i precepts. The nearly defunct aspiration that rulers should apply jihad, zakat, or *hadd* regulations came to life in the twentieth century as Muslim peoples reclaimed the public arena. When the masses entered political life, Islam came with them.

Not all social elements had an equal role, of course; the more educated and urban citizens—school teachers, government clerks, shopkeepers, and industrial workers especially—had an influence far greater than the less educated and rural. Popular movements which accompanied modernization reflected the concerns of Muslims most in contact with modern life and who bore modern identities. It was they who joined movements such as the Muslim Brethren in Egypt, the Jama'at-i Islami in Pakistan and India, and Masjumi in Indonesia.

Other developments contributed to the increased emphasis on the Shari'a in public affairs. As traditional life disappeared, law became the main reminder of old ways. "As younger generations increasingly lost touch with any wider Islamicate heritage, the Shari'ah and the associated legal and societal outlook become the one point at which they could clearly identify themselves as Muslims and dissociate themselves from the West."[66]

Four approaches to the Shari'a co-exist in modern times. The most basic division is that between traditionalism and the three modernist approaches; traditionalism met premodern needs but was steadily replaced by reformism, secularism, and fundamentalism as exposure to the West increased. As the traditionalist understanding of the Shari'a lost appeal, other attitudes took its place: reformists saw the sacred law as an embodiment of liberalism, secularists resented the way it obstructed Westernization, and fundamentalists turned it into an ideology. At the heart of this change was a de-emphasis of the *Hadith* Reports in favor of the Qur'an; just as the Protestants rediscovered the Bible and modern Jews pushed aside the Talmud, so Muslims dwelt on the Qur'an. In each case, going back to scripture signaled an unwillingness to accept the interpretations of the patriarchs and showed an intent to redefine religious practice.

Each of the three modernizing schools responded primarily to a single aspect of Western culture. Attracted by Western *values*, reformists brought the Shari'a into conformity with them; intent on adopting Western *customs*, secularists facilitated the process by limiting the Shari'a to private life; and fundamentalists, concerned to stave off European *ideologies*, transformed the Shari'a into a rival. No less than the others, fundamentalists were influenced by the modern age, for self-conscious rejection of the West changes a Muslim as much as adopting its ways. Despite their archaic models, Maududi and Khomeini are thoroughly modern men.

A second division is between the three non-fundamentalist types of Muslims, all of whom are flexible on the question of implementing Islam's public ideals, and the fundamentalists. Traditionalists would wish to live up to Shar'i standards but know better; reformists adjust those standards to accord with Western ways; and secularists are indifferent to them. These three types of Muslims admit to other political concerns beside Islam and none of them is prepared to overthrow the existing order in pursuit of Shar'i ideals. Fundamentalists alone possess an exact Islamic program inspired by abstract ideals and wish to impose it on everyone else. Their conspicuous devotion to Islam makes fundamentalists a natural focus of attention whenever the topic of Islam in politics arises; yet their activities must not obscure the other, equally important, aspects of the Islamicate political legacy which apply to all Muslims, regardless of personal inclination. Autonomism, pan-Islamic solidarity, hostility to Europe, disdain toward dhimmis, and a host of other Islamicate features continue to play a vital role in the public life of every Muslim people; these are the topic of chapters 7 and 8.

7

Responses to Western Political Ideologies

Islam today is a stranger; no one
knows it fully.
—*Imam Ruhollah Khomeini*

THE SACRED LAW is only one portion of Islam's legacy; no less important
for public life today are those features not required by the Shari'a but characteristic of Muslim life. Deriving from three sources—"fences" around Shar'i
precepts, the medieval synthesis, and a thousand years of historical experience—Islamicate features described in chapters 3 and 4 shaped the actual patterns of Muslim life.

On a formal level, at least, nearly all Muslim states abandoned Islamicate
political culture in favor of that of the West. Except for a handful of states
on the Arabian peninsula, their governments boasted of constitutions, elections, political parties, voluntary associations, mass armies, and many of the
other institutions of distinctly Western provenance. European legal systems
replaced the Shari'a in all matters except personal status. Muslim states widely
promoted Western ideals such as democracy, socialism, social egalitarianism,
popular sovereignty, and personal freedom. They accepted international law
and recognized the permanence of non-Muslim states. In theory, a total transformation of public life occurred.

But beneath this patina of Western forms, Islamicate sentiments and attitudes were nearly as strong as ever. Context and style changed far more than
substance; the force of Islamicate impulses remained strong, and no analysis
of Islam in politics is complete without taking them into consideration. Islami-

cate patterns changed less than did Islamic laws. More Muslims continued to act under the influence of Islamicate ways, which willy-nilly affect the whole umma, than lived by the law, which requires energy and will to fulfill. (As of old, the Islamicate patterns were most felt in the Middle East.) Only the devout are Islamic, while everyone is Islamicate. Despite its pervasive effect, however, the Islamicate legacy is usually ignored by analysts of Islam, for it is diffuse and un-selfconscious.

In the modern age, that legacy has frequently been decisive in shaping the Muslim response to Western civilization. Western ways that meshed with Islamicate patterns were readily assimilated; those that clashed were impeded. This chapter traces the impact of the Islamicate political culture on three levels of activity: the domestic, the Islamic and the international.

Participating in Politics

MUSLIMS

In premodern Dar al-Islam, the medieval synthesis kept Muslims away from public life; in Dar al-Harb, kafir rule had the same effect. In sum, nearly all Muslim subjects kept away from politics and became actively engaged only when they had a chance to apply the law or to battle non-Muslims. This Islamicate pattern—customary withdrawal punctuated by bursts of activity—survived into the modern period. Despite the adoption of Western ideologies which call for regular citizen participation, Muslims continued to avoid politics and warfare except when galvanized by issues relating to legalism or autonomism. "Almost every Islamic movement, in almost every part of the Muslim world, throughout [the modern] period has been in some way a variation on this double theme" of protest against "internal deterioration" and "external encroachment."[1]

The context was changed, however. In premodern times, before the Shari'a had rivals to contend with, every legalist and autonomist effort was directed to living by God's precepts. For fundamentalists this continued to be the case in modern times, but for other Muslims the introduction of Western ideologies created choices: they could act on behalf of the law or else on behalf of goals compatible yet different from it. Ideals reminiscent of the Shari'a but not specifically tied to it came to activate Muslims; diffuse impulses replaced the Shari'a's precise requirements. Legalism in premodern times meant applying the sacred law; in modern times, it included any appeal to justice, including some (like Marxism) that are inherently anti-Shar'i. Autonomism once aimed at establishing Muslim rule only for the purpose of applying the law; now it meant self-determination as such, without necessarily including the law at all. Justice and Muslim rule, once the means to live in accordance with God's wishes, became ends in themselves. The spirit was sometimes changed completely, but the political imperatives remained similar to what they had always Shar'i precepts receded, yet their legacy remained.

The first of these, the appeal to justice, was widely popular and often capable of mobilizing the masses. A leader who called for an end to exploitation, favoritism, corruption, arrogance, and the unfair distribution of wealth could win great popular support. The theme of combating "internal deterioration" played a prominent role in every successful effort to involve Muslim citizens in domestic politics, including pan-Arabism, the Algerian Revolution, the anti-Bhutto movement of 1977 in Pakistan, and the Iranian Revolution. The leaders of virtually every coup d'etat in Islamdom articulated this same appeal for justice and regeneration, including those that led to a major change in regime, as in Iran in 1951, Egypt in 1952, Iraq and Pakistan in 1958, Turkey in 1960, North Yemen in 1962, Indonesia in 1965, Libya in 1969, Afghanistan in 1973, Bangladesh in 1975, and Iran in 1979. Coups that failed also stressed these same concerns. In contrast, Western themes unrelated to legalism did not move Muslim peoples to action: democracy, freedom of expression, independent political parties, or civilian rule rarely impelled Muslims to the streets.

The concept of the citizen—an enfranchised, participating member of society who pays taxes, joins voluntary associations, elects government officials, and serves in the military—fitted awkwardly in Islamdom. Arising from the direct democracy of ancient Greek cities, the elections of the Roman Republic, and the representation of nobles at the kings' courts in medieval times, citizenship is another uniquely European idea. Although Islamdom knew nothing comparable, Muslim states of the twentieth century adopted Western institutions derived from the concept of citizenship—elections and militias especially—and mixed them with Islamicate institutions derived from the pattern of withdrawn subjects. The combination produced odd and volatile results.

Almost all Muslim states adopted elections in the twentieth century (the Arabian peninsula excepted), though nowhere did they become part of a democratic process as known in the Occident. Rather than viewing citizen participation as a means to make the government legitimate and stable, Muslim leaders saw it more as a way to prod the populace for support. Practices that came into use after World War II betrayed this difference: one-party elections in Albania and Syria; ballots for lesser officials but not for the head of government in Kuwait, Bourguiba's Tunisia, Qadhdhafi's Libya, republican Egypt and Iraq, and Iran under the shah; political parties representing religious or communal groups in Lebanon and Malaysia; democracy alternating with military rule in Turkey, Nigeria, Pakistan, and Bangladesh; manipulated elections in Senghor's Senegal, revolutionary Iran, and Indonesia. In some countries, such as both Egypt and Lebanon before World War II, oligarchs took the parliament over and exploited it for their own ends.

In Qadhdhafi's "state of the masses," the peoples' councils and his own lack of a formal title did not disguise the fact that as ruler he enjoyed absolute power. The initiative, as ever, came from the top. Muslim populaces understood the authorities' purpose and responded warily to democratic and populist claims. Citizens stayed away; when they did show up at the polls, expectations were modest. "After the centuries of despotism," writes V. S. Naipaul, Muslim populaces "really believed . . . that the state was something apart, something that looked after itself and was ever restored."[2] Imam Khomeini put it with his usual concision: "The main problem of the Muslims is the governments which rule over them."[3] Frustrated, wanting to consolidate their political bases, the rulers tried to induce participation by raising the decibel level; this accounted for much of the shrill rhetoric that characterizes political discourse in Islamdom, and especially in the Middle East.

The withdrawal from politics also impaired the ability of Muslim peoples to articulate new political theories of their own. "Long centuries of submission to secular government induced a tradition of political quietism which cannot easily or quickly be shaken off," writes H. A. R. Gibb; that tradition, he goes on, "still further inhibited the development of political thought and its application to changing circumstances."[4]

Efforts to alter the premodern pattern of recruiting soldiers from outsider groups had little success. As of old, the best soldiers continued to come from beyond the cities and farms—from the mountains, deserts, and steppes. Compare the indifferent regular armies of Jordan and Saudi Arabia with their superior Bedouin corps, the Arab Legion, and the National Guard. This was also the case in Morocco, Lebanon, Syria, Yemen, Afghanistan, and Pakistan.

NON-MUSLIMS

European powers of the nineteenth century worked hard to eliminate the dhimmi status, both as a way of improving the standing of Christians and to strengthen liberal ideals. In response, beginning with the Hatt-i Sharif of Gülhane, an Ottoman edict dating from 1839, Muslim governments began to adopt the Western practice of granting equal rights and equal duties to all citizens of their territories. Non-Muslims won the right to pay no more taxes than Muslims, to appear before the same courts with the same standing, to serve as soldiers, and to hold political offices—all of which conflicted with the Shar'i regulations about dhimmis. As European control over Islamdom expanded, non-Muslims gained further, for the colonial administrators distrusted Muslims and preferred to rely on almost anyone else for help. As a result, Muslims in regions such as northern Africa, the Levant, and India often ended up with the lowest social status, well below that of the Jews, Christians, and Hindus they had long ruled.

With independence and the Muslims back in charge, another reversal took place and the standing of non-Muslims fell despite the retention of laws assuring equality for all citizens. Changes were especially dramatic wherever non-Muslims had collaborated with the European powers; after years of enjoying a favored position, the end of colonial rule exposed them to the anger of the Muslim majority. In Algeria, for example, almost the entire indigenous Jewish population fled the country along with the French authorities in 1962, fearful of the retribution that would befall them if they stayed. Ironically, elimination of the dhimmi status by colonial governments often undercut the legal position of non-Muslims and jeopardized their security. Most importantly, the traditional permission for dhimmis to remain living in Dar al-Islam came into question. Many Greeks and Armenians of Turkey, Jews of North Africa and the Middle East, Hindus of Pakistan, and Chinese of Southeast Asia were forced to leave their native lands; and those who stayed often encountered new obstacles to the free exercise of their religions.

Regulations against kafir rule over Muslims originally developed out of a concern for the application of the law; the assumption was that only Muslim leaders would make the effort required to govern in accordance with Islam. Even as many modern Muslims lost interest in the Shari'a, the Islamicate mistrust of kafirs in positions of authority remained. Once again, the Shar'i justification disappeared but the attitudes it engendered stayed alive. Where non-Muslims held high positions in independent states—Christian politicians in the cabinets of the Arab East, Baha'i military officers in Iran, Chinese officials in Malaysia—this provoked displeasure among the majority Muslim populace. The political role of suspect groups such as the 'Alawis in Syria and the Ahmadis in Pakistan, both of whom adhere to an Islam rejected by mainstream Muslims, was also a source of discontent. The question of the head of state was even more delicate, for he determined the cast of the whole government. A dominant Muslim majority acquiesced and even advanced the rule of a non-Muslim in only one country: this was Senegal, where Leopold Senghor, a Catholic, served as president from 1960 to 1980 (and then was succeeded by a Muslim). Senegal may be unique; even in so highly secularized a government as Albania's, it is difficult to imagine Muslims accepting a non-Muslim as ruler.

Defining Borders and Loyalties

Just as monotheism and the alphabet first emerged in the Middle East, philosophy in Greece, and mysticism in India, so did political ideology originate exclusively in West Europe. No other region knew of anything resembling the systematic arguments concerning "who gets what when and how" that developed there. Diverse political ideologies were available by the twentieth century, including republicanism, anarchism, Marxism, and fascism. They were initially as alien to other civilizations as China's Mandate of Heaven, India's Artha, or Islamdom's Shari'a would have been to the West. Nonetheless, every one of these "isms" quickly attracted non-Europeans, for they expressed moral principles and mobilized citizens and increased the power of the government. Their role in helping to build the power of the European states also increased their attraction. Colonization, trade, education, and religious conversion made political ideologies available outside West Europe; first they spread to East Europe and Russia, then around the world.

Some of these doctrines fitted rather well in Islamdom: democracy, capitalism, and liberalism, for example, could mesh with Shar'i principles, though they did run up against prevailing Islamicate patterns. Others, such as socialism and secularism, contravened Shar'i precepts too. But none fitted so badly as nationalism; indeed, no facet of Western political culture posed so many problems for the umma as nationalism, the stress on loyalty to the nation and the nationality above all other loyalties. Fundamentalists and others opposed to borrowing from the West often saw nationalism as a symbol for the problem of blending civilizations. They even went so far as to see the export of nationalist doctrines as a European plot to undermine Islamic unity and conquer the umma. Imam Khomeini, for example, called it "a stratagem concocted by the foreigners who are disturbed by the spread of Islam."[5]

NATIONALISM

Nationalist ideology requires that the deepest political loyalties be directed to the nation as a whole rather than to the tribe, village, city, social class, or religious community. But what is the nation? Ideally, it is a group sharing common origins, customs, language, and historical experience; Portugal is one such example. This combination rarely appears in clear form, however, and the demarcation of lines between nations is often a matter of enormous controversy—no less than five countries laid claim to Macedonia in the years before the First World War.

148

However ill it fitted, nationalism spread anyway, for it aroused strong popular responses and it offered advantages to rulers; no other ideology could mobilize citizens as effectively. As nationalism spread and nations appeared, the tribal and imperial structures that had dominated politics for millennia almost disappeared; the Soviet Union and China are the only surviving empires of great size, while Rwanda, Burundi, Lesotho, and Swaziland are among the few remaining tribal states. Indeed, nationalism caught on so strongly that it was frequently more virulently felt outside Europe (think of Vietnam or Argentina) than within it.

Premodern Muslims had no concept corresponding to the nation. Though acquainted with regional units such as Tunisia, Cyrenaica, Sind, and Bengal, these defined cultural areas, not political affiliations. Premodern Muslims no more identified with such cultural areas than does anyone today: Who would sacrifice his life for Latin America, New England, or the Confucian world? The transformation of amorphous cultural areas into nations changed the whole tone of politics.

For one, it gave the state a new role. As we have seen, premodern Muslims ascribed scarcely any meaning to the fact that they happened to be living in one kingdom and not another. What did it matter that the Ghaznavids, Saʿdis, or Zaydis were in power? Whereas Muslims were merely resident in a kingdom, the importance was that they were citizens of the umma. Kings, capitals, and state structures had little hold over the loyalties of their subjects. This changed with the impact of European ideologies. The idea of the state as the representative of the people developed in eighteenth-century France and made the government the focus of public aspirations. No longer merely a collection of powerful persons, the state turned into the nation and was seen as the embodiment of the general will of its citizens. This idea too came to full fruition in the French Revolution.

When the European nations attacked Islamdom, Muslims responded the only way they knew how, by turning to Islam. Having minimal allegiance to their governments, Muslim populaces relied on Islamic autonomism to bond them together and to provide leaders, networks of organizations, rallying calls, and goals. Virtually every organized effort to keep the imperialists out depended on Islam, if only because Muslims had no alternate ideology. "As a rule, the struggle against the West was for Islam and by Islam."[6] But Islam failed; old-style autonomism did not keep the Europeans out and Muslims therefore were receptive to trying the ways of their conquerors, adopting nationalism.

By the late twentieth century, every Muslim state used nationalist ideas to bolster its claim to the allegiance of its citizens. The national order had prevailed over the Islamicate one. When nationalist ideas reached Islamdom, they brought a wholly new way of viewing politics. Rulers, hitherto despised as dynastic autocrats, claimed to lead their people and represent their territories. In a word, "the sultans in Morocco became Moroccan kings."[7] Nationalism permitted rulers to claim the loyalty of the ruled, making it easier to win their cooperation.

If fundamentalists like Khomeini suspect the Europeans of foisting nationalism on the umma to divide it, the truth is that imperial powers would have been better off had their Muslim subjects remained ignorant of nationalism. This would have facilitated imperial rule and allowed it to last longer. "Nationalism is the answer of the East to Europe, more truly than it is the gift of Europe to the East."[8] Yet the colonial powers did a poor job of hiding it. They administered the colonies as proto-nations, defining the boundaries with unprecedented precision, building up their communications and transportation, and using regional names as national and ethnic designations. What with the East India Company, the India Office, the Indian Railways, and a myriad of lesser institutions, subjects of the British raj inevitably came to think of themselves as Indians. The imperialists made few efforts to disguise their own nationalist spirit and educated colonials quickly picked it up. Territorial divisions acquired meaning with time; inhabitants of Tunis, Sousse, Sfax, Gabes, and Gafsa began to see themselves as Tunisians and confronted the French administration as such. Further, they realized that as Tunisians they could do little for their Algerian or Libyan neighbors. The struggle for independence had the effect of bestowing unprecedented importance on geographic regions within Islamdom.

In a few cases, boundaries drawn by the European powers closely corresponded to existing cultural areas: Morocco, Egypt, and Iran acquired newly precise definitions and political import. In many more cases, however, colonial boundaries bore little, if any, relation to existing divisions, either human or natural. This was especially the case in Africa, much of which was divided in the Berlin Conference of 1884. As they drew boundaries on sometimes blank maps, diplomats from the fourteen Western countries attending the conference paid no more attention to the tribes and peoples of Africa than to the distribution of the bird species there. Elsewhere, too, wherever the Europeans found no clear units, they created new ones: Iraq, India, and Malaysia, for example. Unlike the boundaries of West Europe, which had acquired meaning through centuries of warfare and population movement, these imposed divisions were arbitrary; nonetheless they acquired significance with time.

Jordan, which accidentally came into existence in 1921, was an extreme example of arbitrariness. After Prince 'Abdallah ibn Husayn, a British protégé, appeared in Amman to launch a campaign installing his brother as king in Damascus, the Colonial Office dissuaded him and temporarily settled him on the east bank of the Jordan River. When it became clear that the French authorities would not allow his brother to rule Syria, the British convinced 'Abdallah to settle where he was in Transjordan. To satisfy his ambitions, they made him ruler of this area, established its borders, and paid him a monthly subsidy. Born as an artifice of the British Colonial Office (headed at that time by Winston Churchill), Jordan nonetheless acquired all the trappings of a modern nation. "The Jordanians" are now spoken of in the same way as "the Dutch," their national character discussed like that of the Italians, and their history traced back to ancient times, like that of the Germans.

IMPEDIMENTS TO NATIONALISM

The establishment of national states demanding their citizens' allegiance confronted Muslims with a conflict between two loyalties, the Islamicate and the Western. Whereas Islam called for a single Muslim state, nationalism divided the Muslims into territorial units. Nationalism made paramount exactly those territorial divisions Islam ignored. As citizens of both the umma and a nation, Muslims found themselves torn between two powerful and incompatible loyalties. The consequences of this clash were numerous and go far to explain the endemic instability of politics in Islamdom since independence.

Fundamentalists, of course, found nationalism unacceptable. "Any Muslim who has pledged himself to the devil of nationalism has been divorced by the angels of Islam."[9] But even non-fundamentalists, persons willing to accommodate Western ideologies, had trouble making the national bond paramount. Lacking a tradition of loyalty to the region or the government, they held back, seeking something larger and more akin to their traditional loyalties. The longing for a unified umma had retained its appeal through eleven hundred years of disappointment; it would not just disappear with the advent of nationalism. Even rulers who might be expected to emphasize the national unit exclusively also had ambivalent feelings, as is shown by their efforts to combine these into larger structures. For nearly all Muslims, "the trappings of modern statehood were a sort of borrowed finery, fitting awkwardly upon the ancient Islamic body politic."[10]

The states that emerged from the colonial era tended to conform to the boundaries between Muslims and non-Muslims; most of them included either a great majority of Muslims or a small minority. As figures in the appendix show, nearly 70 percent of Muslims lived in countries where they made up at least 85 percent of the population, where they controlled the government, and where they were unequivocally a part of Dar al-Islam. At the other end of the spectrum, a bit more than 20 percent of Muslims lived in states in which

151

they constituted less than 25 percent of the population, making them clearly part of Dar al-Harb. A surprisingly small number of Muslims, only about 10 percent, made up a middle portion, from 25 to 85 percent, of the population.[11] All three groups had to come to terms with conflicting demands for their loyalties, but the terms differed in each case. Muslims living in Dar al-Islam (including both majorities and moieties) will be considered in this section, those of Dar al-Harb in the next.

Muslim reluctance to accept divisions between Muslim states compares to the German unwillingness to see the border between the Federal Republic and the Democratic Republic become permanent. Just as all Germans, regardless of ideological viewpoint, feel their country has been truncated and wish to have it whole again, so do Muslims feel their patrimony has been artificially divided. Both the People's Republic of China and the Republic of China hold back from seeing Taiwan as a separate country because both insist that China must not be divided. Just as North and South Korea, North and South Vietnam, and the two parts of Ireland got involved in each other's affairs, so do Muslim countries feel they have rights over each other. The ideal of unity between Muslims remains strong, even though unfulfilled since the eighth century; just as Italy and Germany in the nineteenth century were divided cultural regions in search of political unity, so is Islamdom unfulfilled in the era of nation-states.

And as in the other divided countries, the Muslim aspiration for unity creates special tensions. In each case, the same questions arise: On whose terms will unification take place? Which leadership will prevail, and which will be pushed aside? The divergence of political systems and the perpetuation of vested interests make it extremely difficult to put a divided country together again. This occurs either through clever diplomacy backed by the threat of force, as in Bismarck's unification of Germany, or by brute force, as in Vietnam in 1975. Everything about the relations between these divided peoples is more complex and difficult than among neighbors who consider themselves to be separate peoples.

This is true of the Muslim states in general and the Arab ones in particular, all of which have some moral hold on the others. The goal of unification, though always remote, has a direct influence on the daily conduct of Muslim governments. Two important consequences follow from this: they have difficulty accepting the limitations of national boundaries, and they are unwilling to refrain from meddling in the affairs of other Muslim states.

Pakistan dramatically illustrates the reluctance of Muslims to accept the geographic constraints of national statehood. As India's independence grew near, those Muslims who feared becoming a permanent minority in a Hindu-dominated Indian republic convinced the British to partition India into

Hindu and Muslim parts. As a result, the Muslim state of Pakistan came into existence in 1947. Muslims were concentrated one thousand miles apart, at the far western and eastern ends of north India, and were remote from each other in everything from language and high cultural traditions to diet, costume, calendar, standard time, and social customs. Still, the visionaries who created Pakistan ignored these differences and made all Muslims part of a single state. They counted on pan-Islamic sentiments to bind the two wings into a single whole. But they failed; even a fervent Islamic spirit could not prevail against geography. Mounting tensions led to the civil war of 1970–71 and to East Pakistan's declaration of independence as the state of Bangladesh. The pan-Islamic dream eventually collapsed, but it did temporarily vanquish nationalism and it did keep the Indian subcontinent in a state of turmoil for a quarter-century.

Muslims in India tried to fit themselves into a unit smaller than the whole of Islamdom but larger than the Pakistan and Bangladesh of today. They attempted to bridge the conflicting demands of the umma and the nation by opting for an intermediary. This had the virtue of being politically appealing yet smaller in size than the whole of the umma; it had the drawback of being artificial (What made the Muslims of those two areas a people?) and of not fitting into the territorial units bequeathed by the European colonizers. If the Indian Muslims could not unite into one country, how would the Somalis or Iranians, spread out among three countries each? Or the Fulanis, Hausa, Berbers, Kurds, or Malays, living in some five countries each? Much less the Turks in nine countries (stretching from Yugoslavia to China) or the Arabs in over twenty-five?

The Arab case holds special interest, for pan-Arabism, the ideology calling for a union of all Arabic speakers, has had the greatest regional and international repercussions. In his study of pan-Arabist politics, Malcolm H. Kerr begins by admitting the puzzle of this topic: "Why the idea of unity is so strong among Arabs—so much more than among Latin Americans, for instance, or the English-speaking nations—is a mystery that neither Arab nor western historians have satisfactorily explained."[12] From an Islamicate perspective, however, the Arab urge for unity is simply accounted for. Pan-Arabism rather exactly includes pan-Islamic and nationalist elements; it is a nationalized version of pan-Islamic solidarity. Its appeal to the unity of Muslims recalls pan-Islam, while its stress on language as the definition of political identity recalls nationalism. The idea of Arab unity taps a key Islamicate tradition. It is no coincidence that the pan-Arabists refer to the Arab nation as the *umma 'Arabiya,* the Arab umma.

Pan-Arabism shares other important qualities with pan-Islam. Just as the ideal of a single Muslim state undermined premodern kingdoms, so pan-Arabism harmed the independent Arab states of the twentieth century. To see this connection, read "pan-Islam" for "pan-Arabism" in Fouad Ajami's discussion of recent events and note how exactly it applies to premodern times:

> At the height of its power, pan-Arabism could make regimes look small and petty: disembodied structures headed by selfish rulers who resisted the sweeping mission of Arabism. . . . Allegiance to the state was "tacit, even surreptitious," while Arab unity was "the sole publicly acceptable objective of statesmen and ideologues alike." What this meant was that states were without sufficient legitimacy. Those among them that resisted the claims of pan-Arabism were at a disadvantage—their populations a fair target for pan-Arabist appeals, their leaders to be overthrown and replaced by others more committed to the transcendent goal.[13]

Nationalism changed the context, but the old problem of allegiance to rulers remained nearly the same.

The pan-Arabist impulse inspired many attempts to combine Arab states, even among those that are not contiguous. The first and most important effort was that of the United Arab Republic, the union of Egypt and Syria which lasted from 1958 to 1961. Its failure was a crushing disappointment. Syria later discussed unification with Iraq and Jordan; Egypt and the Sudan took steps toward confederation; the Yemens made plans to unite shortly after each of their intermittent wars; but it was Muʿammar al-Qadhdhafi of Libya who attempted the most bids at unification, trying but failing with each of the Western Sahara, Morocco, Mauritania, Tunisia, Chad, Malta (only Qadhdhafi would see Malta as Arab), Egypt, the Sudan, and Syria. Through all these maneuvers, Arab leaders who advanced the interests of their own citizens, ignoring the demands of pan-Arabism, made themselves vulnerable to the propaganda and the plotting of other governments. As in premodern times, the existing states had a vaguely disreputable standing, and this led to a stunting of the bonds between rulers and ruled. Pan-Arabism explains the exceedingly volatile nature of Arab politics, especially during 1956–67, the decade of its heyday.

The Islamicate drive for unity disrupted politics in another way too, by weakening the dichotomy between domestic and foreign affairs and encouraging the interference by one state into what would normally be considered the internal affairs of its neighbors. Here too, the Arab case is outstanding; Arab leaders believed they had the right, even the duty, to get involved in the politics of other Arab states. Algeria supported a government-in-exile against Sadat; Egypt and Saudi Arabia sponsored armies in North Yemen's civil war between 1962 and 1967; Libya, Egypt, Saudi Arabia, Syria, and Iraq backed factions in the Lebanese civil war; Algeria supported the Polisario against Morocco; Iraq received military and financial aid from Egypt, Jordan, Saudi Arabia, Kuwait, and other Persian Gulf states during its recent war with Iran; and so forth. In each case, outside involvement transformed a local quarrel into a regional issue.

Most impressive by far, however, were the activities of Libya, Saudi Arabia, and Iran during the 1970s, many of which will be detailed in chapter 10. Suffice it to note here that their combined influence probably touched every Muslim community and certainly affected every Muslim government. No less revealing than the activities themselves was the near absence of protest against them; however much the Arabs and Muslims deplored such interference (especially Qadhdhafi's brand of mischief), they rarely disputed one Muslim's right to intervene in the affairs of others. The Islamicate legacy led them to feel—as in the Germanies or the Chinas—that they had claims on each other. As a result, Muslims generally and Arabs specifically involved themselves intensely in each other's affairs, praising, denouncing, plotting coups, sending troops, and much more.

It was this, for example, which transformed the question of Israel's existence from a minor quarrel between the Arabs and the Jews of Palestine into the most consequential territorial dispute of the late twentieth century. Anti-Zionism became the showcase cause of pan-Arabism, the vehicle for leaders to show their pan-Arabist credentials, or a way to protect themselves from those possessing them. The conflict with Israel provided an open-ended justification for interference in a neighboring ruler's affairs, on the grounds that he was not suitably fervent. Israel's existence served as the means for ambitious regimes such as Gamal Abdul Nasser's to augment their power, and destabilizing the entire Middle East. Thus is the region permanently in flux; it is probably the only portion of the globe where hardly a single border is mutually and permanently accepted. The combination of Islamicate and nationalist loyalties made Middle Eastern politics perhaps more intricate than anywhere else in the world.

Nationalism also altered the old ideal of unifying Dar al-Islam. Efforts to eradicate borders between Muslims and revive the caliphate collapsed in the 1930s, probably for good. The proliferation of independent Muslim states with national aspirations meant the replacement of pan-Islamic urges with the more modest ambition of fostering close relations between existing states. International Islamic organizations that emerged after the Second World War accepted the permanence of Muslim nations and aspired only to harmonize their relations, not to unite them. The establishment of such institutions as the Islamic Conference, the Islamic Defence Institute, and the Islamic Solidarity Fund roused hopes among Muslims that Dar al-Islam could be forged into a bloc, at least vis-à-vis non-Muslims. But it is one thing to long for unity and quite another to form more than loose bonds; these organizations provided an infrastructure for cooperation, not alliance. Muslim states showed the most solidarity on issues unrelated to their immediate concerns. Although Muslim solidarity was strong enough to impede the development of bonds to the state, it was rarely translated into positive political action.

Relations with Non-Muslim Governments

On the international level, Islamicate political culture provided the context for relations with Dar al-Harb in both peace and war. Peaceful relations were markedly distant and warfare especially common.

ALLIANCES WITH THE SUPER-POWERS

The dichotomy between Islam and non-Islam keeps Muslims away from kafirs and inhibits close associations with non-Muslim governments. Muslim rulers form tactical alliances with the great powers but maintain a careful distance from them. In recent years, very few Muslim states—Turkey and South Yemen are the clearest exceptions—have placed themselves firmly in the camp of a super-power and then remained there (and in South Yemen this was a decision made by a small minority, subsequently enforced by the Soviet Union). Muslim leaders generally try to reap the benefits of protection by a powerful patron without becoming committed to that patron's ideology or bloc. In relation to the super-powers, the Islamicate legacy tends to foster three patterns: neutralism with some bias in favor of the Soviets; a disengagement from Soviet-American rivalries; and massive domestic opposition to overly close relations with one power or the other.

Neutralism. A pattern of reluctance makes the Middle East (and, to a lesser extent, other Muslim regions) uniquely disengaged from the great rivalry of the age. Confronted with a world order in which two Western countries and two Western ideologies dominate, the Islamicate impulse is not to get involved. Muslim states prefer not to commit themselves wholeheartedly to either super-power, for Muslims find it distasteful to become auxiliaries to a conflict directed by non-Muslims. Why get caught up in a struggle between kafir systems and kafir peoples? The Islamicate impulse encourages them to stay away and find their own solutions to the problems of the day.

The impulse toward neutralism runs deep. Abdul Nasser epitomized it by playing the United States and the Soviet Union off against each other, knowing just how far he could go and extracting maximum benefits from both sides. It is mostly Muslim leaders who followed Abdul Nasser in this characteristically Islamicate skill—for example, the Algerians, North Yemenis, and the pre–1978 Afghan leaders. Muslims were also in the forefront of efforts to organize a neutralist counterweight to the great powers. "Without Islam the Afro-Asian movement would probably have aborted. And without the Afro-Asian movement there would have been no 'non-aligned' group of nations, and without that group there would not have been the economic Group of Seventy-Seven, the underdeveloped South in the current North-South dialogue."[14] The very notion of joining America, Europe, Russia, and Japan into one unit, "the North," bespeaks a Muslim point of view.

But neutralism does not require precise equidistance from the two blocs; just as the non-aligned movement as a whole tilts toward the Soviets, so too do Muslim states, for two reasons. First, Islamdom's relations with West Europe are longer of duration and more problematic in quality than those with East Europe and Russia. This was already true in premodern times, but it was colonialism that involved West Europe most intimately in Muslim affairs; even today, cultural and financial ties to West Europe and America remain by far the most important for most Muslim countries. Consequently, Muslims reserve their strongest feelings for the industrial democracies and are relatively indifferent to the Communist states, still largely outside their purview. The modern Muslim experience is so wrapped up with the need to respond to West Europe and America, forming alliances with them is almost inconceivable. The angry exhilaration that characterized the Organization of Petroleum Exporting Countries, (OPEC) meetings during the 1970s, when Muslims briefly dictated terms to their chief nemesis, showed this very clearly.

Even though the Russians pieced together the largest empire on earth, much of it formerly part of Dar al-Islam, "imperialism" is nearly synonymous with West Europe and "neo-imperialism" with the United States. Muslims remember Britain and France for their colonial rule, and the Soviet Union for succoring independence movements. Muslims and Marxists led the assault on European power earlier in this century; later, the Muslim members of OPEC and Soviet armed forces presented the main threats to the economic and political well being of the West. No other religious or ideological groups challenged Western civilization so intensively, nor do any others watch with equal frustration how the West prospers. Muhammad brought a message claiming to supersede Christianity and Marx thought his theories would bury the capitalist economies of Europe, yet the Christian, capitalist civilization continue to prosper, to the annoyance of both Muslims and Marxists. This bond will last so long as the West thrives.

Second, the Islamicate heritage may predispose Muslims slightly toward

157

Marxism over liberalism. True, liberals respect those institutions that Islam holds most dear, including religious faith, the family unit, and private property, while Communists call for historical materialism, state control, and communal property. But this is superficial; a closer look shows that Islamicate patterns also resemble Marxism in important ways.

To begin with, both Islam and Marxism make claims to the whole truth. Their holy books include regulations that create a social order deriving from their visions of the righteous life, directing the lives of individuals down to the smallest details. In both cases, scriptures, not governments, have the ultimate authority; governments exist to mold society in conformity with old texts. Specifics differ profoundly between the two, of course. Islamic regulations begin with the private sphere and extend to control the public, whereas Marxism moves in the other direction; but in the end, both cover nearly every aspect of life. Most activities—drinking liquor or painting abstracts—have political implications and involve government control. Both discourage dissent and severely punish those who refuse to cooperate. In contrast, liberalism has no political agenda but allows each citizen to find his own way by giving him the opportunity to make his own choices.

Unlike liberalism, with its mundane and practical goals, Islam and Marxism aim high. Islam calls for a society in harmony with God's laws, Marxism envisages a social order in harmony with scientific principles. Each program calls for humans to modify their behavior in dramatic ways to meet the requirements of its principles and laws. Islam forbids war between Muslims, and Marxism requires first loyalty to the class, but neither of these have been implemented. To reduce economic exploitation, Islam outlaws interest on money in transactions between Muslims, and Marxism prohibits profits, yet neither succeeds; interest and profits can only be disguised, not eliminated. Islam's social precepts fail because they depend upon the "ethical exhortation of individual believers" while they are blind to "the power of organized interests in society."[15] Marxism expects harmony of purpose, rationality, generosity, goodwill, mental health, far-sightedness, and intelligence; it fails when human qualities intrude. In contrast to these noble goals, liberalism harnesses self-interest (the free market) and flourishes in conjunction with democracy, which presumes that no one has the ability to know another person's best interests; it does not attempt to mold humans but works with their foibles.

The point of drawing these similarities is to argue not that an Islamicate background favors Marxism, but that a Muslim can turn to Marxism as readily as to liberalism. Which ideology appeals to him more has nothing to do with Islamicate political culture but is a matter of personal temperament and circumstances. Traditionalist rulers, including the Moroccan, Libyan, Saudi, Kuwaiti, Omani, Jordanian, and Afghan monarchs, pursued pro-British or pro-American policies for the simple reason that the Soviets threatened their crowns. Reformists and secularists are entirely unpredictable, with some of each found in each super-power camp. Fundamentalists bristle with hostility toward both sides but their radicalism leads them more often to prefer the Soviet Union.

Staying away. Although Anwar as-Sadat warmly espoused Western interests, he rejected American attempts to secure bases in Egypt, allowing only "facilities" for pre-positioned equipment. Egyptian officials explained that an extreme sensitivity to foreign soldiers, dating from the days of British and Soviet bases, would make the presence of Americans in uniform in Egypt very unpopular. Although a member of the North Atlantic Treaty Organization, Turkey refused to permit the use of American bases in Anatolia in connection with the Persian Gulf or Iran, a decision that showed the clear distinction Turks drew between strategic issues regarding the Soviet Union and regional ones involving Muslim states. Saudi Arabia enjoyed a "special relationship" with the United States going back to the 1930s and involving such diverse components as oil sales, technical assistance, and military training. Despite these ties, American troops were emphatically unwelcome in Arabia after 1961 and efforts to convince the Saudi leaders that they needed American protection failed. Riyadh chose to rely on its own manpower, however thin, and spent untold billions on armaments. So eager were the Saudis to keep the Arabian peninsula clear of American soldiers that they pressured Sultan Qabus of Oman to deny bases to the Rapid Deployment Force in 1981 and offered him $1.2 billion to replace the sum he would have received from the United States.[16] Bahrain restricted American access to its docking facilities, also under Saudi prodding.

The Soviet Union has suffered from similar problems in its attempts to win Muslim allies. If anything, its troubles exceeded America's, for Middle Eastern leaders used the Soviet connection largely to balance Western influences, not out of sympathy for Soviet goals. For example, Col. al-Qadhdhafi broke Libya's military ties to the West and turned to the USSR for arms; he even threatened occasionally to join the Warsaw Pact.[17] But he abused Marxists with relish and pursued his own policies around the globe, even if some of them (such as giving aid to the Afghan rebels) hurt Soviet interests. Iraqi leaders acted in like manner; having signed a Treaty of Friendship and Cooperation with the Soviet Union in 1972 and generally promoted Soviet goals internationally, they periodically asserted their independence from Moscow by executing Iraqi Communists, buying arms from the West, and sponsoring charters that called for the expulsion of all non-Arab forces from Arab lands. For twenty-five years, Russia supplied Egypt with generous help—the Aswan Dam, a rebuilt military after 1967, excused debts, and wide political support—but had

little to show for it. Nasser and Sadat took what they could get and gave minimally in return. Islamicate neutralist impulses even help explain the maverick
behavior of Albania, the one Muslim state with a full-fledged Marxist government. Claiming to hold strictly to true Communism while all other parties
became "revisionist," the Albanian leadership reviled the USSR as bitterly as
the United States. Its Islamicate background was one explanation for this
otherwise perplexing hostility.

Attempts to bring Dar al-Islam into the super-power rivalry usually failed.
The United States and Britain persuaded four Muslim states (Turkey, Iraq,
Iran, and Pakistan) to sign the Baghdad Pact in 1955, hoping this would block
the Soviets from the Middle East. But the Pact precipitated just the reverse;
Abdul Nasser responded to this attempt to control Muslims by drawing closer
to the USSR, taking many other radicals with him. In Iraq itself, the accord
created a furor which contributed to the leftist coup against the monarchy in
July 1958. The Reagan administration's early plans for a "strategic consensus"
against the Soviet Union met an even quicker and more ignominious end than
did the Baghdad Pact. Many commentators pointed out the impossibility of
finessing the Arab-Israeli conflict and other regional problems by re-orienting
attention toward the Soviet Union; they might also have noted that the Baghdad Pact's failure showed how Muslim reluctance to choose sides had doomed
this plan even when Middle East disputes were less polarized along East-West
lines. Iran under Khomeini provided an extreme example of the unwillingness
to get involved: despite concerted efforts by the super-powers to win influence
in the country, the government continued to maintain unbending hostility toward both the United States and the Soviet Union. For years, Khomeini's government required Iranians who assembled for any purpose to chant, "Praise
the Lord! God is Great! Khomeini is Great! Death to America!" and this was
usually followed by "Death to the Soviet Union and to All Superpowers!"[18]
"Neither East nor West" became its most prominent political slogan.

Most Muslims view cooperation with non-Muslims as tactical only, for
long-range goals differ too profoundly for any real common purpose with kafirs. Their attitudes can be compared to those of the U.S. government joining
forces with Stalin against Nazi Germany or aiding China against Brezhnev's
regime; these were alliances forged for specific goals and without expectation
of friendship or common motives, where aversions had to be overcome before
the alliance could be arranged. Muslims approach cooperation with
non-Muslims with a similar spirit of Realpolitik; in a world dominated by two
countries perceived by most Muslims as unfriendly to themselves, they respond to outside pressure by taking sides with whomever appears to threaten
less. Which country has less malevolent intentions, which must be accommodated more? Aversions to liberalism and Marxism, to the United States and

the USSR being about equal, Muslims who must choose a bloc commit themselves only slightly.

Although nonaligned nations exist everywhere, only in the Middle East do *even the aligned nations hold back,* unwilling to aid the United States or the USSR more than minimally. The reluctance of a Saudi Arabia or an Iraq contrasts with the behavior of aligned regions in other regions, for example, the Germanies, the Koreas, Thailand and Vietnam, Zaire and Mozambique, or El Salvador and Cuba. American and Soviet attempts to induce greater involvement generally failed in the Middle East in the face of an Islamicate reluctance.

Domestic Opposition. Sharp local reaction often follows should a Muslim government associate itself too closely with either of the super-powers. This is what happened in Iraq in the 1950s and the presence of American and British air bases in Libya was a major factor in the overthrow of King Idris in 1969. In Iran, Shah Mohammed Reza Pahlevi viewed Soviet intentions in the Persian Gulf with a suspicion similar to Washington's; in cooperating with America, however, he became so closely identified with U.S. interests that his enemies could convincingly portray him as a puppet of Washington, a ruler who had sold out to foreign interests. This accusation acquired great importance in the late 1970s and contributed directly to the success of the revolution. A similar feeling of betrayal motivated Anwar as-Sadat's assassins, who saw him giving American interests priority over those of Egypt. Anti-NATO sentiments have always been strong in Turkey, though poorly represented in he government. Close American ties to Morocco in the early 1980s threatened to provoke a domestic reaction.

Syrian leaders agreed, after years of acrobatic non-alignment, to sign a friendship treaty with the Soviet Union in 1980 and they began to toe Moscow's line more closely after that (for example, voting with the Soviets on the Afghanistan issue at the United Nations). Hafiz al-Asad made these concessions at a moment of weakness, when economic woes, internal opposition, over-commitments in Lebanon, poor relations with Iraq and Jordan, and tension with Israel made it hard to resist Soviet pressure. Violent anger against these close relations subsequently increased within Syria, leading to the assassination of high-ranking Soviet officials and spurring anti-government disturbances. When the pro-Soviet Afghan government which took power in 1973 drifted toward neutralism, Moscow had a key role in arranging for a more friendly regime to take over in 1978. Afghans showed massive opposition to the new government through the mujahidin rebellion. The more Kabul relied on Russia for assistance, the less support it could mobilize at home. Mujibur Rahman of Bangladesh was seen to be drawing too close to India and the USSR, contributing to the coup against him in 1975.

161

Attempts to establish a partnership between Muslims and the West, assuming anything more than a short-term community of interests, are grievously mistaken and both sides lose—a lesson that should have been learnt from the American relationship with the shah or with Sadat. It would be even more of a mistake for the democracies to rally Muslim states against the USSR, an idea that won some support following the Soviet invasion of Afghanistan. Any feelings aroused against the Communists, whether of a legalist or autonomist nature, would then rebound against the West too; kafirs have no business meddling in these highly charged domains. Muslim and non-Muslim alike are better off with such passions subdued.

CONFLICT

Emotionally, Muslims distinguish sharply between war within Dar al-Islam and war outside it. Simply put, fighting against Muslims feels wrong, against non-Muslims it feels right.[19] This sentiment does not prevent intra-Muslim war, *fitna,* but embues it with a reluctance that is absent when Muslims fight kafirs. At some level, all Muslims are attached to the umma, its unity, and its internal peace. When Muslims do go to war against co-religionists, such as Jordan and the Palestine Liberation Organization (P.L.O.) in 1970, East and West Pakistan in 1971–72, Iraq and Iran in 1980, and the Yemens every so often, both combatants regret spilling the blood of fellow-believers. The sanctions Arab states took against Egypt in 1979 to punish it for the peace treaty with Israel were specifically aimed at government, not the populace. Muslims at war with each other always emphasize that they are fighting only an evil regime, not its subjects; Iraq pinpointed Khomeini and his clique as the enemy and Iran inveighed against the "Saddamists," while both sides praised the other country's fraternal population. This distinction was taken to an extreme in January 1983, when the Iraqi vice-premier, Tariq 'Aziz, visited an Iranian opposition leader, Mas'ud Rajavi, in exile outside Paris and the two issued a joint statement condemning the aggressiveness of Khomeini's regime. Only because the two leaders had full confidence in their populaces feeling affection for each other, despite the war, could they make this meeting public.

The umma's response to intra-Muslim warfare tends to be cheerless but helpful—efforts are made to bring the fighting to a quick halt by sending peace missions, convening Arab and Islamic bodies, and bringing moral pressure on the warring parties to end their hostilities. Muslims consider such wars to be the result of misunderstandings, for Muhammad's people have no disputes that must be settled by force of arms. Similarly, Muslim populaces almost never find the prospect of fighting co-religionists appealing; they go to war when ordered to, but without enthusiasm. Hostilities against Muslims do not serve as a means to mobilize the people or to tie them to the government. Muslim solidarity is exhibited against non-Muslims only.

Wars against kafir governments do feel proper, being part of a millennial struggle. Even when Muslims have no intention of applying Shar'i precepts, some Islamicate elements exist. The goal might be to win booty, advance a career, further communal interests or national power, but a sense of jihad is always present. For example, the predominantly Muslim faction in the Lebanese civil war espoused a leftist ideology inimical to the Shari'a, yet an autonomist spirit pervaded its conflict with the Christians for control of the country. The same spirit inspired the leftist Muslim rebels in Chad, Eritrea, the Ogaden, Afghanistan, Thailand, and the Philippines, as well as the Marxist Muslims of the P.L.O. It made little difference who the non-Muslim enemy was: Christians aroused the most widespread hostility, but so too on occasion did Jews, Hindus, Buddhists, Confucians, and animists. The great popularity of jihad makes it useful for Muslim rulers trying to gain support or to mobilize the citizenry. For many years, posturing against Israel served this function throughout the Arab countries; in more local ways, Ethiopia and India filled the same role; and the United States and the Soviet Union provided an external target anywhere the need was felt.

Conflicts with non-Muslim governments are of several recurring types; these are listed here from the most offensive to the most defensive.

1. Attack non-Muslims. A military attack on portions of Dar al-Harb where no Muslims at all live is theoretically possible in the twentieth century, but this type of war has disappeared. Probably the last major military offensive by Muslims into a new area was going into southern India in the sixteenth century; since then, the umma has been on the defensive. Farfetched as it sounds, there is some sentiment to reclaim Spain, lost to Isabella and Ferdinand in 1492, represented by the Society for the Return of Islam to Spain.

2. Dominate non-Muslims (small minority). Where Muslims constitute under one-quarter of the population, they sometimes try to rule, usually in regions that had once been part of Dar al-Islam. Idi Amin's efforts to assert Muslim control of Uganda fitted this pattern as did the Arab struggle with Israel. In both cases, Muslims constituted about 10 percent of the population, yet they felt entitled to rule because of their earlier claims. Other places where this sentiment had force were Cyprus, Zanzibar, and India. For example, Fazal Karim Khan Durrani wrote as late as 1944 that "India, the whole of it, is . . . our heritage and it must be reconquered for Islam."[20] Cameroon, where Muslims make up only one-sixth of the population, was ruled for over two decades by a Muslim, making this probably the smallest Muslim community of recent times peaceably to control a country.

3. Dominate non-Muslims (moieties). Muslim populations making up be-

tween 25 and 85 percent of the country usually try to rule. In Nigeria, the Muslims had an unsteady control of the government most of the time after independence in 1960. Muslims had no say in the central government of Chad at the time of independence from the French, but they took it over through a civil war starting in 1968. The Sudanese government fought for almost seventeen years to assert its control over the non-Muslim region in the south of the country. Muslim impatience with Christian domination was the critical factor in the Lebanese civil war which began in 1975. In Malaysia, keeping control of the central government in Kuala Lumpur was a constant preoccupation of the Muslim political parties.

4. Secede from non-Muslim rule. Where non-Muslim control of the central government is unshakeable, Muslims opt out of the state by fighting for their independence or by attaching themselves to an existing Muslim state. Secession efforts are most likely among Muslim populations who live in compact areas; thus did the scattered Turks of Cyprus retreat to one portion of the island in 1974. For funds, materiel, and safe haven it helps to live close to some part of Dar al-Islam; and the perception of being backward also spurs armed revolt.

Besides Cyprus, recent Muslim attempts to gain autonomy have taken place in the Eritrean and Ogaden districts of Ethiopia, in the far northeast of Kenya, in the Indian province of Kashmir, in the Thai province of Pattani, and on the southern Philippine islands. Efforts in this direction have not gone beyond the riot stage in the Kosovo region of Yugoslavia, in the West Bank and Gaza areas under Israeli control, and in the Arakan region of Burma. Any of these, however, can quickly escalate. Annexation into an existing state of Dar al-Islam has not recently been pursued, though it is a possibility in several parts of Islamdom. Muslims of Kenya and Ethiopia could join Somalia, Cypriot Turks could become a province of Turkey, the Muslims of Lebanon could become Syrians again, and the Muslims of Thailand have considered joining Malaysia.

Muslim minorities tend to find rule by distant kafirs more tolerable than rule by neighboring kafirs; better to be part of a European empire than to be under the thumb of traditional antagonists. Quiet under the British Empire, Muslims in Cyprus, Palestine, and India rebelled at the prospect of becoming a permanent minority in a democratic state dominated by Greeks, Jews, or Hindus. In the first two cases, their efforts were facilitated by assistance from, respectively, the independent Turkish and Arab states.

5. Win a better deal. Where the non-Muslim state is too strong or Muslims are too diffuse for a revolt, Muslims often seek to improve their status by pressuring the authorities, sometimes violently, for more political representation, more government spending, and increased cultural rights. This was the case

in the province of Bosnia in Yugoslavia, among the Arabs living in Israel proper (notably in the Galilee), among the Turks and Iranians of the Soviet Union, among the non-Kashmiri Muslims of India, the Moors of Sri Lanka, the Rohingyas of Burma, and the Turks and the Hui of China. Muslims are more inclined to organize along confessional lines in such circumstances than are adherents of other religions.

6. Defend Muslim rule. Just as modern Muslims no longer attack territories where no Muslims live, so did kafir attacks on Dar al-Islam nearly come to an end after World War II (though they had been extremely common during the colonial era). The Afghan rebellion after the Soviet invasion of December 1979 stands out as an exception.

Warfare against non-Muslims brings out pan-Islamic impulses, prompting Muslim leaders to help their co-religionists, sometimes even at great distances. The Arab conflict with Israel received the widest, most voluble international backing; in some form, every Arab state and many non-Arab Muslim states participated, if only to the extent of economic boycott and verbal solidarity. The Algerian revolt against the French received help from several Arab states, especially Tunisia and Egypt; Turkey aided the Cypriot Turks to win autonomy from the Greeks; Egypt, the Sudan, Syria, Iraq, and Saudi Arabia supported Eritreans against the Ethiopian government; Egypt, Saudi Arabia, Iran, and Pakistan helped the Afghan mujahidin; Libya, Saudi Arabia, and Malaysia sustained the Pattani and Moro revolts. Arab states of the Middle East supplied most assistance for fighting non-Muslims, especially Egypt in the 1960s and Libya and Saudi Arabia in the 1970s.

Confronted with the Islamicate drive for autonomy, non-Muslims respond in similar ways. Indeed, the consistency of their reaction provides striking testimony to the thesis that Muslim actions follow like patterns. Non-Muslims object to living under Muslim rule about as much as Muslims resent non-Muslim rule. In many cases, the two populations disengage from each other, either through territorial division or through the exchange of populations. Non-Muslims living in Dar al-Islam sometimes extricate themselves by moving the boundaries. Maronites and other Christians of Mt. Lebanon convinced the French mandatory authorities to split their territory from Syria's so they would escape Muslim domination. Singapore, with a Chinese majority, went its separate way as independent city-state rather than stay part of Malaysia with its Muslim majority. The southern Sudan, inhabited by Christians and animists, failed to win a separate independence either at the time of the British withdrawal or subsequently through force of arms against the Muslim North. Other unsuccessful efforts included those by the Ibos in Nigeria (the Biafran war), the Armenians in Turkey, and several of the non-Muslim peoples in Indonesia.

165

Alternatively, Muslims and non-Muslims exchange populations and move to more hospitable states. When, after World War I, Greece and Turkey wanted to expel each other's population, they made religion, not language, the determinant factor: Greek-speaking Muslims went to Turkey and Turkish-speaking Christians to Greece. On Cyprus in the 1970s, Turks and Greeks again exchanged populations along religious lines. Huge transfers of population accompanied the partition of India in 1947, significantly reducing the numbers of Hindus in the areas that became Pakistan but leaving large minorities in India and Bangladesh. Jews and Arabs moved in about equal numbers during the years surrounding the establishment of Israel.

A contrary strategy is for non-Muslims to wrest a region from Dar al-Islam by settling it. In the nineteenth century, Frenchmen settled in Algeria, Ethiopians in the lowlands neighboring their territories, Russians in the Caucasus and Central Asia, and Chinese in Kansu and Sinkiang. The success of this policy is shown by the fact that except for the French in Algeria, all the other colonists are still present. In the twentieth century the Philippine government encouraged Christians to move to Mindanao to reduce its Muslim character and the Thais urged Buddhists to the Pattani region. The Zionists used settlements as the way to establish their hold over Palestine before independence, and after 1967, the Israeli government followed similar policies in the territories captured from Egypt, Jordan, and Syria.

Non-Muslims who rule Muslims often seek strategems to temper or eliminate autonomist urges. They have two broad options: to crush all signs of an independent spirit or to win the loyalties of Muslims as full citizens. Harsh treatment is tried more often and proves less successful. The French hoped to keep Algeria as a part of France by destroying Islamic culture, running a repressive state, and excluding Muslims from power. In Chad, the Christians and animists who ran the government after independence followed a similarly unsuccessful approach to the Muslims of the North. In Ethiopia, Christian control over the country was nearly total and consistently repressive. In Cyprus and Lebanon, Christians excluded Muslims from the power that was commensurate with their numbers; in Burma and Thailand, Buddhist majorities pursued stern policies. The ineffectiveness of this approach can be seen in the fact that in each of these cases Muslims took up arms.

More flexible policies work better. The Yugoslav authorities made special economic concessions to Muslims, especially those living in Kosovo; similarly, the Israeli and Soviet governments bettered the Muslims' standard of living in the hope of preventing political discontent. The Congress Party of India went out of its way to cultivate the Muslim vote, with some success; in return, Muslims won advantages such as being able to retain the Shar'i personal laws and having the president of the country chosen twice from their number. Philippine governments alternately pursued harsh and lenient policies toward the Moros since the sixteenth century; the latest attempt to win Muslim support followed the signing of a treaty with the Moro forces in 1976. In China, Muslims fared well or ill along with the many other minorities; the Communist regime at first gave them privileges, cut back on these during the late 1950s, then reinstated them after the Cultural Revolution. Muslims, for example, were not subject to the draconian laws restricting population growth which were applied to the Han peoples.

Behind the more flexible approach lay an assumption that education, economic opportunities, and freedom to maintain Islamic traditions would attract Muslim allegiance. For example, one writer concludes a history of the Muslims in southern Thailand with this observation: "The problems of the Thai-Muslims in the four southern provinces will remain [perennially] so long as the Government [in Bangkok] maintains its negligent attitude and thus reveals its inability to apply the right medicine to this socio-political malady."[21] But this is expecting too much; whereas liberal treatment of Muslims clearly keeps them more content, it is illusory to expect such a policy to win a kafir government the ultimate loyalties of Muslims; this contravenes the Islamicate legacy too directly. The problem arises most acutely when Muslims watch their non-Muslim rulers make war against a Muslim state, creating acute dilemmas of divided loyalty. Muslims in Singapore were not expected to perform military service. The Israeli government did not require its Arab citizens to serve in the military, nor did the Ethiopians use Muslims against Somalia. Soviet Muslim soldiers fraternized with the Afghans, prompting their recall and substitution by non-Muslim troops, while Indian Muslims served near China far more often than along the Pakistani or Bangladeshi borders.

Flexible treatment of Muslims aims more at making them docile than at winning their loyalty. Keeping Muslim citizens tranquil in Dar al-Harb requires a constant vigilance; the policy most likely to succeed is one tolerating multiplicity within a strictly national context. Too much tolerance or too much strictness spells trouble. Raphael Israeli's observation about China applies everywhere: "The two opposite extremes of 'crash integration' and 'lax liberalization' have historically brought about the same result—the rise of Muslim separatism."[22] The "political indigestibility" of Muslim subjects makes them a permanent source of concern to non-Muslim rulers.[23]

The Islamicate legacy is the prism through which modern Muslims perceive public life; while the size of that prism varies from one region to the next, the Middle Eastern one being the largest, its shape is remarkably similar throughout Islamdom. The next chapter assesses how the distortions of that prism affected Muslim efforts to modernize.

8

Muslim Anomie

> The fundamental *malaise* of modern Islam is a sense that something has gone wrong with Islamic history.
> —*Wilfred Cantwell Smith*

WHEN THE EUROPEANS set out to explore the world, they encountered peoples at two levels of development, the primitive and the civilized. Primitive peoples were those who lacked written languages, cities, and bureaucracies; who had weak resistance to diseases; and who had meager military, financial, and technical resources. They could not resist the encroachment of European armies or culture. Indigenous folkways (such as basket weaving or story telling) remained but almost everything else—art forms, literary languages, political culture—were heavily influenced by Europe. The Indians of the Americas, Africans south of the Sahara, and the peoples of Oceania and Siberia adopted much from the West, including its religion.

In contrast, the civilized peoples were those participating in high cultures, who put up more resistance to Europe, both militarily and culturally, and who encountered more difficulty in coming to terms with Western ways. Until 1800, Chinese, Indian and Islamicate civilizations enjoyed roughly the same social power as Europe and possessed full civilizations—with cities, classic traditions, written languages, historical records, and formal institutions—which could compete with Europe's. Of these three peoples, the Muslims had much the hardest time coping with Europe's primacy, however; factors that mitigated the European impact for others were absent for them, and virtually anything that could present problems did so. Civilized peoples faced more difficulties than primitive peoples and Muslims faced more than the other civilized peoples. In short, Muslims experienced the greatest travails in coping with modernity; this was the special Muslim dilemma.

Two points bear emphasis. First, this dilemma did not follow necessarily from the religion of Islam, but rather from the interaction between Islam and the Muslim historical experience; attitudes and institutions burdened the umma much more than did the Qur'an. Second, the causes of the dilemma corresponded, not surprisingly, to the legalist and autonomist categories which are being discussed throughout this book. Culturally, specific qualities of Islamicate civilization were incompatible with those of the West; politically, the drive for autonomy and the hostile legacy with Europe inhibited Muslim acknowledgment of Europe's primacy. Let us begin with the latter.

Hostility with Europe

Mutual antagonism obstructed Muslim adaptation to modernity by keeping the Europeans away, and therefore making them unavailable to the Muslims as models; and by making it psychologically extremely difficult for Muslims to accept the ways of these enemies.

MUSLIM RESISTANCE TO EUROPEAN RULE

Islamic autonomist impulses made Islamdom a special place in European eyes and prompted northern Europeans to avoid it during the centuries between the crusading fervor of the 1400s and the age of imperialism in the 1800s. For some three centuries, they settled and traded mostly in places where the Muslims were not, such as the New World, sub-Saharan Africa, and East Asia. The pattern of avoidance was striking; the Dutch, British, French, and Russians ruled remote territories in Asia and the Americas before they confronted their neighbors in North Africa and the Middle East, just across the Mediterranean Sea or the Kazakh steppes. It was not until 1830—four centuries after the Portuguese reached sub-Saharan Africa, three centuries after Saint Francis Xavier went on missions to India and Japan, two centuries after colonists founded Plymouth, Massachusetts, and Capetown, South Africa, and one century after the Russians surveyed the whole Siberian coast—that the French invaded Algeria; even then, they needed seventeen years just to pacify the coastal region. The remainder of the North African littoral fell to European control yet later: Tunisia in 1881, Egypt in 1882, southern Algeria in 1900, Libya in 1911, and Morocco in 1912, and the Muslims offered resistance in each of these regions. The Middle East fell still later: Palestine in 1917, Lebanon, Syria, and Jordan in 1918, and Iraq and parts of Turkey in 1919.

169

Europeans went around Islamdom because Muslims resisted foreign control with more determination and constancy than did non-Muslims. Occasional encounters with Muslims along the coasts of West and East Africa, India, and the islands of Southeast Asia foreshadowed the bad relations that were to follow. Islamic autonomism accounted for this in part. Also, the hostility initiated in the Mediterranean reappeared later in distant places; battles begun in Palestine and Spain were subsequently resumed in Goa and Sumatra. Christians instinctively treated Muslims as adversaries, and Muslims responded with steady resistance. The first region in which Europeans attempted to subjugate Muslims was the Philippines, a country whose history exemplifies the dramatic contrast between Muslim and non-Muslim reactions to European expansion.

Muslims first arrived on the Philippine archipelago as traders in the tenth century and were followed by Islamic missionaries about three hundred years later. Many tribesmen of the southernmost islands were converted, so that by the mid-fifteenth century the island of Sulu had emerged as a leading center of Islam. In subsequent decades, Muslim rule reached as far as Luzon, the northern island, though when the Spanish explorer Magellan arrived in 1521, the Islamic faith had gained a firm hold only in the south. The Spanish government under Charles V (r. 1517–56) virtually ignored the archipelago but Philip II (r. 1556–98) did take an interest—as the name of the country commemorates to this day. In 1564 Philip dispatched Miguel López de Legazpi to pacify the islands and make them Christian. Legazpi won Manila from the Muslims in 1571 and then captured all of Luzon. Other islands fell in rapid succession and by 1600 most of the archipelago had submitted to Spain. The pagan inhabitants accepted Spanish dominion with little resistance; after the conquest, they quickly accepted the Spaniards' language, religion, culture and institutions.

Only the Muslims resisted. Located on the islands of Mindanao, Palawan, and on the Sulu chain, the Moros (the name for Filipino Muslims, from the Spanish word for Moors) turned away all attempts at pacification or conversion during one-third of a millennium, much after the rest of the country had settled into docile tranquility. Unlike the pagans, they fought Spain in long and vicious wars. In the sixteenth century, the Spaniards pursued a strategy of containing Islam's expansion and in the seventeenth they tried to Christianize the south; in 1700–50 they tried but failed to tempt the Moros with a policy of lenience and attraction; Spanish attacks temporarily broke Moro power at times during 1750–1850; from 1850 to 1890 Spain tried again to subdue the Moros through force; and in 1890–98, the last years of Spain's presence, the occupation was marked by panic and intolerance as the Philippines slipped from Spain's grasp. When the United States took control of the country in 1898, it inherited the Moro problem (viewed as a variant on its Indian troubles at home), and two years later launched a full-scale assault on them. At last, in 1913, General John Pershing of World War I fame subjugated them, using the full array of modern technology, including steamships, the .45 caliber revolver, and dumdum bullets. After three and a half centuries, the Muslims had finally been vanquished. Even this was not permanent, however, as violence broke out anew in 1972, once again over the issue of Manila's control over the Muslim regions in the south.[1]

Uneager to get embroiled in struggles of this sort, the Europeans did not try to control Islamdom, except for the Balkans, parts of Central Asia, and some coastal areas. Only in the late eighteenth century, when their power had become overwhelming, did the Christians challenge the umma head on. Even then, Islamic autonomism made the governance of Muslims especially difficult. Hoping to avoid the problems associated with kafir rule and Dar al-Harb, the Europeans experimented with different methods of indirect rule. Napoleon controlled Egypt through local intermediaries and Lyautey left the monarchy intact in Morocco. But it was the British who developed indirect government into a system and made it standard practice in Islamdom. They began this in Calcutta, where the Nabob of Bengal reigned while the British ruled. As British control extended to the whole of India, the same procedure was followed; thus, even as the Mughal emperor accepted funds for his household expenses from the British Resident, coins continued to be minted in his name, replete with his ornate titles. The British subsequently used this technique in northern Nigeria, Egypt, the Persian Gulf statelets, Iraq, southern Iran, Malaya, and other Muslim regions. And the Russians followed suit in Central Asia.

For similar reasons, the Europeans encouraged application of the Shari'a, often increasing its scope and authority from what it had been under Muslim rule. Colonial administrators understood the law's central importance to Muslim life and tried to avoid antagonizing Muslim sentiments by ignoring it or altering it. European rule brought printing and other methods of communication which encouraged standardization of the Shari'a; it also brought improved transportation, thus allowing Muslims to travel in greater numbers to Mecca and putting them in touch with the fundamentalists centered there. Also, as rulers, the Europeans found a single written code more manageable than a multiplicity of oral ones, so they encouraged application of the Shari'a. To make the law more practical, they even reworked it; British scholars in India and French scholars in Algeria codified the Shari'a, introducing legal practices from their own countries and making it into a national law applied by the government along the lines of a European state law. But the Europeans did not apply all parts of the Shari'a, only those useful to their rule; they ignored provisions irrelevant to them (the ban on alcohol), repugnant to them (slavery or the cutting off of hands as punishment), or restricting their authority (the ceilings on taxation).

Recognizing the vital role of Islamic autonomism in inspiring opposition to colonial rule, imperial administrators treated the religion seriously and with great care. Many great colonial careers were established by coping with Muslim antagonism, such as those of Robert Clive and Warren Hastings in Bengal, Thomas Raffles in Indonesia, Evelyn Baring (Lord Cromer) in Egypt, Louis Lyautey in Morocco, Frederick Lugard in several parts of Africa, especially Nigeria, and Christiaan Snouck Hurgronje in Indonesia. T. E. Lawrence in Arabia had a similar assignment. Most of the administrators saw Islam as an implacable enemy of European control and responded by devising strategies to neutralize its force. Probably the best articulated of these was Snouck Hurgronje's Ethical Policy, which was implemented by the Dutch government in the East Indies between 1896 and 1906. Snouck Hurgronje, an eminent Orientalist, made a distinction between Islam as a private devotion and Islam as a political bond, encouraging the first and repressing the second; thus he promoted private Shar'i precepts and banned the public ones. In effect, he adopted the policy that Muslims apply to Christians under their control as dhimmis and reversed it. Muslims could freely practice their religion on the condition that they remained politically submissive. But this policy failed even in Indonesia which was remote from the Muslim heartlands and only weakly Islamicate. Proof of its ineffectiveness came only a few years later, in 1912, when Muslim activists founded the Sarekat Islam organization to expel the Dutch. Neither the Ethical Policy nor other maneuvers succeeded in defanging Islam; Muslims resisted rule by Christians regardless how the Europeans imposed it.

Areas of Islamdom settled by Europeans, namely, Algeria, Israel, and Central Asia, persistently resisted European control. All three had been part of Dar al-Islam since the first years of Islam, all of them had long traditions of city culture, including literacy, higher education, complex political institutions, and access to high Islamicate culture. In the late nineteenth century, the Europeans moved into these regions, drawn by relative human emptiness and fine farm lands (or, in the case of Palestine, nationalism). The French, Zionists, and Russians attempted to re-orient these regions away from Islam and toward Europe by imposing their own languages, laws, mores, and religions (or, in the Soviet period, atheism). These efforts all met great resistance; even when Muslims spoke French or Russian (Hebrew was spoken only rarely) and lived in a Westernized context, they still preserved a distinct culture. Muslims kept their distance from Western culture, very infrequently adopting such European traits as personal names, laws, languages, or religion. By tacit accord, Europeans and Muslims hardly intermingled: there were very few conversions from Islam, little intermarriage, and scarcely any political alignment with the outsiders. As a result, Muslims could maintain their identity and not lose sight of the ultimate goal of rejoining Dar al-Islam. The Algerians eventually ousted the French; the Palestinians began agitating against Zionism in the 1920s; and while the Central Asians have been quiet since the Basmachi revolt in the 1920s, some day they too will undoubtedly also try to evict their European masters.

The religious gulf was especially important. Outside Islamdom, Christian missionaries from Europe usually succeeded in making converts. Whether for spiritual reasons or material ones, substantial numbers of American Indians, Africans, Hindus, Buddhists, and Confucians accepted the Gospels. But Muslims did not; the umma rejected Christianity. The pride of being Muslim and the severe legal and social consequences of apostasy daunted all but a tiny number. The few communities of Muslims to apostacize did so under duress or with expectation of specific gain. In seventeenth-century Russia, a regulation prohibiting non-Christians from owning serfs led to the conversion of rich Tatars, including the ancestors of such luminaries as the musician Sergei Rachmaninoff, the poet and historian Nicholas Karamzin, and the novelist Ivan Turgenyev. Around 1700, some ruling families among the Sunni Muslims in Lebanon converted to Christianity to increase their political standing. But such cases were extremely rare.

Subjugation to Europe worsened Muslim feelings about the Christians. If a Lyautey or a Snouck Hurgronje carefully avoided arousing Islamic autonomist sentiments, most imperial administrators allowed their personal hostility for Islam to show, provoking anger among the colonized Muslims. Worse yet, Europeans often pressed their religion on the Muslims and ignored the outraged Muslim responses. The mere presence of Christian missionaries in solidly Muslim areas, especially in the Middle East, incensed Muslims, who saw them as part of a plan to destroy Islam. Missionary schools, which molded the minds of the young, appeared particularly dangerous. Muslim fears were not mitigated by the paucity of converts; to many, "it was missionary activities closely allied with the expansion of imperial power that represented the real challenge to Islam."[2]

EUROPEAN HOSTILITY TO ISLAM

When the Christian states subjugated Islamdom, the old Islamphobia was replaced by disdain. Islam lost its sting. Dominion over Muslims permitted lighter, even whimsical attitudes; the Orient became a subject of romance and playful intrigue in the early nineteenth century.

As anti-Christian strains of thought developed in the Enlightenment, traditional forms of Christian hostility lost their hold. Enlightenment thinkers saw Islam as no more false than Christianity itself and some of them, such as Voltaire, even preferred Islam to Christianity. Their attitudes led to other reassessments: intellectuals came to see Islam as a vehicle for their disaffection, leftists espoused Muslim causes against European imperialism, and Orientalists made efforts to study Islam and the Muslims with a detached, scientific spirit. As these new views spread, popular attitudes became less antagonistic and less excitable. The old fear of violence by Muslims subsided, as did the anger at the deceit of their religion and the offense at their sexual practices.

They subsided but did not disappear: Christian attitudes retained their historic cast, in large part due to persistent Muslim resistance to Western armies and civilization. The states of Europe found it especially difficult to subjugate Muslims. Just as the Spanish failed to conquer the Muslim Filipinos, other colonial powers also encountered special difficulties in Islamdom: the French faced strenuous resistance in parts of Muslim West Africa, as did the Germans in East Africa, the Russians in the Caucasus, the British in Afghanistan, and the Dutch in Sumatra. The Muslims' resistance gave them a bad name in Europe. Worse yet was when Muslims threatened Westerners, causing archaic stereotypes to resurface. Incidents such as the Black Hole of Calcutta in 1756, the Indian Mutiny of 1857–58, the Bulgarian Horrors of 1876, and the murder of Charles ("Chinese") Gordon by the Sudanese Mahdi's troops in 1885 aroused atavistic hostilities (as even the hysterical language used to describe these events implies).

Ironically, even when the umma fell to the Europeans, anti-Muslim feelings were exacerbated. Conquered Muslims resisted Western culture, confirming European mistrust. Their unwillingness to accept the Gospel was most important in this regard. Muslims had never apostacized in numbers, but so long as Islamdom enjoyed rough political and cultural parity with Europe, conversion had not been expected and its absence was not an issue. The Crusades, the Spanish *reconquista,* and the Holy Alliance of 1815 aimed more to expel Muslims than to win them over. In the course of the nineteenth century, however, an expanding and confident Europe expected converts from Islam, and the fact that so few came over became a source of increasing resentment. Muslim tenacity especially exasperated the missionaries—those interlocutors who so influenced European attitudes toward the rest of the world. Not being able to convert more than a handful of Muslims through a lifetime of effort generated a bitterness among missionaries which was then transmitted to other Europeans. Thus, "empire increased the inherited suspicion of Islam."[3]

To make matters worse, Islam continued to expand to new areas. Sufis and traders won about as many converts to the Crescent as did the Christian missionaries to the Cross, much distressing the latter. Although Islam had steadily attracted converts in the Balkans, Africa, India, and Southeast Asia in prior centuries without arousing West European ire, again these appeared differently in the nineteenth century, when Europeans expected to roll Islam back. Even today, the two religions compete for the souls of heathens in parts of Africa and Southeast Asia, and Islam remains Christianity's only rival. The effect of all this was to repulse Europeans. As Norman Daniel observes, "actual experience of a religion and culture which, even when it welcomed progress, resisted assimilation, did nothing to modify existing disapproval, except on occasions to intensify it."[4]

Adopting to new circumstances, the medieval attitudes toward Islam were transformed and modernized. It often happens that old prejudices are adapted to new contexts; the rationale for animosity changes but emotions remain constant. This was, for example, what happened to the anti-Jewish legacy among Christians. What was traditionally anti-Judaism (hatred of the Jews' religion) evolved in the Enlightenment into anti-Semitism (contempt for the supposed racial characteristics of Semites) and after World War II became anti-Zionism (obsessive hostility toward the state of Israel). The image of the Jew changed from Christ-killer to moneylender to imperialist and the animus changed from theological to racial to national; but basic feelings about Jews remained fundamentally unchanged.

Christian attitudes toward Muslims developed in similar ways, at about the same times. Long-standing religious hostility lost its force in the eighteenth century, replaced by a cultural antagonism, as Europeans manifested an "awareness of their higher material civilisation, the belief in their higher moral system, and the application of a double standard of judgement."[5] Muslims had long represented a force poised to destroy Christendom; now they appeared poor, blighted, backward, and in need of European supervision and rule. "The myths of empire took the place of the myths of Crusade."[6] Muslims became less frightening, to be sure, but not less unpleasant. "A doctrinal hostility was superseded by a vaguer disapproval that arose in the course of actual contact."[7] Disdain lost ground after the Second World War and the breakup of the West European empires. Having developed in the heydey of colonial rule, Europe's self-assured feelings lasted only so long as Muslims remained unthreatening. When the umma increasingly reasserted itself, traditional Western attitudes re-emerged. The violent rejection of Israel by the Arabs, the Algerian war of independence, Abdul Nasser's nationalization of the Suez Canal, P.L.O. hijackings, the aggressive pricing policies of OPEC, the Arab oil embargo of 1973, the kidnapping of a French female anthropologist in Chad, and the Iranian Revolution all contributed to the sense that Muslims had resumed their historic role as a peril for the West.

Even though the religious element had a much smaller role than in previous centuries, "the medieval concept [of Islam] remained enormously durable [and] is still part of the cultural inheritance of the West today."⁸ For many Westerners traditional themes (false belief, violence, licentiousness, and fanaticism) still characterized Islam and the Muslims. Islamic doctrines aroused ridicule even among non-believing Europeans and Americans; and age-old myths—Muhammad an epileptic, Arabs burning the library at Alexandria, "the Koran or the sword"—yet had life in them. Lascivious fantasies about Muslims continued to captivate: veiled women with mischievous eyes, life in the harem, and the "white slave trade" which shipped innocent blonds off for ravishment by Arabs. Sexual associations gained even greater currency during the oil boom with the publication of sensational exposes about "the secret lives of the oil sheikhs."⁹ The theme of violence also flourished, as warfare and terrorism made the Middle East especially volatile. The ongoing acrimony concerning Israel's existence made Arab aggressiveness a front-page story for decades. Photographs of Afghans armed only with rifles attacking Soviet helicopter gunships confirmed Occidental stereotypes. And the fact that Muslim disputes often spilled into the West—the assassination of Robert Kennedy, the Olympic massacre in Munich, bloodshed in the streets of London and Paris, an attempt on Pope John Paul II's life—did not diminish this image.

On both sides, the Muslim-Christian relationship was a source of unique animosity. Although premodern Muslims had no special concern with Europe, they reacted most sharply against Western control of their lands; for their part, Christians had long singled out the umma for concentrated hostility. Muslims reacted worst to colonialism and Christians reacted worst to Muslims. This mutual hostility impaired the umma's ability to take advantage of opportunities that became available through European conquest.

Male-Female Relations

Conflicting customs in private life also affected Muslim attitudes toward Europe and modernity. The pervasive antinomianism of the West sapped the force of most laws, instilling fears in Muslims that their traditional social restraints would weaken to the point that the influence of the West on relations between the sexes would prevail. Here, as in the political sphere, the two civilizations almost perfectly mismatched and European and American influences caused special anguish in Islamdom. And because Islamicate civilization ties sex directly to the public domain, this had immediate political significance.¹⁰

Until recently, it was assumed in the Christian Occident that men and women experience sex differently. The male was seen as actively undertaking the hunt, seduction, and violation, while the female was thought not to enjoy sex but only to endure it. Only lately, as the West moved further from Christian culture, did the idea gain currency that women too have active sexual desires. When one considers the Muslim reputation for backwardness, it is ironic to note that Islamicate civilization not only portrays the woman as sexually desirous, but sees her as more passionate than the man. Indeed, this understanding determined the place of women in traditional Islamdom.

In the Islamicate view, men and women are seen as partaking of the same sexuality. Both desire intercourse, during which their bodies undergo similar processes, bringing similar pleasures and similar physical climaxes. Unlike traditional Western views of the sexual act, as a battleground where the male exerts his supremacy over the female, Muslims see it as a tender, shared pleasure. Sexual gratification was celebrated by Abu'l-Hamid al-Ghazali (1050–1111), whom many consider the key thinker of Islamicate civilization, as "a foretaste of the delights secured for men in Paradise" and as "a powerful motivation to incite men . . . to adore God so as to reach heaven."[11] Sexual satisfaction leads to a harmonious social order and a flourishing civilization.

Unlike the traditional Western view that women do not enjoy sex, Muslims believe female desires to be yet greater than those of the male. Muslims often see "the woman as the hunter and the man as the passive victim" of her ardor; indeed, sexual needs make her the "symbol of unreason, disorder, the anti-divine force of nature and disciple of the devil."[12] This view may derive from the woman's greater physical capacity for sex or it may go back to Muhammad's experiences. But whatever its origin, female sexuality is thought of as being so powerful that it constitutes a real danger to society. At the same time that Islamicate civilization encourages sexual satisfaction, it also considers unrestrained females the most dangerous challenge facing males trying to carry out God's commands (for it is the men who have the far heavier religious burden). In combination, their rampant desires and their irresistible attractiveness give women a power over men which rivals God's.

Left to themselves, then, men might well fall victim to women and abandon God. *Fitna* would result, that is, civil disorder among believers. Just as distress over the *fitna* between Muslim rulers characterized Muslim attitudes to politics, so did the fear of *fitna* dominate private life. "There is no tension between Islam and sexuality as long as that sexuality is expressed harmoniously and is not frustrated. What Islam views as negative and anti-social is the woman and her power to create *fitna.* "[13] Revealingly, in Arabic, *fitna* is also the term for a beautiful woman, for "whenever a man is faced with a woman, *fitna* might occur."[14] Muslim fears that female lusts would bring on anarchy leads Fatima Mernissi to put women on a par with *harbi*s: "The Muslim order faces two threats: the infidel without and the woman within."[15] If believers feel little distress about sex acts as such, they are obsessed with the dangers posed by women. "The whole Muslim social structure can be seen as an attack on, and a defense against, the disruptive power of female sexuality."[16]

Two points follow from this, both crucial for modern times. First, Islamicate restraints on sexual activity are motivated more by a concern to preserve the social fabric than by moral considerations. Second, Islamicate society developed an array of institutional mechanisms for repressing female sexuality, a "whole system . . . based on the assumption that the woman is a powerful and dangerous being."[17] Its principal elements were keeping women away from men, obstructing romantic love, and rendering females powerless.

Islamicate civilization begins with the assumption that women will seduce any available men, and it structures society in such a manner as to prevent this from happening by creating separate spaces and reducing contact between the sexes. According to the Shari'a, a man and woman who are left alone together in private must be assumed to have engaged in sexual relations; therefore, everything must be done to prevent such situations from occurring. (These expectations are self-fulfilling, of course; Muslims who think they cannot control their sexuality may not even try to.) A physical separation of the sexes thus characterizes daily life in Islamdom; any man and woman considered potentially attractive to each other sexually are kept apart.

Islamicate civilization encourages women to stay indoors and holds up as an ideal the woman who has the servants, home facilities, and social stature so that she need not step outside for decades at a time. Any man who can afford to do so, keeps his women at home. The house itself is structured to keep women out of the way of unrelated men. Islamicate houses have walls on the outside and windows on inner courtyards, thus increasing privacy. Within the house, the harem separates the woman from male areas in the building into which unrelated men may enter.

The veil—"an expression of the invisibility of women on the street"[18]—removes the female from the male space she traverses, for the outdoors belongs to men. As such, she is a trespasser:

A woman is always trespassing in a male space because she is, by definition, a foe. A woman has no right to use male spaces. If she enters them, she is upsetting the male's order and his peace of mind. She is actually committing an act of aggression against him merely by being present where she should not be. A woman in a traditionally male space upsets Allah's order by inciting men to commit *zina* [fornication]. The man has everything to lose in this encounter: peace of mind, self-determination, allegiance to Allah and social prestige.[19]

Women should venture outside only for specific reasons, such as shopping, bathing, or visiting relatives.

If casual contacts between unmarried men and women threaten *fitna*, the equivalent danger among married partners is that of romantic love. It is possible that a man can become so consumed by passion for his wife that he might neglect his duties to God. "Heterosexual involvement, real love, is the danger which must be overcome";[20] Islamicate life therefore undermines the development of strong emotional ties between husband and wife. It reduces contact between them by sharply dividing their interests: men concern themselves with religion and work, women with house and family. The wife usually does not eat with her husband, she does not accompany him outside the house, nor do they spend time with their children together. The husband's wide powers over his wife unbalances their relationship; she is often more his servant than his companion. He can repudiate (divorce) her without notice, or he can marry another woman. Polygyny reduces the probability of developing a single strong bond. Arranged marriages, especially between older men and young girls, reduces the likelihood of companionship. The strength of feeling between mother and son often obstructs relations between the son and his wife; and the latter in turn looks to her son for the fullest emotional bond. To the extent that Islam had an influence, it causes spouses to spend little time together and to reduce their emotional bonds.

Powerlessness also serves to contain a woman's ability to threaten the bases of society. A husband can divorce his wife at will; but to divorce him, she must plead her case before a male magistrate and convince him to pressure the husband to grant *her* a divorce, for she herself cannot undertake legal action against him. A woman acts through a male guardian, her father, husband, brother, or another relative. On her own, she may not travel or work. She even depends on her guardian to get married; in many Islamic wedding ceremonies it is not a man and a woman who make vows to each other but two men, the groom and the bride's guardian. The guardian can annul a marriage she contracts without his permission. The Shari'a values her testimony in court at about half a man's (putting her on a par with slaves and non-Muslims). Other signs of powerlessness include virilocality, the custom of having the wife move to the husband's family, where his interests overwhelm hers, and patriliny, stress on the importance of sons and on physical paternity. Thus, "all sexual institutions (polygamy, repudiation, sexual segregation, etc.) can be perceived as a strategy for containing [female] power."[21]

On the whole, Muslims lived up to the Islamic ideals for male-female relations; and they worked. "The traditional coherence between Muslim ideology and Muslim reality" in matters sexual gave the umma a satisfaction in private matters that was lacking in the public ones.[22] Men did devote more attention

179

to God on the whole than to women, but this required constant vigilance; the fear always persisted that women might break out of their restrictions, lure men away from the Shari'a, and ruin the community. These fears multiplied when Islamdom fell to European control.

Western patterns of male-female relations during recent centuries nearly always conflict with the Islamicate ones, creating a gulf between Islamic ideals and Muslim realities. Westerners do not divide the world into male and female spaces: women go about visible to men, they share the entire house, and they do not shy away from windows facing on the street. Men and women mix socially and adults often find themselves alone with a member of the opposite sex. Keeping women indoors is not an ideal, but romantic love is, encouraging strong bonds between husband and wife. Monogamy, more cumbersome divorce laws, the nuclear family, and marriage between partners of about the same age also encourage the conjugal unit. Western women gradually won legal equality with men, gaining the right to live, work, travel, and marry as they wished. Recent developments in the West go even more directly contrary to Islamicate ways: female tourists traveling alone in Islamdom, mixed bathing in hotels and resorts throughout Islamdom, scanty swim suits, fashionably tight clothing, toleration of public displays of affection, sexual innuendoes in advertising, and pornography in books, movies, and video cassettes.

Each side tends to see the other's practices as barbaric: if Western promiscuity appalls Muslims, King 'Abd al-'Aziz of Saudi Arabia's three hundred wives shock Westerners no less. These differences are not haphazard, but arise from a basic contrast between the Christian and Islamic religions: the stress on ethics versus the stress on laws. Controls on sexual activity directly reflect this difference.

The West restricts sex primarily by embuing men and women with standards of morality and enforces sexual inhibitions through a "strong internalization of sexual prohibitions during the socialization process."[23] Christians have long associated sex with wickedness. "The internalized ethics of premarital chastity and postmarital fidelity will ordinarily suffice to prevent abuse of their liberty through fornication or adultery whenever a favorable opportunity presents itself."[24] Among Westerners for whom the old morality no longer holds, new ethical and personal considerations take its place; although more lax, these too usually restrict sexual activity to a small percentage of possible opportunities.

Muslims, in contrast, depend on "external precautionary safeguards" to restrain the sexes, "secluding their unmarried girls or providing them with duennas or other protective escorts when they go out in public, and to check adultery by such external devices as veiling, seclusion in harems, or constant

surveillance."[25] As has been seen, rather than instill internalized ethical principles, Islam establishes physical boundaries to keep the sexes apart and punishes
transgressions harshly, making it extremely difficult for unmarried persons of
the opposite sex to meet, especially in urban areas. Whereas Western civilization relies on private guilt to deter misdeeds, the Islamicate depends on feelings
of public shame.

This difference creates problems for people who look to the sacred law for
guidance in daily life, for they often lose their bearings when confronted with
internalized ethical restraints. Accustomed to the innumerable regulations of
the Shar'i way of life, Muslims expect to be checked by their environment.
Not surprisingly, Muslims of both sexes who find themselves in Westernized
circumstances often misunderstand the ground rules, interpreting the freedom
there as license to do what they please; this can lead to unacceptable behavior.
Thus might a Muslim man misunderstand the apparent availability of Western
women and be astonished by their outraged reactions to his advances.

Western practices invariably attract some Muslims, including women who
want the freedom and rights of their Western counterparts and men lured by
the excitement of greater contact with women, both spatially and emotionally.
(It might be noted, however, that Muslim men often expect to keep their old
power intact.) Others deeply fear the effects of Western influences: for fundamentalists, bringing the sexes together threatens to undermine the male ability
to keep the Shari'a; non-fundamentalists see the problem in more diffuse, Islamicate ways—yet for all, unregulated contact between men and women
threatens the foundations of communal life. Resistance to Western influences
has less to do with morality than with fears of unleashed forces that would
destroy Islamicate society. Reluctance to accept Western ways is thus inspired
mostly by political concerns and Muslims see "any change in male-female relations [as] a threat to the Umma's strength."[26] Apprehension about the political
dimension of relations between the sexes permeates Muslim life. Thus, a Moroccan man wrote in a letter to a counseling service in 1971, describing the
difficulties he faced marrying the woman he loved: "I cannot conceive of my
life without this girl anymore and if I try to part with her I might find myself
in a situation which is dangerous not only for me but for the Muslim Umma
as well, and for the Muslim religion too." When a scandal involving factory
girls posing for nude pictures came to the attention of the chief minister of
Selangor State in Malaysia, he responded by calling it a matter "as dangerous
as communism and the threat posed by criminals."[27]

Western influences on relations between the sexes affect much more than
personal life; by undermining the Islamicate order as much as any political
ideology they cause many Muslims to fear everything connected to the West
and modern life. The West poses not just an external threat as the infidel; it

also erodes Islamicate mechanisms for coping with the internal threat, woman.

Western antinomianism has similar effects in other areas of private life too, eroding Shar'i prohibitions on pork, alcohol, drugs, gambling, and interest. Muslims who abandon the law often do not replace it with a code of personal ethics but allow themselves unrestrained gratification. Mistaking freedom for license and personal ethics for indulgence, some lapsed Muslims then go on to disregard even more basic moral precepts, such as those concerning trust, respect, and honesty. These habits understandably give Western customs a bad name. The amorality of non-observant Muslims confirms the determination of pious Muslims to live strictly by the Shari'a, splitting Muslim societies into two factions, the fundamentalists and the Westernized, the religious and the anti-religious, the moral and the amoral, the self-controlled and the hedonistic. Only a few persons (and most of them tend to come from the upper classes) find a place in the Western-style middle niche of ethical but non-religious behavior. Unlike the political arena, where many Muslims settle in the fuzzy middle ground of reformism, private styles are polarized, dividing and destabilizing the umma.

Avoiding Reality

It would be difficult to imagine a turn of events more disastrous to the umma than the European assault of the nineteenth century. Everything—foreign invasion, cultural backwardness, poverty, and psychological humiliation—went wrong at once. The long-established connection of Islam with power and wealth had created an assumption that God rewards the faithful with bounty on earth; Muslims "had an innate respect for the force that triumphs for there is no success other than what is wished for and blessed by God."[28] But the link between the umma and worldly success was broken, challenging the traditional sense of superiority vis-à-vis non-Muslims. If premodern Muslims had been able to disdain kafirs and concentrate on their standing before God, their nineteenth-century heirs had to contend primarily with Christian overlords.

The result was cultural crisis. "Military defeat was defeat not only in a worldly sense; it also brought into doubt the truth of the Muslim revelation itself."[29] Failure left the Muslims uncomprehending. The Franks' success posed many dilemmas, few of which received satisfactory answers: What had happened to leave the umma defeated and poor? If, as Muslims had so long permitted themselves to believe, God indicated His approval by granting mundane satisfactions, why then had Muslims lost their strength and their well being? Had the centuries-old association between Islam and high worldly standing been permanently broken? Was it that Muslim devotions had become inadequate, that their faith had lost validity, or that the Europeans subscribed to a faith that had won more favor in God's eyes? Muslims had to account for what Wilfred Cantwell Smith terms "the discrepancy between their faith and their contemporary history," between past triumphs and current disappointments.[30]

Understanding what went wrong and finding responses became the central intellectual concern at the time of the European conquests and remains so ever since. "The fundamental problem of modern Muslims is how to rehabilitate [their] history: to set it going again in full vigour, so that Islamic society may once again flourish as a divinely guided society should and must."[31] Earlier in this century, many Muslims answered this question by looking inward, analyzing their society, admitting weaknesses, and considering ways to solve them; Kemal Atatürk and two Egyptian thinkers, Ahmad Lutfi as-Sayyid and Taha Husayn, still stand out for their serious efforts to find the reasons for Muslim backwardness. Since the 1930s, however, the predominant approach has been to look outside the umma and to blame Westerners (or other non-Muslims) for all that has gone wrong. This effort usually entails two steps: shifting responsibility for Muslim troubles onto kafirs, then praising everything connected with Islam. One process involves conspiracy theories, the other apologetics.

Conspiracy theories make it possible to account for misfortune without having to come to terms with it; they fill a need in modern Islamdom and flourish especially in the Middle East. Rumors, whispers, cabals, plots, and devils permeate politics, excusing virtually any unfavorable development, be it a single incident (the October 1980 massacre in a police station at Batu Pahat in Malaysia by Muslim extremists was called a plot to discredit Islam) or the grand sweep of history (in the eyes of many Indonesians, "modernization is another conspiracy of the West").[32]

For Arabs, the inability to destroy tiny Israel prompts the belief that sinister forces must be backing the Jewish state. While some Arab commentators made serious critiques of their military defeats, especially after the setbacks of 1948 and 1967, most governments and writers preferred to avoid the actual situation and rely instead on conspiracies to explain their losses. One theory, based on *The Protocols of the Elders of Zion,* involved a Jewish plot using Israel as a base to take control of the entire world; a second saw the West using Israel as a tool for subjugating the Middle East; a third suspected Soviet-American collusion to use Israel as a way to create a need for their weapons in the Arab states. Soon after Israel caught Egypt's air force on the ground and destroyed it on the morning of 5 June 1967, Gamal Abdul Nasser spoke by telephone with King Hussein of Jordan (according to an Israeli interception of the call). The two leaders agreed to hold the United States and Britain responsible for what happened, accusing them of sending planes to help Israel—a claim that was at the time widely believed in the Arabic-speaking countries. Such theories serve several purposes at once: they explain away humiliating defeats by a small enemy, making him part of some dark international force; they deepen hatred for the enemy; they inflate the threat he poses, rallying citizens to the government; and they absolve the leadership of its failures.

Beginning with Imam Ruhollah Khomeini himself, Iran around the time of the Islamic revolution was a most prolific source of wildly imaginative conspiracy theories. Khomeini saw the success of European imperialism resulting not from Europe's power but from their successful sabotaging of Islam:

> The British imperialists penetrated the countries of the East more than three hundred years ago. Being knowledgeable about all aspects of these countries, they drew up elaborate plans for assuming control of them. . . . They felt that the major obstacle in the path of their materialistic ambitions and the chief threat to their political power was nothing but Islam and its ordinances and the belief of the people in Islam. They therefore plotted and campaigned against Islam by various means. . . . The agents of imperialism, together with the educational, propaganda, and political apparatuses of the anti-national puppet governments they have installed, have been spreading poison for centuries and corrupting the minds and morals of the people.[33]

If Europe got where it did through chicanery, the implication was clearly that Muslims have little to learn from it.

Conspiracies also served to explain Muslim resistance to fundamentalism and their opposition to the Iranian government. When Muslim extremists captured the Great Mosque in Mecca, Khomeini saw the event as an Israeli and American plot to destroy the holy places of Islam, perhaps because he found the notion of Muslims committing such an outrage unbearable; sufficient numbers of Pakistanis concurred with his view to the point that they killed four of the U.S. embassy staff in Islamabad. Within Iran, some blamed every piece of bad news on the United States and Israel, including the unrest among the Kurds, Baluchis, and Azeris, the assassination of pro-Khomeini political and religious figures, and the Iraqi invasion of Khuzistan. The Islamic Republic of Iran may be unique in having a constitution that mentions conspiracies, which it does twice. The Preamble refers to the White Revolution (the shah's land-reform program) as an "American plot . . . a ploy to stabilize the foundation of the colonialist government [of the shah] and strengthen Iran's . . . ties with world imperialism." A second reference promises good treatment of non-Muslim Iranians so long as they "do not get involved . . . in conspiracies hatched against the Islamic Republic of Iran."[34]

Iranians saw foreign influences on a more mundane level too:

A Teheran taxi driver explained that he thought the city's notorious traffic jams were the handiwork of American agents. "They get people to do unnecessary things and make the drivers frustrated and lose their temper," he said. When shopkeepers complained that itinerant vendors were setting up tables in front of their stores and demanded their removal, there were allegations that the Central Intelligence Agency was behind the frictions.

The use of narcotics in Teheran, which has not diminished since alcohol was prohibited, are also part of a plot by the superpowers, according to Ayatollah Khomeini. He explained last month that "a heroin addict cannot think about politics" and would be useless in time of military invasion. . . .

The skyrocketing oil prices that helped push the United States into an economic recession are the result of a plot by its own Central Intelligence Agency, according to one of the many conspiracy yarns making the rounds. . . . The C.I.A. realized that the Western European countries were forging ahead of the United States in economic growth and contrived the jump in oil prices to punish the Europeans.[35]

One reason for taking over the American embassy in Tehran was to ferret out the "den of espionage" controlling all these activities; but some Iranians who opposed the takeover argued that even this was part of a conspiracy: Washington arranged for the seizure of its own diplomats as hostages to isolate Iran internationally! Conspiracies multiplied in the fever of fundamentalist excitement in Iran, creating a level of political discourse in the country, complete in itself and immune to rational argument. They also became a routine device for political infighting, as cliques accused each other of plots in the battle for power. And the government used the threat of plots when this proved convenient; for example, it kept the United Nations Secretary General, Kurt Waldheim, out of public view during his visit to Tehran by discovering a plot against his life at an opportune moment.

Conspiracies prove useful when events are too painful to be faced rationally; just as farfetched notions about the assassination of John F. Kennedy appealed to the many Americans who could not come to terms with his death, so Muslims avoid distressing reality. Here the Islamicate legacy of power and wealth proves most detrimental to modern Muslims. Blaming the hidden hand allows them to escape responsibility for their predicament of weakness and poverty, permitting them to believe that they would still enjoy their former superiority over Europe were it not for Western intrigues against Islam. The self-image implicit in this is of an umma powerful but naïve, enervated and exploited by tricky Western agents. However myopic, such views do assuage insecurities and reduce humiliation.

All this is at a cost, however, for not confronting realities means not identifying critical problems, much less solving them. To the extent that the Arabs see Israel's strength deriving from clandestine support or that the Iranians believe their internal troubles to be manipulated by foreigners, Arab military success and Iranian domestic tranquility will remain elusive. On a larger scale, if Muslims really believe that Europe derived its strength by plotting against the umma, they cannot respect or emulate the West, nor can they grow strong themselves. Conspiracies spawn a paralyzing climate of suspicion. If oral contraceptives are part of a plot to reduce the number of Muslims, how will Egypt contain its population? If foreign investment is designed to prevent Muslims from industrializing, modernizing efforts will suffer. If foreign visitors are spies, relations with the outside world will be restricted.

Whereas conspiracy theories provide the means for Muslims to blame their predicament on kafirs, apologetics—proving what one already believes to be true—provide the means to praise Islam. Worried that Westernized Muslims view Islam as ineffective and will fall away from the Islamic identity or way of life, apologists are devoted to enhancing the appeal of Islam. Their efforts being directed at Muslims already attracted by the West, they promote Islam *in Western terms.* This can lead to strange results. Nonetheless, Westernized Muslims, who feel inferior about their civilization, do often grasp at this reassurance.

Shamelessly distorting and exaggerating the past to suit their needs, apologists use the historical record as "a storehouse of precedents for foregone conclusions."[36] They revel in the achievements of medieval Muslims, especially in the acclaim given them by Western writers; they also derive special satisfaction from the fact that premodern Islamdom culturally outshone West Europe. Apologetics are based on a skewed contrast which holds Islam outside and above history and sets off its ideals against the sordid realities of its rivals—Christianity, liberalism, and Marxism. Stress on a glorious past proves that Islam is a winning force, even if it has been recently in eclipse, and implies that the current imbalance is temporary.

Muslims often disguise their borrowing from the West by claiming Islamicate origins for what they take from abroad. Algebra was first discovered by Muslims in about the ninth century,[37] and Ibn Khaldun (d. 1406) is sometimes called the father of sociology; on this basis, apologists claim that modern mathematics and social science are derived from (or even stolen from) the Muslims. In other disciplines, Muslim apologists strain the truth yet further, finding "some reference, moot or indirect as it may be, to the Western concept in the Quran or the sayings of the Prophet, even if this entails rendering a new meaning to Arabic words. Employing this method, a great deal of theories in such fields as agriculture, chemistry, and physics was found to have an origin in Islam."[38]

Apologetics have been sharply criticized by Western analysts. H. A. R. Gibb characterizes their tone as "the argument of defending counsel" and describes their efforts as "the outcome of intellectual confusion."[39] Wilfred Cantwell Smith regrets that the need for a vision for the past to assuage present difficulties led to a disregard for historical accuracy; he observes that "relief of distress is sought not in a revision of doctrine but in a redressing of history."[40] For apologists, Islam served as an identity more than as a faith; a home team to root for more than a means to personal salvation.

The apologetic impulse has had widespread influence: "Most books and speeches on the faith by those within it today are defensive" and are marked by "the endeavor to prove, to oneself or others, that Islam is sound."[41] Gustave E. von Grunebaum notes that apologists express what they want to believe: "It cannot be overemphasized that whatever the modern Near Easterner has to say about his own background and about the West is primarily a political judgment. His presentation is meant to influence rather than describe."[42] For von Grunebaum, the source of this problem lies in the discrepancy between ideal and reality: "A certain reluctance to confront the realities of a historical situation where it involves the recognition of its conflict with the norm . . . has stayed with a majority of the Muslims through intellectual humiliation and the perpetual crises of the last century."[43] As a result, "modern Muslim society is as a whole lamentably ignorant of the origin, development, and achievement of its civilization."[44] It is difficult to disagree with von Grunebaum's assessment that the religion of these apologists is a "tired faith."[45]

Despite its intellectual bankruptcy, the apologist effort has had both practical success and a certain value. It *has* convinced many Westernized Muslims of the validity of their religion and kept them closer to the faith. "Were it not for this apologetic, it is certain that the proportion of athiests, apostates, and merely nominal Muslims would be much higher than it actually is."[46] Apologetics also eases Westernization by making the process more palatable; even if it is intellectually dishonest, the claim that modern science is stolen from the Muslims makes borrowing it less of a tribulation, and expedites the process of modernization.

The Travails of Modern Islam

Many reasons have been offered for the difficulties Muslims face in modernizing; it may help to recapitulate these before drawing conclusions.

The great majority of the problems took form before the rise of Western Europe in the eighteenth century; the context in which Muslims acted already existed well in advance of their encounter with the modern West. The following characteristics, all of which subsequently caused Muslims difficulties, predated the European intrusion:

- The withdrawal of subjects, the gulf between ruler and ruled, and the reliance on outsiders conflicted with the democratic bent of European ideologies.
- Pan-Islamic solidarity and other non-territorial loyalties conflicted with nationalism.
- The success of the medieval synthesis engendered a cultural conservatism after the thirteenth century and reduced Muslim receptivity to new ideas, especially those coming from outside Islamdom.
- Inexperience with competing cultures made Muslims unprepared to contend with a rival that excelled them in both military power and cultural achievement.
- The tendency to divide all things along the lines of Islam and non-Islam created a psychological dichotomy unconducive to learning from kafirs.
- Eighteenth-century fundamentalist movements increased Muslim adherence to Shar'i and Islamicate ways, reducing the willingness to experiment with non-Muslim innovations.
- The autonomist impulse created special problems when Europeans conquered.
- Autonomism kept Europeans away from Islamdom until late in the imperialist era, reducing Muslim contact with modernity.
- Europe's long-standing aversion to Islam made rule of Muslim lands by Westerners a particularly unpleasant experience for Muslims, who responded by shying away from contacts with their rulers and learning slowly from them.
- Traditional Muslim scorn for Europe obstructed the process of learning from the West.
- Expectations of worldly success led to a particularly traumatic loss of confidence when Muslims became weak and poor, causing some Muslims to despair of their faith and others to ignore the real problems they faced.
- The tradition of living by laws caused Muslims to resist the antinomianism that accompanies Western civilization.
- Depending on separation of the sexes to keep society stable meant that Muslims became anxious when Western social and sexual practices impinged.

It would be wrong, however, to conclude from this list that nothing Islamicate fitted Western patterns, for some did, such as a resistance to inherited rights and an acceptance of social mobility. Also, political concepts such as justice and freedom were not incompatible. Overall, however, compared with other non-Western civilizations, the Islamicate background is the least propitious for modern life; Muslims faced greater obstacles than did the Indians,

Chinese, or Japanese. This can be illustrated by a comparison with non-Muslims with regard to two key matters: conquest by Europe and nationalism.

Falling under the control of Europe affected Muslims more severely than other peoples. In the first place, Islamicate civilization places an especially heavy emphasis on the control of land, so that loss of control to Europe had an alarming effect. India and China had for centuries been under foreign control before the Franks came, ruled by Turks and Manchus, respectively; both had accommodated to this fact and maintained their cultural integrity while subjugated. British conquest did relatively little damage to Hindu civilization, either in India itself or in its outposts abroad. China had an extremely powerful political tradition which had many times overwhelmed and absorbed foreign conquerors; if a Briton had ruled in Peking, even he may have eventually fit its structures and ways. As it turned out, the predicament of Confucian lands was eased by the fact that most of them escaped direct European control. Muslims lacked such versatility; conquest by Europe meant passing from Dar al-Islam to Dar al-Harb, with all the trauma that implied.

Second, Islamic autonomism provided Muslims with a unique drive to defy foreign domination. Other colonized peoples resisted the Europeans initially; then they accepted colonial rule without much protest. It was not until they learned about Western ideologies such as nationalism, liberalism, and democracy that they were aroused to action again. In contrast, the autonomist impulse made Muslims resist foreign control more consistently and it caused them more suffering. Because Islam requires its adherents to wield political power, the colonial experience especially bruised Muslims.

As for nationalism, it was incorporated by non-Western peoples other than the Muslims without great tribulation. The political units of East Asia—China, Japan, Korea, Mongolia, Vietnam, Cambodia, and Laos—fit the framework of the nation-state far more easily than do those of East Europe. In India, sub-Saharan Africa, Southeast Asia, and the Americas, indigenous political traditions were usually too weak to resist nationalism, which reigned supreme and almost unchallenged after World War II. Even in Africa, where the state boundaries have an especially arbitrary quality, they have acquired a sacrosanct character and are rarely questioned. The Organization of African Unity (O.A.U.) established as its cardinal rule the preservation of existing borders, a decision that has given the continent a certain stability. Africans accept the status quo, regardless of its inadequacies, because they have no alternate vision to it, because no other political order rivals the national ideal left behind by the Europeans. What were once arbitrary lines on the map drawn by European diplomats lost the colonial associations and became almost universally accepted.

In contrast to the O.A.U. decision to preserve existing borders, members of the League of Arab States chafe at boundaries bequeathed by the imperial powers and devise one scheme after another to eradicate these vestiges of the colonial era. Instead, the Arabs dream of building a single Arab state from the Atlantic Ocean to the Persian Gulf. Arabs envision a political order that emphasizes cultural and religious bonds over territorial ones; as Muslims, they are heir to a powerful tradition of political ideals different from the European ones. Pan-Islam and nationalism must conflict: either cultural or territorial bonds can have paramount importance, but not both. Thus, the more influenced by Islamicate patterns, the more acutely a people feels the dilemma of its political identity.

As a result of these obstacles, Muslims experienced the most difficulties with Western and modern life. They have had relatively few achievements. Except for the petro-rich, Muslims are poor, having neither fully industrialized nor developed other modern infrastructures. Politically, Muslim states enjoy little legitimacy or stability, and their military record is indifferent. Scholarship is derivative and the culture has minimal influence beyond the bounds of Islamdom. Its writers and artists rarely win international acclaim or distinction; the exceptions usually reside in the West.[47]

The contrast with other non-Western peoples, especially the Japanese, is striking. After having quarantined their country from Europe for over two centuries, from the 1630s onward, Japan's rulers responded to the mid-nineteenth-century threat of Western invasion by initiating a crash program of industrialization. It proved so successful that by 1905 Japanese forces defeated Russia's in war, marking the first occasion in modern times that a non-Western country beat a European power using modern methods; then three years later, the Japanese invaded Korea. In the 1930s, Japan overran much of China and then became Germany's most powerful ally during the Second World War. Today, Japan not only has the world's second strongest industrial machine, but it has mastered much of Western culture, including its technology and arts. Japan's novels and films win as much acclaim as its motorbikes and television sets, and its musicians have achieved international stature in the classical repertoire of Europe. Much of Japan's culture, including no, kabuki, jujitsu, haiku, netsuke, and Zen Buddhism, has acquired a following far beyond the country's borders. Although limited since 1945 to a self-defense force, Japan built up a large and very well-armed military machine. Organizations such as the political party and the business corporation were absorbed from the West and refashioned in distinctively Japanese ways. The emperor became a constitutional monarch similar to those of northern Europe and nationalism was made the basis of Japanese political life. Many Japanese extolled their traditional ways, yet very few seriously wished to return to premodern conditions.

While no other country outside the West achieved quite the success of Japan, non-Muslims generally outperformed Muslims. India adopted a Western political philosophy (liberal democracy), attained fair political stability, created an indigenous scientific establishment, built a large, well-equipped armed force, and boasted artists of international repute. Hong Kong, Taiwan, and Singapore became economic powerhouses. The Vietnamese incorporated modern military techniques so well that they defeated the French and American forces. South Korea and Brazil entered the path to full industrialization, and so forth.

The Muslims' lesser record is most clearly seen within the context of single nations. In Yugoslavia, Bosnians and Albanians are the poorest of the country's many ethnic groups. While Christians in Lebanon identified for centuries with France, their Muslim neighbors kept away from European contacts and fell behind the Christians as a result. In Nigeria, Muslims adhered to the old ways longer, leaving most modern endeavors to non-Muslims. Muslims of Chad resisted French conquest most strenuously and lost ground to the animist Christians. Hindus outperformed Muslims in India after the British conquest, reasserting themselves after many centuries of Muslim rule. Muslims in the Soviet Union lagged behind the country's other ethnic groups. Malays had little economic success compared to the Chinese and Hindus. In Thailand and the Philippines, Muslims remained far behind the majority populations according to most indices. Exceptions to this pattern are few and can be explained by special circumstances; in East Africa, South Africa, and Burma, for example, immigrants from India raised the general level of the Muslim community, making it a leading force on the local scene.

Noting Islam's correlation with volatile politics, economic backwardness, and cultural stagnancy, outside observers often ascribe the problem to Islam itself. The fact that the area most influenced by Islamicate patterns, the Middle East, has the most political difficulties of all seems further to confirm this correlation. Because Muslims cling to ancestral ways, passively accept conditions Westerners find intolerable, and act in ways which appear illogical, outsiders tend to conclude that Islam is retrograde, fatalistic, and irrational, a faith that discourages economic development, opposes rationalism, and obstructs modernization. The spectacle of an Imam Khomeini— a bearded, robed, and turbaned religious patriarch calling for Muslims to return to "medieval" ways—confirms the Western suspicion of Islam as hopelessly reactionary.

But this is nonsense. Islam, as all religions, is neutral with regard to such matters. Concerning economics, "there is nothing to indicate in a compelling way that the Muslim religion prevented the Muslim world from developing along the road to modern capitalism, any more than there is anything to indicate that Christianity directed the Western European world along that road."[48]

191

Were Islam inimical to advancement, how then did the medieval umma lead its contemporaries in wealth, science, and war? Muslims once wrote better books, planted crops more productively, knew more about the skies, and fielded stronger armies. If Islam imbues fatalism, how then does one account for the powerful surges of Muslim activity from the Arabian conquests of the seventh century to the Iranian Revolution? Muslims are as capable of progress, decisive action, and logic as anyone else.

The religion of Islam does not account for the predicament of modern Muslims; rather, this is a consequence of changes in historical circumstances. Muslim responses to modernity were shackled by conditions in Islamdom in the eighteenth century, the legacy of hostile relations with Europe, and the contrast between Islamicate and Western ways. Islam obstructed efforts to modernize not because of its inherent qualities but because of its relationship to Europe and European civilization. More concisely, Islamic values do not oppose modernization, but Islamicate traditions oppose Westernization. Islam does not conflict with modernity but its civilization conflicts with that of the West. This may be seen by contrasting the actual progress of the umma with what might have happened had the Turks or the Chinese, rather than the Europeans, made the breakthrough to modernity.

Had it been some Muslims, say the Ottoman Turks, who forged ahead culturally and conquered much of the world, the entire umma's standing would be wholly different from what it is. Muslim rulers would resist conquest by Turks no less than by Europeans, but the Islamic autonomist impulse would be absent; once conquered, Muslim peoples would accept Ottoman rule without difficulty. The power holders would be displaced but the subjects would offer little resistance. Poor government might provoke revolts or local notables might attempt to gain power for themselves, but such rebels would not seek complete independence from the Ottoman Empire, only local rule within it. Ottoman culture would cause few difficulties for the umma; what one Muslim people devised, others could imitate, for it would fit Islamicate patterns and thus meet only minimal psychological resistance. Inventions and ideas spread easily from one Muslim people to another; where one Muslim country surges ahead, others follow. Had the Ottoman Turks first developed modern ways, the whole umma would have shared its benefits.

Although the Chinese are kafirs, a modern and expansionist China would also have been easier for Muslims to accept than Europe. Its religious tolerance would have greatly facilitated Muslim acceptance of Chinese culture; the absence of a Chinese religion rivaling Islam, much less one with missionaries to spread it, would have done much to create a more friendly atmosphere. In contrast to their scorn for the Franks, Muslims long respected Chinese culture and acknowledged its wisdom; an oft-quoted *Hadith* Report, for example, advises the faithful to "seek knowledge even unto China." Middle Eastern contact with China was too infrequent for strong feelings about it to develop; the principal encounter was a single battle in Central Asia in A.D. 751, which the Muslims won. (Its long-term significance was that the Muslims captured Chinese paper makers, who soon afterwards introduced their product to the Middle East.) Whatever problems the Muslims of China faced (and these included some terrible massacres), they were unknown beyond the empire's boundaries. And unlike European phobias, the Chinese paid Islam little attention.

Western observers of modern Islamdom are prone to judge harshly, interpreting its turbulence and lack of achievement as proof of an inferior civilization. This is wrong, however. Islam is not anti-modern, but being Muslim means having a harder time coming to terms with Western civilization. Islam is not by nature anti-progressive, but being Muslim entails greater difficulty accepting the skills that lead to wealth. Islam is not xenophobic or irrational, but autonomism and legalism complicate the task of Muslims trying to cope with the West. The religion of Islam, its civilization, and its adherents are not deficient; they are the victims of circumstance.

Outsiders glibly condemn Islam; they might instead sympathize with the Muslim predicament. Westerners can understand this by imagining how they would feel were the roles reversed, and Arabs, Persians, and Turks had made the breakthrough to modernity and Christendom were forced to adjust. In this case, Europe's distress and reluctance would probably equal that of the umma's. If Middle Eastern states had divided Europe among them and ruled it until just a generation ago; if Iraq had conquered Rome and if Paris had been subject to Saudi laws; if Muslim rulers had encouraged Islamic missionaries to set up schools in Europe to weaken the Christian faith; if Muslim rulers had imposed on Europe customs such as the veil, the harem, and polygyny; if they had banned alcohol, the theater, and monasteries; if Egypt and Pakistan possessed the world's most powerful armed forces and the largest arsenals of nuclear weapons; if European and American graduate students traveled to the Middle East not just to learn science and technology but also to learn about their own history and culture; if the greatest authority on Aristotle were a Yemeni and the outstanding critic of Shakespeare a Moroccan; if Arabic and Persian were the international lingua franca; and if dinars, dirhams, and riyals dominated foreign-trade markets—Westerners would be no less upset than are Muslims.

The West in general and the United States in particular enjoy a vital but rarely noted luxury; being at the cutting edge of modernity, the question of whether or not to advance, or in which direction, is culturally neutral. Because standards for such diverse matters as computers, weaponry, popular music, clothing fashions, and literary movements are all set in the West, responses to change within the West hinge mainly on the merits of each case. In the non-Western world, however, the same decisions are more complex, involving sensitive matters of cultural influence. An American responds to Hollywood fare largely on aesthetic grounds; an African's views also involve his feelings about U.S. policies toward his country, his views about the Western way of life, and so forth. Adopting computers to a business is a straightforward financial decision in the West; in the Middle East, it also involves many social and emotional factors, making the choice a symbolic one involving much more than matters of profit and loss. A computer is not just a technical instrument in Islamdom, but a cultural outpost of the West; buying one has many implications. And this is far more the case with decisions involving personal matters such as the use of contraceptive pills or wearing Western clothes. Every choice has an emotional and political dimension of which Westerners are unaware. The question of Westernization complicates the process of modernization everywhere but in the West.

Conclusion:
Muslim Ambivalence

A consensus on the measure to
which Westernization is necessary
for survival, or desirable for the
resurgence, of the [Muslim]
community has not yet been
reached.
—*Gustave E. von Grunebaum*

THE DECISION to modernize ultimately comes down to a question of
whether to adhere to the Shari'a and Islamicate patterns or to try out Western
ways: fundamentalism, reformism, and secularism represent the principal responses. Which of the three the umma adopts will determine, more than anything else, its success with modernization.

The Shari'a itself does not impede modernization so much as do attitudes
toward the West; after two centuries of exposure, Muslims are still reluctant
to acknowledge the West's power and cultural leadership. The result is what
Naipaul terms the "Muslim disturbance," that is, admiration for what the
West does mixed with resentment for the fact that it fares so well; a desire
to imitate its results but an unwillingness to emulate its actions:

The West, or the universal civilization it leads, is emotionally rejected. It undermines; it threatens. But at the same time it is needed, for its machines, goods, medicines,
warplanes, the remittances from the emigrants, the hospitals that might have a cure
for calcium deficiency, the universities that will provide master's degrees in mass media.
All the rejection of the West is contained within the assumption that there will always

195

exist out there a living, creative civilization, oddly neutral, open to all to appeal to. Rejection, therefore, is not absolute rejection. It is also, for the community as a whole, a way of ceasing to strive intellectually. It is to be parasitic; parasitism is one of the unacknowledged fruits of fundamentalism.[1]

What holds truest of the fundamentalists holds true, in milder form, for the umma as a whole.

Two nearly parallel phenomena exist here: on one side, a religion that has strict requirements (the Shari'a) and a penumbra of cultural implications (the Islamicate way of life). On the other, a process of change (modernization) with its own penumbra of culture (the Western way of life). In theory, a Muslim faces few conflicts when he tries to reconcile the Shari'a with modernization, for they overlap only rarely—mostly in economics; with a few adjustments, he should be able to make the two compatible. The presence of so few areas of conflict between the Shari'a and modernization encourages some Muslims, the fundamentalists, to believe that they can become modern without Westernizing, that they can avoid most of those features of Western life that cause them such anguish.

But this belief is illusory; if modernization is theoretically distinct from Westernization, the two are in fact inescapably intertwined. The chances for becoming modern without Westernization are about as good as conceiving children without sex. A Muslim intending to work as a jet pilot, for example, will not become adequately technicalized unless he is Westernized as well. Modernization is not some abstract principle but a very real force projected by teachers, administrators, investors, and writers from the Occident. The jet pilot's training has to be carried out in a Westernized environment either by Westerners or by Westernized persons. Also, Westernization is necessary because Muslims are influenced not only by the Shari'a but by the whole of Islamicate civilization. Even if the Shari'a rarely conflicts with modernization, Islamicate civilization differs from Western civilization on a wide array of issues.

An outsider can easily see the faulty logic behind fundamentalism and reformism. Fundamentalism assumes that Muslims can modernize without Westernizing, leading to the contradictions Naipaul exposed; reformism holds that the two processes are compatible, leading to the falsehoods that so many scholars have noted. But secularism also fails, for even when Muslim leaders do dispense with the Shari'a itself, the Islamicate legacy persists. Formally giving up the idea of a caliph has hardly eased the predicament of Muslim governments vis-à-vis nationalism; nor has outlawing the veil (as the Iranian authorities did in 1936) achieved much more than heighten Muslim fears of social and sexual anarchy. Muslims are tied to the Islamicate legacy; even when they disavow the Shari'a and try to technicalize, Islamicate elements remain, holding them back from fully Westernizing.

The result is disarray and ambivalence. In the words of a Pakistani lawyer, "Our people emotionally reject the West. Materially, we may be dependent on the West."[2] Equivocation of this sort paralyzes Muslims and prevents them from decisive action. Individuals and governments muddle along, rarely willing to devote themselves either to a secular program or a fundamentalist one. Reformism, with its hesitations, empty rhetoric, false promises, misrepresentations, sleights of hand, tortured logic, and flights of fancy, wins by default. It demands the fewest commitments and tolerates the most contradictions, offering a vacuous but optimistic middle ground for Muslims unable to decide on fundamentalist or secularist programs. Reformism does not satisfy, but the alternatives do not attract. Secularists and fundamentalists offer sharper, more persuasive programs, but few Muslims wish to experiment with them. Except in a few states, notably Turkey and Albania in one direction, Iran and Pakistan in the other, Muslim leaders have avoided committing themselves to clear-cut solutions. The result is cultural stagnancy and political volatility.

Another result is the acceptance of inconclusive compromises. The unitary umma conflicts with nationalism, so nations exist, but in limbo. Dhimmi disabilities clash with the Western ideal of equal citizenship, so non-Muslims may enter the government and the military but not become head of state. The Islamicate tradition of withdrawal from politics goes contrary to the ideals of democracy, the civic society, and the militia; skewed elections, weak voluntary associations, and recruitment from small portions of the population result. Shar'i court procedures differ fundamentally from the British Common Law, the Code Napoleon, or any other European legal system, so elements from several systems are drawn on at the same time and mixed freely, satisfying no one. These compromises neither preserve the old ways intact nor thoroughly assimilate those of the West. They cause the umma to drift ideologically, seeking a program true to its traditions yet helpful for dealing with modernity, seeking a niche between the two super-powers, and hoping somehow to regain the successful self-image of old.

To escape anomy, Muslims have but one choice, for modernization requires Westernization; the fundamentalist option is illusory, with most of its proposals "too unsophisticated to be of any value in solving the complex issues now facing the world."[3] Islam does not offer an alternate way to modernize. So long as the umma insists on looking for solutions to current problems with patched-up versions of archaic programs, it will remain poor and weak. Secularism cannot be avoided. Modern science and technology require an absorption of the thought processes which accompany them; so too with political institutions. Because content must be emulated no less than form, the predominance of Western civilization must be acknowledged so as to be able to learn from it. European languages and Western educational institutions cannot be avoided, even if the latter do encourage freethinking and easy living. Only when Muslims explicitly accept the Western model will they be in a position to technicalize and then to develop. Secularism alone offers escape from the Muslim plight.

A comparison with the modern history of the Jews suggests that Islam is likely to witness a weakening of the law over time. Today's debate over the observance of the Shari'a corresponds roughly to the Jewish debate about a century ago; then as now, advocates of Westernization were gaining strength, just as adherents of the law held strong. The Jewish experience indicates that legalist forces, however strong, numerous, and well-organized, will fail, for they are defying the prevailing ethos of the age, antinomian Westernization. Too much occurring in life today undermines adhesion to the law; it is inconceivable that Muslims can withstand Westernization any more than Jews could.

If they accept Westernization, it is the opinion of some that the essence of Islam will be lost and the religion forsaken; as M. Jamil Hanifi sees it, abandoning the Shari'a means "an all-powerful Allah without adequate guidance concerning his will, a holy book without agreed upon interpretations, a religious emotion without clear ethical and social consequences, and authority in the community without traditional legitimacy."[4] H. A. R. Gibb sees it in even starker terms: "To reject the Sharia *in principle* is . . . in some sense apostasy. . . . With the maintenance of the Sharia is linked the survival or disappearance of Islam as an organized system."[5] But this is overly rigid: religions, like all human institutions, survive through adaptation, and if Islam must discard the law and adopt faith and ethics, as Judaism did, it will do so. It can flourish too, for a Protestantized Islam will serve Muslims no less well than a legalized one; decline in the law need not impair the relations of men to God. This said, the efforts of those Muslims who do persevere in keeping the law deserve respect, for they are maintaining important traditions in the face of great challenge.

If Shar'i precepts often conflict with Western ways, so too do Jewish ones, at least in the private sphere, where the Halakha outdoes the Shari'a in the number and scope of its regulations. Even the Christian churches advocate precepts that differ form the customs of the modern West (such as the Catholic prohibition of divorce). All three religions discourage or prohibit taking interest on money, yet this does not hinder the free use of interest payments in the West and in Israel. In some ways, the sacred law has helped the Jews modernize; devotion to Talmudic studies is widely credited with giving Jews literacy and analytic skills which proved of great value outside the ghetto or shtetl.

CONCLUSION: MUSLIM AMBIVALENCE

The eventual adaptation of Jews to modern life makes it clear that attitude, not sacred law, is the key. Whereas most Jews accept Western ways and work hard to incorporate them or adjust to them, Muslims too often attempt to finesse Westernization and become modern without it.

To prosper again, the umma faces an inescapable set of demands: worldly success requires modernization; modernization requires Westernization; Westernization requires secularism; secularism must be preceded by a willingness to emulate the West; and this willingness will gain acceptance only when Muslims are unalterably convinced that it is their only choice. Westernization is an unpleasant prospect which Muslims will not pursue unless all other efforts fail. Thus, were the Westernizers to flourish and the fundamentalists to fall behind, Westernization would look good and attract more Muslims. But it was precisely this that did not happen in the 1970s, when changes in the umma dramatically increased the power of fundamentalists and weakened that of the Westernizers. This was the worldwide phenomenon known as the Islamic revival.

PART III

*Islam in
Current Affairs*

9

The Islamic Revival:
A Survey of Countries

In the contemporary Arab world, Islam has simply been by-passed.
—*Hisham Sharabi,* 1966

Islamic conservatism is at present the dominant ideological force in Arab society.
—*Hisham Sharabi,* 1979

THAT an Islamic revival took place in the 1970s few dispute, but what exactly it was remains a matter of disagreement. Was it an increase in piety, in legalism, or autonomism? Did it indicate a surge in traditionalist or fundamentalist strength? Was it restricted to things Islamic or did it also include the Islamicate? Did the turn to Islam affect just one region, several regions, or all parts of Islamdom? Did it occur simultaneously or at different times?

To answer these questions, this chapter provides a review of events in the whole of Islamdom over a fifteen-year period, from the late 1960s to the the spring of 1983, focusing on changes in the role of Islam as a political force. Every country for which information was available is covered: omissions include several states on the Arabian peninsula (the Yemens, Oman, and Qatar), Djibouti, and Brunei, and most of the states of West Africa. The following accounts have a dual purpose: to portray the political context of Islam in each country and then to document the revival by highlighting Islam's changed role in recent years.

The countries are arranged in three separate listings depending on the proportion of Muslims in the population:

1. Dominant majorities: where Muslims constitute more than 85 percent of the total and where fundamentalism increased almost everywhere in the 1970s. The countries covered are: Afghanistan, Algeria, Bangladesh, Egypt, Guinea, Indonesia, Iran, Iraq, Jordan, Libya, the Maldive Islands, Mauritania, Morocco, Niger, Pakistan, the Persian Gulf statelets, Saudi Arabia, Senegal, Somalia, Syria, Tunisia, and Turkey.

2. Moieties: those relatively few countries where Muslims make up between 25 and 85 percent of the population. In many of them, Muslims and non-Muslims were engaged in a contest for control of the government. Moieties discussed here include: Albania, Chad, Ethiopia, Lebanon, Malaysia, Nigeria, and the Sudan.

3. Small minorities: where Muslims are less than 25 percent of the population and where autonomism, either defensive or secessionist, usually grew stronger in recent years. These include: Bulgaria, Burma, Cambodia, Cameroon, China, Cyprus, Greece, India, Israel, Kenya, the Philippines, Rumania, Singapore, the Soviet Union, Sri Lanka, Thailand, Uganda, the United States, Yugoslavia, and a scattering of other countries.

Dominant Majorities: The Fundamentalist Surge

In countries where Muslims greatly outnumber non-Muslims, Islamic sentiment is usually expressed through legalism. Muslims already in charge, the main concern is to transform society along Shar'i lines. During the 1970s, fervent Muslims—usually but not always fundamentalists—took power in two countries, Pakistan and Iran; they won a major political role in Libya, Egypt, Turkey, Syria, and Saudi Arabia; and they acquired greater weight in virtually all other predominantly Muslim states. Autonomism rivaled fundamentalism only in Afghanistan after the Soviet invasion.

AFGHANISTAN

Afghanistan's rugged terrain and the prowess of its warriors had assured the country's independence throughout the modern era. Both Russia and Great Britain gave up after several attempts at subjugation and eventually the country became a buffer zone between them. As a result, traditionalist Islam remained unchallenged in most of the country.

Thus it is not surprising that the leftist, pro-Soviet coup of April 1978 met with massive resistance, especially outside the cities. Land reform, changes in the status of women, and other measures spurred the beginnings of a fundamentalist movement. The anti-government rebellion then took on an autonomist tone in December 1979, when the Soviet Union sent nearly 100,000 troops to support the government in Kabul. The rebellion expanded, fueled partly by the desire to preserve a way of life, partly to place true Muslims in power, and partly to further nationalist goals. The government sought unsuccessfully to appease Islamic sentiments by taking such steps as eliminating offensive Marxist slogans, having the president promise "freedom for all religions, sects, national customs, and traditions,"[1] and by broadcasting Qur'anic verses on radio and television. Also, green, the color of Islam, was again included in the Afghan flag.

The rebels divided along tribal, territorial, religious, ideological, and personality lines into about one hundred groups. Whereas some of these rebel groups had secular orientations, most fought within an Islamic framework of jihad and considered themselves *mujahidin* ("fighters of jihad"). They differed, however, in their conception of Islam: of the six most important groupings, four had a fundamentalist orientation (the Islamic Party of Afghanistan, headed by Gulbuddin Hekmatyar; the Islamic Party, headed by Muhammad Yunis Khalis; the Islamic Society of Afghanistan, headed by Burhanuddin Rabbani; and the Islamic Revolutionary Movement, headed by Muhammad Nabi Muhammadi), one had a reformist outlook (Sayyid Ahmad Gaylani's National Islamic Front of Afghanistan), and one a traditionalist outlook (Sibghatullah Khan Mujaddidi's National Liberation Front of Afghanistan). Unable to unite, these groups formed shifting coalitions; at times, however, as in the summer of 1981, fighting between Muslims was so intense that the war against the Soviets was temporarily stopped. Such conflicts presaged the disputes that would probably follow a withdrawal of Soviet forces. As far as the fundamentalists were concerned, they were engaged in an effort to institute a fully Islamic way of life; as Gulbuddin Hekmatyar put it in 1981, his troops were "fighting to establish a pure Islamic society and government in Afghanistan."[2]

Changed Role of Islam in Recent Years. Leftist governments and foreign troops compelled Afghans to deal with modernity as they had never had to before; thus a fundamentalist movement emerged where hardly any had existed a decade earlier.

ALGERIA

As with everything else in independent Algeria, Islamic developments must be seen against the colonial experience, undoubtedly the most violent and disruptive in the annals of modern Islamdom. Both the conquest by France from

1830 to 1848 and the war of independence from 1954 to 1962 cost hundreds of thousands of Muslim lives. During the period of colonial rule, Algerian high culture nearly disappeared: French replaced Arabic as the written language and Islam retreated from school curricula, the legal system, and daily life.

Leaders of the independence movement responded to this assault by stressing Arabic and Islamic themes. When the French left in 1962, the new government spared no effort for the monumental task of re-orienting the country away from Europe and toward the Middle East. It brought teachers of the Arabic language and Islamic religion from the Arab countries, eliminated public use of written French (including government papers, street names, outdoor signs, and so forth), made Friday the day of rest, adopted a civil code from Egypt, and, in 1976, decreed Islam the religion of state.

But the authorities' vision of Islam had no Shar'i content; colonial legislation had undermined the sacred law and the rulers of independent Algeria did nothing to revive it. They saw Islam as an identity and a way to mobilize the populace for developing the country, not as a legal system or a way of life. "The connection of their Islam with Algerian national consciousness made religious feeling a major political factor, even though the Islamic law had no influence on political structures and the ulama had no power in the state apparatus."[3] Algeria remained fully secularized even after independence.

Fundamentalism gained force slowly. Starting in 1973, isolated incidents indicated that legalist impulses were not dead, though the occasional attack on a brothel or bar, street demonstration, university riot, or attack on an immodestly dressed woman fell for short of a coherent political movement. Fundamentalist ambitions quietly grew, however, and came to light in an attempt to take over the government in November 1982. Riots at the Ben Arkoun campus of Algiers University led to the throwing of acid in the faces of unveiled women and the death of two fundamentalist students. Literature distributed at that time called for the formation of an Islamic government and the replacement of the National Charter with the Qur'an. In the aftermath of the violence, twenty-nine students were arrested, classes were boycotted, and a rally staged by the fundamentalists was heavily attended. The government responded by dismantling the Islamic organizations at the university, arresting the minister of religion, and accusing the fundamentalists of trying "to impose ideas which have no relation to the true faith."[4] Massive dragnets and spectacular shoot-outs followed. The authorities made it very clear that they were willing to employ whatever force was required to quell legalism. One sign of their success was the fundamentalists in Algiers shaving off the beards which they had previously flaunted as a sign of their religiosity.

After fifteen years of incarceration and enforced silence, Algeria's first president, Ahmed Ben Bella, surprised many when he finally spoke out publicly in 1980. Though a pro-Soviet socialist when in power, he studied and memorized the Qur'an during his years in prison and became convinced that Islam provided the answers to Algeria's political problems. His views had no discernible practical effect, but Ben Bella commanded great prestige, and his shift in views greatly enhanced the visibility and prestige of the Islamic faction.

Although rarely recognized as such, Algeria's colonial experience made it the most secularized and non-Shar'i country of all Dar al-Islam. Even more than Turkey, Albania, or South Yemen, it had abandoned the traditional Islamic way of life and thus had to confront the full force of the West. For this reason, its experiences probably foreshadowed those of other Muslim peoples. Were the government not so repressive, Algerian intellectuals would be in a position to play a key role in the formation of a secularist Islamic thought; but until now, Islamic cultural life in independent Algeria has been nearly moribund.

Changed Role. Hesitantly at first, more confidently later, legalist sentiments in Algeria increased through the 1970s and early 1980s.

BANGLADESH

Bengali Muslims joined with their co-religionists in western India to push for the creation of Pakistan, but they never had quite the same resolve.[5] Bengali nationalism was stronger than territorial feelings in West Pakistan; thus, as the Bengalis became disillusioned with the notion of Pakistan, they rebelled against an Islamic ideal and affirmed their own national identity. The independence movement that led to the breakup of Pakistan in 1971 had anti-Islamic overtones, for rejecting the Pakistan union meant choosing Bengali nationalism over Muslim brotherhood. When West Pakistani troops slaughtered East Pakistanis in the name of Islamic unity, the Bengalis were even more alienated from pan-Islam; and the fact that some fundamentalists in East Pakistan resisted the drive for independence and in some cases colluded with the West Pakistanis to prevent it discredited pan-Islam even further.

Thus, the new nation of Bangladesh emerged as a firmly secular state and its leaders were resolved to keep Islam out of politics. Reliance on the Soviet Union and India, two nations hostile to Islam, confirmed this orientation. During the country's first years of independence under Sheikh Mujibur Rahman, the government stressed nationalism and hardly ever spoke of Islam. The 1972 constitution made secularism one of four principal ideals (along with nationalism, socialism, and democracy) and called for the elimination of "the abuse of religion for political purposes." This, and declaring that the country derived its identity from its "language and culture,"[6] signaled a dramatic end to the twenty-five-year period when Islam had defined the nation.

The coup d'etat of August 1975 had a legalist component—Bangladesh was briefly declared an "Islamic Republic"[7]—as did the coup in November which brought General Ziaur Rahman to power. The new leader's sympathy for Islam led to a reversal of the legislation enacted during the previous years. A new constitution in 1977 eliminated secularism as an ideal and replaced it with an assertion of "absolute trust and faith in the Almighty Allah."[8] Ziaur Rahman permitted Islamic political parties to organize and released many of the fundamentalists held in prison since 1971. In 1979 he issued regulations prohibiting alcohol and gambling and making religious education compulsory in the schools. The leader of a failed coup attempt in May 1981 (in which Ziaur Rahman was killed) tried to win more support for his cause by appealing to even stricter fundamentalist ideals.

By the end of Ziaur Rahman's rule Islam still had far to go to regain the favored place in society that it occupied when Bangladesh was East Pakistan. In the 1979 elections, an alliance of fundamentalists received only 10 percent of the vote and won but 20 out of the 300 contested seats in parliament. But Bangladesh began its return to legalism as the memory of the Pakistan fiasco faded. And in the opinion of one analyst, Islam's political rehabilitation is inevitable, for "so long as the great majority of its citizens think of themselves as Muslims as well as Bengalis, Bangladesh must pursue Muslim [that is, legalist] ideals as well as Bengali ones, if it is to pursue any ideals wholeheartedly." Further evidence of this came in January 1983, when the country's new leader, General Hussain Mohammed Ershad, declared that his foremost goal was "to fight the enemies of Islam and turn Bangladesh into an Islamic state."[9]

Changed Role. After a sharp turn away from Islam as a political force at the time of independence, Bangladesh gradually returned to moderately legalist policies.

EGYPT

Egypt is the most important single country for Islamic political action in the twentieth century. Although poor and only moderately populous, it became the key to Islamic developments for several reasons: Egyptians led in the effort to develop the Islamic response to modernity, featuring such thinkers as Muhammad 'Abduh, Muhammad Husayn Haykal, and Sayyid Qutb, who exerted an influence far beyond their nation's boundaries. Located in Cairo is Al-Azhar, the international university of Islam (and the oldest continuously operating institution of higher learning in the world) founded in 970. In 1928, Egyptians organized the first mass fundamentalist movement, the Muslim Brethren, which was much imitated in following years. As Arabic speakers, Egyptians use the language of the Qur'an and their writings are available to anyone educated in Islam. Egypt's concerns are those of the mainstream. Unlike Turkey or Saudi Arabia, absorbed by their own special circumstances, Egypt struggles with basic issues in ways meaningful to most Muslims. Finally, Egypt's open society, its central location, and its hospitality are responsible for its attracting a disproportionate share of attention from foreigners, journalists and scholars, Muslims and non-Muslims alike. As a result, the question of Islam in politics is often seen as a reflection of developments in Egypt.

As in many Arab states, the current move toward Islam began in the difficult days that followed the June 1967 defeat by Israel, a calamity that discredited the prevailing ideology of pan-Arabism and caused many Egyptians to seek solace in their faith. Abdul Nasser's death in September 1970 and Sadat's succession accentuated this trend, for Sadat recognized the new climate and encouraged Islamic sentiments. Friendly relations with fundamentalists served him well in his struggle with Nasserists and increased his popularity.

Over the next decade, Sadat played a complex balancing game on Islamic issues, allowing fundamentalists to gain in some areas, attacking them in others. His pro-legalist measures included the creation of a new government post, that of Deputy Premier for Religious Affairs, in 1973; the establishment of a Supreme Committee for Introducing Legislation According to the Shari'a in that same year; the submission to parliament of bills prohibiting alcohol consumption and instituting Shar'i penalties for robbery and slander; and the mandatory teaching of religious classes in 1978. A 1978 referendum approved a ban on freethinkers and athiests:

Anyone known to hold principles harmful to the official religion [Islam] will be banned from jobs in the top-level administration of the state or the public sector. Moreover, he will not be allowed to be a candidate for the board of directors of public and labor organizations, nor write for a newspaper, work in the mass media or have any position that could influence public opinion.[10]

Another referendum, in May 1980, changed the Shari'a from *a* main source of legislation (as it was in Sadat's first constitution of 1971) to *the* main source. A Supreme Islamic Council was established in 1979 with the mandate to promote Islamic missionary work in the country. It in turn established an Institute of Islamic Economics in early 1981 to introduce interest-free banking. Over the years, the Sadat government appointed several prominent fundamentalists to high positions in the religious establishment, such as the deputy minister of Waqfs and the head of Al-Azhar University in April 1981. It also took some symbolic steps, such as banning alcohol on the national airline.

But much of what the government gave fundamentalists proved to be empty promises. Most of its proposals for Islamic legislation—including bills to make apostasy from Islam punishable by death, banning usury, and Shar'i punishments for theft and adultery—never became law. Fundamentalist hopes were repeatedly raised and frustrated. Other Shar'i provisions that were formally enacted—flogging for dealing in or drinking alcohol, for example—were dead letters from their inceptions. Worse yet, the government pushed for family legislation contrary to the Shari'a: the July 1979 revision of the Law on Personal Status gave wives non-Shar'i rights in divorce.

Fundamentalists expressed their disappointment by resorting to violence. Not the Muslim Brethren however: the extremist organization of a generation earlier, had become legal and its leaders enjoyed the benefits of associating freely and publishing openly. As the Muslim Brethren became mellow, new groups inherited their earlier tactics, starting in 1974 with the attack on the Military Technical College outside Cairo by a shadowy organization known as the Islamic Liberation Organization or as Muhammad's Youth. And although the Cairo food riots of January 1977 initially had no Islamic component, the sacking of bars and nightclubs indicated that fundamentalists had directed the violence along Islamic lines. When a group known as Atonement and Flight abducted a former minister of Waqfs in June 1977 and executed him, the Egyptian government started to take extremist groups more seriously; a few months later, members of other fringe outfits, the Soldiers of God and New Jihad, were arrested. Student groups went on strike and rioted at the Universities of Minya and Asyut throughout much of early 1979. These disturbances led to stepped up security precautions as well as increases in salaries for members of the official religious establishment to ensure their continued loyalty to the government.

Of all fundamentalist actions, however, the treatment of Egypt's indigenous Christian population, the Copts, had the most inflammatory consequences. Communal relations in Egypt had been relatively smooth for some decades, until the growth of Islamic sentiment in the early 1970s. Violence first occurred in November 1972 with the burning of a Holy Bible Center and the stoning of Christians (including a bishop). Many isolated incidents followed, increasing Coptic apprehensions, setting the stage for the summer of 1977, when the government proposal to reinstate capital punishment for apostasy from Islam produced alarm among the Christians. The ease of an Islamic divorce had led many Coptic men to convert temporarily to Islam and then, once the divorce proceedings were finished, to return to the Christian faith. The new law threatened to force them all to become Muslim again, permanently this time, breaking up families. Church leaders responded to this proposal by calling for a five-day fast of protest by all Copts. The Coptic leader, Pope Shenouda III, and forty-four bishops cloistered themselves in the Cathedral of St. Mark in Cairo in September 1977, threatening to remain there until the apostasy bill was withdrawn. They came out only after a visit by the prime minister, who promised government opposition to the bill.

Many more Muslim-Christian incidents followed. A priest was murdered for trying to win back to the fold a Christian who had converted to Islam. University disturbances regularly included the persecution of Copts. On the Coptic Christmas Eve in January 1980, two bombs went off in Alexandria churches, Muslims in Minya prevented Copts from holding services, and a caroler was stabbed in Asyut. Not long after, Muslims burned down a cinema showing a film about Jesus. Inflammatory literature regularly appeared in pious Muslim neighborhoods, supposedly written by Copts; one proclaimed that Christians "do not accept Islam as a religion" and another called Islam "the lie of lies."[11] To protest these assaults and harassment, the Coptic leadership curtailed Easter festivities in April 1980. Tensions came to a head in June 1981 with Muslim-Christian rioting in Cairo which left eighteen people dead and which was quelled only with the arrival of several divisions of riot troops ordered to shoot on sight. Feelings ran high again in August when the bombing of a wedding ceremony in a Coptic church killed several people.

On 3 September 1981, President Sadat struck back against the fundamentalists, arresting (by official count) 1,536 persons, most of them extremist Muslims, and declaring the Muslim Brethren an "illegitimate" entity.[12] While the communal riots of June 1981 were offered as the immediate cause for this move, the crackdown really had to do with the fundamentalists' increased strength. Islamic groups responded by staging massive demonstrations in Cairo on three successive Fridays in September, including a march on the Coptic cathedral. The government ordered that all mosques be placed under its direct control to put a stop to inflammatory sermons. By mid-September, Egyptian politics had entered a crisis.

According to official accounts, members of the New Jihad group planned to assassinate President Sadat on 26 September but were foiled by the government crackdown. They took advantage of his next public appearance, the review of a military parade on 6 October, to gun him down. The assassins intended to kill not only Sadat but the whole Egyptian leadership sitting around him, then to strike again during their funeral and yet again at the swearing-in ceremony of the new president. After taking over key military and communication facilities, they planned to declare Egypt an Islamic republic along Iranian lines. The authorities arrested more than 2,500 fundamentalist Muslims in their investigation of the assassination, imposed martial law, and purged the military of all those with connections to extremist groups. Two hundred and eighty members of New Jihad went on trial in December 1982, charged with plotting an Islamic revolution. More fundamentalist violence followed the assassination, especially the three-day riots in Asyut which left eighty-two people dead, and a gunfight with a leader of New Jihad near the Pyramids.

Sadat's successor, Husni Mubarak, revived Sadat's pre-September 1981 strategy of distinguishing between peaceful and violent Islamic groups and he too tried to make peace with the former. To this end, he released the Muslim Brethren leaders imprisoned in September (but he kept the Coptic pope restricted to a monastery) and promoted a new program to spread reformist Islamic views in the schools. Also, Mubarak counted on public exposure to show the inadequacies of the fundamentalist program, hoping that challenging the Muslim Brethren and the others to convert slogans into specifics would expose their inadequacies and disillusion most of those who saw Islam as the answer to Egypt's problems.

Changed Role. Though numerically small, extreme fundamentalists alarmed the Copts, threatened non-fundamentalist Muslims, and killed the president of Egypt. The much larger body of devout Muslims gave Egyptian society and politics a new tone during the decade of the 1970s.

GUINEA

After independence in 1958, Ahmed Sékou Touré experimented with increasingly radical ideologies and pushed Islam to the side, culminating with the overtly Marxist program adopted at the 8th Congress of his ruling party in 1967. A change in attitude occurred a few years later. By 1975, Sékou Touré called a jihad against those merchants he accused of being "the gravediggers of the economy"[13] and in 1977, he came near to declaring himself the mahdi. A year later, Islamic Councils were instituted in the country's thirty-four administrative regions and on the national level, with the head of the latter enjoying the rank of minister. Sékou Touré himself went several times on the pilgrimage to Mecca and became visibly active in Islamic causes (serving, for example, as the head of an Islamic mission charged with mediating the Iraq-Iran conflict). The government enforced such Shar'i provisions as the prohibition on alcohol, pork, and the public consumption of food during the Ramadan fast; it also gave half days off on Friday and carried out Shar'i justice for sexual offenses. Persistent speculation holds that Sékou Touré will proclaim an Islamic republic in Guinea.

Changed Role. Guinea's government turned from Marxist socialism to partial fundamentalism.

INDONESIA

Muslims in Indonesia split into two types, the "statistical" believers and the devout ones, known in Indonesian as the *abangan* and the *santri. Abangan* remained attached to the region's indigenous and Indic cultures and steadily resisted *santri* efforts to impose a legalist version of Islam on the country. *Santri* included observant Muslims of all types, traditionalist, reformist, and fundamentalist. The tension between these two factions was long a major theme of politics in Indonesia: *santri* organizations wielded considerable power but failed to shift the balance of power in their favor, with the result that they were increasingly frustrated. And a surge of Islamic sentiments in the 1970s exacerbated their feeling of powerlessness.

Although the *santri* initiated the nationalist challenge to Dutch colonial rule at the beginning of this century, it was taken over by the *abangan*. Secularist groups led the fight to expel the Dutch in 1945–49; as a result, the leadership that emerged at independence was more oriented toward Western ideologies than Islam. Despite enormous legalist pressure, the constitution said nothing about Islam, much less about the Shari'a, but referred only to "belief in the One and Only God." In reaction to the *abangan* success in establishing the Republic of Indonesia as a secular state, some fundamentalists began a guerilla war, known as the Darul Islam Rebellion, from the mountains of West Java. This began in 1948 and continued until the execution of their leader in 1962; on other islands, the rebellion began later and went its own way. The *santri* hoped to win a majority of votes in Indonesia's first general elections in 1955, but the Islamic parties together (including reformist ones) received only 43.5 percent of the vote, far too little for them to be able to impose Shar'i legislation.

Fundamentalist participation in another rebellion, known as the PRRI revolt, led to a deterioration of relations between the Islamic leaders and President Sukarno and the declaration of martial law in 1957. In 1960, Sukarno banned Masjumi, the largest fundamentalist political organization. Nonetheless, the *santri* helped the armed forces five years later to suppress the Communists after a coup attempt in October 1965. Both this cooperation and the coming to power in March 1966 of a new president, Suharto, gave the *santri* hopes of participating in the government, only to be disappointed again. The military leaders who shared in the power with Suharto included almost no *santri;* many officers were *abangan* who feared that the efforts of legalist Muslims would suppress Javanese traditions, divide the country, and undermine the nationalist ideology that held it together; other officers, Western in outlook, regarded the *santri* as backward-minded obscurantists.

Suharto's policies after 1967 aimed at keeping devout Muslims politically docile by following practices reminiscent of Snouck Hurgronje's Ethical Policy at the turn of the century. Just as the Dutch had encouraged personal piety but opposed any role for Islam in public affairs, so did Suharto: his government gave financial assistance for the pilgrimage to Mecca, mandated religious instruction in school, and kept a close watch on the activities of

213

Christian missionaries. It closely monitored the 'ulama and put pressure on any who spoke out, even indirectly, against the government; the more insistent and braver ones ended up in jail. During the 1970s, the authorities responded to increased legalist sentiments by closing nightclubs in Jakarta, banning casino gambling, and taking other measures favorable to the Shari'a. Like the Dutch, too, Suharto tried to undermine the power of Islamic institutions in politics. He compelled nine Islamic parties to combine into one, the United Development Party (PPP), in the hope of blurring their distinctiveness and weakening them. The minister of religion, for years a traditionalist picked from the religious hierarchy, was now chosen from the military leadership, assuring that he had the government's interests more in mind than those of the *santri.* The state cut aid to Islamic schools and restricted Shar'i court jurisdiction as part of its efforts to reduce the strength of Islamic institutions.

Suharto's mixing of piety on the personal level with quasi-secularism in the public sphere succeeded; Islamic parties won only 27.2 percent of the national vote in the 1971 elections, a large drop from the previous vote in 1955; and their proportion increased only slightly to 29.3 percent in 1977 before falling back to 28.4 percent in 1982. Harold Crouch concludes an analysis of these election results with the observation that "the basic dilemma of political Islam in Indonesia arises from its inability to muster more than minority support from a people the overwhelming majority of whom describe themselves as Muslim."[14]

Hidden behind these static election results, however, was a major surge in legalist feeling. According to an Indonesian observer in 1978, "all the evidence points to a widespread and deep-rooted Islamic revival in Indonesia," while an American wrote in 1980: "The last decade has seen a strong upsurge of orthodox Islam. The numbers of mosques and *mushollahs* (local prayer houses) built has risen sharply; the attendance at weekly Qur'an reading sessions has gone up; Friday sermons in the mosque are addressed to packed houses."[15]

Unable to translate these changes into electoral victory, fundamentalists increasingly went outside the political structure and took direct action. They forced the government in 1973 to back down from a proposal to Westernize the marriage laws by provoking mob violence in the capital, including the occupation of the floor of Parliament by youth groups who disrupted a debate on this issue. The followers of an extreme fundamentalist, Imran Mohammad Zain, attacked a police station in Bandung in March 1981 and later that month hijacked an airplane. A secessionist movement grew in Indonesia's most legalist province, Aceh. The Aceh Liberation Front proclaimed independence for the region in May 1977, just three days after the national elections indicated that the *santri*s again would not prevail. A shadowy group called Darul Islam is claimed by some to run "a parallel administration that is the effective government of Aceh, especially in matters of law and order."[16] A key factor inspiring these and other actions directed against the federal government was the pervasive feeling that Suharto had become dependent on the support of Chinese merchants. As a result, despite making up 90 percent of Indonesia's population, autonomist worries of Muslims persisted during the 1970s.

The government has been suspected of sponsoring some of the extremist activities in the hope of discrediting all fundamentalists. Why, it is often asked, would fundamentalists bomb mosques or set fire to them, as happened several times in Indonesia? A terrorist organization called Komando Jihad came to light in the late 1970s and over a thousand of its members were arrested, but its existence was not established; some observers suggested that the government had made it up. When a leader of Komando Jihad confessed receiving arms from an unnamed foreign country through a submarine drop on the southern coast of Java, he did little to increase the government's credibility![17] The authorities also showed too much haste in their effort to exploit the March 1981 hijacking to discredit all fundamentalists; within weeks of the incident, the government had plans for a major local film to be made about the event.

Fundamentalists can be expected to continue to exert their will over the government, provoking general resistance, for reasons well summarized by Donald K. Emmerson:

> So long as practicing Muslims remain a qualitative minority in a statistical majority, in a diverse society, in a fragmented environment, the temptation to enforce piety from the "top down" will remain. And because of those very conditions, non- and nominal Muslims will continue to fear that "political solution."[18]

Changed Role. Fundamentalist frustration with the political process prompted a modest but distinct growth of Islamic political action.

IRAN

Khomeini and his supporters have had the most spectacular, the most renowned, and the most influential success of any fundamentalist movement in modern times; accordingly, their fate has special import for the future of fundamentalism.

The story of Khomeini's rise to power has been retold often enough not to require details here. Shah Mohammed Reza Pahlavi made only nominal gestures to Islam during his reign from 1941 to 1979; at no time until his final months did the government pay much attention to religious concerns, being far more interested with the consolidation of domestic power, military prowess, industrialization, oil sales, and the like. On several occasions, the shah weakened ʿulama power, notably by dispossessing them of land holdings in the early 1960s, though he also made efforts to win their allegiance by distributing funds and other benefits to religious causes.

As economic turmoil and the shah's tyranny provoked restiveness in the late 1970s, Iranians found in Islam a way of expressing grievances and their political demands increasingly took on legalist and autonomist tones. Islam had numerous advantages: standing for traditional Iranian ways, it contrasted most sharply with the Western features of the shah's rule. It provided a haven for the distressed and a bond for the outraged. The autonomist theme directed antagonisms against foreigners in the country (Americans especially) and non-Muslims in the government (Baha'is especially). The mosques offered the opposition movements a network of religious institutions in all regions of Iran which could be forged into a base for national political action.

On this last point: Iran differed from most other Muslim states in having a strong, independent religious establishment. Twelver Shiʿi leaders did not accept the medieval synthesis as fully as their Sunni counterparts, but they retained an impulse of opposition to the authorities; as a result, Iranian ʿulama settled less easily into the passivity of the Sunni traditionalists.[19] Outside Iran the state typically paid the religious leaders their salaries, in return for which it received their political cooperation; in Iran, the mullahs (Iranian ʿulama) retained their independence by taking money directly from their congregations. This made them more sensitive to the concerns of the populace and also permitted them to take positions on public issues. Thus, the mullahs played a central role in most of their country's modern political history; more than anywhere else, Islamic leaders in Iran were popular spokesmen and powerful figures.

These factors came together in early 1978, when Ruhollah Khomeini, the shah's most persistent and unbending critic, emerged as the leader of the opposition. In contrast to the *gharbzadegi* ("West-toxication") of the palace clique, he represented Islamic values; in contrast to its opulence, he personified the interests of the masses. By exploiting the longing for traditional ways and his access to the 180,000 or so mullahs in Iran, Khomeini directed a year of street demonstrations and strikes from abroad with brilliant skill. He made the armed forces the main target of his appeals and he fomented agitation in the ranks of labor. Overwhelmed, the shah left Iran in January 1979 and one month later Khomeini returned from fifteen years in exile. Many Iranians supported Khomeini as a symbol of opposition to the shah without actually wanting his fundamentalist programs put into effect. Their underestimation of his eagerness to make Iran fully Islamic seems astonishing in retrospect, for Khomeini, of course, did not give away the power he had won but immediately set about establishing a government that would restructure Iran along Shar'i lines. Khomeini ordered a Shar'i court system put in place, brought the school system into conformity with Islamic ideals, punished moral offenses (especially sexual ones), expelled non-Muslims from government service, prohibited interest on money, put pressure on women to wear purdah, and even tried to ban music.

As Khomeini carried through with a legalist program, many of his former allies broke ranks and went into the opposition. For some, having expelled the shah was an end in itself; and on reaching power, they were ready to resume politics fairly much as usual. This was the approach of Western-educated men such as Karim Sanjabi, Mehdi Bazargan, Ibrahim Yazdi, Sadegh Ghotbzadeh, and Abolhassan Bani-Sadr. But for the Khomeinists, expulsion of the shah merely set the stage for the real revolution, the full application of Islamic principles. Leading advocates of this approach included Mohammed Beheshti, Hossein Ali Montazeri, Mohammed Ali Raja'i, and Ali Akbar Hashemi Rafsanjani. The Western-educated leaders proved politically less skillful than the mullahs and within two and a half years of Khomeini's return, by the summer of 1981, mullahs controlled virtually the entire government. Opposition to them came principally from the Mujahidin-e Khalq, a radical Islamic reformist group with an anti-mullah orientation. They, like many other Iranians, favored implementation of Shar'i regulations yet reacted negatively to the prospect of the religious authorities running the government; indeed, it was Khomeini's concept of "the rule of the Islamic jurists (*faqih*s)" that made the Iranian experiment unique.

In Khomeini's opinion, the religious scholars should rule for they are best qualified to carry out God's mandate—a novel idea but not without logic or persuasiveness. To begin with, he defines Islamic government as "rule by sacred law," and argues that the establishment of a policy that acts in conformity with the Shari'a is essential to Islam. "Anyone who claims that it is not necessary to form an Islamic government denies the need to implement the Islamic precepts . . . and consequently denies the comprehensiveness and eternality of the faith of Islam."[20] For Khomeini, living by the law is central to the Islamic faith and he, like all fundamentalists, insists that the state be involved in executing those laws.

Where Khomeini differs from others is in his extreme emphasis on the importance of knowing the law. For him, the Islamic jurists are entitled to positions of power because they know best the ways by which the umma should live and how the state should act. In a key passage, he begins by quoting a

217

Hadith Report, "the Islamic jurists rule over kings," and then he goes on to draw the following conclusions: "If the political leaders are pious, then they must promulgate acts and decisions as decreed by the jurists. In this case, the jurists are the true rulers and the political leaders are merely their agents."[21] Thus, Khomeini's constitution,[22] promulgated within weeks of his return to Iran, puts the 'ulama in the two top positions: guardian *(velayat-e faqih)* and members of the Council of Guardians. The guardian is a religious man "enjoying the confidence of the majority of the people as a leader" (Principle 5) who has "charge of governing and all the responsibilities arising from it" (Principle 107). He appoints the Council of Guardians, all the highest juridical authorities, and the commander of the armed forces. He approves the presidential candidates, confirms the president in office, and has the right to dismiss the president (Principle 110). If no one fills the requirements to be guardian, a Leadership Council of three or five members takes his place (Principle 107). As for the Council of Guardians, it is made up of six "just and religious persons" appointed by the guardian and six lawyers chosen by the legislature (Principle 91)—many of them 'ulama. This body of twelve has the power to approve the credentials of the legislators, to assure that bills passed by the legislative "conform with the Islamic standard and the constitutional laws" (Principle 94), to interpret the constitution (Principle 98), to supervise elections (Principle 99), and to appoint the guardian or Leadership Council (Principle 108).

√ In short, Khomeini called for a theocracy (a government ruled by the religious authorities), something almost without precedent in Muslim history. In accepting the medieval synthesis, premodern men of religion had removed themselves from politics or government service; when religious figures did become involved, it was invariably to rouse their followers against the existing authority. Premodern 'ulama resisted serving as judges, stayed away from money tainted by politicians, and even avoided public facilities built by the authorities, on the grounds that they had been made possible through illicit gains. Many of "the more pious ulema refused to serve the government in any capacity."[23] As Claude Cahen observes, scholars of the Shari'a "were always more interested in the duties of the cult, in private law, in penal law, than in public law and in the organization and functioning of the administration and the character of its leaders."[24] Jurists were even less interested in taking over the reins of power themselves, a notion never seriously considered until Khomeini proposed it. Duran Khalid is thus correct in concluding that "from any point of view, Khomeini represents something new."[25]

Changed Role. From the shah's Westernization to Khomeini's extraordinary fundamentalism, Islam moved from the periphery to the center of Iranian politics.

IRAQ

If Islamic action be defined as legalist or autonomist movements, Iraq had very little of it during the 1970s. As a predominantly Muslim country unthreatened by non-Muslims, autonomism had no role; as a country ruled by secularists who faced few challenges from fundamentalists, legalism was also weak. Instead, Islam figured in the public life of Iraq as the key to communal tensions between Muslims.

The Muslims of Iraq divide into three major groups: Shiʻi Arabs, Sunni Arabs, and Sunni Kurds. Shiʻis of the Twelver sect constitute a majority of the population, about 55 to 60 percent and live predominantly in the southern half of the country; as a community they enjoy much less than their share of the nation's wealth and power. Sunnis make up about 35 to 40 percent of the population and in turn are divided rather evenly between Arabic and Kurdish speakers, with Arabs mostly in the northwest and Kurds in the northeast. Sunni Arabs have dominated politics since the sixteenth century, maintaining a hold on power through all changes in government from the time of the Ottoman Empire to the period of Baʻth socialism. Although they represent only one-fifth of the population, their cohesiveness and organization made it possible for them to exclude the Shiʻis politically. The secular ideology of the Baʻth party did not diminish the Sunni Arab grip on power, for although the Baʻthists included members of all communities when they first came to power in 1963, Sunni domination became more narrowly based than ever by the 1970s, when much of the top military and political leadership came from a single Sunni Arab town, Takrit.

As minority rulers, the Sunni Arabs were preoccupied with the prospect of losing power to the Shiʻis. (Kurds rebelled constantly but sought merely to win their own autonomy, and thus posed much less of a threat.) In the attempt to defuse Shiʻi resentment, the government supported such innocuous, non-political facets of Shiʻi Islam as celebrating the birthday of Muhammad's son-in-law, the great Shiʻi figure, ʻAli ibn Abi Talib, as a national holiday, and spending money on Shiʻi shrines. The president after 1979, Saddam Husayn, also claimed descent from ʻAli ibn Abi Talib.

Iraqi Shiʻis organized into two principal organizations, the Islamic Call (founded in 1968–69, probably aided by the Iranian government) and the Mujahidin (founded in 1979). A law passed in 1980 made mere membership in either organization punishable by death, and according to figures of the Islamic Call, about 500 members of its organization were executed between 1974 and 1980.[26] Despite these draconian measures, the Shiʻis were very far from threatening the Sunni control of the state. Shiʻi discontent erupted in February 1977

219

with riots, apparently organized by the religious leaders, in the Shi'i holy cities of Najaf and Karbala. The government became especially worried about a Shi'i challenge to its authority after Khomeini came to power and made it clear that he planned to rally his fellow-sectarians against the atheists ruling in Baghdad. Riots broke out simultaneously in June 1979 in Kufa, Najaf, Karbala, and in other towns throughout the country, leading the Iraqi government to suspect Iranian involvement. In the south, some of these disturbances were not quelled until armored divisions were brought in. The government then arrested many of the leading Shi'i religious figures, including Ayatollah Muhammad Baqir as-Sadr. Marches protesting these arrests were violently crushed and Baqir as-Sadr was executed in April 1980, presumably because the authorities feared he would fill a role in Iraq comparable to Khomeini's in Iran.

Changed Role. While Iraq experienced no increases in legalist or autonomist action, the emergence of Shi'i organizations presaged future changes.

JORDAN

Jordan allowed the Muslim Brethren to function, but only as a cultural association, a fiction which suited everyone, especially as the Brethren's principal political activity seemed to be aiding its colleagues in Syria. The Syrian authorities found this aid so troubling that it attacked a Muslim Brethren camp at Ajloun in Jordan in December 1980 and threatened further hostilities unless it was ended. Within Jordan, fundamentalists embarrassed the government by revealing sex scandals involving high state officials.

LIBYA

Libya's experience with Islam was shaped in the modern period by the Sanusi order, a fundamentalist Sufi brotherhood. Founded in 1837 near Mecca by Muhammad ibn 'Ali as-Sanusi, the Sanusi order was soon after headquartered in Cyrenaica, where the leader of the order acquired great political power. The Sanusis led the resistance to Ottoman rule in the nineteenth century and to Italian conquest in the twentieth. At independence in 1951, the United Nations commission in charge of establishing the new state made the then Sanusi chief, Idris, king of the country. The Sanusi movement became diluted with time, losing its fundamentalist edge and becoming tamely traditionalist. After independence, the government of King Idris retained Italian laws from the colonial period and allowed non-Muslims living in Libya to go about their business. In the international sphere, it permitted Great Britain and the United States to maintain military bases and disregarded Islamic autonomist causes, including the conflict with Israel.

Colonel Mu'ammar al-Qadhdhafi's bloodless military coup d'etat in September 1969 suddenly ended the era of mild, traditionalist government and replaced it with turbulent domestic change and wild international activity—much of which had some connection to Islam. In a sense, Qadhdhafi brought a return to the early Sanusi spirit. Although he denounced the Sanusis as non-Muslims and banned their order, he also espoused ideas resembling theirs. He

proclaimed a "purified" version of the main Sanussi principles (without so naming them): *Ijtihad* [individual initiative to understand Islam], return to pristine Islam as a way of life for all the people, spreading Islam, holy war *(jihad)* (conferring religious justification for his military build up) and manual work ("Islam is the religion of power and work"). Like the Sanussis, Qadhafi considers his regime as having a pan-Islamic mission: "The Libyan revolution is a revolution to reform Islam . . . and acts to reform Islamic religion."[27]

More than any other single event, Qadhdhafi's coup marked the beginning of the Islamic revival, for he reversed the trend of decades by becoming the first Muslim head of state to turn his government away from Westernizing goals and proudly to proclaim his allegiance to legalist Islam. This public intent to reinstate the Shari'a "came as a startling break with the overall pattern of legal development" in Islamdom.[28] Soon after coming to power, Qadhdhafi's government prohibited alcohol, banned lewdness in public performances, made the Arabic language and the Islamic calendar mandatory in all public communications (including the passports of visiting foreigners), closed churches, nightclubs and cafés, and—most surprising to the rest of the world, including Muslims—applied Qur'anic punishments for theft, brigandage, fornication, false accusation of fornication, and alcoholic consumption. In addition, the state prohibited gambling, interest on money, and stated its intent to collect zakat.

While these dramatic measures received great attention in Libya and abroad, and symbolized for some the inauguration of a new era in Islamic history, they were hardly ever applied. (In this sense, they did accurately symbolize the new era; most Shar'i laws proclaimed with fanfare quickly passed into oblivion.) Indeed, at the same time as it passed these "much vaunted Islamicizing enactments," the government drastically decreased the scope of the Shari'a by abolishing the family waqf and eliminating the separate jurisdiction of Shar'i courts. Ann E. Mayer, perhaps the most knowledgeable observer of Qadhdhafi in the West, writes that

it was easy to assume that a government that would adopt such extreme measures [as the Shar'i criminal code] would not hesitate to enact the less controversial portions of the *shari'a* into law, but, in fact, the Islamicizing process did not go much beyond the reinstatement of the Quranic criminal penalties—and these were only reinstated in a modified form.[29]

This apparent inconsistency is explained by the fact that Qadhdhafi did not acknowledge the Shari'a, but only those laws directly deriving from the Qur'an itself; he rejected most *Hadith* Reports and the whole system of law elaborated by the 'ulama; as noted in chapter 6, he took reformist logic to its extreme by dispensing with all Islamic laws except for the very few and elusive precepts found in the Qur'an.

With time, Qadhdhafi's opinions became yet more eccentric and less Islamic. By 1976, he began to interpret the Qur'an on his own authority, ignoring the 'ulama completely; by 1978, he dispensed with the entire body of Shar'i jurisprudence and all the 'ulama who interpreted it, arguing that the Qur'an provides all the laws a Muslim needs and that each believer with faith can interpret the Qur'an on his own. Stranger changes followed, such as making the Islamic calendar start in 632 (when Muhammad died) instead of the standard date of 622 (when he founded the umma). Qadhdhafi also argued that Islamic law concerns the private sphere alone, regulating personal morality and the afterlife, but offering no guidance in public matters. For the public sphere, Qadhdhafi offered his own ideas, embodied in three pamphlets making up *The Green Book,* which covered political, economic, and social questions. Compelled to read and acclaim *The Green Book,* Libyans irreverently called it "The Watermelon," referring to its being green (the color of Islam) on the outside and red within.

By the mid-1970s, Qadhdhafi thought of himself as becoming almost a mahdi or a new prophet. He denigrated the Prophet Muhammad: "What has Muhammad done that I have not? It is I who liberated you [Libyans] and gave you international standing." He made fabulous claims for *The Green Book:*

Qadhdhafi: The Green Book is the guide to the emancipation of man. The Green Book is the gospel. The new gospel. The gospel of the new era, the era of the masses. . . .

Oriana Fallaci: Well, then, you're a kind of messiah. The new messiah.

Qadhdhafi: I don't see myself in those terms. But the Green Book is the new gospel, I repeat. In your gospels it's written "In the beginning there was the word." The Green Book is the word. One of its words can destroy the world. Or save it. . . . My word. One word and the whole world could blow up.[30]

At the same time, Qadhdhafi funded the Children of God, an American-based Jesus movement which regarded him as a messianic figure and described him as "one of God's chosen ones. . . . the only world leader who is talking in the name of God, and . . . chosen by God to be a world leader."[31] When *The Green Book* was finished and first applied to Libya, Qadhdhafi decided, his own task finished, to withdraw from active politics. His abdication from power was reminiscent of a mahdi's, who restores the umma in its moment of crisis, then retires from public affairs.

By the late-1970s, Qadhdhafi had imposed an Islam on Libya which bore little relation to the mainstream religion. Two strangely contrary events had occurred simultaneously: while Qadhdhafi became internationally a symbol of resurgent legalism, domestically he moved Libya far from the Shari'a. He made Libya a major factor behind the new push toward fundamentalism, taking an active role throughout Islamdom from Senegal to Malaysia (details of this are in chapter 10); yet in Libya, he "precluded revival of the *shari'a* as law by denying that it has potential viability as a legal order for today's Muslim societies and relegating it to the role of a scheme of ethics."[32] Appearances to the contrary, Qadhdhafi secularized Islam in Libya, withdrawing the Shari 'a from public affairs and replacing it with his own vision.

The singular developments in Libya did not go unremarked in Islamdom. An Egyptian thinker noted disapprovingly that Qadhdhafi's links to the Children of God movement showed he "is trying to portray himself as some kind of new mahdi figure."[33] In November 1980, the Supreme Council of the Ulema of Saudi Arabia considered Qadhdhafi's notions about Islam. It noted his ridiculing pilgrims to Mecca as "guileless and foolish," his rejection of the truth of *Hadith* Reports, his doubts about the veracity of the Qur'an's contents, and his criticisms of the Prophet Muhammad; in response, the Council labeled him a "deviator from the principles of Islam and the brotherhood of Believers." It condemned his "perjury and lies" and accused him of striving "to abrogate the Shariah." Declaring Qadhdhafi "to be completely anti-Islamic," it recommended that he be ostracized from Islamic activities and that Muslims make efforts to combat his ideas.[34]

Ann Mayer writes that "if a campaign on behalf of Islamic revival is launched in Libya, it will be in opposition to the policies of the Qadhdhafi government rather than one that emerges under its auspices";[35] yet Qadhdhafi's program may permanently secularize Islam in Libya. Qadhdhafi's ability both to signal the start of the Islamic revival internationally and to undermine legalism domestically must be considered the most remarkable Islamic development of the 1970s.

Changed Role. From a force for moderation and tradition, Islam under Qadhdhafi's regime became part of a sweeping and eccentric force for change.

MALDIVE ISLANDS

After taking power in 1978, Maumood Abdul Gayoom gave public life in the Maldive Islands a new Islamic tone. A scholar of Islam who had studied in Cairo and taught in Nigeria, he reversed the secular policies of many decades, becoming, for example, the first Maldive head of state in over eight centuries to lead the Muslims at prayers.

MAURITANIA

The turn toward Islamic law began in June 1978, near the end of Mochtar Ould Daddah's rule, when he announced that, in the effort to return to the true Maurianian "personality and authenticity," existing laws would be modified to conform with the Shari'a. The military government that came to power in July 1978 pursued a fundamentalist program. Despite brave plans to implement the entire Shari'a ("For us Muslims, the Shari'a . . . is more modern than the so-called modern law"), only portions of it were actually put into effect.[36] Shar'i criminal courts were established in May 1980 and Islamic punishments—including the death penalty for murder, cutting off of hands for thievery, and flogging for lesser crimes—soon followed.

MOROCCO

That fundamentalist sentiments did not coalesce into a major political movement in Morocco was largely due to King Hasan II, for he, more than any other non-fundamentalist Muslim ruler, set the tone for Islam in his country. The monarch in Morocco has two principal religious roles: as Commander of the Faithful, he leads the Muslims and as a *sharif* (a descendant of Muhammad), he inherits the prestige of the Prophet's family. So great was his standing that even fundamentalist critics refrained from direct attacks: "He is a descendant of Our Master Muhammad; criticize him and you cast a slur on the family of the Prophet," said one of them, who instead blamed the king's advisors, especially those ministers "who give him bad counsel."[37] The king did not return the favor but publicly insulted the fundamentalists, calling them "those little devils in burnoose" and referring to the surge in legalist Islam as an "extremely disturbing phenomenon."[38]

The government carefully maneuvered to defuse the growing fundamentalist movement during the 1970s, for example, by creating a council of 'ulama under the king's chairmanship with authority to consider government policies in the light of Islamic precepts. Most spectacular was the "Green March" into the Western Sahara; in November 1975 for several days 350,000 volunteers, 90 percent of them civilians, filed into this disputed territory, brandishing Qur'ans and marching under the Prophet's colors. The march won no territory for Morocco but it did gain the king popularity at home and became a major proof of his Islamic credentials in subsequent years. The event was celebrated in all the public media, and even a cigarette brand named "The Green March" appeared. In February 1980, the king sent to the Western Sahara the Badr and Uhud divisions (named after Muhammad's first two military victories), again reinforcing the Islamic nature of Moroccan involvement there.

Fundamentalist opposition remained weak and fractured in this still predominantly traditionalist country. One extremist had a role in the assassination of the socialist leader Omar Benjelloun in December 1975 and then fled to Saudi Arabia; four years later he was arrested in connection with the attack on the Great Mosque in Mecca. The editor of a fundamentalist magazine, *Al-Jam'a,* wrote an open letter to the king, urging him to respect Islamic precepts more carefully, an act which landed him in jail. Other "fanatics" were arrested in late 1979 and then released. In dealing with fundamentalists, "the Moroccan government does its best to consign them to a marginal position; to make them look outdated and reactionary; to implicate some of the most representative leaders in criminal affairs; to suspend *al-Jama'a* and ban meetings; or to contrast national Maliki [the madhhab, or legal rite, in Morocco] orthodoxy to the bigotry, intolerance, and charlatanism of a handful or extremists."[39]

Changed Role. While fundamentalism increased, it did not seriously threaten existing political structures.

NIGER

Islam had so small a role in the first years after independence in 1960 that the Catholic church, although it had only a symbolic presence (650 citizens out of over 3 million), enjoyed an official status in the country. By the 1970s, however, the government became more attuned to the religion of the mass of its citizens. "Every observer notes an acceleration of the Islamization movement from the time of independence, so that Islam became one of the major elements in the Nigerien identity."[40] The most dramatic changes occurred soon after the military coup of April 1974, which brought the establishment of the influential Islamic Association of Niger, a government-sponsored organization to promote Islamic values. In addition, the new leaders made Islam the virtual state religion and took hesitant steps toward applying the Shari'a.

PAKISTAN

Pakistan suffered special problems with fundamentalism, for the state came into being as a result of autonomist efforts; yet legalists tried to take it over, leading to a profound and interminable crisis. Muhammad Ali Jinnah and the other leaders of the Muslim League who convinced the British to separate the Muslim regions of India into Pakistan were Western-oriented professionals favoring a Muslim state in large part because it would provide them with a way to retain political standing; they feared disappearing in an independent India dominated by Hindu politicians. Muslim Leaguers did not intend to create a state that would apply the Shari'a, a legal system they saw as archaic; they were reformists and secularists. For them, Islam was an identity much more than a faith. Ironically, fundamentalists and traditionalists in pre-partitioned India overwhelmingly opposed the Pakistan movement, which they saw as a nationalist effort contrary to the spirit of Islam. In the fundamentalists' view, Muslims owed allegiance exclusively to the unitary Muslim umma; carving out yet one more state hardly appeared to them a step in the proper direction. With the establishment of Pakistan, however, the fundamentalists had a change in attitude, seeing the new state as a unique opportunity to implement their programs. Whereas the founders of Pakistan had autonomist motives, the fundamentalists had legalist ones; the latter could never be content with autonomy for Muslims, which they saw merely as the precondition for applying the Shari'a.

A struggle between non-fundamentalists and fundamentalists has dominated Pakistani political life from the beginning, subsiding only during the period from 1958 to 1970 when their dispute was temporarily settled. They debated basic questions of Islam and politics with eloquence and careful reasoning. Writings such as the Munir Report (on the anti-Ahmadi riots of 1953 in the Punjab) for the non-fundamentalists and the works of Abul Ala Maududi, founder of the Jama'at-i Islami, for the fundamentalists, laid out the alternate positions on an unparalleled intellectual level. Whoever wishes to understand this argument will find the fullest and most articulate discussion in Pakistan. In part, this is due to the high caliber of the intellects engaged in the debate and the freedom of expression they enjoyed; in part too, their argument reflected the urgency of the problem, for Pakistan is the one state that must resolve these issues and cannot defer them, its very identity being indivisible from them. Egyptians also wrote at length on the political role of Islam, but they often sidestepped the most intractable problems, a luxury not available to the Pakistanis. As a state founded for causes deriving from faith, Pakistan faced a domestic debate over religion and politics that perhaps only Israel could fully appreciate. (Zionists too had founded a state on the basis of religious identity, not sacred law, and they too had to deal with the tensions between the two.)

The dispute between non-fundamentalists and fundamentalists took many forms: conflict over the "Objectives Resolution" of March 1949 which laid down the framework for the nation's constitution; the 1953 riots against Ahmadis and the inquiry which followed; debate over the constitutions of 1956 and 1962; the Muslim Family Laws Ordinance of 1961 which modified Shar'i regulations on polygamy, divorce, and so forth; and the composition of the government board for applying the Shari'a, the Advisory Council on Islamic Ideology. In each case, Western-oriented political leaders (including many military, legal, and intellectual figures) fought off the demands of fundamentalists trying to impose Shar'i regulations. Eventually, the two factions reached a stalemate and a tacit compromise: the non-fundamentalist leadership paid lip service to the forms and symbols of Islam, while the fundamentalists allowed public life to continue substantially in the British tradition inherited from the colonial administration. For example, as Aziz Ahmad writes, the constitution of 1956 envisioned "the law and administration of the state as . . . modern, even broadly secular. But the constitution theoretically endorsed the concept of an Islamic state."[41] Non-fundamentalists thus prevailed in the short-term at the expense of their long-range position. Over the years, they conceded that Pakistan should be Islamic, not just Muslim, encouraging expectations that the Shari'a would eventually be implemented; the fact that implementation never seemed to get closer created an atmosphere of frustration and extremism. Islamic elements were incorporated segmentally into politics, in isolated bits that could be produced to prove good intentions, without actually affecting public life. This stalemate had profound consequences for Pakistan, keeping the national identity in limbo, creating instability and unrest, and lending Islam to manipulation for political ends.

The deadlock was broken in 1971 with the secession of East Pakistan, leading to an increase of Islamic spirit in the Western region during the 1970s. The breakup of the union meant, first, that political tensions between East and West, a constant feature of Pakistan's early years, disappeared, thus highlighting the question of Islam and the Pakistani identity. If East Pakistan seceded because of cultural and ethnic differences from the West, what, given its own diversity, was to hold West Pakistan together? What defined the Pakistani nationality? Second, because West Pakistan had the stronger fundamentalist movement and fewer Hindu citizens, the secession of the East increased the fundamentalists' influence. Third, dropping the East wing re-oriented the West away from the Indian subcontinent and toward the Middle East, encouraging Pakistani fundamentalists. The strengthening of ties with the boom states of the Persian Gulf after 1973 further confirmed this tendency. In all, "the reassessment of Pakistan's national identity that followed in the wake of the catastrophic events of 1971 has sensitized the people of 'new Pakistan' to the appeals of a resurgent Islamic ideology."[42]

Fundamentalist pressure grew so strong after 1971 that the government of Zulfikar Ali Bhutto, despite a secular orientation, felt it had to accede. Bhutto dubbed his socialist program "Islamic socialism" and claimed that it derived from Islamic ideals, not Western ones. He made many gestures toward Islam, such as hosting the Islamic Conference Summit Meeting in 1974, relaxing restrictions on pilgrims to Mecca, and punishing printing errors in the Qur'an. These initial actions aroused little opposition among non-fundamentalists, but when he declared in 1974 the Ahmadis (a splinter group which recognizes the nineteenth-century figure Ghulam Ahmad as a prophet) to be non-Muslims, a long-standing goal of the fundamentalists, one-half million Pakistanis became dangerously disenfranchised and the fundamentalists' appetite was whetted for more. In April 1977, Bhutto went further, banning alcohol, gambling, horse racing, and nightclubs. Sunday replaced Friday as the official day of rest, the Red Cross became the Red Crescent, Arabic language courses were added to the school curricula, and so forth. He went so far as to promise a fully Shar'i legal system within six months. Bhutto tried to give an Islamic tone to his whole administration, even in matters unconnected to Islam. For example, after India exploded a nuclear device in 1974, he justified Pakistan's efforts to follow suit with this remarkable reasoning: "There was a Christian bomb, a Jewish bomb, and now a Hindu bomb. Why not an Islamic bomb?"[43]

But these efforts were to no avail; the fundamentalists distrusted Bhutto and were never satisfied by his efforts to appease them. When nine opposition parties joined forces as the Pakistan National Alliance to contest the March 1977 elections, the three religious parties in the Alliance set the tone for the entire coalition by rallying their supporters with a call for *Nizam-i Mustafa* (which translates roughly as "The Prophet Muhammad's System"). Fearing defeat, Bhutto rigged the elections, leading to an even greater outcry, massive demonstrations, and a coup d'etat against him in July 1977. Bhutto's non-fundamentalist orientation made it impossible for him to win the approval of fundamentalists, but his actions did contribute vitally to the momentum for legalism.

General Mohammad Zia-ul-Haq, the army chief of staff who took over from Bhutto and imposed martial law, had the religious credentials Bhutto lacked; personally pious, he had long been associated with the fundamentalists. Further, as a military dictator, he lacked Bhutto's political stature and depended on Islam to legitimate his rule. From the first, he took steps to implement the Shari'a, by appointing prominent fundamentalists to high government posts and to positions on the Advisory Council on Islamic Ideology. Islamicate place names replaced British ones, Urdu took the place of English in the schools and in much of the media, and textbooks were revised to reflect fundamentalist attitudes. In December 1978, Zia announced the Shariah Bench Order which required that Pakistan's laws be brought into line with the sacred law. On the Prophet's birthday in February 1979 Zia declared: "I am today formally announcing the introduction of the Islamic system in the country," though little more than Shar'i criminal penalties were decreed at that time.[44] Subsequent regulations required that employees be given time off to pray and to attend the mosque on Friday noon. Nineteen eighty saw the establishment of a Federal Shariah Court, state collection of zakat and '*ushr* (a tithe on agriculture), and a law punishing the defilement of the names of the Prophet or the first caliphs. Interest-free banking began in 1981 (called the Profit/Loss Sharing Scheme), artists were encouraged to work within Islamiguidelines, and two lovers were sentenced to death on charges of fornication. (Revealingly, Shar'i rules of procedure were not followed in this case; four righteous men had not witnessed the couple in the act of intercourse; instead, the court relied on circumstantial evidence, the woman's pregnancy.) The first step toward Zia's goal of "Islamic democracy" was taken in January 1982 with the convening of an advisory council made up of 288 members and bearing a Qur'anic-sounding name, the Majlis-i Shoora. Although the Shari'a says nothing about such an institution, Zia plucked the word *shura* ("counsel") out of the Qur'an (42.38) and made it the basis for this body.

Zia's Islamic measures threatened to bring the fundaments of Pakistan's public life into question. In September 1979, a retired Supreme Court justice and occasional advisor to Zia, B. Z. Kaikaus, filed a suit in a High Shariah Court Bench arguing that the democratic elections required by Pakistan's constitution have no basis in the Qur'an and are therefore un-Islamic: "The rule of people's representation was not there in the Holy Quran."[45] On these grounds, Kaikaus called for a change in Pakistan's system of government—in effect, seeking sanction for Zia's autocracy. Although the case was dismissed in December 1980, it opened the possibility of other challenges to the existing political order, thus further putting in doubt Pakistan's identity.

Attempts to implement the Shari'a inevitably created problems and generated widespread dissatisfaction. The Jama'at-i Islami and other leading fundamentalist organizations stayed away from Zia's efforts. They found the process of Islamization too slow and erratic, and they were distressed that their program should be exploited by a military ruler to enhance his political standing. They particularly disapproved of Zia's arrogating the title Majlis-i Shoora for a toothless council intended to prop up his rule. At the same time, non-fundamentalists were unhappy with the legalist program Zia instituted, which they considered burdensome, intrusive, and ineffective. Women, who found career and social opportunities reduced, took to the streets in March 1983 to protest a proposed law that would, in accordance with the Shari'a, make their testimony in court equivalent to half that of a man's. Shi'is resisted the Islamization effort too, seeing it as a covert way to compel them to adopt Sunni customs. Their displeasure came to a head in early 1983 when riots over the building of a Shi'i shrine in Karachi led to the deaths of seventy-two persons.

Islamization made cultural life increasingly bland and whittled away personal freedoms without bringing commensurate gains. The Central Zakat Fund, supposed to eradicate poverty, had negligible effect; corruption in high places remained a plague; and Zia was perceived as manipulating Islam for his own benefit. He claimed to be building an "Islamic democracy" but the Shari'a knows no such concept, and that left him a free hand to claim Islamic legitimation for any steps he took. After thirty years of waffling between Western ideologies and fundamentalism, from 1947 to 1977, the government finally made a whole-hearted move to resolve the question of Pakistan's identity and ideology. Zia-ul-Haq chose Islam; but historical experience suggests that this decision will not stick and that the Pakistanis will soon again face the old dilemma of identity, only next time with less innocence.

Changed Role. The Islamic revival began in 1971; fundamentalists took control of the government in 1977 with the intent of applying the full range of Islamic law.

PERSIAN GULF

Kuwait made modest moves in the direction of bringing its laws into conformity with the Shari'a. Fundamentalists swept Arab nationalists out of the National Assembly in the February 1981 elections and became the leading voice of the opposition. In January 1982, the Assembly voted against female enfranchisement by a 3-to-1 margin. Organizations to further Islamic goals appeared in Kuwait, such as the Social Reform Organization and as-Salifiya, but without much political impact. Fundamentalist groups acquired increasing influence after 1974, led by the Islamic Enlightenment Society, a Shi'i group. The United Arab Emirates also decided in 1980 to bring its laws into conformity with the Shari'a and prohibited alcohol and other non-Shar'i indulgences. Several events in April 1981 marked a swing toward Islam: a bomb went off in Dubai's newest luxury hotel in protest against indiscriminate selling of alcohol (that is, to Muslims as well as non-Muslims); the sexes were ordered completely separated in all United Arab Emirate schools, and a Shar'i court in Abu Dhabi sentenced two adulterers to be stoned to death. Just before Christmas, 1982, Kuwait, the U.A.E., and Qatar barred public celebrations of the Christian holiday.

SAUDI ARABIA

The Saudi state owes its existence to the doctrines of Muhammad ibn 'Abd al-Wahhab (1703–91), one of the most extreme fundamentalists in Islamic history. In 1745, he concluded an alliance with a tribal leader of central Arabia, Muhammad ibn Sa'ud, forming the nucleus of the Saudi state. Just as religious ideology gave the Arabians in the time of Muhammad the Prophet the means to organize and conquer, so did Wahhabism serve them eleven centuries later by ending their internecine feuds and marshalling their energies. By the late eighteenth century, the Wahhab-Sa'ud alliance had won a large, if ephemeral, empire in Arabia—at one point nearly the size of today's state. The capture of Mecca in 1803 and the subsequent massacre led to an Egyptian intervention that destroyed the first Wahhabi kingdom in 1818.

A second and smaller kingdom came into existence two years later and lasted until 1891, with little impact on its neighbors. A third kingdom was initiated in 1902, when 'Abd al-'Aziz ibn as-Sa'ud captured his ancestral home of Riyadh and used it as a base from which to re-establish the Wahhabi realm. 'Abd al-'Aziz spent the next third of a century, until 1934, conquering those regions that had once been ruled, however briefly, by his ancestors.

From 1745 to 1934, virtually every battle the Wahhabis fought was against Muslim enemies; they justified their expansion by refusing to recognize the Islamic credentials of non-Wahhabi Muslims. Unlike most other examples of Muslims reading their opponents out of Islam—an obvious tactic almost never effective—the Wahhabis genuinely considered other Muslims untrue to the faith and therefore proper objects of jihad. Religious differences motivated these wars and were not merely a cover for other reasons. 'Abd al-'Aziz depended heavily on settled tribal nomads, the Ikhwan, for most of his military support; their ruthless fanaticism grew from a very real devotion to Wahhabi principles.

And those principles were uncompromising. Muhammad ibn 'Abd al-Wahhab intended to re-create the exact way of life of the Prophet; to achieve this, he rejected nearly every innovation subsequent to the seventh century, including Sufism, scholasticism, and saint worship. In their fundamentalist fervor, the Wahhabis exluded much that is Islamic and nearly all that is Islamicate. By stripping away eleven centuries of accretions they discarded much of what had made Islam the basis of a great and diverse civilization. Instead, "quaking with a noble determination to allow no corner of public or private life to escape the rigorous if benign sway of the divine law,"[46] the Wahhabis devised their own regulations for Islamic life. Two practices that most distinguished Wahhabi rule were those of requiring mosque attendance by men and suppressing tomb-side prayers (which they saw as intercession with God, a heathen practice). Both caused unceasing difficulties with non-Wahhabi Muslims who felt the state had no right to interfere with private faith, either to compel prayers in the mosque or to prohibit them from praying by the side of a tomb. And so, by destroying tombs and sacred enclosures wherever they could, even in the holy cities of Mecca and Medina, the early Wahhabis aroused enormous enmity.

Wahhabi fundamentalism began to soften in the 1920s, especially after ʿAbd al-ʿAziz conquered Mecca and Medina in 1925, an event that transformed him from rustic bedouin chief into king of cosmopolitan cities. He had the political insight to realize the necessity of accepting the validity of the faith of non-Wahhabis in the holy cities. (Ironically, it was Islam's sacred shrines, with their international populations and their urban vices, that softened the faith of the Wahhabis.) Also, by conquering so much of Arabia, ʿAbd al-ʿAziz eliminated his tribal rivals and ended up abutting on established governments, including the British Empire in Jordan, Iraq, and the Persian Gulf; the encounter with sophisticated and powerful neighbors compelled him to think along diplomatic lines and to employ foreign innovations such as cars and rifles. The Ikhwan, unconcerned with diplomacy or modern technology and determined only to expand God's rule, rebelled against ʿAbd al-ʿAziz in 1928–29. He, however, retained the loyalty of enough tribes to vanquish them, and with this victory, the relaxation of Wahhabi doctrine became assured. From that time on, the Saudi government became more flexible, even allowing female education and television broadcasting; slavery was abolished in 1962 and in 1981 grooms were given permission to see their brides before their marriages. Aside from these modest changes, most of the Sharʿi order according to the Hanbali rite remained on the books, including prohibitions on alcohol, gambling, the mixing of the sexes, and so forth.

Because the Saudis tried to retain the fundamentalist spirit at the same time that they were the beneficiaries of extraordinary oil wealth, they found themselves having to improvise methods to reconcile Western and Islamicate ways. Combining the most modern appurtenances, technical education, and international travel with the harshest interpretation of Islam's sacred law produced a remarkable mélange of practices. The ban on male-female interactions led banks to open branches staffed by women only, for female customers only, high rise apartment buildings had elevators for women only, and male professors taught female students through closed-circuit television. The Saudi government continued to sponsor Islamicate institutions long forgotten elsewhere. It established a *mazalim* court in 1955 which, in contrast to its premodern namesake, was restricted to government affairs and did not deal with cases under Sharʿi jurisdiction. A morals police force, "The Committee for the Promotion of Virtue and the Punishment of Vice," applied private Islamic precepts such as those concerning female modesty and male mosque attendance.

Saudi efforts to apply the Shariʿa met with fair success. In part, this was due to the gradual moderation of fundamentalist aims, easing some of the least applicable ones (such as interest-free banking) and not even attempting to live up to others (such as the prohibition on warfare between Muslims). In part, the fact that Arabia had not been colonized by Europe made it easier to maintain traditions intact; the simple ways of most Saudis also helped, as did the vast wealth that oil sales provided. But the Saudi leaders could not deviate too far from the Wahhabi ideology or the raison d'être of the state would be threatened. Whatever public realities or their private views might be, they had to espouse Wahhabi doctrines, just as Soviet leaders have had to utter Marxist-Leninist pieties. This led to some spectacular hypocrisy, especially in the era of the oil billions: alcohol was prohibited in the kingdom while Saudi embassies abroad served liquor in abundance; movie houses were banned for reasons of public morality but pornographic video cassettes were widely available to the affluent; an ordinary citizen could have his hand cut off for stealing some small item while members of the royal family received kickbacks in the hundreds of millions of dollars.

Unlike most fundamentalist experiments, which went brittle and sour, special circumstances allowed the Saudi effort to turn gently into a more traditionalist type of Islam. The remoteness and primitiveness of the population, the flexibility of the leadership, the firm but restrained pressure from the outside world, and the enormous sums of free money all eased a transition to a modern version of the medieval synthesis.

But not everyone agreed to this move toward traditionalist Islam. A nephew of King Faysal's, Khalid ibn Musa'id, led the attack on the newly installed television station in Riyadh in 1965, losing his life when he drew a revolver and was shot dead by a policeman. (His brother Faysal killed King Faysal ten years later, perhaps in part to avenge this event.) But the major challenge to the drift toward traditionalism came in November 1979, on the first day of the year 1400 by the Islamic calendar, popularly reckoned to be the start of the fifteenth century. At the dawn prayers that morning over two hundred armed persons forcefully occupied the Great Mosque in Mecca, Islam's holiest spot. Seizing the mosque's microphone, they claimed the mahdi had arrived and urged the 40,000 people praying in the mosque to join them or to leave; then they closed the building's doors and spread out to defend their position from government attack. The authorities responded slowly and ineffectually, needing a full two weeks to flush the raiders out. A month afterwards, sixty-three of them were beheaded, including forty-one Saudis, ten Egyptians, six South Yemenis, three Kuwaitis, and a single Iraqi, Sudanese, and North Yemeni.

Although the group proclaimed one Muhammad ibn 'Abdallah al-Qahtani to be the mahdi, the real leader was Juhayman ibn Muhammad ibn Sayf al-'Utaybi, a tribesman of the 'Utayba confederation. Born into a settlement of Ikhwan around 1940, he served in the National Guard, rising to corporal. He

233

left military service in 1974 to attend lectures on the Shari'a at the Faculty of Law in Medina. Disappointed by the willingness of his professors to abide by and even support the Saudi regime, 'Utaybi quit the university and with about ten disciples returned to his home region, Qasim. His preaching against non-Shar'i practices attracted a growing band of followers. Two years later, they moved with him to the capital city, Riyadh, where they preached, published, and plotted. 'Utaybi and ninety-eight followers were arrested in 1978 but were released after several weeks of interrogation.

About that time, 'Utaybi wrote a short treatise, *Rules of Allegiance and Obedience: The Misconduct of Rulers,* in which he expressed his views on politics. As a fundamentalist, he upheld Wahhabi doctrines and used them to incriminate current Saudi rulers, arguing that they did not maintain the Shari'a and therefore deserved to be eliminated. 'Utaybi viewed Saudi history exactly as one would expect a child of the Ikhwan to, believing that the country's problems began with the relaxation of standards under King 'Abd al-'Aziz:

> Ever since the rule of King Abdel Aziz has settled down in the peninsula, you find that people have become ignorant in the ways of Islam, . . . suspending jihad in the alliance with Christians and in the pursuit of worldly things [a reference to the petroleum industry]. Our belief is that the continued rule [of these leaders] is a destruction of God's religion even if they pretend to uphold Islam. We ask God to relieve us of them all.

In 'Utaybi's view 'Abd al-'Aziz's having "allied himself with the Christians and stopped the Jihad outside the peninsula"[47] made him virtually a traitor. 'Utaybi wrote bitterly of the immorality that consumed the ruling class and accused the 'ulama of joining them: "Where is it that the *ulema* and sheikhs find their money, except through corruption?"[48]

√ Faced with such a dramatic reassertion of its own doctrines, the Saudi government increased the enforcement of existing Shar'i legislation. It prohibited women from traveling alone or working with men and non-Muslim foreigners, from dressing immodestly, wearing crosses openly, or holding hands in public. Newspapers could no longer publish pictures of women (except with their faces blackened). There was also talk of introducing democratic institutions and eliminating corruption, though with few results. The Saudi government was caught in a political bind; while proclaiming a steady devotion to fundamentalist principles to its subjects and the outside world, it had in fact gradually settled into a traditionalist pattern of accommodation and compromise. Despite government efforts to portray the Meccan zealots as anti-Islamic, the fact could not be hidden that 'Utaybi and his followers were judging the monarchy by its own standards. Saudi leaders have probably not seen the last of this problem; contradictions inherent to a conservative government promoting a radical ideology will continue to haunt the kingdom.

√ *Changed Role.* The Meccan affair reversed a long trend toward relaxing Shar'i restrictions.

The leaders of the Sufi orders, known in West Africa as marabouts, have retained a major role in Senegal's political life and wielded a wide influence over their followers. Over the years, extensive economic interests have made marabouts of the four major orders (the Tijaniya, Mourides, Layanne, and Qadiriya) increasingly worldly-minded and traditionalist. Despite Senegal's overwhelming Muslim population, they supported as president a Catholic, Leopold Senghor, after independence in 1960; then in 1962 they helped Senghor survive a severe challenge to his rule. In turn, Senghor rewarded the marabouts by according them economic, religious, and social privileges. When Senghor resigned at the end of 1980, his Muslim successor, Abdou Diouf, retained these policies.

In the early 1970s, new Islamic forces arose to challenge the predominance of these conciliatory marabouts and their close relations with the government. A group of Arabs and Arab-trained Senegalese led efforts to spread a fundamentalist vision of Islam. Writers, educators, and intellectuals organized the Union Culturelle Musulmane and gained an important voice. Within a few years, "the theme of purifying Islam and returning to the sources [was] no longer only that of a small minority," but appealed to "large portions of the population." The marabouts responded by becoming more fundamentalist themselves. As a result, "the religious leaders [had] a new audacity and a freedom of action in relation to the state" greater than before.[49] In contrast to their earlier passivity, the marabouts pressured the government in the 1970s for programs such as an Islamic Institute in Dakar and Arabic classes in the schools.

One fundamentalist leader, Sidi Lamine Niasse, tried to take advantage of political liberalization under Abdou Diouf to register a fundamentalist party, the Assembly for National Salvation, to contest the forthcoming elections. Because Senegalese law forbade a political party to identify with a religion, the name of this party and its explicit principles did not indicate its Islamic goals; even so, the government disapproved its application.

Sidi Lamine Niasse's brother Sheikh Ahmed Khalifa Niasse took a more radical tack and founded an illegal group, the Islamic Party, to oppose the government. Working out of the town of Kaolack, he called for an immediate,

235

complete, return to Shar'i regulations, a break with the country's pro-Western policies in favor of Islamic-oriented neutralism, and a trial of Senghor on charges of "squandering the nation's prosperity."[50] In these and other ways, his program so closely resembled Khomeini's that admirers and detractors alike began calling him the "Ayatollah of Kaolack." The first issue of a journal he published in 1979, *Allahou Akbar,* posed the question on its cover, "For or Against the Islamic Republic of Senegal?"[51] Ahmed Khalifa Niasse fled to Paris in 1979 (where he further imitated the real ayatollah by recording speeches calling for Islamic revolution on cassette tapes and then having them smuggled into Senegal) and went on to Libya in February 1980. According to reports from Senegal, Qadhdhafi planned to use Libyan forces to overthrow Senghor and to place Niasse in power, but Niasse's efforts came to at least a temporary end in April 1981 with his arrest in Niger on charges of recruiting soldiers for Libya.

Changed Role. Legal and illegal groups appeared in the 1970s to challenge the quiet power of Muslim leaders in Senegal.

SOMALIA

When Muhammad Siad Barre's government introduced legislation in 1975 guaranteeing equal marital rights for men and women, many Somalia 'ulama resisted the bill. In response, the government rounded up thirty of the leading religious authorities, exiled some of them, executed ten, and confined the rest. Rarely in modern history has any Muslim government felt strong enough openly to confront the religious establishment in this manner; and Siad's confidence did not last long. A rising sympathy for legalist Islam forced him quickly to tread more carefully. By the late 1970s, religious authorities attended government meetings to make sure state decisions accorded with Shar'i precepts, the official newspaper included a page in Arabic, and Siad himself talked about the community of interests between Islam and his ideology, socialism. "If you read the Qur'an properly and believe in it," he claimed, "then you have to be a socialist."[52]

The opposition to Siad also took on an increasingly Islamic tone. Mijerteyn tribesmen had formed the Somali Democratic Action Front after Siad took power away from them; to tap the legalist revival, they changed its name to the Somali Salvation Front and added Shar'i goals to their program. One of the 'ulama exiled by Siad in 1975, Sheikh Muhammad Hajji Dualeh, directed the Islamic Party of Somalia from London.

Changed Role. Government and opposition forces both moved away from leftist forms in favor of Islamic ones.

SYRIA

After 1963, a military clique belonging to the 'Alawi sect and the secularist Ba'th party ruled Syria, to the distress of most Sunni Muslims. The 'Alawis are a Shi'i group that broke away from mainstream Islam in the ninth century and were traditionally viewed as beyond the pale by Muslims. Numbering about half a million in Syria, 12 percent of the population, the 'Alawis' uncertain status meant that the Islamic opposition to the regime wavered in its attack, sometimes pressing for legalist measures (as though the 'Alawis were Muslim), sometimes inciting autonomist revolt (implying they were non-Muslim).

If the rulers' faith was puzzling, their attitude toward religion was not; Ba'thist ideology calls for the exclusion of Islam from politics. This viewpoint was hardly ever expressed openly, however, due to the widespread opposition it aroused. The vehement response to a magazine article calling Islam "a mummy in the museum of history" has already been noted (p. 122); when the People's Assembly adopted a permanent constitution in January 1973 which did not require that Islam be the religion of the head of state, riots followed in many cities. The government reacted by adding an amendment to the constitution stating that "Islam shall be the religion of the Head of State" (neatly affirming the Islamic credentials of the incumbent 'Alawi president, Hafiz al-Asad) and by massively distributing Qur'ans bearing the president's portrait as a frontispiece.[53] Also, the president paid frequent visits to mosques (something 'Alawis do not normally do) and actively sought the support of Sunni religious authorities. That these moves did not appease Islamic sentiments was made clear by the new round of riots three months later, on the occasion of the Prophet's birthday.

The Syrian government's aid to the Lebanese Christians in their civil war with the Muslims and Palestinians prompted dark talk of a conspiracy between 'Alawis and Christians to subjugate the Muslims, leading to a campaign of assassination of prominent 'Alawis. Low-intensity terror by fundamentalists persisted for years after 1976, irritating the Asad regime without threatening it. A more active effort against the government began in June 1979 with the Muslim Brethren's massacre of fifty or more cadets at the Artillery School in Aleppo (where 'Alawis constituted about 96 percent of the class), followed by about an incident each day for the next several months. The conflict further escalated in early 1980 with the bombing of an Aeroflot office and attacks on Soviet military personnel, including some of the highest ranking officers on duty in Syria, perhaps in retaliation for a Soviet role in the torture of Muslim Brethren. A new level of ferocity followed with the assassination of a promi-

237

nent Sunni religious figure (because he cooperated with the government), attacks on state property, full-scale riots, and an attempt on Asad's life in June 1980.

In response, the regime used all the force at its disposal, including dragnets, exemplary punishment, and the execution of prisoners. In July 1980, it announced that "any member of the Muslim Brethren will be considered a criminal punishable by the death sentence,"[54] and in December of that year, it crossed into Jordan to attack Muslim Brethren camps. Violent reprisals continued on both sides, degenerating into a pattern of cruelty: but the opposition was not suppressable, the government not unseatable.

The conflict between government and fundamentalists reached a climax in February 1982 with the destruction of Hamah, a city of about 150,000 residents. It began when 300 'Alawi soldiers searching the city for Muslim Brethren hideouts and caches of arms were ambushed, and nearly all were killed. The authorities sealed off the old quarter of Hadhir and reportedly brought in up to 12,000 troops, 100 tanks, 130mm artillery cannons, helicopter gunships, and even jet bombers. After shelling the city for some days, the troops moved in for house-to-house fighting; civilian casualties were estimated at anywhere between 3,000 and 35,000. After the fighting, little of the city center remained standing. Asad's actions in Hamah proved his determination to subjugate the Muslim Brethren regardless of cost, presumably winning for his reign a new lease on life. His actions also marked a rare example of a Muslim leader trying to destroy his fundamentalist opposition through naked force. The success of his efforts could have important implications for other rulers confronted with similar enemies.

Changed Role. Fundamentalist opposition to the secularizing, semi-Muslim regime of Hafiz al-Asad surged dramatically during the 1970s, becoming the key domestic issue.

TUNISIA

With a fling at secularism after independence followed by a turn toward fundamentalism in the 1970s, Tunisia was archetypical of the countries where Muslims predominate. As leader of the nationalist opposition to French colonialism, Habib Bourguiba relied heavily on Islamic symbols, leading many to believe, once independence was won, that he had "a mandate to work for the establishment of an independent national community committed to Muslim values."[55] He made it appear that autonomism was a prelude to legalism; but when Bourguiba did take power in 1956, he enacted a program that quickly made Tunisia one of the most secular Muslim states. A new Personal Status Code replaced the Shari'a for family affairs, the government expropriated waqf properties, religious schools were closed, and the Ramadan fast was discouraged on economic grounds.

The rise of fundamentalism is usually traced back to 1970, the year when the Society for the Preservation of the Qur'an became widespread and influential through its cultural programs, public relations efforts, and pressures on the government. Its growth may have been encouraged by the government as part of an effort to weaken the left-wing forces.[56] Over the years, the fundamentalists' assertiveness increased. During Ramadan of 1975, a female professor of philosophy caused a stir when she appeared fully veiled on national television (and before a live audience that included President Bourguiba), and called for women to return to Islamic ways.[57] In August 1977 members of a fundamentalist group attacked cafés in Sfax and roughed up customers they found drinking alcohol.[58]

But it was not until 1979 that fundamentalists acquired real political force. In that year, several leaders emerged—Rashid al-Ghanushi, 'Abd al-Fattah Muru, and Hasan Ghudbani—who had the stature to pressure the government on the national level. They founded magazines, organized students, spoke in mosques, and led rallies. One project of theirs that particularly worried the government was a strike by high school students in February 1981 in which the students carried placards with Islamic themes such as "God is great" and "Islam is our way, Muhammad is our leader."[59] At the University of Tunis, students who were disappointed not to get the new mosque they had requested held the dean of sciences hostage and made him sign a confession before the police rescued him. In March 1982, fundamentalists at the university deployed knives, bottles, chains, and crowbars in a pitched battle against leftist students.

The authorities responded with increasing concern. Ghanushi was arrested in December 1979 and his magazine, *Al-Mujtama'a,* was banned six months after its inception; other fundamentalist magazines, including *Al-Ma'rifa* and *Al-Habib,* were closed down by the police as well. Prime Minister Hedi Nouira subsequently warned that the mosques were being used as "pulpits for inflamatory speeches by the opposition for manipulating the feelings of the faithful, for provoking hatred and sowing seeds of fanaticism."[60] The director of the government political party accused the fundamentalists of acting "in a manner prejudicial to the interests of religion" while "under the cover of religion."[61]

Fundamentalism took on greater strength in June 1981 with the establishment of the Islamic Movement of Tunisia, an amalgam of three distinct organizations. Headed by Ghanushi and Muru, it came into being at a time when the government had allowed other opposition parties to become legal. But on 18 July 1981, the very day that the government lifted an eighteen-year ban on the Communist party, the police arrested Ghanushi, Muru, and eighty-nine others in the Islamic Movement; quick justice followed and the leaders were sentenced to as many as sixteen years in jail. When Tunisia's first multiparty elections were held in November 1981, the Islamic Movement was not allowed to participate. Tunisia's fundamentalists had little prospect of winning more power as long as President Bourguiba lived; but his passing could allow them a significant voice in national politics.

Changed Role. Leadership of the opposition passed from the leftist forces to the fundamentalist Muslims in the 1970s.

TURKEY

The rise of fundamentalism in Turkey has exceptional interest because its government was the first to embrace secularism and the only one to attempt completely to eliminate Islam from public life. Under the leadership of Kemal Atatürk, the country underwent a series of reforms in the 1930s and 1940s (see on p. 122) that replaced Islamicate forms with European ones. Atatürk did all he could to Westernize Turkey, for example, replacing Turkish words of Arabic and Persian origin with words of French derivation; he even installed pews in the mosques. After his death in 1938, the secularist legacy was carried on by the military. Keeping Islam out of politics required constant vigilance on its part, to the point that the soldiers made Atatürk's program into something resembling a civil religion.

Secularism always had opponents, but they laid low during Atatürk's life-time and for years after his death. The state did retreat from some of his more excessive policies (such as requiring that the call to prayer be in Turkish rather than Arabic) and the gradual democratization of politics in Turkey meant that the parties had to accommodate Islamic sentiments; but fundamentalism did not acquire a political voice until 1970, when Professor Necmettin Erbakan and others founded the Party for National Order. While this movement had a program that avoided specific references to Islam, its goal was clearly to bring the state in line with Shar'i precepts. If the vague and guarded formulations of its policies did not make this clear, then a heavy reliance on Arabic words did (for these have an Islamic ring in modern Turkish). The Party for National Order was judged to be in violation of Turkey's constitution, which prohibits any organization from trying to influence "the basic social, economic, political or judicial orders of the State [according] to religious principles and beliefs," and was dissolved in May 1971.

Having learned from this experience, Erbakan tried again and five months later he founded the National Salvation Party (NSP). A cautious program, a low profile, and a well-planned organization not only kept it out of court but won it surprising success at the next elections. In October 1973 the NSP won 48 out of 450 seats in the Grand National Assembly, enough to make it the junior partner in a coalition with the Republican Peoples Party—ironically, the secularist party founded by Atatürk. From this position of influence, NSP members worked to implement the fundamentalist agenda in national politics and autonomism in international affairs (especially in Cyprus), clashing frequently with their nominal allies. After only a year, the coalition floundered but the NSP participated in several more governments before losing half its seats in the June 1977 elections and going into the opposition in 1978.

The NSP advocated a more militantly autonomist position for Turkey in the Cyprus dispute and had an important role in the decision to send the Turkish army there in 1974. Fundamentalist pressure also spurred the government to sign the Charter of the Islamic Conference in 1976, just before the Islamic Conference met in Istanbul. Because this accord contradicted the principles of secularism enshrined in the Turkish constitution, the constitution had to be amended.

Fundamentalism made great gains outside the government as well. Turkish imams (prayer leaders) so effectively made use of the Iranian practice of giving political sermons that the government banned all political statements by the religious authorities, even outside the mosque, in February 1980. Fundamentalist pressure compelled the government to re-establish two prominent symbols of Islam in Turkey. Hagia Sophia, the ancient Byzantine church which had been turned into a mosque in the fifteenth century, was made into a museum in 1945; then, in August 1980, it opened once again for Islamic prayers (though not the main building, only an annex, the Sultan's Loge). The authorities also reinstituted the practice of reciting the Qur'an in a pavillion at the Topkapi palace; but whereas in Ottoman times, it had been recited around the clock, the reading was this time limited to seven and a half hours per day.

Fundamentalists had a major part in the political violence that swept Turkey in the late 1970s. Students of the left and right fought long-running battles in hundreds of incidents each year. Whereas these fights took on a feuding quality and acquired a life of their own apart from ideological disputes, they did in some sense reflect a debate over the vision of society, with about half the rightists intent on a Shar'i order for Turkey (and the others seeking a fascist order along European lines). This left-right split also acquired a communal character, leading to violence between Shi'is and Sunnis in many parts of the country. Shi'is in Turkey (called Alevis) tended to prefer secular policies because these de-emphasized their religious difference; thus, the Alevis gravitated toward the leftist parties. The worst communal violence occurred in December 1978 at Maraş where over one hundred people were killed following an incident that began with the bombing of a cinema and then grew so violent that military reinforcements had to be called in. Martial law was subsequently imposed on thirteen of Turkey's sixty-seven provinces.

These and other fundamentalist activities no doubt had a major part in the generals' decision to evict Turkey's elected leaders from office and to establish a military government in September 1980. Because the armed forces had shown a special devotion to the secular legacy of Atatürk it came as no surprise when the generals, upon seizing power, took measures against the fundamentalists. Among these was a ban on all political statements by the 'ulama and a prohibition against women wearing kerchiefs on their heads in school, except during Qur'anic classes. Professor Erbakan, head of the National Salvation Party, was arrested and detained on flimsy charges for months before his trial began in March 1981. The indictment (echoing the constitution) accused him of attempting "to replace the fundamental legal, social, economic and political principles of the state by religious principles."[62] Erbakan denied all the charges, claiming that he had never called for the application of the Shari'a, but he and twenty-three aides were found guilty in February 1983 and sentenced to prison terms.

Even the military government could not entirely contain the fundamentalists, however. It did stop prayers at Hagia Sophia and Qur'anic recitals at the Topkapi palace, but in each case it relied on the lame pretext that the buildings were in need of urgent repairs. On one major issue, the generals felt compelled to give into a fundamentalist demand that all prior governments had resisted, namely, that of making religious education mandatory in the schools. Such concessions not only pointed to the strength of fundamentalism but also revealed the ideological stagnation of secularism. The generals took over the government to preserve Atatürk's vision, yet they treated it as a kind of divine authority, not daring to make the adjustments it needed to stay attractive. Promoting secularism for its own sake, they caused it steadily to lose popularity, while fundamentalists won support through the dynamism of their ideas and the currency of their policies.

The outside world had a glimpse of the turmoil in Turkish politics when a young Turk, Mehmet Ali Ağca, was arrested for shooting Pope John Paul II in May 1981. Although the idea for the assassination attempt probably came from the Soviet Union, Ağca's own motives involved a wild autonomist fury against the pope as the most visible leader of Christendom. Ağca sent a letter to a Turkish newspaper in November 1979, just before the pope visited Turkey, which made this sentiment clear:

> Out of fear of seeing Turkey and its Arab brothers create a new political, economic, and military force across the Middle East, the West has sent John Paul II to Turkey as commander of the crusades. If this untimely and meaningless visit is not canceled,

I will certainly kill the pope. . . . Someone has to pay for the attack on the Great Mosque of Mecca in 1979, provoked by the United States and Israel.[63]

His younger brother supposed that Ağca wanted to kill the pope "because of his conviction that the Christians have imperialistic designs against the Muslim world and are doing injustices to the Islamic countries."[64] Ağca's defense lawyer from a previous murder charge in Turkey suggested that Ağca "might have wanted to kill the pope because the Pontiff held prayers in Hagia Sophia," while his Italian lawyer argued that Ağca was a "religious fanatic."[65] Whatever the exact motives, Ağca clearly felt he was striking a major blow for Islamic autonomism.

Changed Role. Fundamentalists acquired a political voice in 1970, they participated in the government for five years, and they became engaged in street violence and other non-democratic activities, all of which eroded the secularist nature of the state in Turkey.

In all but Iraq and Algeria, fundamentalism surged in countries with large Muslim majorities, creating new problems for the authorities and impeding the process of modernization. From a comparative standpoint, five nations held the greatest interest: the major fundamentalist and theocratic experiment in Iran; the eccentricities of Qadhdhafi's Libya; the rigorous debate and the imposition of fundamentalism by military fiat in Pakistan; the mixture of fundamentalist ideology and traditionalist way of life in Saudi Arabia; and the stark contrast between a stagnant secularist government and a dynamic fundamentalist opposition in Turkey.

In Iraq, divisions between Muslims overshadowed fundamentalist efforts; this situation could change with a shift in the power distribution. Algeria, however, holds special interest. Is it really the first Muslim country to have entered a post-Shar'i era or will the Shari'a return through influences from outside the country? The answer could have important implications for the future course of Islam.

Moieties: A Greater Drive to Rule

In the situation where neither Muslims nor non-Muslims can achieve uncontested political superiority, a long-term struggle for power tends to color all aspects of public life. During the 1970s, this was the dominant concern in Chad, the Sudan, Lebanon, and Malaysia; and it was less obvious but still centrally important in Albania, Nigeria, and Ethiopia. These differences had a violent cast in all of these countries except Albania.

ALBANIA

From the moment the Communists seized power in November 1944, they waged a campaign against religion. Moderated during the first fifteen or so years by its weakness, in the 1960s the government was strong enough to directly confront the religious institutions. By September 1967 it had closed all religious edifices in Albania, including 2,169 mosques, churches, monasteries, and so forth, making Albania officially "the first atheist state of the world."[66] Two months later, the People's Assembly annulled earlier laws guaranteeing the freedom of worship. Then religious ceremonies and holidays were replaced by state festivals and atheistic missionary work was stepped up. The violent suppression of clandestine religious practices was carried out by such means as executing transgressors or cross-examining children in school the day after religious holidays about the food and activities of the night before. In 1976, the government even went so far as to suppress personal names with religious connotations: "Citizens who have inappropriate names and offensive surnames from a political, ideological, and moral viewpoint are obliged to change them."[67] Whoever did not agree to this voluntarily would have a new name decided for him by a committee.

Despite the Communist framework of political life, the rulers of Albania appeared to be as keen as Muslims elsewhere to monopolize power. Judging by personal and family names, most of the government and party leaders were of Muslim origins. Indeed, it would appear that they held more than 70 percent of the top positions and thus enjoyed more influence than their percentage of the population entitled them to. This fact has two implications for Islamdom at large: first, an Islamic background is not proof against Communism; and the autonomist urge holds even among Muslims who utterly reject their religious patrimony.

Changed Role. The Islamic revival had apparently no effect in Albania, where legalism remained outlawed and autonomism remained moderate.

CHAD

When the French occupied Chad at the beginning of the twentieth century, they did their best to destroy all indigenous political institutions in the north, the Muslim region. Upon leaving the country in 1960, French authorities took steps to ensure that Muslims would not wield power. They transferred the government apparatus to the Christians and animists of the south, virtually excluding Muslims from representation; Muslim efforts to win a role in the government led to the banning of their political party in 1962 and the arrest of their leaders a year later. Also, the French army stayed on in the north until 1965, five years after independence, keeping tight control over the Muslim population. Only with its departure could Muslims rebel, organizing under the banners of the Front for the National Liberation of Chad (FROLINAT). By 1968, the Muslim resistance had turned into a civil war; but FROLINAT unity was broken early in that year when its leader, Ibrahima Abatcha, was killed, leading to a proliferation of FROLINAT factions. By 1977, the Muslims fielded five independent forces.[68]

Through a kaleidoscope of splits and alliances, two processes went gradually ahead: first, the Muslims gradually increased their hold over the entire country, destroying the Christian and animist forces and winning control over the south as well as the north by February 1979. Second, as the non-Muslims receded, inter-Muslim fighting grew worse, opening the country to outside manipulation. What began as a Muslim autonomist effort ended as a melée between armed Muslim factions following an assortment of personalities and ideologies. As a result, the Islamic quality of the fighting diminished, though it never disappeared. "The pogroms which took place in the south against the Muslims testify to the persistently religious character of the conflict, even if FROLINAT and the various northern factions forsook Islam as a symbol and became more oriented toward ideological and political goals than religious ones."[69]

Changed Role. As an Islamic autonomist rebellion gained victory, it turned into a feud between Muslims.

ETHIOPIA

Although a state ruled by Christians since late antiquity, conversion to Islam and the nineteenth century conquest of Muslim areas eroded the Christian majority of Ethiopia. As a result, the country's population is by now nearly half Muslim. The government in Addis Ababa, however, both imperial (until 1974) and revolutionary (after then), refused to recognize this fact and tried to suppress Muslims through persecutions, appropriations of property, and harsh social measures. Both regimes excluded Muslims from power and systematically discriminated against their interests. In reaction, Muslims in several regions of Ethiopia took up arms in the effort to win autonomy or independence.

Eritrea, a province on the Red Sea near the Sudan with a near majority of

Muslims, fell to Italian control during the 1890s and remained separate from Ethiopia until linked with Addis Ababa in a nominal federation in 1952. Just before the federation was abolished and the region came under direct Ethiopian rule ten years later, a rebellion led by the Eritrean Liberation Front broke out. Although it began as an Islamic autonomist movement, the need to win participation by the Christian Eritreans impelled the rebels to de-emphasize the Islamic dimension of their struggle. The secessionists came close to expelling Ethiopian forces in 1978 when massive aid from the Soviet bloc, including Cuban soldiers, helped push them back.

For Muslims in other parts of Ethiopia too, Islam served as the premier symbol of resistance to Christian domination. In response to government resettlement programs, the Oromo peoples in the south launched an Oromo Liberation Front in the late 1970s, and other Galla peoples also showed increased desire for autonomy. To the east, Muslim rebels of the Western Somalia Liberation Front, assisted by regular forces from the Somali army, invaded the Ogaden region in 1977 but were repulsed in 1978, again with Soviet and Cuban aid. Somali government troops were officially withdrawn from the Ogaden in March 1978, but Western Somalia Liberation Front forces continued to fight, probably with covert help from the regular Somali army, certainly with the full diplomatic support of the Somali government.

Changed Role. Many of Ethiopia's Muslims took up active efforts to free themselves of Christian rule in the 1970s.

LEBANON

Outsiders disagreed about the identities of the factions in Lebanon's civil war which erupted in 1975 and then became a way of life. The fighting pitted conservatives against radicals and Christians against Muslims and Druze, but not along clearly defined lines. Although usually not discussed by foreign observers in terms of Islam, the conflict had deep autonomist roots. Sa'ib Salam, a leader of the Muslim Lebanese for half a century, summed it up in 1982: "All the [political] parties in Lebanon are nonsense to me. In Lebanon there are only Christians and Muslims."[70]

Of Lebanon's many Christian sects, the Maronite Catholics were politically pre-eminent, for the most part due to their centuries of cultural and commercial ties to the West, especially to the Vatican and France. In Ottoman times, French intervention on the Maronites' behalf won them a separate province, Mt. Lebanon, where Christians made up 80 percent of the population. In 1920, shortly after France occupied the Levant, the French added other regions to

246

Lebanon, doubling its area. Although intended to favor the Christians (giving them a larger, more viable state), the new regions also reduced the Christian majority to 53 percent, according to the census of 1932.

Sunni Muslims (20 percent by that same census) were especially unhappy about being separated from Syria and Dar al-Islam and at being made part of a Christian country. Shi'is (18 percent) and Druze (6 percent), who would be minorities in any state, were less involved. Differences of view between Christians and Sunnis over the independent existence of Lebanon, and its size took on an ominous tone in the 1930s with the formation of para-military organizations along communal lines. Conflict was averted, however, by the conclusion of an unwritten compromise in 1943, known as the National Pact. In return for Muslim acceptance of the independence of Lebanon and its territorial integrity, the Christians ended their reliance on French protection and agreed that Lebanon become an Arab state (that is, join the Arab League and oppose the Jewish presence in Palestine). As for internal politics, the 1932 census became the basis of a complex distribution of power along communal lines: six Christians to every five non-Christians in the parliament, a Maronite president, a Sunni prime minister, a Shi'i speaker of the parliament, a Druze minister of defense, and so forth.

Although the National Pact held for over thirty years through innumerable challenges, the para-military organizations founded in the 1930s did not disband. Muslim dissatisfaction with the existing order grew over time, in part because Christian leaders refused to permit a new census, thus maintaining the Christian edge in power and nullifying the dramatic surge in the Muslim population. (Estimates saw the Christian proportion of the population in 1980 drop from 53 to about 40 percent, the Muslims increase from 38 to 49 percent, and the Druze increase from 6 to 9 percent.) An influx of Palestinian refugees in the late 1940s further increased the numbers of Muslims, while the arrival of the P.L.O. in 1970 added significantly to the Muslims' military potential.

Palestinian use of Lebanon as a base for operations against Israel eventually brought internal Lebanese tensions to a crisis: whereas Sunnis supported P.L.O. use of Lebanon, despite the Israeli policy of retribution, Christians were opposed. Frustrated with the static nature of Lebanese politics and the impossibility of advancing their position through legal means, the Muslims joined forces with the Palestinians and opted out of the National Pact in 1975, activating the communal militias and leading to the partition of Lebanon into Christian and Muslim regions. The various factions reverted to their pre-1943 positions: the Christians distanced themselves from Arabism (as symbolized by their growing cooperation with Israel) and the Muslims strove for a state of their own, free of Christian domination—they no longer wished to join Syria after witnessing the political life there through thirty years of independence. The Israeli invasion of June 1982 exacerbated these tendencies, making it even more unlikely that the country would resume its former political structure; yet no generally acceptable alternative appeared to replace it.[71]

Changed Role. The Muslims' dissatisfaction with the existing division of power led to a protracted civil war, during the course of which they took over large parts of the country.

MALAYSIA

The political role of Islam in Malaysia was particularly varied and complex. To begin with, the country's demographics are unusually intricate, for the population divides between the Malays, who are Muslims and constitute roughly 47 percent of the total, and three major non-Muslim groups: the Chinese (33 percent), Indians (9 percent), and tribal peoples (11 percent, including Christians and animists). As relative newcomers, the Chinese and Indians are not fully accepted by the Malays. Until the mid-nineteenth century, the Malays dominated the Malay Peninsula; it was not until the British encroached upon this region that they encouraged the Chinese and Indians to emigrate, providing manpower for the British economic ventures, especially tin mining and rubber growing. So many Chinese and Indians moved in that by 1920 they numbered about the same as the Malays and they dominated business activities. Malays remained farmers and fishermen, largely isolated from modern life, often characterized as lazy, shiftless, and uninterested in economic growth—"nature's gentlemen" was one of the kinder epithets. A division of labor along racial lines facilitated British control and was welcomed by the colonial authorities.

In the 1950s, as independence drew near, the ethnic groups began to jockey for power. Malay, Chinese, and Indian leaders avoided polarizing the country along racial lines by creating the Alliance (after 1972 called the National Front), a coalition of political parties representing each ethnic group which controlled the government from independence on. The Muslims were represented in the Alliance by the United Malay National Organization (UMNO), and Muslims consistently filled the key official positions. But although Malays ran the government, they were virtually excluded from the country's wealth: in 1970, they were estimated to own a mere 4.3 percent of the equity capital in business enterprises in Malaysia, while the Chinese and Indians held 34 percent and foreign interests, mostly British, owned 61.7 percent.

The Islamic revival in Malaysia began with the race riots which erupted on 13 May 1969 in Kuala Lumpur, the capital city, and which deeply changed the nature of the country's politics. The riots resulted from Malay resentments of the Chinese. They left 196 persons dead and 439 injured and destroyed the notion that Malays accepted their lot. The government was compelled to take a more active policy toward helping the Malays; most important, one year later, it adopted the "National Economic Policy," a plan to place 30 percent of Malaysia's equity capital in Malay hands by 1990. To keep the Chinese within the Alliance, UMNO promised to work toward this goal by creating new sources of wealth and by buying out foreign interests—not by expropriation. This well-devised program was fairly successful and by 1979 the Malay share of equity capital had increased to 10.3 percent, the Chinese and Indian to 43.7, and the foreigners' had declined to 46 percent.

The relative poverty of Malays made Islam a central subject in any discussion of economic life in Malaysia, as Malay backwardness was usually attributed to religion. Many Islamicate characteristics were held to be inimical to modernization: "fatalism" discouraged the development of a work ethic, some of the Islamic rituals (the Ramadan fast) hurt productivity and others (the many festivals and the hajj) required too many costly outlays. Indeed, influential Muslim voices did espouse views harmful to economic growth. Parti Islam opposed the National Economic Policy on grounds that it was a capitalistic plan and therefore unsuitable for Muslims; at the same time, Parti Islam promoted the notion that no one needs wealth to be a good Muslim. Also, when the government established a national unit trust (the Amanah Saham Nasional), promising a minimum annual dividend of 10 percent, some fundamentalist groups condemned the plan on the grounds that fixed returns resembled interest and were therefore contrary to the Qur'an. Members of extremist Islamic organizations threw such possessions as radios and television sets into a river, calling these forms of wealth forbidden by Islam. The minister of commerce and industry was compelled in 1979 to justify his efforts to attract foreign investment to the country against the opposition of fundamentalist groups which claimed that this program was contrary to the teachings of Islam.[72] These fundamentalist views gave credence to the government argument that Malays could achieve material well-being only by de-emphasizing Shar'i precepts.

Leading the opposition to the UMNO policy of stressing Malay nationalism was Parti Islam (also known as the Pan Malaysian Islamic Party or by a variety of initials: PI, PMIP, or PAS). From independence until 1972, Parti Islam served as the principal opposition group in the parliament; then in December 1972 it joined the National Front, as UMNO attempted to attract the growing Islamic sentiments to support of the government. Parti Islam quit the coalition in December 1977, expecting to ride the international Islamic wave and hoping to win more seats in parliament than UMNO and thus to take over the government.

But the Islamic revival did not translate into parliamentary strength. Parti Islam, far from challenging UMNO's appeal, lost ground. In the March 1978 state elections in Kelantan, where Parti Islam had ruled since 1959 and where it entered the elections with 22 of 36 seats, it emerged with only 2 seats, a rout termed "incredible" by the correspondent for the *Far Eastern Economic Review*. [73] In the national elections which followed in July 1978, Parti Islam's representation in the 154-seat parliament dropped from 13 to 5, and its leader, Datuk Asri Muda, lost his seat. Again four years later, in April 1982, Parti Islam had high hopes for the national elections, but it only retained its 5 seats. The inability to gain from the surge of fundamentalism was undoubtedly due to the fears this movement created among non-fundamentalists and non-Muslims. The closer Parti Islam appeared to challenge UMNO, the more its opponents voted for the National Front. In addition, the party's appeal was reduced by its lack of a clear program to deal with Malaysia's economic and racial questions.

The 1970s witnessed a proliferation of fundamentalist organizations called *dakwah* groups. *Dakwah* derives from the Arabic, *da'wa* ("call to Islam"), and, like their evangelical Christian equivalents, they called on Muslims to live more in the spirit of Islam and urged non-Muslims to convert. A "mushrooming of dakwah groups" occurred around 1970 and by 1974 they had achieved a clear impact, especially in the cities. [74] Of the two most important groups, Darul Arqam founded a utopian community in Sungai Penchala, a town where the faithful attempted to live just as Muhammad and his companions had, and Jam'at Tabligh, an Indian-based organization encouraged its members to retreat from society.

Outsiders condemned these groups for "piety parades" and espousing the "glamour value" of living by the Shari'a. [75] The government attempted to dilute their appeal by establishing its own missionary agency, PERKIM (the Islamic Welfare Organization of Malaysia) and by increasing the Islamic content of the school curricula. Worried that the *dakwah* movements would impair Muslim efforts to advance economically and undermine the careful UMNO policy of combining favoritism for Malays with co-existence with non-Malays, the authorities banned Indian, Pakistani, Indonesian, and other foreign teachers from entering the country.

UMNO had an "ambivalent attitude toward the rising tide of Islam in the country," favoring the impulse to strengthen the Islamic identity while wary of its destabilizing effects. The government hoped, writes Mohamad Abu Bakar, to usurp "the fundamentalists' role as champion of the Islamic cause in society" by sponsoring rival organizations "more inclined to interpret religious rulings in a manner . . . compatible with government policies." On the whole, the government placed "a higher premium on Islam as a threat to its position than ever before."[76] Caught between aggressive fundamentalist Muslims and apprehensive non-Muslims, the ruling coalition trod a narrow path, trying to indulge the Muslims while assuaging the non-Muslims, aware that alienating either side could lead to communal disaster.

By 1974, an organization known by its acronym as ABIM (the Muslim Youth Movement of Malaysia) emerged as the country's most dynamic Islamic institution, and posed special challenges to the government. Founded in 1972 by Anwar Ibrahim (then twenty-five years old), ten years later it boasted 40,000 members in addition to a large following in the universities (students were not permitted to join). Ibrahim criticized the *dakwah* groups and PERKIM for encouraging mindless ritual practice and unthinking observation of Shar'i laws. He worked to raise Muslim consciousness and to make Islam a vibrant way of life by developing a system of social justice. In contrast to the *dakwah* groups, Ibrahim emphasized social and economic concerns and stressed only those Shar'i precepts which he considered advantageous to Malaysia. For example, in the matter of relations with non-Muslims, ABIM urged the end of the National Economic Policy (which, contrary to Islamic tenets, discriminated between races), proposing, instead, the establishment of programs to help all the poor of Malaysia. Ignoring the Shari'a, he advocated full participation by non-Muslims in the government. Anwar Ibrahim mixed the spirit of the fundamentalist with the flexibility of the reformist and the result was a distinctively new approach to Islam in politics. This, combined with outstanding confidence and charisma, led increasing numbers of Muslims to believe that Ibrahim could mold Islam into a viable way of life. He seemed likely to remain the key figure in Malaysian Islam for decades to come.

In April 1982, Ibrahim became a powerful political figure as well. He joined UMNO and won a seat in parliament, then he became a deputy minister in the Prime Minister's office and was elected leader of UMNO's youth wing. In a by-election at the end of 1982, Ibrahim's campaigning for the UMNO candidate was widely credited for the UMNO victory over Parti Islam. He was behind the founding of an international Islamic university, the Islamic Bank Act, 1982 (which created the non-interest-paying Bank Islam Malaysia), religious programming on television, courses on Islam in all schools, and a ban on gambling. Under his influence, the government developed plans to establish an Islamic insurance company and even Islamic pawnshops.

Other developments reinforced the atmosphere of rising Islamic piety. The government banned liquor at its receptions, thus imposing an Islamic prohibition on Chinese, Indians, and others. The state government of Kedah sent a delegation to the Middle East to study ways to implement the Shar'i punishments. A leader of the socialist Parti Rakyat, Kassim Ahmad, lost his office when he published a book entitled *Problems of Modern Islamic Social Theory*

251

in which he called for the application of the Shari'a. The Malayan Communist party, which drew its support almost exclusively from the Malayan Chinese, paid Islam a backhanded compliment when it set up the Malayan Fraternal Islamic Party in an effort to lure Muslim support.

But fundamentalists met disappointments too. Students at all the major universities had voted fundamentalists onto their campus councils during the 1970s. Then, without warning, the students voted them out of three leading universities in the space of one month, July 1980, provoking national comment. PERKIM and the other *dakwah* groups won about 30,000 Chinese and Indians and 100,000 natives into the fold of Islam, but in June 1979 the senior figure of Malaysian politics (a former prime minister, the first secretary general of the Islamic Conference, and the chairman of PERKIM) revealed that 20,000 new Muslims had apostacized. He blamed their readiness to revert to their original religions on the extremism of some Islamic groups.

A climate of growing fundamentalist strength fostered clandestine and violent activities. The Movement of the Forces of Allah apparently urged its members to prepare for conflict with the Chinese and Indians. In August 1978 Hindu guards clubbed and stabbed to death four Muslims they had caught desecrating a Hindu temple in Kerling, thirty miles north of Kuala Lumpur. An investigation showed that the same four had broken into a different Hindu temple each night during the preceding month, which was Ramadan. The messianic claims of Mohamed Nasir Ismail, a recently arrived Muslim from Cambodia (possibly a convert), seemed to be the reason behind the attack in October 1980 by fifteen Muslims dressed in white robes and wielding *parang*s (the razor-sharp machetes used for splitting coconuts) on a police station at Batu Pahat, a small town in southern Malaysia. They butchered everyone they could find in the station, killing fourteen and wounding twenty-three, while in the process, six of them perished.

In addition to a wide range of domestic legalist issues, Malaysia was also peripherally involved in two autonomist problems. In Thailand, Pattani Muslims fighting the central government were ethnic Malays, and some of them hoped to secede from Thailand and to join Malaysia. In the Philippines, the Moros at war with the authorities had close relations with some of the peoples in the nearby province of Sabah, Malaysia. Both these conflicts generated wide support in those regions of Malaysia near the fighting and among fundamentalist groups, pitting them against the authorities in Kuala Lumpur, which were intent on maintaining good relations with the Thai and Filipino governments.

Changed Role. Fundamentalism increasingly permeated the politics of Malaysia, threatening to destabilize the country, as powerful Islamic organizations made demands certain to upset the non-Muslim half of the population.

NIGERIA

Muslim regions of northern Nigeria have a legacy of strong states dating from before the British colonization in the early twentieth century. The Muslims retained enough of the old organization to play a predominant role after the British left in 1960; with the exception of a few months in 1966, the northerners always had a decisive voice in independent Nigeria. Their rule had geographic, tribal, and religious overtones, provoking resentment among the mostly Christian and animist peoples of the south. Although often ignored, the religious aspect of the north-south conflict underlay many of the tensions in Nigerian politics. Ibo attempts between 1967 and 1970 to break away and form the independent state of Biafra had a religious significance; as non-Muslims, the Ibos found rule by the northerners repugnant. The fact that Muslim states supported the central government, while Christian organizations and Israel aided Biafra accentuated this difference.

For years, autonomism was an end in itself. Muslim domination of the government was not followed by attempts to bring the state into conformity with the Shari'a, if only because of the acute sensitivities of non-Muslims. But the mood changed in Nigeria, as elsewhere during the 1970s, and legalist sentiments increased. A brief but bitter debate over the Shari'a flared up in 1978 during the preparation of a new constitution, and to satisfy Muslim wishes to live by Shar'i regulations, rather than Nigeria's secular laws, the draft constitution included a proposal for the establishment of a Sharia Court of Appeals on the federal level. But, fearing this would further divide Nigeria's already heterogeneous population, a parliamentary committee at the Constituent Assembly deleted the provision. In reaction, eighty-seven Muslim members of the Assembly withdrew from the legislature for the rest of its session, raising alarm about the prospect of Christian-Muslim confrontation.

While non-Muslims suspected the government of trying to impose the Shari'a, fundamentalists found its policies unsatisfactory. Islamic groups such as the Society for the Victory of Islam, the Islamic Trust, and the League for the Elimination of Heresy proliferated during the 1970s. They became a focus of public attention at the end of 1980 when members of one extremist group, Yen Izala, went on a rampage in Kano, the largest city of the Muslim north. Yen Izala had created minor disturbances more than a dozen times after 1977, but the group became violent in October 1980 when some of its members, possibly thinking themselves protected by magic, attacked the police, killing one officer. The governor of Kano State ordered the Yen Izala leader, Alhajji Muhammadu Marwa Maitatsine, and his estimated 4,000 followers to leave the state within two weeks. Rather than obey these orders, Maitatsine used the interim to plan a takeover of Kano's central mosque. In December he and his followers launched an attack which overwhelmed the police and forced local authorities to call in the armed forces. Yen Izala and the military fought pitched battles, devastating the entire quarter in which the mosque stood. The army called on residents of the area to leave, then (with the help of air force reconnaissance flights) killed everyone who remained behind during the next two days by shelling them, engaging in hand-to-hand fighting, and executing truckloads of prisoners in nearby fields. According to official figures, 4,200 persons died in the rioting, including Maitatsine himself and 11 policemen.

Yen Izala's example seemed to encourage other extreme fundamentalists to violence. In April 1982 alone, for example, fighting provoked by extremists broke out in four states of Nigeria (Kano again, Bauchi, Borno, and Gongola). The government released about 1,000 of Maitatsine's followers on 1 October 1982 and within days they took up preaching their cause again. By the end of October, major riots broke out in three northern Nigerian towns, Maidaguri, Kadura, and Kano, leaving over a thousand dead. On several occasions, the rampages were directed against churches and bars.

Changed Role. As the autonomist issue of Muslim rule in Nigeria lost urgency in the 1970s, the legalist impulse strengthened.

SUDAN

The Sudan faced an unusually delicate Islamic problem: powerful forces of proven capabilities threatened to break the country's unity, some by insisting on implementation of the Shari'a, others by resisting it. Although such conflicts existed elsewhere too (notably in Malaysia, also in Egypt, Pakistan, and Indonesia), nowhere they did they have quite the urgency they presented in the Sudan. The slightest misstep by the government in Khartoum could unravel Ja'far an-Numayri's finely balanced policies and draw the country into civil war.

Anti-Shari'a pressures were strongest in the Sudan's southern provinces, where the population is about 90 percent Christian or animist. Memories of Muslims as slave traders and invaders had left a legacy of bitter resentment against the northern Sudanese, who are predominantly Muslim and Arabic-speaking. Southern fears of northern political control and the imposition of Islam led to the outbreak of a rebellion in August 1965, half a year before Sudanese independence. By 1963, this had developed into a full-fledged guerrilla movement known as the Anya-Nya. For sixteen years kafirs fought to avoid Muslim control and Muslims tried to keep them within Dar al-Islam. Then, frightened by a Communist-backed coup attempt in July 1971, Numayri sought to broaden his base of support by reversing government policies and settling the dispute with the South. In a peace accord signed in February 1972 the South agreed to remain in the Sudan in return for autonomy in its local affairs and the right to restrict the missionary and commercial activities of northerners in the South.

Two organizations dominated the pro-Shari'a side, the Ansar and the Khatmiya. The Ansar traces its origin to the Sudanese Mahdi, Muhammad Ahmad, the man whose followers killed General Charles Gordon in 1885 and then went on to establish a fundamentalist government. After the Ansar was defeated militarily by the British in 1898, it reorganized into a nationalist movement. In 1944, the Ansar founded the Umma party to put pressure on the colonial administration; in the early 1970s, it counted about 2 million members (including Numayri) and 200,000 armed tribesmen. The Khatmiya order was founded in the early nineteenth century in the Sudan and grew to become the region's largest and most powerful Sufi brotherhood. From the 1880s on, its interests clashed with the Ansar's (it being on the whole less fundamentalist and more traditionalist), though its political arm, the People's Democratic Party (founded in 1956) cooperated with the Ansar's Umma Party. Together, these two organizations dominated Sudanese politics until 1964, when a coup brought leftists to power.

Numayri, who came to power in May 1969 with leftist backing, faced virtually annual coup attempts or armed rebellions by Islamic groups. In March 1970, after an Ansar attack on Khartoum failed, its forces retreated to Aba Island south of the city. The air force then bombed them, killing between 5,000 and 12,000 persons. In July 1976, the Ansar and other Islamic groups failed in another major invasion; their strong showing, however, convinced Numayri to sign a pact of "National Reconciliation" with the Ansar leader, as-Sadiq al-Mahdi, in July 1977. Mahdi returned from exile, as did Hasan at-Turabi, leader of the Muslim Brethren in the Sudan, though ash-Sharif al-Hindi, a politically important religious notable, stayed away.

Having made peace with both the South and the fundamentalist organizations, Numayri's policy after 1977 sought to balance these groups by involving them both in the central government and giving each of them reason to maintain the status quo. Southerners and fundamentalists both filled key positions; thus did Turabi became attorney general, a critically important position for the fundamentalists. The Shari'a stood at the heart of the balance, representing the most irreconcilable difference between non-Muslims and fundamentalists. Each side continuously jockeyed to improve its position. Turabi used his influence to appoint a committee to revise Sudan's laws along Shar'i lines and included several Muslim Brethren among its members, but no southerners. Non-Muslim fears increased further when Turabi's intentions became appar-

255

ent: "I know that this country will become Islamic," he once said, "either gradually or by a coup."[77]

To a large extent, however, this was bluster: Islamic groups were unable to win more than lip service from the government to apply the Shari'a, and several years after the National Reconciliation, Sudan's laws had hardly changed, nor would they be likely to in the future. What John Voll wrote in 1973 continues to be true:

> In a unified Sudan, the old issue of an Islamic constitution becomes a dead one. The majority of the northern Sudanese probably want a unified Sudan without a civil war more than they want an Islamic constitution. This also means that specifically Islamic legislation, such as prohibition, is also very unlikely.[78]

(Another way of putting it would be that the autonomist urge outweighs the legalist one.) But acceding too much to the South's concerns ran the risk of alienating the fundamentalists and their foreign backers. Only great political acumen by the government could prevent the two sides from taking up arms again.

Changed Role. Growing fundamentalist power imperiled the unity of the Sudan.

Moieties are inherently unstable at a time of Islamic revival. Autonomist urges to win political control increased where there was non-Muslim rule or insecure rule by Muslims as in Chad, Ethiopia, Lebanon and Nigeria. Legalist impulses to apply the Shari'a grew more powerful where Muslims already ruled securely, as in Malaysia and the Sudan. In either case, Islamic causes were inimical to political balance.

Small Minorities: Increased Autonomist Demands

In the large number of countries where Muslims constitute less than a quarter of the population, autonomist impulses far outweigh legalist ones. In recent years, autonomism was signaled through secession (as in Thailand and the Philippines), cultural self-assertion (in Yugoslavia and the Soviet Union), or a combination of the two (in Israel and India). Fundamentalists sometimes leavened these autonomist efforts with a vision of the wholly Islamic society, but legalism rarely had much impact in circumstances where the Muslims' first concern was either to unburden themselves of kafir rule or, even more defensively, to safeguard their cultural heritage.

BULGARIA

Through five centuries of Ottoman rule, a substantial Muslim population appeared in Bulgaria, four-fifths of it Turkish-speaking and the rest, known as Pomaks, speaking Bulgarian. The Communist government recognized the Islamic faith of the Turks but not that of the Pomaks, claiming that the Pomaks' ancestors had been forcibly converted to Islam. (Communist regimes often betray positively medieval attitudes such as this.) An estimated 500 Pomaks were imprisoned in the Belene camp in the mid-1970s, and an anti-Islamic campaign began in late 1976 with press criticism of the Ramadan fast. Riots occurred when the government refused Pomaks the right to emigrate to Turkey.

BURMA

Although the Muslims of Burma were on the defensive, especially after 1978, their plight was related to the surge of Islamic political action in other regions. A million Muslims make up about 4 percent of the population in Burma, yet only one quarter of these, called the Rohingyas, have ethnic and territorial solidarity conducive to political activism. The fact that they live in the province of Arakan which borders on the Muslim country of Bangladesh also made it easier for them to organize. The Rohingyas launched a struggle in 1948 to win independence from the Buddhists who ran the central government in Rangoon. Known as the Mujahids' Rebellion, the active phase of this war ended in 1954, although the conflict dragged on until 1961. More recently, the Rohingya Patriotic Front pushed politically for Islamic autonomism and the Arakan Liberation Army was active in 1974–75.

Throughout the 1970s, hostility toward the Rohingyas and suspicions about their loyalty to Burma led the government to expel some of them to nearby Bangladesh. In 1978 this became a massive campaign, called "Operation Dragon King," in which about 200,000 Muslims were ejected across the border to Bangladesh. Rangoon justified its actions on the grounds that the Muslims were not Burmans but immigrants from India. (Although partially correct, even the immigrants among the Muslims had lived in Burma for generations.) Islamic organizations and Muslim states publicized this expulsion and brought enough pressure to bear on Rangoon to compel the repatriation of Rohingyas that began in September 1978. But the return went slowly, with the Burmese officials unwilling; the last refugees arrived only at the end of 1979. United Nations sources estimated that 190,000 persons were repatriated and 10,000 died. The Bangladesh army forced refugees in Bangladesh to return to Burma, though many resisted; on one occasion, the Bangladesh police opened fire on a group of disgruntled refugees, killing some of them.

Failing to expel the Rohingyas in this direct manner, the central government came up with a different, more subtle plan in December 1979, even as the refugees were still returning. President Ne Win announced a new category of citizenship; in addition to the full citizenship of "pure blooded" Burmans, there would also be a category of second class citizens of "mixed blood." The definition of this second category clearly was formulated with Muslims in mind. One Muslim source speculated that "the scheme is now to take away their citizenship rights on the grounds of racial purity and then to disperse them thinly all over the country."[79] More than two-thirds of the Muslims were expected to become "naturalized citizens" and thereby to lose their right to participate in public affairs. Before long, groups of Muslims began leaving Burma by sea, landing in Thailand and Malaysia.

While the Rohingyas experienced just the opposite of an Islamic revival, the general surge in Islamic political action around the world heightened Burmese Buddhist concern about the Muslims of Arakan. The authorities in Rangoon, noting the debilitating effect of Muslim insurgencies in Thailand and the Philippines and their roughly comparable circumstances to those in Burma, perhaps decided to pre-empt the danger of autonomism by expelling the Rohingyas or redistributing them around the country.

Changed Role. The Burmese government anticipated an increase in Islamic autonomism by persecuting its Muslim population.

CAMBODIA

The Muslims of Cambodia, known as the Chams, underwent the most horrific experience of any Muslim peoples in recent years—very much the opposite of a revival. When the Khmer Rouge took over in April 1975, the Chams numbered somewhere between 85,000 and 250,000; by the time the regime fell to Vietnamese troops four years later, an estimated two-thirds of them had been killed, a monstrous percentage even by the standards of Pol Pot's regime. The Communist government targeted all minorities for extinction and especially the Muslims because of their conspicuous religious practices. The Muslim nations failed to aid the Chams in any way, partly due to ignorance of their very existence.

CAMEROON

Although making up only 17 percent of the country's population, Muslims controlled the presidency from independence in 1960 until November 1982. Alhaji Ahmadu Ahidjo won French support for his candidacy by virtue of moderate policies and the Muslims constituting the single largest ethnic bloc in the country. Muslim power increased with the years as Ahidjo's stature grew and as his co-religionists won an expanding share of government positions, especially in the armed forces. A group of Muslim extremists attacked the police at Dolle, in the north, in 1979, apparently under the impression that they were invulnerable to bullets. Except for this and a few other fundamentalist activities, however, Islamic efforts were devoted to autonomism.

CHINA

Muslims in China divide into two broad groups, the Hui, who are Han Chinese living mostly in Yunnan province in the south, and the Turkic peoples of the northwest. Although the Hui identify strongly with Islam and the umma, their ethnic and linguistic ties to the government in Peking make them feel less of a separate identity and less inclined to initiate autonomist action than the Turkic peoples, who consider themselves to be conquered peoples and who have been often quick to revolt.

The Cultural Revolution was a great trauma for the Muslims, as for all Chinese. From the early 1960s until after Mao Tse-tung's death in 1976, the practice of Islam was persecuted. For example, in the autumn of 1966, two of the wall posters in Peking made these demands:

Close all mosques;
Disperse [religious] associations;
Abolish Koran study;
Abolish marriage within the faith;
Abolish circumcision.

Immediate abolition of all Islamic organizations in China;
Moslem priests must work in labor camps;
Moslem burial practices must be replaced by cremation;
Abolish observance of all Moslem feasts and holidays.[80]

To a considerable extent, these demands were implemented. Except for mosques in Peking and Canton (maintained for foreigners), every mosque in China was closed. A leading Chinese scholar of Islam, Muhammad al-Amin, was in the process of translating the Qur'an and the *Hadith* Reports into Chinese when the Cultural Revolution broke; he was imprisoned, his house repeatedly ransacked, and his manuscripts were destroyed except for those saved by fellow Muslims. A thousand Muslims were killed in a mosque in Shajien (Mengzi county, Yunnan province) in July 1975 following a quarrel between local Muslims and the army commander in their district. Also about that time,

259

Muslim villages in Yunnan were bombarded when the peasants refused to raise pigs, as the authorities in Peking demanded.

The end of Mao's rule brought relief. Mosques re-opened, Islamic associations became legal again, and scholarship resumed. For the first time since 1964, sixteen Muslims went on the pilgrimage to Mecca in 1979 and a Qur'an in Chinese translation was published. Restrictions on the Arabic script, intended to cut Muslims off from their written heritage, were less rigorously applied. A Muslim, Yang Ching-jen, became minister in charge of national minority affairs in 1978 and then vice-premier from 1980 to 1982.

Muslims also undertook direct political action to protect themselves from the excesses of the Cultural Revolution. In 1974, Muslims rallied in the capital of Yunnan province to protest the prohibition of Islamic rituals, wearing burial shrouds to show the seriousness of their intent; about 1,700 Muslims lost their lives. Even after the death of Mao, conflicts with the authorities continued—for example, disturbances were reported during 1980 in the far northwestern cities of Kashgar and Aksu.

Changed Role. Persecuted in the early 1970s, the Muslims became more secure and more willing to stand up for their identity later in the decade.

CYPRUS

Cyprus, inhabited by Christian Greeks for over a millennium, fell to the Ottoman Turks in 1571. Greeks converted and Turks migrated in the course of the next three centuries, bringing a Turkish-speaking Muslim community into existence. Comprising almost one-fifth the island's population, the Muslims lost their favored status when Britain conquered Cyprus in 1878. By the time Cyprus won its independence in 1960, the Greeks were firmly in charge of the government. As the Turks struggled for more power, tensions between the two religious groups increased, leading to the communal violence in 1963–64 and 1967, and to a partial division of the country enforced by the United Nations. (Turks could move freely about Greek areas but Greeks could enter the Turkish sections only with permission of the U. N. guards.) The continued exclusion of Muslims from power precipitated the invasion of Cyprus by the Republic of Turkey in July 1974, leading to full partition. Although the Muslims subsequently set up their own state, they were in reality little more than a province of Turkey—and happy to be so; moving from Dar al-Harb to Dar al-Islam outweighed the desire for independence.

Changed Role. The long-standing wish of the Turkish Cypriots to win their autonomy from the Greeks was achieved in 1974.

GREECE

In a massive transfer of populations after World War I, Muslims living in Greece moved to Turkey and Christians in Turkey went to Greece. In exchange for the patriarchate of the Orthodox Church remaining in Istanbul where it had always been, a deal was struck to spare two communities from this transfer: Christians living in Istanbul and Muslims in Western Thrace, the region of Greece bordering on Turkey. Thracian Muslims are mostly Turks, but they also include some Pomaks (Bulgarian-speaking Muslims) and Gypsies. The Greek government allowed the Muslims to stay but made life difficult for them, hoping they would leave for Turkey. (In like manner, the Turkish government harassed the Christians of Istanbul.) In the prefecture of Rodop, for example, Muslims were required to get permission to travel to other parts of Greece, while foreigners were denied entry. In all three predominantly Muslim prefectures, the authorities tried to erase the Islamicate cultural heritage by changing place names, banning written materials in Turkish, and prohibiting the repair of mosques or schools.

The Muslims of Greece were largely passive until the 1970s, when they formed such organizations as the Western Thrace Turkish Solidarity Association to protect their interests. Despite this, conditions in Western Thrace deteriorated further after the Turkish invasion of Cyprus in 1974 and the economic squeeze was stepped up in 1979 with the virtual expropriation of waqf lands. These developments prompted Ankara to take up the issue of West Thrace with Athens in high-level talks between the two governments. Although broken off in 1982 with none of the disputes resolved, these did have the effect of bringing the Thracian Muslims to international attention. Worried by this, the Greek government added still more repressive measures. Like the Rohingyas of Burma, the Muslims of Greece paid a price in the 1970s for the assertiveness of their co-religionists elsewhere.

Changed Role. A new autonomist assertiveness developed in the 1970s, accompanied by worsened conditions.

INDIA

In India more than anywhere else, the autonomist impulse characterized the political history of Islam; ironically, special circumstances have almost entirely denied the possibility of autonomism in the Republic of India. During the millennium following the first incursions by the Arabians in 711, Muslims conquered territory in South Asia before settling in or converting the inhabitants to Islam. Power came first; ruling the Hindus became so routine that political

261

ascendance came to be seen as a Muslim prerogative. Muslims lost control to Britain, however, starting with the East India Company's initial concession of 1608 and ending with the proclamation of Queen Victoria as Empress of India in 1857. Hard as it was for Muslims to accept British dominion, this was at least mitigated by the fact of the Hindus being subjugated as well; rule from London kept the Hindus out of power and Muslim hopes of eventually recovering the old power remained alive.

These hopes dimmed in the years after World War I, however, as the prospect of an independent and democratic India increased. Barring the improbable—very different reproductive rates or large-scale conversions to Islam—Muslims realized that they would always number about one-quarter of the total population. In democratic India, they would be permanently excluded from power. But the autonomist legacy in South Asia was too strong for Muslims to accept this fate, and by 1940 their leading organization, the Muslim League, adopted a program splitting the two most predominantly Muslim regions (today's Pakistan and Bangladesh) from the rest of India to form the new state of Pakistan. This idea caught hold and in the final years of British rule, as Hindus struggled for independence from Britain, Muslims struggled for independence from Hindus. Separation of over one thousand miles and dissimilar cultures did not deter the Muslim League, which expected the bonds of Islamic solidarity to prevail over all differences.

Islamic autonomism proved unstoppable. Pakistan was proclaimed as an independent state on 15 August 1947, the same day that India became independent. Although millions of Muslims living outside the designated borders of this new state migrated to Pakistan (and about as many Hindus left it for India), most Muslims stayed where they were and became citizens of the Republic of India. Scattered throughout India, they numbered about 35 million at the time of partition (and 76 million in 1982), making India the country with the second or third largest Muslim population (and making the Muslims of India possibly the largest single minority group anywhere in the world).

Like their co-religionists in Cyprus and Israel, the Muslims of independent India lived in an area historically part of Dar al-Islam but with ancient ties to a non-Islamic civilization. Like them, the Muslims of India came under British rule and then were forced to contend with the fact that British withdrawal would not permit them to return to Dar al-Islam. But unlike the Muslims in Cyprus and Israel who turned to autonomism, this option was precluded to the Muslims of India. If they wished to live in a state ruled by Muslims and strive for Shar'i goals, they would have to move to Pakistan, otherwise, if they stayed in India, they had to accept becoming citizens of a secular, democratic, and overwhelmingly Hindu state. Not going to Pakistan meant renouncing autonomism (and, by implication, legalism too). Yet, India was a democracy and Muslims had a voice with which to make their wishes felt (indeed, Muslims twice became president of the republic, twice chief justice, and once head of the air staff). This presented the Muslims of India with a unique dilemma:

> The question of political power and social organization, so central to Islam, has in the past always been considered in yes-or-no terms. Muslims have either had political power or they have not. *Never before have they shared it with others*. . . . The Muslims of India in fact face what is a radically new and profound problem; namely, how to live with others as equals. This is unprecedented; it has never arisen before in the whole history of Islam.[81]

Strife between Muslims and Hindus on the local level (known in India as "communal tensions") flared up periodically after independence, though their character changed over the years. Most clashes followed the same pattern: occurring mainly in the urban areas within the Hindi-speaking region of northern India, they were typically set off by some trivial incident (a pig in a mosque, music during the Islamic prayers, the killing of a cow, disputes over water at a public faucet). Before the mid-1970s, Hindus had usually provoked the incidents and Muslims, outnumbered within India and feeling vulnerable, did little more than defend themselves. In the late-1970s, however, Muslims went over to the offense, attacking policemen, storing arms, and calling for federal investigations of local incidents. Other changes also occurred: whereas fighting previously had been localized, in the 1970s it spread from town to town (the Moradabad riot of August 1980 quickly reached twenty other urban areas); and whereas fighting had been between the faithful on both sides, the Muslims now made the police their principal target. These changes augured a new sense of self-confidence among the Muslims and possibly indicated the beginning of a new era for them in Indian politics:

> Years of political inaction and administrative ineptitude have brought the Indian Muslims to the point of no return; they have begun to take up cudgels for themselves, like other sections of Indian society, who find it harder to believe, much less rely on, their political leaders or the apparatus of state machinery. They are coming out of their self-imposed exile, and making their demands heard after drifting without a sense of direction. For the first time they are confronting their future in India full in the face.[82]

Shar'i personal law continued to apply to Muslims in India and was popular among them as a symbol of cultural separateness. Ironically, while Islamic Pakistan Westernized its Shar'i regulations in 1961, secular India retained them unchanged from the colonial period. In all likelihood, they will remain unchanged, for few politicians wish to risk alienating the Muslim vote by challenging them. Islamic organizations called for special Shar'i courts to apply the Shari'a, instead of regular courts, and several Communal Tribunals applied fundamentalist prohibitions to Muslims in their localities. For some reason, women attending movies or the circus, even with their husbands, particularly offended these guardians of morality.

Conversions to Islam increased in the late 1970s. While only 1,500 persons in the state of Tamil Nadu converted in the period 1944–80, 2,000 persons did so in the first eight months of 1981 alone. But it was the June 1981 conversion of 1,150 out of 1,400 Untouchables in one town of Tamil Nadu, Meenakshipuram, that raised an uproar. Everyone wanted to know what had happened in Meenakshipuram. A Home Ministry official observed sarcastically: "From February to July over 2,000 people have visited Meenakshipuram; the locals never saw so many VIPs and cars in their village before."[83] Reporters, sociologists, religious dignitaries, and community leaders went to the town, and various agencies of the government wrote reports on the conversions. In response, Hindu leaders promised to eradicate vestiges of prejudice against Untouchables. A Hindu revival movement started in late 1981, the Greater Hindu Society, then promised to remove the causes of the Untouchables' discontent.

These and other conversions emboldened Muslim leaders; at the 1981 annual meeting of the fundamentalist group, Jama'at-i Islami Hind, a call was made for massive conversion campaigns to increase the Muslim population of India to 200 million within the decade. This goal can be explained in light of the inability of Indian Muslims to pursue autonomist or legalist goals, but it aroused strong Hindu reactions. An opinion poll taken by a magazine in fifteen major cities after the Meenakshipuram incident found that 57 percent of the respondents favored government intervention to prevent mass conversions of Untouchables to Islam.[84] If this poll had any validity, Muslim missionaries would not go far.

The province of Jammu and Kashmir in the far northwest, near Pakistan, differed from the rest of India on account of its Muslim majority, the autonomist urges of the Muslims living there, and Pakistan's claim to it. For thirty-three years, the Kashmir issue bedeviled relations between the two countries, even taking them to war—but the Kashmiris themselves were quiescent. Then, in August 1980, riots protesting Indian control of the province broke out in Srinigar, apparently instigated by the Jama'at-i Islami Hind. The mood had changed in Kashmir, and Islamic autonomism became newly fortified. Defining the new attitude, a Muslim leader in Kashmir declared, "India is not our country and the Indian Constitution is not applicable to us."[85]

Changed Role. Islam's role increased in many ways through the 1970s: Muslims took the offense against Hindus in riots, fundamentalists pressed for more Shar'i laws, converts increased in numbers, and autonomist agitation in Kashmir emerged as a new factor.

ISRAEL

Israel faced increased autonomist sentiments among Palestinians abroad, in the occupied territories, and in Israel proper. The resistance to Jewish settlement in Palestine had had powerful Islamic overtones from 1922 to 1951, when it was led by Amin al-Husayni, Mufti of Jerusalem and head of the Supreme Muslim Council. In the era of Abdul Nasser and the heyday of Arab nationalism, however, Western and secular themes prevailed. This ended with the Arab defeat in 1967 and the emergence of the Palestine Liberation Organization (P.L.O.). The principal constituent of the P.L.O., al-Fatah, relied on Islamic motifs and symbols more than Israel's neighbors—the very name of the organization in Arabic means the Muslim conquest of non-Muslim lands. Many of al-Fatah's leaders, including Yasir 'Arafat, had been involved with the Muslim Brethren; 'Arafat himself was related to Amin al-Husayni. The P.L.O. routinely made use of the Islamic theme of jihad and emphasized the special role of Jerusalem in the Islamic religion.

Israeli occupation of the West Bank and Gaza after 1967 created optimal conditions for the development of anti-Israel sentiments and legalism made great progress in both regions. The observance of Islamic rituals increased markedly and fundamentalist groups gained in strength, culminating in university riots and clashes with leftist students.

The 1967 war also transformed the attitudes of the Muslim Arabs living within the boundaries of Israel proper. Before 1967, they had been almost entirely cut off from other Arab and Muslim peoples, but Israel's victory brought them into contact with the West Bank, Gaza, and beyond. At the same time, defeat in war had the effect of discrediting pan-Arabism and led to a re-emphasis of the Palestinian identity. The notion that Palestinians formed a people of their own (and not just a small part of a single Arab nation) gave the Muslims of Israel an enhanced sense of their own importance and had the effect of politicizing them. The candidates they elected to office increasingly promoted Islamic autonomist themes. Legalism also grew, but more slowly. In February 1981 the Israeli police uncovered a fundamentalist Muslim group in the Galilee called the Family of Jihad. In addition to the usual fundamentalist concerns—modest dress for women, no music at weddings, etc.—it had accumulated a large arsenal of stolen weapons. Israeli authorities suspected the Family of Jihad of being a P.L.O. front intended to attract support from Muslims unsympathetic to the P.L.O.'s secularist ideology. Twenty members of the group were later sentenced to jail terms.

Changed Role. As Palestinians everywhere—in Israel proper, the occupied territories, and beyond—became more involved in the autonomist cause against Israel, the appeal of fundamentalist solutions increased.

KENYA

The Northern Frontier District Liberation Front attacked Kenyan government installations in late 1980, hoping to wrest this predominantly Somali and Muslim region from the control of non-Muslims in Nairobi. A state of emergency was called and the Kenyan government accused Somalia of interference in its internal affairs, probably with good reason. The Kenyan government refused to recognize the political character of the rebellion, calling the rebels bandits (*shifta*s).

PHILIPPINES

Muslims of the southern islands of the Philippines have a tradition dating back to the sixteenth century of resisting control by the central government in Manila. It was then that the Spanish conquered the pagans of the northern provinces with relative ease but met fierce and protracted resistance from the Moros (as the Filipino Muslims are called). Moro territories were not subdued by the Spanish despite centuries of effort; the United States only accomplished this, and then still incompletely, in 1913. Even after 1913, Moros remained outside the mainstream of Philippine life and occasionally agitated for their autonomy.

From 1903 on, Christians from the north were encouraged to settle in the south, for both economic and security reasons. Until the late 1940s, they lived apart from the Muslims, but, as open land ran out, they came increasingly into conflict with the Moros over property and resource rights. As contacts multiplied, tensions sharpened and the Moros felt ever more threatened. A number of Muslim soldiers lost their lives in March 1968, in an incident known as the "Corregidor Massacre," provoking the Moros to organize the Muslim Independence Movement which called for a separate Moro state. Violent encounters between Moro guerrillas and government forces became a major problem about 1970 and were a major factor in President Ferdinand Marcos' decision to impose martial law in September 1972. Government attempts to disarm the Muslims backfired and pushed them instead into a full-scale rebellion. The Moro National Liberation Front (MNLF) emerged as the leading Muslim organization and its military wing, the Bangsa Moro Army, did most of the fighting. Conflict between the Moros and the government peaked in 1974, when it even included the destruction of whole cities. The civil war remained intense through 1976.

The Muslims fought for autonomy, the application of Islamic law, political control over the Christian settlers in the south, and economic advancement.

Moro strength in battle convinced the politicians in Manila to try discussing the differences between them, and in December 1976 Nur Misuari, leader of the MNLF, and President Marcos signed a peace agreement in Tripoli, Libya, calling for Muslim regional autonomy in return for the laying down of arms. The ceasefire held for some months, until disagreements over the manner in which Marcos carried out his obligations led to a resumption of fighting in 1977. Hostilities continued sporadically after that. Even with half the Philippine army stationed on the southern islands, the government made little progress toward subjugating the Moros. By the end of 1978, official estimates put the number killed in the war at 50,000.

Although Marcos felt confident enough to declare that the rebellion "is no longer a problem" in January 1980, increased violence (arson, bombings, ambushes) in the next two months led the government in March to declare the Tripli peace agreement invalid. In turn, Misuari announced that the MNLF would struggle "for complete self-determination and freedom from Philippine colonial rule"[86]—meaning full independence, not autonomy. On paper, the antagonists had reverted to their original positions, more bitter and unlikely to compromise than ever before; in reality, the rebellion wound down as the government used the incentives at its disposal to lure the Moro fighters out of the jungle.

Changed Role. From a minor source of unrest in 1970, Moro autonomism quickly developed into one of the Philippines' most pressing internal problems.

RUMANIA

The Muslims of Rumania, both Turks and Tatars, experienced an almost unbroken decline, cultural and demographic, from the time of independence in 1877 until the 1970s. Their schools were closed in 1957, the Islamic seminary of Mejidiye disappeared in 1967, Islamic publications were shut down, and the Muslims were cut off from their co-religionists abroad. In the mid-1970s, however, Muslim conditions improved, as the government took steps to please the Muslim oil-exporting states. Muslim contacts with the outside world resumed in 1973 and pilgrims were allowed to go to Mecca. Qur'anic schools reopened and the authorities authorized the import of Qur'ans.

SINGAPORE

Singapore became part of Malaysia in 1963 but withdrew from the federation two years later because its predominantly Chinese population did not want to live in a state ruled by the Muslim Malays. Singapore thus shares with Lebanon the distinction of being a state that came into existence specifically because its inhabitants rejected living in Dar al-Islam. This context made the position of Muslims living in Singapore (17 percent of the population) especially delicate.

The Chinese majority discouraged the practice of Islam and reacted with extreme nervousness to any signs of Islamic autonomism. Thus, Muslims did not serve in the armed forces and the authorities watched closely for any attempts to rejoin Singapore to Malaysia. Even calls for application of the Shari'a spurred fearful responses. Ten persons described as "Muslim fanatics" were arrested in 1979 on the grounds of planning an Islamic revolution.[87] Another ten persons, members of the Singapore People's Liberation Organization, were arrested in January 1982 as they prepared to distribute leaflets which accused the Singapore authorities of "suppressing the Malays and [their] language and culture," calling on Muslims to act: "It is the duty of every Muslim to protect the morality of Islam by whatever means. True Islam does not fear death." From this, the authorities implausibly claimed the group intended "to overthrow the government through use of arms."[88]

Changed Role. Increased Muslim confidence prompted agitation for more rights, alarming the government.

SOVIET UNION

Most of the Muslim peoples now living in the Soviet Union fell under Russian rule during the nineteenth century, in an expansion that paralleled West Europe's conquests at that time. But unlike the British, French, and other empires, the Russian empire was not dismantled in the years after World War II. It remains solidly in place, though with some important changes. Ironically, Moscow's support for "anti-imperialist movements" around the world has had little bearing on its own peoples, including a Muslim population recently estimated to number about 45 million persons, or about one-sixth the entire Soviet Union.

Before 1917, the Bolsheviks condemned all European imperialism, including Tsarist control over the Muslims of Central Asia and the Caucasus, but when they came to power, a change of heart took place. Not surprisingly, the Communist authorities did everything in their power to hold on to the colonies, even reconquering them when they rebelled. To justify this about-face, the Bolsheviks modernized the ideology of imperialism, calling the colonies "autonomous republics" and giving them the trappings of independent countries. All the while, non-Russians remained strictly under Moscow's control. In the new divisions, Muslims predominated in one autonomous region of Russia, Bashkir

A.S.S.R., and in six republics: Azerbayjan, Kazakhstan, Kirgizia, Tajikstan, Turkmenistan, and Uzbekistan. From the vantage point of the Muslim subjects, these adjustments changed very little; the evolution from explicit colony to "autonomous republic" still left them under Russian rule. The government's shift of support from Orthodox Christianity to atheism did not diminish its campaign against Islam. In short, Central Asia and the Caucasus remained in Dar al-Harb; even the occasional rise of a born Muslim in the Soviet hierarchy—such as Gaidar Aliyev in Andropov's administration—did not suffice to change this attitude.

After a brief period in the 1920s, repression and isolation ended all Muslim autonomist efforts. Soviet Muslims subsequently became silent, passively accepting their subjugation (except for some pro-German activities during the World War). But silence did not mean stagnancy. Just as in Algeria during the 1950s or in Israel in the 1970s, a mood of Islamic piety developed which probably presaged an increase in autonomist spirit. In the Caucasus, Sufi orders had organized most of the Muslim resistance to Russian rule before disappearing after 1928. They turned up again after World War II in a less political form, concentrating their energies on mystical pursuits; according to Alexandre Bennigsen, a leading analyst of Soviet Islam, this is "the appropriate posture for periods when Islam is recouping its forces for another round against the infidels."[89] The Sufi orders espoused "a very conservative form of Islam [whose] goals are those of the traditional *jihad*"—namely, expelling the Russians.[90] Sufi orders grew in importance from the 1950s, exercising a deep influence on public opinion and becoming increasingly responsible for giving spiritual sustenance to Muslims of the USSR, especially in the North Caucasus. The orders became a mainstay of Islamic faith, "one of the main reasons why Islamic beliefs, traditions and customs continue in the USSR," in some cases even constituting "a parallel 'church' without which the Muslim faith could not have survived the onslaught of scientific materialism [Soviet atheistic propaganda]." In Bennigsen's view, these Sufi orders are "among the most intractable and dangerous adversaries of the Soviet regime because [they] are *the only authentic anti-Soviet mass organizations in the USSR*" and the likely "nucleus for communal and even national movements in the Muslim regions of the USSR."[91]

Parallel with other Islamic movements, these organizations acquired "a new vigour" during the 1970s. According to Geoffrey Wheeler, "despite Soviet efforts, perhaps even as a result of them, there has of recent years been a great increase in national consciousness among Soviet Moslems."[92] In part, this was a result of the Muslim birth rate being three times that of the rest of the Soviet population's, giving Muslims a feeling of confidence about their future. Bennigsen believes this to be a reason for short-term inactivity, as the Muslims do not wish to risk provoking the Soviet authorities in the meantime: "that is why there is currently no insurrection and why the Muslim community keeps quiet."[93] Even so, reports of occasional incidents reached the West, such as the riots in Kazakhstan touched off by the burial of Muslim soldiers in a Russian cemetery in March 1980 or the assassination of a high-ranking Kirgiz Communist party official of Muslim origins, rumored to have been carried out by "Muslim nationalists."[94]

By late 1982, the invasion of Afghanistan had had a growing impact on Central Asians. In addition to the tales of Soviet Muslims helping the mujahidin or even defecting to them, reports from Tajikistan indicated discontent with a war against brothers in the faith.

Soviet authorities viewed such developments with obvious concern. The first secretary of the Kazakhstan Communist party complained in 1981 that even Communist officials observed Islamic ceremonies and that mullahs were free to do as they pleased in parts of southern Kazakhstan.[95] Worried about current trends, the government devoted many studies to Islam in politics and the way to defuse it. Moscow faced one problem which prior European colonialists did not: of the dozens of independent Muslim countries, several closely monitored Soviet activities and were willing to protest on behalf of their co-religionists in the 1970s. If domestic requirements called for repressing Islamic activities, foreign pressure called for restraint.

Although the significance of these developments may still lie far in the future, the Muslims of the Soviet Union will eventually awake to the fact that they are the last major bloc of third world peoples under European rule; and when they do, the spirit of Islamic autonomism will spur their efforts to shake kafir control. The implications of such a movement are immense: by challenging the Soviet authorities at home, Muslims would severely hamper Moscow's position abroad, leading to a possible realignment of the international order.

Changed Role. Quiet changes in the 1970s brought Islamic autonomist movements closer to realization.

SRI LANKA

Living on an island where they never ruled, where they constitute only 8 percent of the population, and where the two predominant ethnic groups (Sinhala Buddhists and Tamil Hindus) were engaged in a long-term ethnic struggle, the Muslims of Sri Lanka enjoyed a remarkably tranquil existence. It was they who often provided the minister of religion, when a Buddhist or Hindu appointment would create problems, and they mediated between the two sides on occasion. Yet even here the Islamic revival touched the Moors (as the Muslims of Sri Lanka call themselves) by giving them greater pride in their heritage, spurring efforts at legalism and contributing to occasional outbreaks of violence between Muslims and Buddhists. In 1982, the minister of foreign affairs, a Muslim, visited Pakistan to gather information about the Zakat Act there to use as a model for Sri Lanka's Muslims.[96]

THAILAND

As in Burma, the Muslims of Thailand make up about 4 percent of an otherwise overwhelmingly Buddhist country, and those Muslims who are concentrated in a single region count the most politically, for they alone pose an autonomist threat. In Thailand, 700,000 Muslims live in the historic region of Pattani in the far south, near the border with Malaysia, where they constitute 80 percent of the population. Muslims of the south are Malays, ethnically identical to the majority of Malaysia's citizens, speaking the same language, sharing customs and religion with them.

Thai kings claimed Pattani as early as the thirteenth century, but the government in Bangkok won direct control of the region only at the turn of the twentieth century. Autonomist movements flared up repeatedly after that, as Muslims refused to accept incorporation in Dar al-Harb. Sometimes their efforts were directed at joining the Malays to their south; the high point of this drive was a remarkable petition to the United Nations in 1947 calling for union with Malaya, reportedly signed by half the adult Muslim population of some southern provinces.[97] At other times, and especially in the 1970s when Malaysia's leaders discouraged efforts at union, the Thai Muslim forces appeared more interested in establishing their own state.

During the 1940s, officials in Bangkok launched a campaign to eradicate every distinctive custom of the Malays living in Thailand, including those features associated with Islam. The government abolished Shar'i family regulations, it prohibited the Malay language, Malay dress, and Malay names (many of which were Islamic); it even compelled Muslims to kneel down before statues of the Buddha. Muslims were prohibited from such distinctive practices as chewing betel nuts or carrying loads on their heads.[98] This trauma ended in 1945 but it remained a vivid memory among Muslims and poisoned Muslim-Buddhist relations in Thailand for decades afterwards. It fulfilled the Muslims' worst fears about living in Dar al-Harb, namely the prospect of the systematic elimination of Islam by determined enemies. Muslims suspected the government of waiting for an opportunity to repress them again; with somewhat more justification, they viewed government programs settling Buddhists in the south as aimed at undercutting Muslim strength and reducing the autonomist threat.

271

The recent autonomist movement gathered force in 1975 with two acts of violence against Muslims. On one occasion, Thai marines stopped a car with six Muslim passengers inside and, according to a survivor's account, murdered all the passengers but himself. Then, at a rally protesting these deaths, Thai soldiers threw grenades at the mourners and killed thirteen more Muslims. In response, some 50,000 persons staged a demonstration at the central mosque in Pattani which was called off only after 45 days, when the government agreed to a list of demands. Buoyed by this show of solidarity, the Muslims pressed for more concessions from the government.

At about the same time, some Muslim autonomists organized a campaign of terror to force the government to leave the Muslim regions. The Pattani National Liberation Front (BNPP), the National Revolutionary Front (BRN), the Pattani United Liberation Organization (PULO), and Sabil-illah ("The Path of God") all participated in these attacks. They engaged in kidnapping, robbery, and extortion, and they bombed such targets as a railroad station, the airport in Bangkok, as well as the royal couple (who escaped injury). In all, observers estimated that the autonomist forces numbered no more than several hundred. By forming occasional alliances with bandits and Thai or Malay Communists, however, they kept southern Thailand in a state of ceaseless flux.

Islamic autonomism also threatened to disrupt relations with Malaysia. When Muslim rebels in March 1981 captured an area previously held by Communists, the ensuing turmoil forced about a thousand Muslims to flee into Malaysia for refuge. Many fundamentalists in Malaysia dearly wished to exploit this occasion to rally support for the Pattani rebels, and it took supremely careful diplomacy by the Malaysian leaders to avoid a severe crisis in relations with Thailand.

Changed Role. A long-standing ongoing autonomist rebellion became active again in 1975.

UGANDA

When Idi Amin overthrew the government of Milton Obote in January 1971, he was commander of the army, and from then until his defeat by Tanzanian troops in April 1979, he depended primarily on the armed forces and the security services to stay in power. Amin solidified control over both branches by systematically eliminating officers and men who belonged to tribes suspected of sympathizing with Obote, and replacing them with foreigners and with members of tribes deemed friendly to himself. (In 1977–78, one-fifth of the army came from the southern Sudan.) These purges brought a disproportionate number of Muslims to power. Although they made up only about 6 percent of the population in Uganda, they held seventeen out of twenty-two top military posts in 1977–78.[99] This bias reached a point where "the army and security apparatus that . . . ruled Ugandans resembled an alien and mercenary occupation force, distinct from virtually all Ugandans in language, culture, religion and regional origins."[100] Muslims also staffed more and more civilian appointments, and the government provided them an opportunity to enrich themselves at others' expense (they profited disproportionately from the expulsion of the Asians in 1972). Islamic institutions received state subventions while Christian ones suffered persecution; much of the Christian hierarchy was killed or in exile by the end of Amin's reign. The government, always seeking loyal supporters, searched the remote bush areas to find Muslims and encouraged them to practice their faith.

Amin's fall from power in 1979 meant that Ugandan Muslims lost all they had gained during the 1970s, and more. Revenge hit them hard; in the words of a sympathizer, they were "mercilessly slain, recklessly ousted from position and power and forcibly evicted from their homes, looted, raped and indiscriminately thrown into prisons."[101] Some Muslims hid their faith by adopting Christian names, hoping this would help them avoid persecution. After a visit to the country in late 1980, the secretary general of the World Muslim Congress, Inamullah Khan, feared that many Muslims might abandon Islam altogether: "Unless their confidence and self-respect are restored and the feeling of helplessness and frustration checked immediately, we might lose them as Muslims forever."[102] Idi Amin echoed this sentiment in early 1981, predicting that unless he were returned to power, "Uganda will be lost to Islam."[103] What had initially appeared as a boon for the neglected Muslims of Uganda, in the end proved devastating.

Changed Role. An ambitious attempt by its small Muslim minority to control Uganda ended in terrible failure.

UNITED STATES

The West's largest indigenous Muslim community, the Black Muslims, once hoped to establish settlements of its own and withdraw from the United States, but these autonomist notions slowly died out. Instead, the movement made a dramatic shift toward legalism. During the 1970s, the Black Muslims abandoned their wildly eccentric "Nation of Islam" doctrines and adopted those of Sunni Islam.

273

The Black Muslim movement originated in Detroit in 1931 when an itinerant silk merchant of uncertain origins, one Wallace D. Fard, taught the rudiments of Islam to a thirty-four-year-old black laborer, Elijah Poole. Poole, who later changed his name to Elijah Muhammad, became the leader of the Nation of Islam after the disappearance (or occultation) of Fard in 1934 and won tens of thousands of followers. Although called Islam, his religion was almost entirely of his own making. Aside from a few terms such as "Islam" and "Allah," the Nation of Islam's doctrines shared almost nothing with mainstream Islam. Some of the outstanding differences included:

1. An anthropomorphic God. According to Elijah Muhammad, God is a corporate being, equivalent to the collective body of the Black Nation. All Blacks are God and one of them—the most powerful Black scientist of the age—is the Supreme Being. God is a man, a Black man; Wallace D. Fard was "God-in-person." This understanding not only contradicts the Islamic emphasis on a single God, but it reveals evident Christian themes.

2. Prophethood after Muhammad. The seventh-century prophet Muhammad is virtually neglected in favor of Elijah Muhammad, prophet of God (that is, of Wallace D. Fard), contradicting the Islamic insistence on Muhammad as the final prophet.

3. Racism. The world is divided into Blacks and Whites, with only the Blacks allowed to become Muslims. If Blacks adhere to Islam, they will eventually destroy Whites (who are devils). Whites are inherently inferior to Blacks, both morally and physically. In contrast, mainstream Islam condemns racism and stresses the suitability of the faith for all peoples.

4. Disregard of the Shari'a. Coming from a Christian environment, the Black Muslims had no understanding of sacred law. Elijah Muhammad ignored most Islamic precepts and made whimsical changes in the ones he kept: the Ramadan fast conveniently became a December fast, prayer rituals were altered, and many American Negro dishes (soul food) were prohibited.[104]

Had Elijah Muhammad merely tacked on a few Arabic motifs to his otherwise novel religion (something like the Shriners), it would have developed on its own into something new, but he called his religion Islam and this simple fact of nomenclature had profound effects on its evolution. As Black Muslims learned about the practices of mainstream Islam in Africa and the Middle East, and as Middle Eastern leaders took interest in the remote outpost of Islam centered in Chicago, pressures inexorably welled up to bring the Nation of Islam into conformity with mainstream Islam. Two forms of contact with the Middle East had the most importance in this transformation: first, the travels of Malcolm X made him aware of the gross disparity between real Islam and the American version. Disagreements with Elijah Muhammad led to a break by Malcolm X, splitting the Black Muslims. Second, Elijah Muhammad sent several of his sons to study Islam at Al-Azhar University in Cairo where they learned Arabic and became learned in mainstream Islamic ways. When Elijah Muhammad died in February 1975, his elder son Wallace (Warith ad-Din) Muhammad succeeded him and rapidly changed the Nation of Islam's doctrines and practices, bringing them into line with Sunni Islam. Perhaps most important of all, he announced in June 1975 the end of racial discrimination: "There will be no such category as a white Muslim or black Muslim. All will be Muslims. All children of God."[105]

Changed Role. The leading Muslim group indigenous to the West joined mainstream Islam in 1975.

YUGOSLAVIA

The catastrophic legacy of irredentist disputes which led to the outbreak of World War I made the Yugoslav government especially wary of ethnic claims and nationalist sentiments. Josef Broz-Tito spent decades achieving a fragile unity based on a structure of six republics and two autonomous provinces; the slightest changes in this structure threatened to bring down the whole edifice. Thus, the central authorities responded with alarm to increased autonomism among the two main groups of Muslims in Yugoslavia, the Bosnians and Albanians.

Bosnian assertiveness in the 1970s was connected in part to the jockeying for power in anticipation of Tito's death and in part to the increased liberalization of the country. Mosque attendance soared and the leading Islamic periodical, *Preporod,* advocated a more assertive attitude toward the practice of Islam. At the same time, the Muslim position in the province of Bosnia-Herz'egovina was eroded. A semi-official study characterized the Muslim religious leaders of Bosnia before and during World War II as "plunderers" and "traitors to their people," while emphasizing Muslim collaboration with the Nazis—the most powerful accusations that can be made in Yugoslavia.[106] The Latin script used by Muslims began disappearing from the media and the schools, while Muslims lost their positions in the Central Committee of the republic. Though they make up half the population, they filled only one out of seven secretaryships.

Tito, while on a trip to the republic, approved the repression of Islamic sentiments by Bosnian officials:

Although this nationalism [Islam] is propounded by small groups . . . this is dangerous. . . . So it is a good thing that you have now taken severe measures against the undermining activity of some clerical circles. Such attempts should be nipped in the bud, if necessary with severe measures.[107]

275

To combat Islamic sentiments stirred up by the Iranian revolution, the government dismissed the editors of *Preporod,* transferred mosque officials and religious teachers to distant provinces, and publicized condemnations of Islam in politics written by Communist intellectuals of Muslim origins. These efforts, however, did not stiffle all sentiments of Islamic autonomism; in April 1983, eleven Muslims were arrested in Sarajevo under suspicion "of having committed the crime of hostile propaganda from positions of Muslim nationalism"—a circumlocution that betrayed the government's unease with the problem. According to the authorities, the ultimate aim of this group's "hostile activity was to create, as its members stressed, a religiously and nationally pure Bosnia-Herzegovina, an exclusively Muslim state." (It would be hard to find a more exact statement of the autonomist program.) Then would follow "a linkage of all Muslim states." The government-controlled press linked this "self-appointed Muslim elite'" with the activities of the Young Muslims, a clandestine organization which operated in Bosnia-Herzegovina after the Second World War.[108] In the neighboring republic of Croatia, fears of Islamic autonomism reached such a pitch that the chief Islamic official of the republic was pressured to condemn Islamic activism.

At the same time that the government clamped down on ambitions to achieve Muslim solidarity, it made concessions to Islamic sensibilities. For example, it allowed construction of the long-awaited mosques in Ljubjana and Zaghreb and approved the opening of an Islamic seminary in Sarajevo. Besides placating Muslim opinion, this last concession also gave the government closer control over Islamic ideas, for providing higher education in Islamic subjects within Yugoslavia meant that students no longer had to go abroad for an education, where they might become infected with legalist or autonomist notions. The Sarajevo college emphasized devotional aspects of Islam and minimized potential challenges to the state.

Muslims of Albanian heritage make up more than three-quarters of the population in the province of Kosovo, the poorest region in Yugoslavia. During World War II, the Albanians fought unsuccessfully to detach Kosovo from Yugoslavia. Oppression by the Serbs during the 1950s and 1960s led to the establishment of underground organizations. Riots first occurred in 1968 and were followed by repeated outbreaks of violence through the 1970s. While further problems were expected after Tito's death, their size and violence came as a surprise. What began as a rampage by students at the University of Pristina in March 1981 escalated into clashes involving tens of thousands of armed demonstrators. Some rioters called for outright secession from Yugoslavia and unity with Albania, while others demanded that Kosovo's status to be upgraded to that of a republic, which would imply the theoretical right to secede from Yugoslavia. The Kosovo disturbances also had effects in other regions; in Macedonia, the government charged autonomists, including some official religious leaders, with pressuring gypsies, Turks, and all other Muslims to declare themselves as Albanians on the 1981 census forms. In Kosovo itself, twice as many persons declared themselves to be of "Muslim" nationality in the 1981 census than in 1971. Non-Muslims living in Kosovo complained to the authorities of being pressured to emigrate from the region.

In combination, "Bosnia-Herzegovina and Kosovo had become new loci of ethnocentric malaise" in Yugoslavia by the late 1970s. Pedro Ramet notes that Belgrade's fears of Islamic autonomism made "both the Muslim question and the persistent separatist sentiment among Yugoslavia's Albanians increasingly prominent on the political agenda."[109]

Changed Role. Increased identification with Islam in the 1970s threatened to unravel the carefully balanced political structure in Yugoslavia.

THE FURTHER LANDS

The Islamic revival also occurred in countries far beyond Islamdom's traditional boundaries, where it was not so much legalism or autonomism that gained, but the Islamic faith itself. In East Asia, West Europe, and North America especially, new Muslim communities and Islamic institutions appeared during the 1970s. The Qur'an and *Hadith* Reports were translated, mosques and schools were opened, and Islamic associations proliferated.

Possibly the largest new community of Muslims developed in South Korea, where Turkish soldiers stationed in the early 1950s had become engaged in missionary work. Thirty years later, Korean Muslims numbered about 50,000 and the symbol of their dynamism was the newly-established Korea Islamic College in Pusan. A smaller but growing Japanese Muslim community included prominent professionals.

In West Europe, conversions played a much smaller role in making Islam visible than the migration of Muslim workers from the Mediterranean basin. Of a total of about 6 million guest workers in the late 1970s, 1.9 million lived in France, 1.5 million in Great Britain, 1.4 million in West Germany, 800,000 in Italy, and significant numbers elsewhere, including 200,000 in Belgium and 30,000 in Denmark. Muslims outnumbered Jews and became the second largest religious community in most West European countries. In France, Muslims outnumbered all non-Catholics combined, including both Protestants and Jews. The 300,000 Muslims of West Berlin, including the largest number of

277

Turks in any West European city, kept the city economically alive. Turks in West Germany brought with them the political violence of their homeland; in March 1980, for example, an organization called the Grey Wolves was suspected in the political murder of a leftist Turkish teacher.

Mosques proliferated: in addition to resplendent new buildings in the hearts of such capital cities as Brussels, Copenhagen, Lisbon, London, Rome, and Vienna, more prosaic places of worship were established in less fashionable quarters. In 1977 an estimated 300 mosques functioned in Great Britain. A mosque even appeared in Spain, at Marbella, just outside Cordoba, the first public Islamic institution established in Spain in the almost 500 years since the expulsion of the Moors. An interest-free bank, the Islamic Finance House, opened in London in August 1982 to serve pious Muslims. The growth of Muslim populations in Europe brought legalist pressures, as Muslims lobbied to have the Shari'a recognized, especially regulations touching on the family. By a special act of parliament, the Belgian government recognized the Shari'a in July 1974. In Britain, the House of Lords ruled oral pronouncements of divorce along Shari'i lines valid in British courts.

Small Muslim minorities lacked the clear achievements of their co-religionists living in countries where Muslims formed dominant majorities or moieties. Secessionist efforts succeeded in Cyprus but not in Thailand or the Philippines. Muslims in Uganda held power for most of the 1970s but ended up worse off as a result. Israel's external enemies consistently sought too much and ended up with little to show. Political assertion in India provoked a backlash, whereas the Muslims of Greece and Burma suffered from the pre-emptive actions of their governments. Autonomism in Yugoslavia provoked the wrath of the federal government. Muslims living under communist rule in Bulgaria and Cambodia underwent new tribulations. For the long run, perhaps the most successful efforts were those quiet changes toward legalism which took place within Israel, the Soviet Union, and China, three states with powerful central governments and important Muslim minorities.

Characteristics of the Revival

Where Muslims ruled, the revival took the form of fundamentalist efforts to bring the whole country in line with the sacred law. Where Muslims did not rule, several complementary processes occurred: long-standing autonomist efforts revived and took on a more Islamic tone, powerful minorities rebelled, and weak ones asserted their rights more forcefully. The revival in the 1970s led to an increase in fundamentalism relative to its traditionalist, reformist, and secularist alternatives, while the bond of Islam gained relative to its nationalist, ethnic, and class alternatives. This Islamic revival—as any revival—involved *a strengthening of fundamentalist and autonomist impulses.* It also implied greater receptivity to the Islamicate patterns: veils, robes, hostility to Europe, and non-territorial loyalties increased along with mosque attendance and devotion to the Shari'a.

Although not simultaneous, the revival did begin within about a decade most everywhere. It reached all parts of Islamdom, but most dramatically in the east and least in the west. Every Muslim community in Southeast Asia experienced marked changes, as did almost every one in South Asia, while the Middle East saw a less consistent turn to Islam, and sub-Saharan Africa experienced the least of all. Even in Africa, however, the strengthening of Islam as a political force was notable.

One characteristic of the Islamic movements in the 1970s that this survey makes very clear is the minor role of intellectuals. Whether government supporters, loyal opposition, clandestine societies, or rebel forces, whether fundamentalist or autonomist, Islamic groups devoted little energy to constructing consistent theories. Secularism was in retreat almost everywhere, reformism stagnated, and even fundamentalism witnessed few developments other than Khomeini's theocracy. In the view of Habib Boulares, movements which contributed to the revival made "no contribution either to Islamic thought or spirituality."[110] In part, John Voll explains, this was due to the fact that doctrinal problems have less importance in Islam than in Christianity and therefore seem "more real to the Western observer than they are in the actual practice of modern Muslims." As a result, it was the organizers, enthusiasts, and politicians who had the most impact; "the actual revival of Islamic confidence has been the result of the activities of men of action who spent little time theorizing about what they were doing. Here, perhaps, is the location of the present and potential future vitality of Islam."[111]

Analysts of the Islamic revival almost always stress the independent rhythms of each country, and they are right to do so, for wholly distinct events spurred the turn toward Islam. Some of the more prominent developments include: a 1965 coup in Indonesia, a 1968 massacre in the Philippines, 1969 riots in Malaysia and coup in Libya, a 1971 coup in Uganda and attempted coup in the Sudan, the 1974 oil cornucopia in Iran, a 1975 massacre in Thailand and the death of a leader in the United States, the 1976 death of another leader in China, a 1978 coup d'etat in Afghanistan, and a 1979 rampage in

Saudi Arabia. Even when one event affected more than one country (as the 1967 Arab-Israeli war in Egypt and Israel or the 1971 split between Pakistan and Bangladesh), the impact was felt differently.

Granted that each country was most affected by specific internal developments unrelated to the umma as a whole, 1,350 years of Muslim history point to the importance of Islamicate developments. The primacy of local causes does not preclude the contribution of Islamdom-wide factors. Regions always developed on their own, yet within a context established by Islam. Was this also the case in recent years? The final chapter considers what factors may have moved all Islamdom in the direction of fundamentalism and autonomism.

10

The Great Oil Boom

He or she would be a bold and
venturesome prophet who was
ready yet to opine that the increase
in the price of oil will not prove of
significance primarily in the
religious history of the Muslim
peoples.
—*Wilfred Cantwell Smith*, 1975

The main resource to depend upon
after God is oil.
—*King Fahd of Saudi Arabia,*
1983

TWO STRIKING features characterize the Islamic revival. First, it touched
nearly all Muslims, as fundamentalist and autonomist sentiments almost everywhere took on new force. Second, the surge took place within a decade;
Islam had far greater political impact in 1980 than in 1970. What happened
so that the whole umma nearly simultaneously turned to Islam and what was
it that encouraged the Muslims to emphasize Islam as an identity?

The answer to these questions can be of two sorts: it can focus on independent developments across Islamdom or on some connecting influence touching
them all. Although the former explanation depends on an improbable sequence
of coincidences, it does have proponents. According to Thomas Lippman,
"There is no single worldwide 'Islamic resurgence,' but there has been a series
of coincident upheavals in which Islam is the common expression of political
dissent."[1] This approach does not justify serious discussion, however. Not only
is it extremely unlikely that more than forty countries should accidentally experience such similar developments at the same time, but the whole pattern

of Muslim history and Islamicate civilization point to shared rhythms. Claiming that the Islamic revival took place due to mere coincidence is comparable to analyzing the recent worldwide surge in inflation or terrorism by seeing the circumstances of individual countries only and being blind to factors that transcend national boundaries.

If one accepts the second type of explanation, that a few developments influenced most of the umma, then determining the causes of the revival becomes a matter of identifying those developments. Recognizing that each Muslim people has a separate evolution, a unique Islamic complexion, and distinct reasons for turning to Islamic political solutions, *what factors simultaneously and across the whole breadth of Islamdom prompted a surge of Islamic fundamentalism and autonomism?*

We may start with the presumption that whatever happened was sharply positive or negative. As Ali A. Marzui writes, "the political revival of a religion usually comes when the religion is subject to new forms of insecurity or when the followers are beginning to acquire a new level of self-confidence." Mazrui argues—as will I—that "in the case of the Islamic revival both factors have been at play."[2] Of these factors, a number set the stage for changes in the 1970s; and one event decisively completed the turn toward Islam.

Setting the Stage

In its broadest perspective, the Islamic revival is a product of the West's declining power and prestige. Europe began to impose its will over the rest of the globe in the fifteenth century and steadily increased its predominance until about 1900; but in recent years power has ebbed away from Europe to the non-Western world. At the turn of this century, European peoples virtually monopolized modern skills: they alone enjoyed the wealth, political stability, and military might that modernity makes possible. They ruled most of the inhabited regions, and their leaders, sitting in a handful of capitals, made nearly all great international political decisions. Others did little more than respond to their initiatives.

The Japanese were the first to incorporate European skills and to play an active role as a world power. Japan's striking victory over Russia in 1905 began the move toward non-Western assertiveness, while other non-Western peoples also began to learn modern skills. In the course of two devastating world wars (which were largely civil wars among Westerners), a new distribution of power brought on a wave of decolonization which began in 1943 and lasted twenty years. During that time nearly the whole non-Western world (with the important exception of regions under Russian and Chinese control) passed from colony to independent nation. Non-Western countries gained yet greater strength in succeeding decades; contrast the weakness of the oil exporting countries in Mosaddeq's time (1951–53) and their power two decades later. Note too Vietnam's military victories, the assertiveness of the non-aligned movement, and changes at the United Nations.

As the West relinquished total ascendance, its ideals and institutions lost luster. If European ways were indisputably the route to prosperity and power until World War II, they looked less attractive as the twentieth century wore on. In part too, the diminished prestige of European ways resulted from the West losing confidence and sureness of purpose. The most advanced countries betrayed confusion in the 1960s, assailed by doubts about science, progress, capitalism, liberalism, and secularism. These hesitations had an especially powerful impact in Islamdom, where the many persons who had misgivings about Westernization now found support for their views in the West itself. In particular, new religions and mystical trends in the West weakened the attraction of its ideologies and confirmed Muslim reluctance to give up their traditions. Islam began to look far more attractive than it had in previous decades.

The end of the imperial era spurred the revival of Islam in a variety of ways. In the first place, it led to fundamental economic changes. Whereas European colonial administrators saw their territories as sources of raw materials to be processed into finished goods in Europe, the newly independent governments built up industries and cities, even when these made little economic sense. Such efforts used up scarce resources, distorted the economy, harmed agriculture, caused farmers to move to the cities, and created mammoth urban populations of poor, isolated individuals. In Islamdom, megalopolies such as Casablanca, Cairo, Istanbul, Tehran, Lahore, Dacca, Kuala Lumpur, and Jakarta grew wildly, and became home to millions of dislocated peasants. Thrust out from their familiar surroundings, these people often sought solace in Islamic goals and bonds, for Islam was virtually the only aspect of their former identities that could be transferred from the village to the slum.

Changes in education reinforced this emphasis. All non-Muslim colonial rulers (not just the West European states but also Russia, China, Japan, Ethiopia and the United States) deeply feared Islam, correctly sensing that the autonomist impulse would prevent Muslims from ever accepting their control or adopting their customs with the ease of such peoples as the Maoris in New Zealand or the Ibos of Nigeria. To minimize autonomism, colonial authorities discouraged teaching about Islam and sometimes went so far as to replace Islam with the imperial culture. Thus did black Africans learn about "our ancestors, the Gauls." With independence, Muslim children again learned about their own traditions and Islam often recovered a key role in the curriculum. Algeria exemplified this change: before its independence in 1962, the French taught their language and culture. Since then the "democratic and popular republic" has taught Arabic language and Islam to its youth.

Having won their independence between 1943 and 1962, most Muslim states had been independent long enough by the 1970s to draw negative conclusions about the efficacy of Western ideologies. The political stability, social and economic justice, and military success hoped for at independence had not been achieved. Disappointed, they tried alternatives. In the Arab world, repeated failures led to an alternating of Arab nationalism with state nationalism, and several Muslim countries (Turkey, Egypt, Iran, Indonesia) experimented with varieties of capitalism and socialism, while others changed diplomatic alignments, and so forth. As imported ideals consistently worked less well in Islamdom than in their countries of origin, Muslims sometimes turned to Islam, hoping that its totally different program would provide them an escape from the tyranny of Western ways. "People were turning to Islam because everything else had failed."[3] Islam presented simple and confident answers to the umma's most pressing problems, proposing radically different solutions from the Western ones. For this reason, "to an increasing number of alienated Muslims, Islam does appear to provide a practical political alternative as well as a secure spiritual niche and psychological anchor in a turbulent world."[4] After a generation of experimentation, the time had come to try something different. The sequence of "imitation of the West, failure, and anti-Western backlash has repeated itself with remarkable uniformity in most Muslim countries, despite fundamental differences in historical development."[5]

The Islamic revival also had ties to the Arab-Israeli conflict, the most visible Islamic autonomist cause of recent times. Jerusalem's religious significance for the umma meant that Jewish control of the city since 1967 disturbed many Muslims and added an Islamic twist to this conflict; what had been an Arab cause took on greater meaning for the whole of Islamdom. Saudi rulers in particular stressed the need to bring Jerusalem back into Dar al-Islam. A fire at the al-Aqsa mosque in August 1969 provided them with the occasion to convene a long-planned summit meeting of Muslim heads of state a month later in Rabat. The Organization of the Islamic Conference which grew out of this gathering inscribed "support of the struggle of the people of Palestine" in its charter as a fundamental aim.[6] The conference subsequently played an important role in rallying Muslim support for the Arab cause against Israel.

After the terrible defeat of June 1967, the Arabs sought to win back diplomatically the territories they lost militarily. To accomplish this, they for the first time seriously courted international political support. Campaigning for public opinion among non-Arab Muslims in sub-Saharan Africa, the Middle East, South and Southeast Asia, they stressed the Islamic quality of the struggle with Israel. How could fellow Muslims traffic with the foremost enemy of Islam? This is the question al-Qadhdhafi put to the leaders of Chad, Iran, Niger, Senegal, and Turkey in March 1970 at the Islamic Foreign Ministers Conference. Three months later, while visiting Malaysia and Indonesia, King Faisal of Saudi Arabia stated that Palestine was a problem for Muslims everywhere. In 1983, Israel maintained official diplomatic relations with only two countries in Dar al-Islam, Turkey and Egypt.

The calamity of 1967 dealt a final blow to the already waning fortunes of pan-Arabism. Promoted by Abdul Nasser and the Ba'thists in the effort to unify the Arabic-speaking peoples, pan-Arabism attained wide popularity after the Suez War of 1956. But the 1967 war revealed the weaknesses of this ideology, discrediting it for the masses and sending them elsewhere for solace. Many turned to the familiar symbols and ideals of Islam. Nearly all the radical Arab regimes of yesteryear (Algeria, Egypt, Sudan, Syria, Iraq, North Yemen) responded to this change by relying more heavily on Islam to effect policy. Only al-Qadhdhafi maintained support for the pan-Arab goals, and even he mixed them with powerful doses of Islam.

Arab military success against Israel in October 1973 gave further impetus to growth of Islamic sentiments. The Egyptian and Syrian armies, no longer fighting under the pan-Arab banner but for Islam, did much better than expected:

The religious significance of the October 1973 War was obvious since it occurred during the Islamic holy month of Ramadan. The code name for the war was Badr, a reminder of the first Islamic victory under Muhammad in A.D. 623 over the forces of apostasy which, like its twentieth-century counterpart, was fought against seemingly overwhelming odds. In the 1967 war the battle cry of the Arabs was "Land, Sea, Sky," implying faith in equipment and the tactics of the military engagement. In 1973 the cry was more explicitly Muslim, the call of "God is great *(Allahu Akbar),*" with which Islam has spread the message of God through major portions of the world. It is not unusual to find Muslim writers who specifically ascribe the 1973 victory to God and His forces.[7]

The sense of "Islamic holiness" was so acute that some soldiers heard "a thundering voice" from the hills calling out *"Allahu Akbar,"* while others saw those words "vividly written across the sky."[8] Just as the 1967 war was portrayed as a humiliation for the entire umma, 1973 appeared to many as a victory for Islam: Muslims felt that "heightened religious fervor had yielded manifest results."[9] Some observers concluded that the two Arab-Israeli wars gave impetus to "a renascent sense of an international Islamic identity."[10]

285

These are the explanations most commonly proffered for the surge in Islamic fundamentalism and autonomism. To be sure, all of them—the West's declining prestige, its loss of confidence, the end of colonialism, the independent Muslim states' poor experience with Western ideologies, and the wars with Israel—contributed to an atmosphere conducive to the revival. They did not, however, fully account for it. For one, these explanations dwell exclusively on the surge of fundamentalism and pay no attention to the concurrent rise of autonomism. How does the inability of Muslim rulers to achieve social justice spur the Muslim minority to take over Uganda? How do hesitations about Western ideals touch the Bosnians and Albanians in Yugoslavia? Could the Arabs' military defeat inspire the Moros to rebellion in the Philippines? Analyses which ignore the autonomist aspect of the revival neglect the one-quarter of the umma who live in Dar al-Harb and are almost unable to express its convictions through legalism.

Further, these explanations even fall short of accounting for the surge in fundamentalism. Not one of the above-mentioned factors meets the criteria set out in advance, those of simultaneity and breadth. The first four of them did not occur at the same time and the Arab-Israeli wars did not influence the whole of Islamdom. The West lost prestige and power during the course of the twentieth century, but this was largely due to the fact that the non-Western peoples had so well incorporated Western ways, these quite lost their foreign cast. As William H. McNeill writes, "the dethronement of western Europe from its brief mastery of the globe coincided with (and was caused by) an unprecedented, rapid Westernization of all the peoples of the earth."[11] Japan's businessmen, Vietnam's military officers, India's scientists, and Iran's oil technicians had so thoroughly absorbed European techniques that they appeared indigenous. The West may have lost standing, but its culture acquired an international following.

The fact that most Muslim communities achieved independence during the period between 1943 and 1962 makes it reasonable to argue that they turned away from Western culture after a generation's experience had showed its deficiencies. But Muslim peoples who do not fit this timetable turned to Islam in the 1970s no less than those who do. Turkey, North Yemen, Saudi Arabia, Iran, Afghanistan, and Sinkiang never fell under European control, while Iraq and Egypt won their independence in the 1930s, yet most of these regions also recently experienced a marked Islamic revival. The United Arab Emirates stayed a colony until 1971, Muslims in the Soviet Union remain still under European rule, and Muslims in Yugoslavia *are* Europeans, yet they too fitted the revival pattern. The time that elapsed since independence did not noticeably affect a country's turn toward Islam.

Nor did other factors correlate any more closely with the revival. To varying degrees, Islam acquired new force in countries where Westernization ran deep (such as Algeria and Lebanon) and where it existed only on the surface (Mauritania and Afghanistan). Countries that had prospered politically since independence (Tunisia, Jordan) experienced the revival no less than those that fared badly (Syria, Iraq). Economic growth did not further Islam in Iran and Malaysia more than did stagnancy in Egypt and Bangladesh. A government's disposition toward Islam, whether friendly (Saudi Arabia), neutral (Indonesia), or hostile (USSR) made no apparent difference. Similarly, proportion of Muslim population (Libya versus Thailand), great power alignments (Turkey versus Guinea), and other considerations did not correlate with Islam's progress. Countries experiencing a revival of Islamic sentiments were too diverse for *any* pattern of national characteristics, singly or in combination, to account for their changes. The Islamic revival did not depend on attributes to be found only in parts of Islamdom; instead, it had to have been the result of something Islamicate, of some development that touched, to varying degrees, the entire umma.

Arab-Israeli relations cannot have been it, however, for the impact of the 1967 and 1973 wars did not reach beyond the Arabic-speaking countries. Even if Muslims distant from the Middle East felt sympathy for the Arab cause, the actual conflict hardly influenced them. How could the storming of the Bar-Lev line or the establishment of Kiryat Arba directly bear on the course of events in West Africa or the islands of Southeast Asia? Even in the Middle East itself, these events had limited impact on the non-Arab Muslims. The claim that Arab-Israeli affairs affected the umma as a whole should be seen as another consequence of the common tendency to equate Islamdom with the Middle East.

What then did happen in the 1970s that affected the entire umma? Was there an Islamicate event that set this period off from preceding years? Indeed, there was. The great oil boom was an event so profoundly and broadly influential that it provides the key to understanding the surge of Islam as a political force during the 1970s. Oil wealth affected Islam in three principal ways: (1) an enhanced worldly standing improved the attitudes of Muslims toward Islam; (2) Saudi Arabia and Libya acquired the means to promote Islamic causes around the world; and (3) Iranian society was disrupted, paving the way for Khomeini's rise to power and his experiment with Islamic theocracy—which in turn affected Muslims beyond Iran. Prosperity, power, and disruption: petro-wealth redirected Muslims to Islam as a source of ideals and bonds. For these reasons, the oil boom was the paramount Islamicate event of the late twentieth century.

Oil and Islam: A Changed Psychology

Soaring energy prices during the 1970s affected everyone, but it was the umma that netted most of the profits. True, lesser booms took places in regions as varied as Aberdeen, Alberta, and Alaska, and true, more Muslims suffered from paying higher energy bills than benefited from increased revenues; but Muslim domination of the international trade in petroleum inextricably tied oil to Islam. Muslims profited so disproportionately from the sale of oil that this resource altered some of the very premises of the modern Muslim experience. The close, even uncanny connection between oil and Islam existed on four levels, which can be pictured as four concentric circles: Islamdom, the Arabic-speaking world, the skeikdoms, and Saudi Arabia. Were it not obviously illogical, an observer might conclude that the more Islamic a government is, the more petroleum it exports on a per capita basis.

Of the thirteen members in the Organization of Petroleum States (OPEC) after 1975, all but two (Venezuela and Ecuador) were in Dar al-Islam. Eight were Muslim states of North Africa (Algeria, Libya) and the Persian Gulf (Saudi Arabia, the United Arab Emirates, Qatar, Kuwait, Iraq, Iran); Indonesia has a 90 percent Muslim population; Nigeria, about half Muslim, has often had a Muslim head of state; and though Gabon's Muslim population was miniscule, President Albert-Bernard Bongo converted to Islam in 1973, just as the price of oil mounted sharply. OPEC policy was tantamount to decisions made by Muslims, its power was Muslim power. Additionally, many other countries in Dar al-Islam exported sizeable quantities of petroleum without becoming members of OPEC, including Tunisia, Egypt, Syria, Bahrain, Oman, Malaysia and Brunei—bringing the total number of exporters in Dar al-Islam to eighteen. Further, oil reserves in predominantly non-Muslim countries were often located near Muslim areas, as in India and the Philippines.

Because they speak the language of the Qur'an, Arabs have a special visibility in Islamic affairs; for example, among Muslims as well as Westerners, "Arab" and "Muslim" are often used interchangeably, despite their very different meanings. Therefore, the fact that Arabic-speaking countries were also the principal exporters of oil through the 1970s added a second dimension to the oil/Islam nexus. Twelve Arab states had such extensive reserves and such high levels of production, they could control the oil trade. To emphasize a common purpose, the Organization of Arab Petroleum Exporting Countries was formed in 1968.

In the third circle, five states with the largest per capita exports, Libya, Saudi Arabia, Kuwait, Qatar, and the United Arab Emirates, not only spoke Arabic but were renowned for their piety and their resolve to implement Shar'i regulations. Oil revenues helped achieve some legalist goals; for example, they made it possible for governments to tax no more than the zakat rates permit. These richest Arab states led the efforts to institute interest-free banking and to apply Qur'anic penal codes. Several of them, especially the Saudis and Libyans, worked hard on behalf of Islamic unity.

The incomes of each of these five countries so far exceeded mundane needs that ample funds could be devoted to imaginative and attention-gaining projects, such as Kuwait's skating rink or its takeover of the Sante Fe International Corporation. The Saudis built an airport in Jidda as large as Manhattan and costing $7 billion, and they sponsored a conference on the towing of icebergs to supply drinking water. These countries became the leading symbols of petrowealth; an abundance of both oil and Islam made them especially important to the revival. To conjure up these five countries as a group, we shall refer to them as the "sheikhdoms," a not entirely accurate term (for Libya has a "government of the masses" and Saudi Arabia a monarchy), but one that does capture the right image.

In the fourth circle stood Saudi Arabia alone. Its oil revenues far exceeded those of any other country and its steadfast devotion to legalist Islam also had no peer. As the only Muslim country in modern times whose government did not deviate from fundamentalism, as the land of God's and Muhammad's cities (Mecca and Medina), and the sole nation to restrict its citizenship to Muslims, Saudi Arabia epitomized the conjunction of oil and Islam. And as the mainstay of the 1973 oil embargo, it led the umma to a sense of strength.

Muslims in all four circles were thus especially well positioned to take advantage of increases in the price and production of oil on the international market beginning in 1970. Arabian light crude had had a posted price of as much as $2.08 a barrel in 1958 but then declined to $1.80 in 1961 (precipitating the foundation of OPEC in 1960). Oil prices then stayed almost unchanged through the rest of the decade.

It became clear that energy would soon be more expensive in 1969–70, when a confluence of factors combined to transform the trade in oil from a buyer's market to a seller's. Over the years, inexpensive petroleum had encouraged conversion from coal to oil; at the same time, low prices had discouraged exploration for new sources. Production in both the United States and Venezuela began to decline in 1970, simultaneous with a marked economic upsurge in Europe and an increase in the rate of factory conversions to oil. Several supertankers and TAPLINE, the pipeline carrying Saudi oil to the Mediterranean, were damaged by explosions, making the existing shortfalls worse. Growing financial reserves and skilled personnel gave the exporting countries greater independence of action against oil companies and consuming nations. The entry of the "independents," smaller oil companies eager for a share of the Middle East oil market and willing to grant better terms than the "majors," gave the producing countries more leverage in negotiations. Colonel Qadhdhafi came to power in 1969 and was willing to cut Libyan production to exacerbate a shortage. After completing the White Revolution, the shah of Iran was ready for a more aggressive role. British evacuation from the Persian Gulf in December 1971 terminated the Western military presence in the world's chief oil exporting region, giving its leaders a new sense of their own freedom to act. Similarly, British and American troops left Libya in 1970. Finally, there was the American entanglement in Vietnam, which rendered almost inconceivable any direct Western intervention in the Middle East.[12]

These changes turned the petroleum market around. By the end of 1970, producing governments received 99¢ per barrel, a slight but significant increase from the rate of 91¢ per barrel that had lasted for years. From this modest start, government revenues quickly jumped several times more, so that they had more than doubled by September 1973 (that is, just before the Yom Kippur War) to $2.01. After the price rises of October 1973 and January 1974, government royalties per barrel increased another four and a half times, to $9.27. Several years of relative price stability followed, until the shah's government fell and a tight market pushed prices up rapidly to $34 per barrel by the beginning of 1980. Price increases were matched in some cases by large boosts in production. Saudi output soared from 3 1/2 million barrels per day in 1970 to 7 1/3 in 1973 and almost 10 in 1980. The oil boom was a combination of vastly higher prices and sometimes larger production as well, bringing staggering riches to a few countries. Saudi Arabia received $1.2 billion in 1970, $29 billion in 1974, and $101 billion in 1981.

These changes in the oil market brought great power to the sheikhdoms. In the first years after 1973, oil was in sufficiently short supply that the very willingness of the exporting states to sell it in itself constituted a source of influence. So long as the trade in oil was a seller's market and prices climbed, governments of consumer nations did what they could to win guaranteed supplies and moderation of pricing. France, for example, sold arms and a nuclear installation to Iraq in return for oil contracts. The United States held back on filling its strategic oil reserve in deference to Saudi sensibilities. Politicians in Japan, West Europe, and other countries made anti-Israel statements to please Arab exporters.

Later, as the threat of embargo receded, "the oil weapon [was] transformed into a money weapon."[13] Instead of threatening to hold back delivery of oil, the sheikhdoms used the funds at their disposal to pressure foreigners. Because the oil countries acquired huge quantities of goods and services, usually at premium prices, the prospect of winning a contract with them often spelled for a firm the difference between a mediocre year and a great one. OPEC members generated business for everyone: financiers, lawyers, manufacturers, shippers, builders, architects, scientists, academics, advertisers, and even government agencies (such as the U.S. Army Corps of Engineers). Again, this power translated into a widespread concern to placate the sheikhdoms, including support for their favored political causes (especially against Israel) and pronounced concern for their customs. In the United States, for instance, businesses with interests in the sheikhdoms sponsored the National Committee for the Fourteenth Centennial of Islam, a body intended to improve Islam's image. More ominously, the sheikhdoms used their unprecedented influence in Western capitals to create an atmosphere conducive to anti-Semitism.[14]

At a time when other philanthropic sources diminished (in part as a result of the oil price increases), OPEC wealth made the sheikhdoms and the shah's Iran important new sources of grants and low-interest loans. In the West, everyone in search of funds, from American black community leaders to university administrators, made a bid for Arab money. Indeed, the sheikhs' reputation reached such proportions that they acquired an aura of wealth which in itself bestowed influence on them, even when no money was disbursed. The competition for help was keen and one way for potential recipients to ingratiate themselves was by declaring their abiding concern for Islam and whichever Islamic causes the oil sheikhs were believed to appreciate.

Oil wealth gave Muslims the power to raise or lower oil prices, to buy telephone systems from this company or helicopters from that country, to give aid or withhold it. Against all this, the West hardly reacted at all. It made no serious effort to form a consumers' cartel nor did it threaten military action. This passivity heightened the perception among Muslims that a momentous shift in power had occurred, and they were exhilarated by it. Roles were dramatically reversed as the sheikhs dictated terms to past colonial masters and present industrial giants, and the West's homage and even obsequiousness to such Arab leaders as Ahmad Zaki Yamani, the Saudi oil minister, was seen to symbolize a change in the international order, as well as an opportunity to indulge long-held resentments. "For the Saudis," John B. Kelly wrote in 1980, "there is undoubtedly a double satisfaction to be gained from the infliction of humiliating punishments upon Westerners; for not only are they an expression of the power and independence of Saudi Arabia but they also demonstrate, as they are intended to demonstrate, contempt for Christianity and the pre-eminence of Islam."[15] In the view of this same author, "the actions of the Arabs and the Persians before, during and since 1973, if placed in their historical, religious, racial and cultural setting, amount to nothing less than a bold attempt to lay the Christian West under tribute to the Muslim East."[16] As an Arab official succinctly put in December 1973: "It is our revenge for

Poitiers" (a reference to the battle of 732 when the Franks beat back a Muslim advance into northern France).[17] The establishment of oil power cheered not only the nations directly involved but the whole umma; even those Muslims who suffered from higher oil prices derived satisfaction watching the sheikhdoms assert themselves against the West.

Not only could the Muslim oil exporters exert considerable leverage over the West, but—what was yet more critical for the Islamic revival—they acquired an extraordinary stature. Concern not to upset the oil potentates meant that it was bad form to point out the unearned quality of their wealth or to criticize their behavior, and this in turn added enormously to the sheikhdoms' prestige.

Discussions about the nature of oil wealth understandably upset its beneficiaries, who preferred (and who would not in their position?) that their well-being be viewed as no different from anyone else's. They discouraged attention to the fact that Western initiative and expertise had created the demand for oil; that Muslims had played a negligible role in prospecting, drilling, extracting, transporting, refining, and distributing oil; that the small part they did play owed more to political concessions by the oil companies than to need for their help; that oil had value only because non-Muslims were willing to hand over substantial portions of their wealth for this commodity; and that as rentiers they spent wealth others created. In keeping, however, with the general reluctance to upset the oil barons, these facts became virtually taboo. Thus, a Yugoslav film made in the late-1970s about life in Kuwait, for example, showed Kuwaitis at work and play without including a single allusion to the oil trade, as though Kuwaiti wealth derived from the commerce, industry, and study that citizens in the film were shown undertaking. Booklets of slides distributed by embassies of the United Arab Emirate portray factories, construction projects, and elegant hotels, but omit everything related to oil.

Deference to the sheikhs extended so far that they won near-immunity from public criticism. The outstanding example of this occurred in the spring of 1980 and involved a British television film, "Death of a Princess." The film described events surrounding the execution in 1977 of two Saudi lovers, a royal woman and a common man. Called an "unprincipled attack" on Islam by the Saudi government,[18] the film was in fact the account of a journalist's attempt to pursue a news story in a secretive environment. Saudi pressure induced the British Foreign Office to announce that it "profoundly regret[ted] any offence which the film may have caused in Saudi Arabia," while the foreign minister, Lord Carrington, personally apologized for the "understandable offence . . . this particular television film has caused to the royal family in Saudi Arabia, and other Saudis and Muslims everywhere."[19] While Riyadh "studied" its economic ties with the United Kingdom,[20] the government in London pressured the film makers to tone down the offending scenes. In the United States, the Mobil Corporation ran advertisements urging the film not be shown "in the light of what is in the best interest of the United States,"[21] while the acting secretary of state took the unprecedented step of conveying a Saudi letter of protest to the television network which was to air the film. New Zealand television withheld screening of the film for overtly political reasons and even the Dutch government tried to prevent its showing.

Within Dar al-Islam, Saudi influence was yet more effective, extending to fundamentalists as well as to others who criticized the monarchy. Rashid al-Ghanushi, editor of the Tunisian magazine *Al-Ma'rifa*, published a commentary on the Meccan mosque seizure in which he noted that discontent in Saudi Arabia took such an ugly, despicable form because of the country's lack of free expression. The Saudi ambassador vigorously protested this attack and the Tunisian government arrested Ghanushi soon afterward.[22]

When the Philippine press published reports of Filipina maids suffering mistreatment and even rape at the hands of their employers in Saudi Arabia, one columnist, Jess Bigornia, advocated a ban on Philippine women working there. The ever-vigilant Saudi embassy protested this to the Foreign Ministry, complained of a "smear campaign" against the Arabs, demanded an official apology, and insisted on a retraction of Bigornia's article. Bigornia took it all back with alacrity. The acting information minister instructed editors to stop publishing articles about Filipina maids in Saudi Arabia and government officials hinted that the reports had been false to begin with. A few days later, the president's wife, Imelda Marcos, managed to get Saudi oil exports to the Philippines (40 percent of that country's total imports), reinstated after a temporary cutoff.[23]

So powerful was the image of the oil exporters, even with their oil exports down after the revolution, the Iranians could still exact a similar immunity. In Spain, the residents of Valencia celebrate a local festival by displaying life-size effigies of well-known personalities, often in caricature, and then burning them. When the Iranian embassy learned that Khomeini was included among the 611 effigies in April 1980, it told the authorities, in the words of the *Economist,* "that the ayatollah was not for burning. Faster than it takes to say 'oil,' the civil governor of Valencia was ordered to rescue him."[24]

Money transformed Islam's image in other ways too. A fifteenth-century Egyptian Qur'an which would have sold for a pittance a decade earlier went for $140,000 at a London auction in 1982, a testimony not only to the affluence of Muslims but also to the new prestige associated with Islamic artifacts. Along similar lines, the Italian publisher, Fideurart Edizione d'Arte, a specialist in luxury facsimiles of Greek and Latin classics, produced 1,500 copies of a sixteenth-century Ottoman Qur'an for $3,000 apiece and sold them at a brisk pace.

Further, for the first time in modern history, association with Islam brought practical advantages. It had long been that the good things in life came through knowledge of European languages, modern skills, and connections to the West, but oil made Arabic, Islam, and the Middle East sometimes even more rewarding. Competition for scholarships and jobs in the sheikhdoms led to a burgeoning of Islamic sentiments in many regions of Islamdom. It was Muslims primarily, especially in the first years of the oil boom, who serviced the new wealth: Tunisians, Egyptians, Sudanese, Yemenis, Palestinians, Lebanese, Syrians, Jordanians, Turks, Omanis, Pakistanis, and Indians descended on the Persian Gulf and Libya, and they often conspicuously displayed their piety in the effort to win employment. Among Egypt's academics, for instance, "the writing of texts from a specifically Muslim perspective . . . is in part due to the competition among faculty at Egyptian universities for the highly remunerative teaching positions at the new institutions of higher learning in the Arabian peninsula."[25]

Turkey, the country that had strayed furthest from the Islamicate heritage to associate with the West, realigned with alacrity. Western culture had come in the form of loan words, clothing, secularism, membership in NATO, and hundreds of thousands of laborers in Germany. Then, as the advantages of being Muslim and having connections to the Middle East multiplied in the 1970s, these patterns were reversed. Secularism went into retreat with the rise in popularity of religious parties, relations with Israel were cooled to placate Arab sentiments, and Turkey joined the Islamic Conference and hosted its annual meeting in 1976. Workers increasingly went to Libya and the Gulf, where Turkish citizens such as Sarık Tara, head of the Enka Group of construction companies, made fortunes. In the view of Nehemia Levtzion: "The Muslim bloc was no longer the weak and beaten area of the world on which Turkey had turned its back after World War One. The growing importance of Asia and Africa in world politics, the weight of their votes in the United Nations, and the economic power of the oil-producing countries were all assets that Turkey would have liked to be associated with."[26]

Just a few years earlier, the notion that the Arab nations might rank among the world's wealthiest would have been preposterous; when sudden riches came, they appeared all the more awesome and even miraculous for being so unexpected. The sheikhdoms won a renown which extended to the furthest reaches of Islamdom. The Arabian sheikh, characterized by a constant devotion to Islam, possessing more wealth than he could count, lording his power over Westerners, employing his fellow Muslims, and patronizing the finest money could buy, gave Islam a new élan. As a result, many Muslims reconsidered their attitudes toward their religion. Those who previously had associated Islam with poverty and backwardness and considered it an obstacle to coping with modern life, now saw it in a new light.

The psychological effect of all these changes was electric. "Nineteen seventy-three was the year of the oil-price rise, the year when money for Arab oil seemed to come like a reward for the Arab faith. Muslim missionary activity picked up; in a dozen foreign countries, half-evolved Muslim students, until then shy in the new world, hardly able to relate their technical studies to the countries where they were, felt the time had come to proclaim the true faith."[27]

Oil and Islam took off together. Just as the oil trade quietly turned in favor of the Muslim producers, Qadhdhafi came to power in September 1969 and later that month the Saudis finally convened their long-planned summit conference of Muslim leaders—two key events. But it was not until October 1973 that the direct link between oil and Islam was established, when oil prices quadrupled in the midst of the fourth Arab-Israeli war. At the very moment that Muslims finally stood up on the battlefield to their most conspicuous enemy, they also won unprecedented power in the oil marketplace. The conjunction of military resolve, economic muscle, and diplomatic influence gave Muslims around the world a feeling of exultation and a stunning sense of their own prowess. Although the war had nothing to do with the market being able to bear so high a price for oil, fighting did precipitate the OPEC decision to raise prices. These two events became connected in people's minds and Muslims thereafter associated the benefits of more expensive oil with success against Israel.

The Islamic spirit, increasingly intense after 1970, entered a new phase; Muslims felt they had finally stopped, and perhaps reversed, their long decline. Starved for two centuries for some worldly sign of their special standing before God, for Muslims the achievements of late 1973 appeared to be a vindication of their faith and a reward for their long-suffering steadfastness. Of a sudden, they again tasted something of the wealth and power that had so long eluded them. The effect was a heady sense of confidence. Together, Egypt, Syria, and the sheikhdoms had stood up to the non-Muslims and won; what could the umma not do if all joined in? These events marked a turning point in Muslim consciousness, convincing many that the umma had begun its long-awaited resurgence, and improving Muslim attitudes toward themselves, their cultural traditions, and Islam. "Waves of renewed confidence and euphoria" were experienced throughout Islamdom; as far away as Yunnan, China, 1,700 Muslims died in an uprising described as being "led by young people who had been inspired by the worldwide resurgence of Islamic militancy to defend Islam in China."[28]

The surge of power in the sheikhdoms created a mood highly favorable to the two most potent forms of Islamic political action: fundamentalism and autonomism. As the umma felt it again enjoyed God's approval, Muslims approached their own traditions with renewed confidence; after two centuries of tribulation, they rejoiced in the prospect of regaining the correct path. The fact that the greatest winners were piously Islamic further confirmed the new of image of success. Udo Steinbach noticed this connection already in 1974:

Herein lies the significance of petroleum: The dependence of a majority of the industrial world on Arab (and especially Saudi) oil imbued the Muslim Arab with a degree of power and international respect which he needed in order to appreciate the validity of his (political) religion. . . . In this way, he regained his full identity and he found the world once again properly ordered.[29]

Although oil wealth and Islamic faith would seem to be unrelated, drawing connections between them meshed two needs of the Muslims during the 1970s. First, the umma retained the notion that worldly well-being affirms faith; success during the early centuries connected the two and the trauma of modern times came too late to permit a disengagement. The Muslim need for a sign from God of His approval long went unanswered. It was not surprising, then, that the remarkable benefits from oil sales were interpreted as the long-awaited sign. The fact that it was the sheikhdoms, with their most piously Islamic governments, which received the most money made this interpretation of oil all the more convincing. The sheikhdoms' affluence seemed to vindicate Islamic ways. Thus, according to Guy George, a senior French official, Qadhdhafi saw oil "as a gift of God. The badly-behaved Arabs didn't have it, the well-behaved ones did."[30] That demonstrably pious Islamic regimes enjoyed a preponderant share of the oil trade increased the sense of Islam's recompense: according to Bruce Borthwick, "Muslims point out that roughly two-thirds of the world's oil resources lies in Islamic countries, a sign from God of the correctness of their belief"; and a reporter noted "a vague feeling that the oil wealth of the Saudis and Libyans is somehow connected to the Koran, however illogical it may seem."[31]

Second, and not coincidentally, this view of oil wealth also helped the beneficiaries justify what was otherwise an *embarras de richesse*. By choosing to see oil wealth as a sign of God's favor, Arabs and other Muslims could explain their good fortune in the face of the world's laboring poor. Given these needs, it was inevitable that Muslim domination of the international trade in petroleum carried a powerful message and that an accident of geology became a key factor of the Islamic revival.

A vague expectation developed that, just as Islam began among the Arabs in the seventh century and then spread to others, so did the recent change in fortune start with the Arabs before expanding to include other Muslims. Eventually, perhaps, the whole umma would share the sheikhdoms' well-being. All this might appear delusive to an outsider, but modern history made Muslims susceptible to such enthusiasms; after centuries of frustration, they ached for signs of success and a return to the high stature of an earlier age. A stirring of activity in one region of Islamdom, especially in the Middle East, inevitably stimulated hopes everywhere. "Each time the banner of Islam is raised," writes Hamadi Essid, "the Muslims allow themselves to believe that someone has finally come along to help them take revenge for all the centuries of scorn they suffered at the hands of history."[32]

Increased exposure to the West and to modernity made Muslims more receptive to fundamentalist Islam. Oil revenues led to urbanization, it attracted foreign non-Muslim workers, it made Western manufactured products more available; and it funded travel to the West for Muslim students, businessmen, and tourists. In these and other ways, the oil boom brought many Muslims into closer contact with modernity. As oil increased Muslim contacts with the West, many believers reacted by turning inward. They sought refuge in their own tradition rather than contend with the threatening impact of modern culture. Being already somewhat modernized, however, they could not return to traditionalist Islam, and in the 1970s, they were among those Muslims who found fundamentalism increasingly attractive.

But changes taking place in Islamdom were not only psychological. Oil wealth in the Middle East made it possible for activist Muslims in power in several countries, especially Saudi Arabia and Libya, to further the cause of Islam around the world.

Saudi and Libyan Networks

Two major currents of influence, one Western and the other Communist, have dominated international relations since 1945. Both have principal centers (the United States and the Soviet Union), secondary regions (Western Europe and China), and wide networks of allies (such as the two Koreas). In the effort to further its aims, each side gathers support, often from parties which do not share a basic viewpoint but are tactically useful (Pakistan for the United States, Iraq for the USSR). The global struggle is conducted militarily (with standing forces, foreign bases, arms sales), economically (loans, grants, use of currencies), and culturally (language studies, foreign students, books, movies).

On a smaller scale, the oil boom enabled Saudi Arabia and Libya to become centers of a third international current—Islam. They possessed the means to advance Islamic interests after 1970, both legalist and autonomist, in a manner resembling the Western and Communist blocs, by employing military force, economic pressure, and cultural presence. Standing aside from the struggle between liberalism and Marxism, moving toward distinctive goals of its own,

297

Saudi and Libyan influence reached into dozens of countries, seriously affecting many of them.

In contrast to the other Muslim countries with new oil wealth (Kuwait or Algeria, for example), Saudi Arabia and Libya both had heritages of fundamentalist fervor which still influenced their policies in the 1970s. Their rulers—kings Faysal, Khalid, and Fahd of Arabia, and Colonel Mu'ammar al-Qadhdhafi of Libya—were all devoted to Islam and entertained grand aspirations internationally. Despite small populations and simple cultures, these two countries had traditions of influencing Islamic affairs far beyond their borders. They also shared a legacy of territorial expansion (neither country grew so large by accident). Foreigners knew little about the internal condition of Saudi Arabia or Libya; it was hardly noted that neither of their governments was fundamentalist. Saudi and Libyan support for Islam garnered them prestige among Muslims.

The House of Sa'ud was known for its Wahhabi doctrines and control of the Islamic holy cities, its resistance to Westernization and its abiding concern for Muslim political unity. Piety and activism won Saudi leaders a voice in Islamic affairs far out of proportion to their country's population or cultural resources. The abandonment of early Wahhabi fervor and the adaptation to political realities went largely unnoticed. However short they fell of professed fundamentalist ideals, the Saudis' money and propaganda established Arabia in the 1970s as the standard for Islamic behavior. Saudi religious practice became exemplary. *De facto* Saudi success at mixing fundamentalist rhetoric with traditionalist compromises appealed to a broad range of observant Muslims, including the 'ulama and the urban poor, the Shar'i-minded and those disillusioned with Western ideologies.

Although Qadhdhafi could not match this, he did win an Islamic reputation beyond Libyan borders when his government began to apply Qur'anic regulations soon after it came to power. Coming after decades of seemingly irreversible Westernization throughout Islamdom, his actions gave heart to legalists everywhere and attracted worldwide attention to the Shari'a. Early legalist actions bestowed a fundamentalist image on Qadhdhafi which then endured. The growing eccentricity of his rule and the fact that he had weakened the Shari'a more than he had strengthened it were often missed. An Islamic reputation also concealed the manifestly un-Islamic portions of Qadhdhafi's manifesto, *The Green Book*, even though he had implemented it in Libya and pressed it on friends abroad (with the most success in Ghana). Although Qadhdhafi claimed that *The Green Book* served as a way to bring Qur'anic ideas to non-Muslims (in his words, "In the Third Theory, we present the applications of Islam from which all mankind may benefit"),[33] it diverged widely from the

Qur'an—and probably owed more to Jean-Jacques Rousseau than to any Muslim thinker.[34]

Fundamentalists did sometimes question the credentials of the Saudi and Libyan regimes, even when taking their money. The Muslim Brethren in Syria and elsewhere scorned the Saudi leaders' personally lax adherence to the Shari'a and criticized them for paying only lip service to Islam. Qadhdhafi's odd ideas about Islam involved him in arguments with the Shi'i leader of Lebanon, Imam Musa as-Sadr and on one occasion a disagreement between the two probably contributed to Sadr's disappearance and murder. The Muslim Brethren in Tunisia called Qadhdhafi "an atheist, a miscreant, an agent of Communism, and a traitor to the Prophet,"[35] and he reciprocated by banning them from Libya along with Communists, Marxists, atheists, capitalists, and propagandists for the West.

For the most part, however, outsiders ignored internal conditions: Saudi laxity was buried under a show of piety and Libyan eccentricity was less noted than Qadhdhafi's unbending assertion of Islamic political will. Thus, when fundamentalists in Indonesia resisted their government's policy of keeping schools open during the Ramadan fast, the education minister countered with two arguments: that the Shari'a does not forbid study during Ramadan and that Saudi children also attended class through the fasting month. When corrected on the second point by the Saudi ambassador to Indonesia (schools did close in Saudi Arabia), the minister simply gave up trying to justify his view on Islamic grounds—as though he allowed the Saudis to have the final say on matters Islamic.[36] Qadhdhafi stood for the principle that "the international Muslim community should give active and unqualified support to Muslims in their conflicts with non-Muslims, regardless of the particular circumstances of the conflict, and with no regard whatever to diplomatic complications that might result from a foreign policy based on religious considerations."[37]

Other than their orientation toward Islam, however, the two governments differed profoundly in temperament and policy. The Saudis were eminently respectable in speech and deed, cautious and conservative, aiming to establish a quiet world in which to enjoy their riches in safety. In intra-Arab politics, they saw tranquility as the best assurance of their own stability and therefore made it an overriding principle of their diplomacy to soothe and to make peace. Virtually every Saudi move can be explained with reference to Riyadh's obsession with self-preservation. Internationally, they lined up with the United States on most questions, seeing America's interest in preserving the status quo as compatible with their own. In turn, Saudi Arabia, with its huge oil reserves, its high level of oil production, and its key location, figured large in

Washington's strategic thinking. Two quotes summarize the Saudi position internationally: King Khalid, discussing aid for Mauritania with its ruler in 1978, stated that "the defense of Saudi Arabia begins at the coasts of the Atlantic Ocean."[38] The Saudi oil minister, Ahmad Zaki Yamani, explained his government's insecurity noting that never before "has a country had such a valuable resource and been so ill-equipped to defend it."[39]

Saudi Arabia became active in the international arena only after the 1967 war against Israel. Defeat then discredited Gamal Abdul Nasser, brought an end to his meddling in North Yemen, and increased the dependence of all the states fighting Israel on subventions from the sheikhdoms. Saudi foreign policy became increasingly self-assured during the 1970s, working behind the scenes to defuse radicalism and create a moderate atmosphere conducive to Arab unity. After 1973, Riyadh acquired grander ambitions and the House of Sa'ud began to see itself as a leader in Arab and Muslim politics.

Similarly, Libya had virtually no standing internationally before the 1967 war. The crushing defeat by Israel caused many Libyan military men to despise their own government for standing aside from the Arab cause and, worse yet, allowing the British and Americans to maintain bases on Libyan soil despite the widely held belief among Arabs that these two countries had aided Israel during the Six-Day War. After 1967, identification with the Palestinians and hostility toward Israel became synonymous with opposition to the government of King Idris. Palestine came to symbolize an alternate Libyan political identity, away from the United States and Britain, back to the Arab and Muslim fold. Foreign policy became vital to the concerns of the men who took the country over in 1969.

In contrast to the fearful Saudis, their leader, Mu'ammar al-Qadhdhafi, was a firebrand, a colonel prone to tantrums, to whimsy, and to revolutionary turmoil. Always on the offensive, he was more interested in changing the world than in safeguarding his oil fields. He made up neologisms (such as *jamahiriya,* the "state of the masses"), devised new political theories (the Third International Theory), and involved his country in foreign causes (Southwest Africa, Rhodesia, the Canary Islands, the Caribbean, Northern Ireland) far removed from Libyan self-interest. Qadhdhafi prodded and disrupted, not fearing for his regime but instead, eager to take the fight to the enemy's camp. He pursued opposite policies from the Saudis' in intra-Arab politics, taking an extreme and intransigent ideological approach, creating divisions by his adamant refusal to accept any view differing from his own. His repeated attempts at sabotage, political meddling, coups d'etat, unions between states, and territorial expansion made him a source of anxiety for even those Arab leaders inclined to approve of his policies. On the international level, Qadhdhafi sided with the Communist states after 1975, despite his objections to their official atheism.

Libya agreed with the Soviet position or had aims compatible with theirs in places such as southern Africa, Ethiopia, Egypt, and Malta; they may even have cooperated in the May 1981 assassination attempt on Pope John Paul II. Soviet backing for Libya helped deter the possibility of an Egyptian invasion and the Soviet Union would probably depend heavily on its arsenal in Libya for logistical support in conflicts in Europe, the Middle East, or Africa. On several occasions, Qadhdhafi brought up the possibility of Libya joining the Warsaw Pact.

Not surprisingly, Saudi Arabia and Libya had poor relations after Qadhdhafi came to power in 1969. Offended by the overthrow of Idris, a fellow king, the Saudis, who waited for several months, were the only Arab leaders to delay recognizing the new Libyan regime. Subsequently, Qadhdhafi called for revolution in Saudi Arabia to overthrow the monarchy. He probably financed the attack on the Saudi embassy in Khartoum in March 1973 and was involved in the Tabuq conspiracy of 1977, an attempted air force mutiny. Relations then warmed in 1979, only to degenerate again when the United States dispatched AWACS planes to Saudi Arabia in October 1980. Qadhdhafi accused the Saudis of forfeiting their sovereignty by allowing American kafirs to gain control of the holy cities. In return, the Saudis broke diplomatic relations with Libya. The Israeli annexation of the Golan Heights led to an improvement in relations, but then, within a few months, Qadhdhafi was once again calling for the Saudis' overthrow.

The antagonistic foreign policies of Saudi Arabia and Libya placed them in the American and Soviet camps, but they did agree on one matter, the need to promote Islam in politics. Here their differences were complementary and were a source of strength. The two regimes used different methods to achieve similar goals; they tacitly worked together, without intending to but with great effect. Saudi Arabia pressured Muslim governments to apply the Shari'a or to abandon links to the Soviet bloc, it stood above disputes between Arabs, presided over the pilgrimage to Mecca with great ceremony, and sponsored Islamic conferences. Qadhdhafi funded extremist Islamic movements, trained saboteurs, kidnapped enemies, and sponsored terrorism. Temperamental and ideological differences kept the two states apart but their goals were compatible; both fervently supported fundamentalist and autonomist movements. The Saudis preferred behind-the-scenes maneuvers and Qadhdhafi tended toward dramatic action. Saudi Arabia gave economic aid to governments, Libya ran guns; Arabia propped up friends of Islam, Libya brought down its enemies; one provided incentives, the other punished. Between the Saudi anvil and the Libyan hammer, many Muslim communities moved perceptibly toward Islam.

Examples of Saudi Arabia taking the high road and Libya the low are many. (1) In Jordan, Pakistan, and Bangladesh, the Saudis gave money with strings attached, urging the governments toward fundamentalism; in these same countries, Qadhdhafi supported extremist organizations, usually ones plotting to overthrow the government. (2) In Egypt, the Sudan, and Turkey, the situation was similar, except that the Saudis aided both the government and the leading legitimate fundamentalist parties (respectively, the Muslim Brethren, the People's Democratic Party, and the National Salvation Party). Libya funded these groups and also the fanatics. (3) In the Philippines, Libya provided arms for the Moro National Liberation Front, and Saudi Arabia promised the central government aid for solving the Moro problem to Saudi satisfaction. (4) Saudi money helped finance elegant mosques in prominent sections of such international capitals as London and Rome, while Libya located the one anti-establishment Muslim institution in the West, the Black Muslims, and lent it money for a mosque on the south side of Chicago. Despite some exceptions to this pattern (Arabia long plotted against the Marxist government in South Yemen and the Libyans sponsored the Philippine peace treaty in December 1976), the two countries usually acted in characteristically different ways.

In their efforts to promote Islamic causes, Saudi Arabia and Libya faced one major constraint—manpower. Their own peoples being poorly educated, lacking in modern skills, and very few in number, both relied either on foreigners or on money to exert influence. Only the sketchiest figures are available, even for Saudi Arabia, but these suffice for an insight into their largess and impact. During 1975–77, its first three years of operation, the Saudi Fund disbursed the following amounts:

Recipient	Amount in $ million	Percentage
Arab League members	2,924	53
Non-Arab Muslims	1,308	24
Non-Muslims	1,276	23
Total	5,508	100

In these same years, Saudi Arabia also contributed over a billion dollars to the Islamic Development Bank and multinational funds. According to other figures, Saudi Arabia spent more than $10 billion in foreign aid in 1973–75, of which all but 1 or 2 percent went to Muslims. Yet another source indicates that in 1976, 96 percent of Saudi aid went to Muslim countries, and about three-fourths of that to Arab states.[40] That at least four-fifths of Saudi aid went to Muslims reflected the Saudi concern to help brother Muslims and the priority placed on influencing them.

Such enormous sums willy-nilly bestowed formidable political power on the Saudis; recipient countries went to great lengths to please these benefactors. Saudi leaders normally accompanied their money with polite statements and discreet diplomacy, expecting slight hints to convey their wishes. As Henry

Kissinger observed, "contemporary Saudi policy has been characterized by a caution that had elevated indirectness into a special art form. . . . There has grown up a style at once oblique and persistent, reticent and assertive."[41] Only rarely did the Saudis explicitly state conditions or threaten to cut aid; even then, they responded slowly when displeased, exerting the quiet but implacable influence that suited them best.

Perhaps the most imaginative Saudi effort to influence the umma religiously was their utilization of international Islamic organizations. In 1962 they founded the World Muslim League as a channel to all of Islamdom for funding mosques, religious schools, publishing houses, and other Islamic institutions. Lavish state support for the League meant that it could even extend grants to its rivals abroad (including Pakistan's World Muslim Congress, Egypt's Academy of Islamic Research, Jordan's General Islamic Conference on Jerusalem, and Indonesia's International Islamic Organization) and influence their policies. That the Muslim World League emerged as the trend-setting and dominant Islamic organization resulted from a "concerted Saudi campaign . . . carefully attuned to Riyad's policy objectives."[42]

But Saudi leaders had ambitions greater than merely the domination of religious affairs; they aspired to organize forums for every type of Muslim leader. The politicians came first, with the convening of a summit meeting of Muslim heads of state in Rabat in September 1969 and the ensuing establishment of the Organization of the Islamic Conference, with a secretariat in Jidda and annual meetings on the foreign ministerial level. During the following years, as Saudi funding increased and a corps of Islamic bureaucrats emerged, a great many more groupings formed, some related to the Islamic Conference, others not. A number of these groupings concerned political and military affairs, including the Commission for Muslim Cooperation, the Islamic Council of Europe, the Organization of Islamic Capitals and Cities, the International Commission on Muslim Minorities, the Islamic Institute of Defence Technology, the Islamic Solidarity Fund, the Islamic Court of Justice, and the Islamic Council. Economic and business organizations included: the Islamic Development Bank, the Islamic Chamber of Commerce, the International Union of Islamic Banks, the Islamic Reimbursing Bank, the Islamic Economic Conference, and the Islamic Monetary Fund. Cultural and welfare agencies were formed as well: the World Assembly of Muslim Youth, the Islamic Press Union, the International Islamic News Agency, the Pan-Islamic Games, the Confederation of Islamic Solidarity Games, the Islamic Conference on Information and Culture, the World Conference on Muslim Education, the Islamic Science Foundation, the Muslim Health Organization, the Islamic Red Crescent Society, the International Islamic Federation of Student Organizations, the Islamic Cultural Foundation, the Conference on Islamic Cultural Centers, the Islamic Council on Civil Aviation, the Islamic States Broadcasting Organization, the Islamic University, and the International Islamic Foundation for Science and Technology.

Through generous funding and careful nurturing, Saudi Arabia controlled virtually all the Islamic organizations and, as a result, its "strict brand of fundamentalism has become the common tone in the deliberations of the major conferences."[43] These agencies served Riyadh as a means for influencing public life in all regions of Islamdom and "as a basis for coordinating and controlling its financial hold over the conservative forces in the world of Islam."[44] The effects of their patronage were widely felt, as Muslims and non-Muslims alike began to hew to the Saudi viewpoint in the hope of winning Riyadh's favor—or at least enjoying a few days at Saudi expense in a posh hotel discussing issues concerning Islam and the Muslims. For example, in Mauritania, the fundamentalist Islamic Cultural Assembly, founded in December 1979, had three years later received all its financial support from the Saudi-backed Islamic Solidarity Fund. In addition, what Duran Khalid calls "the emergence of a Church-like apparatus"[45] served to extend Saudi ideology. By creating new posts—Secretary of the Muslim World League, Secretary General of the Islamic Conference, Rector of the Islamic University of Medina, Imam of the Ka'ba—all virtually without precedent in Islam, they brought into existence a rostrum of Islamic personalities sympathetic to Saudi aims.

Sizable Saudi contributions for research on Islamic topics strengthened and publicized the fundamentalist view. On the scholarly level, the Saudis "have directed historical and social science research into specific channels, and have fostered a network of authors and professors committed to the pursuit of such research."[46] A proliferation of newspapers, magazines, and journals altered the tone of cultural discourse in Islamdom. In Great Britain alone, the Saudis funded an Arabic daily *(Ash-Sharq al-Awsat),* an Arabic weekly newsmagazine *(Al-Majalla),* an English fortnightly *(Impact International),* an English monthly *(Arabia: The Islamic World Review),* and an English quarterly *(Journal of the Institute of Muslim Minority Affairs).* Saudi-influenced teachers and textbooks assured widespread fundamentalist influence on the Muslim children of the 1970s.

The Saudis supplemented their promotion of fundamentalism by becoming the self-appointed guardians of Islam's values and good name. Hardly a week went by without some activity to promote or protect Islam, be it Saudi money for a prize given for memorizing the Qur'an, a Saudi protest to the Moroccan government for allowing the distribution of tape cassettes of Qur'anic readings set to disco music, Saudi condemnation of a Qur'an printed in Indonesia not in the Arabic script, or Saudi objections to CBS television for allowing a dog to be named Muhammad on the show "Hawaii Five-O." The Saudis managed to identify themselves as the patrons—or the Church—of Islam.

Like the Saudis, Qadhdhafi also faced the problem of meager manpower; also like them, he employed foreigners, training them in camps in Libya to serve as missionaries, soldiers, and terrorists abroad. He too gave away substantial sums of money, though usually less than he promised, and established Islamic organizations such as the Conference for the Islamic Call. Colonel Qadhdhafi's most original method of promoting Islam may have been his personal efforts to exhort non-Muslims to relinquish their faiths and accept the truth of the Qur'an. In some cases, he called on whole peoples to convert, especially Christians in Africa and in the Arab world. In January 1977, on a state visit to the West African state of Togo, he called for a "revolt against Christianity."[47] Subsequently, he appealed to all Arabs to convert to Islam, because "an Arab can't be Christian. . . . They should become Moslems. Otherwise, they will be Israelis in spirit, because Christ was sent as a prophet to the sons of Israel whereas Islam is an Arab religion."[48] (Needless to say, such opinions run contrary to mainstream Islam.)

Qadhdhafi also attempted to convert non-Muslims he met in person. It was his practice to take leave of them saying, "I hope to see you again someday, but make sure you try to convert to Islam!" African leaders were especially targeted: Qadhdhafi offered François Tombalbaye of Chad $2 million for himself and an assortment of projects for his country, if the president would convert. Then he held the following conversation with General Gnassingbé Eyadéma of Togo in November 1973:

Al-Qadhdhafi: As we are friends, I would like you to become Muslim. I will give you whatever you wish in exchange.

Eyadema: Don't you see that you are insulting me? We are friends, so let us leave our religious convictions to the side and talk instead about cooperation between our countries.

Al-Qadhdhafi: No. I insist that you convert to Islam. It is the best religion. I have an [Islamic] name to propose to you. You will be well compensated.

Eyadema (agitated): Why don't you become a Protestant like I am?[49]

At this point, Qadhdhafi angrily ended the discussion. Sese Seko Mobutu of Zaire, Siaka Stevens of Sierra Leone, Juvénal Habyarimana of Rwanda, Marien Ngouabi of the Congo, and Mathieu Kérékou of Benin all refused Qadhdhafi's overtures as well, though Kérékou found on his return home to Benin from a visit in Libya that Qadhdhafi had announced the fact of his conversion and even publicized the Islamic name he had taken.

Qadhdhafi had somewhat more success with Albert-Bernard Bongo of Gabon and Jean-Bedel Bokassa of Central Africa. The former did sincerely convert to Islam soon after returning from a trip to Tripoli in 1973, whereas the latter accepted Qadhdhafi's offer for mercenary reasons. The sophistication of Qadhdhafi's missionary efforts can be gaged from Bokassa's recollection of his conversion:

Bokassa: . . . One must believe in God.

Interviewer for Jeune Afrique *magazine:* Is this why you left Christianity to become a Muslim?

Bokassa (with a mocking smile): No, no. Qadhdhafi came [to Bangui, capital of Central Africa] and declared that I had become a Muslim. But this didn't happen because I didn't accept. Hin, hin, hin.

J.A.: How did he want you to convert?

Bokassa: He said to me, "Accompany me to the mosque in Bangui." We went, everyone, the whole government, my son. When we arrived at the mosque . . . Hin, hin, hin . . . he took a coffee pot . . . Hin, hin, hin . . . he washed my feet and he baptized me. Hin, hin, hin. But he couldn't, because I had already been baptized! [Qadhdhafi really was washing him to prepare him for the Islamic prayers; Islam has no baptism ceremony.]

J.A.: Were you expecting this?

Bokassa: He had said nothing at all. He said, "Come!" I came and he washed my feet!

J.A.: Did he propose anything else?

Bokassa: He wanted Central Africa to become the Islamic Republic of Central Africa . . . [A silence, then again] He washed my feet! Hin, hin, hin![50]

On an earlier occasion, Bokassa contradicted this account with a truer version of what had happened: "You wouldn't believe this comedy! Qadhdhafi thought he had had me. But I am more cunning than he! He offered me a lot of money. I said okay. But as soon as I pocketed it, I told him to go to the devil with his Islam!" Bokassa knowingly converted to Islam and then kept up the act of being a Muslim for several months before reneging. Qadhdhafi's efforts at conversion failed in part because, in the words of one targeted leader, the Africans knew his intent was "to create satellite countries."[51] Still, the efforts did sometimes succeed, when someone desperate or unscrupulous enough was found. After Bokassa was overthrown, for example, Qadhdhafi converted Rodolphe Idi Lalla, leader of the Central African Movement of National Liberation, the main opposition to the government of the Central African Republic—an organization not coincidentally based in Tripoli.

Even such crude and unsuccessful efforts as these contributed to the Islamic revival, for they added to the vitality and expansiveness of Islam. Qadhdhafi brought a flair to the religion which had been absent previously. For all his eccentricities, Qadhdhafi embued Islam with a dynamism which made an impression even on those Muslims most opposed to his activities.

Through a combination of money, arms, and diplomatic pressures, Saudi Arabia and Libya had a widespread impact on the whole of Islamdom. Even if most of their activities took place far from the public eye, enough was revealed to indicate the pattern of their involvements. To show how extensively they promoted legalist and autonomist causes, the following pages survey Saudi and Libyan influence in three types of countries: where Muslims formed a dominant majority of the population or about half of it or a small minority of it.

Before this, however, a word on sources: this survey must unfortunately rely to a considerable degree on rumor, hearsay, and other wisps of evidence, for so much of Saudi and Libyan (as well as Iranian) international influence is clandestine and therefore impossible to verify. If some Saudi and Libyan connections are missed, others are mistakenly imputed. The case of Libya presents especially great problems, for Qadhdhafi's activities won him such great notoriety, he may have been sometimes falsely ascribed responsibility. Bearing these caveats in mind, the following review should be understood more as an indication of broad, almost statistical patterns than as a conclusive account of specific events. By relying on a multitude of facts I hope to reduce the importance of each particular one. Although some details may prove to be inaccurate, the general trend of Saudi and Libyan activities is clear.

MAJORITIES

Outside help had moderate importance for the mujahidin in Afghanistan. Aid from Libya ended with the Soviet invasion of December 1979, after which Saudi diplomatic support, arms, and money provided the bulk of foreign Muslim backing. Within days of the assault, the Saudi foreign minister called on all Muslim governments to "take a clear position to face the blatant Soviet invasion of Afghanistan and to prevent the serious Communist aggression from achieving its goals there."[52] Saudi pressure on rival mujahidin groups made them cooperate and form temporary coalitions. So concerned were the Saudi Arabians about developments in Afghanistan that one businessman, Sulayman ar-Rashid, went on his own initiative to Peshawar, Pakistan, the location of many refugee camps, and handed out 100 rupee notes (the equivalent of $10) of his own money to individual Afghans, explaining that "we Muslims must help one another if we are to fight the Russian enemy."[53]

Libyan influence was discerned behind some of the moves toward Islam in Algeria, especially the Islamic provisions of the 1976 National Charter. On a visit to Algeria in January 1982, Qadhdhafi encouraged the fundamentalists when he spoke at a university of the return to "pure Islam."[54]

When Ziaur Rahman came to power in Bangladesh in 1975, his sympathy toward Islam and his concern for the country's economy impelled him to seek the attention of the oil-rich states. Saudi Arabia, which had refused to deal with his predecessors, responded by quickly establishing diplomatic relations with Bangladesh and shortly thereafter became its fourth largest aid donor; in return, it pressured the authorities to enact Islamic laws. The Bangladesh government exploited the presence of Muslim refugees from Burma in their country to win more financial support from the sheikhdoms. Saudi Arabia and Libya also provided other miscellaneous help, such as financing the airlift of 2,800 Biharis (Pakistanis stranded in Bangladesh after Bangladesh independence) to Pakistan. The desperation of Bangladesh's economy and the abundance of Saudi funds led one analyst to conclude that by the late 1970s, "few countries find themselves so firmly in [Saudi Arabia's] sphere of influence as Bangladesh."[55]

In the first four years after he came to power, Qadhdhafi did his best to cooperate with Egypt, hoping eventually to unify it with Libya. The high point of Libyan involvement was his remarkable eighteen-day visit to Egypt in June 1973 advocating an Islamic "cultural revolution" along the lines announced just two months earlier in Libya. Qadhdhafi's relations with Anwar as-Sadat, always shaky, broke down after the October 1973 war, when Sadat engaged in negotiations with Israel to end hostilities. As relations further degenerated, Qadhdhafi used every available means to strike at Sadat's regime, especially extremist Muslim groups in Egypt. He called for revolution in Egypt in December 1973 and first attempted a coup d'etat there in April 1974. Libyan funds soon flowed into the Islamic Liberation Party, Muhammad's Youth, the Army of God, the Society for Jihad, and other radical groups. Forty-two members of the last-named group were tried in 1977–78 on grounds of attempting to overthrow the Egyptian government. Another group, Flight and Repentance, abducted a former minister of religious affairs in July 1977 and executed him when the government refused to deliver a ransom; its close connections to Libya were subsequently established.

There was no proof of Libyan complicity in the assassination of President Sadat, but the fact that Qadhdhafi had been aiding Sadat's sworn enemies for years pointed in this direction and circumstantial evidence confirmed Libyan involvement. A seemingly pre-programmed outburst of messages from Libyan radio stations called on the Egyptians to rise up against the government, implying Libya's foreknowledge of the plot. Also, some Egyptian military units were suspected of contacts with Libya. A week after the assassination, two bombs exploded in baggage being unloaded in Cairo off an Air Malta jet just arrived from Libya, killing two persons. Husni Mubarak, the new president, revealed that his government had information that the plotters received money from outside Egypt.

Rumors circulated about funds received by the Muslim Brethren from Saudi Arabia and Libya. Figures are naturally hard to come by, but the Saudis apparently gave the Muslim Brethren $100,000 in early 1979, ostensibly for building mosques.[56] The Egyptian government's dependence on Saudi money meant that it could not afford to thwart "the discreet but well-funded efforts of the Saudis to further the return to fundamental Muslim values."[57] The Saudis often worked with 'Abd al-Halim Mahmud, the rector of Al-Azhar University in Cairo and an internationally respected Islamic figure. As a result of his efforts, Islamic groups won greater freedom to organize and to publicize their activities, Al-Azhar University received increased funding for, and legislation to dilute the Shar'i content of Egypt's laws was dropped.

Saudi efforts also reached more prosaic levels. John Alden Williams reports about a female student at Cairo University who said that "she received a small sum of money to hand out head-kerchiefs to her classmates, and more money for every woman she converted to wearing *shari* dress; money which came from a Saudi source. It is said that girls who announce their intention to change dress may have a contribution for the cost of their new clothing from various fundamentalist organizations with mysteriously large supplies of money."[58] There is little doubt that these "mysteriously large supplies of money" came from Riyadh. Egyptians often saw the Saudis as the force behind the dramatic turn by young women toward wearing Islamic clothing. "When asked why *shari* dress is increasing among women, many educated Egyptians are apt to shrug their shoulders, look embarrassed, and reply that they can't imagine. Pressed, they often reply that 'it's all because of the Saudis' . . . who give money to writers and *shaykhs* who will further a fundamentalist version of Islam."[59] More generally, "the influence of the oil embargo and a relative strengthening of the Arab world may have influenced increasing numbers of Egyptian students toward a strict Islamic orientation."[60]

Unable to win enough support from Communist or Western countries, Ahmed Sékou Touré of Guinea turned to the Persian Gulf for aid in the 1970s. He made so many trips there that by 1980 he won more Arab aid for Guinea than any other African country, $371 million in long-term, low-interest loans. To win more money yet, Sékou Touré actively took up the Arab cause against Israel, became active in the Islamic Conference, and demonstrated great piety. Not only were parts of the Shari'a reinstated in Guinea but so thoroughly did Sékou Touré acquiesce to Saudi influence, King Khalid reportedly dissuaded him from declaring himself as mahdi.[61]

Persistent suspicions that Libya aided the extremist fundamentalists in Indonesia could not be confirmed, but the concern was voiced in reference to Komando Jihad, the Aceh National Liberation Front and the March 1981 hijacking of an Indonesian aircraft by Muslim extremists. At the same time, Qadhdhafi let it be known that he was disappointed with the lack of fervency among Muslims in Indonesia. Saudi assistance financed mosques and other Islamic institutions. By making Dr. Muhammad Natsir the director of the Muslim World League regional office in Jakarta, the Saudis enfranchised Indonesia's leading Islamic fundamentalist, establishing him as a major voice.

The shah's pro-Western policies and his close relations with Israel made his rule anathema to Qadhdhafi, who backed many of the opposition movements. In particular, he gave "generous aid" to Khomeini's faction.[62]

Saudi influence toned down anti-Islamic policies of the secularist government in Iraq. This was "strikingly demonstrated" during a 1976 visit to Saudi Arabia by the Iraqi leader Saddam Husayn. His presenting Prince Fahd with a hand-made Iraqi Qur'an was called a "remarkable gesture" by a Saudi newspaper and interpreted as a sign that the Iraqi leader had accepted pan-Islamic solidarity as an element of his foreign policy.[63]

Provoked by Qadhdhafi's anti-Saudi policies, the Saudis responded by attacking the Islamic credentials of the government in Libya. They called Qadhdhafi "a spearhead against Islam and its Islamic sanctities"[64] and convened a special meeting of the Supreme Council of the Ulema of Saudi Arabia to expose Qadhdhafi's deviations from mainstream Islam. The Council distinguished between Qadhdhafi and his subjects noting that "the Libyan people were aware of the controversy into which they have been dragged by this man, and were struggling to return to the Arab and Islamic ranks."[65] It implied that the Libyans should replace their government with a fundamentalist order. Among the many opponents of Qadhdhafi's regime were fundamentalist groups which received Saudi backing.

The Saudis supported Mauritania's military efforts (along with Morocco's) in the Western Sahara against Algeria and the Polisario, and they also funded non-military projects in Mauritania. The critical importance of this aid became apparent early in 1978 when the Saudis' suspicions about the use of their money led to a reduction in funds. By June of that year, President Mukhtar Ould Daddah, fearing the discontent that was growing among his unpaid military officers, became desperate for Saudi money. Toconvince Riyadh of his sincerety and worthiness, Ould Daddah called for the application of the Shari'a to all aspects of Mauritanian life. A leading Mauritanian official visited Tripoli the day before these measures were announced and the Saudi press greated the program with favorable comment.[66] The money did finally arrive in the middle of July, but too late; Ould Daddah had been overthrown on the tenth of July. Subsequent Mauritanian leaders retained the Shari'a plans, hoping thereby to retain Saudi and Libyan favor.

Saudi aid to Morocco helped King Hasan wage war in the Western Sahara; in return, Morocco joined the other Arab countries in condemning the Egypt-Israel peace treaty, despite its having facilitated the contacts that led to Sadat's visit to Jerusalem. Qadhdhafi supported almost every group opposed to the monarchy in Morocco, including some organized by fundamentalists.

After King Faisal's visit to Niger in November 1972, the government's foreign policy became notably more Islamic in orientation. Libyan aid alleviated problems caused by years of drought and was also used to pressure the government in Niamey to adopt Islamic policies.

The fate of Pakistan mattered greatly to the Saudis because, in addition to nearly bordering on the Persian Gulf, it supplied laborers and soldiers. To assure their influence in the early 1970s, the Saudis supported both Zulfikar Ali Bhutto's socialist administration and opposition groups such as Abul Ala Maududi's Jama'at-i Islami (JI). JI convinced the Saudi leaders to make their aid to the government conditional on it becoming more friendly to legalist Islam. So much did Bhutto depend on Saudi largess that he was compelled to placate JI by modifying the Pakistani constitution and altering his policies. Libya, whose many ties to Pakistan gave its opinion weight, also supported these changes.

But nothing Bhutto did pleased JI or the Saudis. Even "constant shuffling to the oil-producing states"[67] did not earn their trust. Firm evidence that the Saudis funded the widespread agitation directed against Bhutto in 1977 is lacking, but it is hard to see where else sums of money to sustain four months of demonstrations could have come from. Further, the Saudis were clearly happy to see him go.

Zia-ul-Haq, the general who replaced Bhutto, was far more to the Saudis' liking. Directly after taking power, Zia visited Saudi Arabia to solicit financial aid, which he received. On his return to Pakistan, he declared that "Islam is our religion and Saudi Arabia is the biggest source of assistance to us"[68]—drawing a closer connection between Islam and oil money than perhaps he intended. Aid came pouring in. The rulers of Saudi Arabia and the United Arab Emirates gave $125 million in personal contributions for the Central Zakat Fund established to help widows, orphans, and other needy Muslims, providing most of the initial capitalization. King Khalid's personal advisor gave the Islamization program added impetus when, reporting the king's pleasure with developments in Pakistan, he promised that "Saudi gold coffers will be open to Pakistan once it has an Islamic government."[69] Islamization also served as a means to enhance the attraction of Pakistanis as laborers for the sheikhdoms.

The more open societies of the Persian Gulf statelets offered temptations to Saudis which were unavailable in their own country; in the 1970s, Riyadh put intense pressure to close these down. Although the small countries had long records of resisting Saudi territorial encroachments, they yielded easily on matters concerning Islam. None applied the Shari'a so strictly as did the Wahhabis, but "under Saudi influence, the application of Islamic law has become common-place in the United Arab Emirates, Kuwait, and the smaller Gulf states."⁷⁰ An institute in Bahrain funded by the Saudis, for example, required women to wear long skirts, contrary to local custom. The Saudis funded groups as Al-Islah, the Bahraini fundamentalist movement founded in 1978. Observers noted Saudi influence behind the ban on Christmas festivities in 1982.

In Saudi Arabia, the single fundamentalist movement against the government, the attack in Mecca in November 1979, apparently had Libyan backing. The two Libyans who took part had connections to the Qadhdhafi government and much of the financing and gunrunning for the escapade was arranged by Libya.⁷¹ Tripoli also attempted to rally Saudi subjects against the monarchy by emphasizing the non-Shar'i indulgences of the rulers. The head of the Libyan news service referred to the Saudi princes as "camels" who "are drinking, gambling, doing everything bad against Islam." He argued that "if you want to judge them by the Koran, most of them have to be killed."⁷² A Libyan-sponsored gathering of "national liberation movements" from the Arabian peninsula in Cyprus in November 1980 included some fundamentalist groups.

Ahmad Khalifa Niasse, the "Ayatollah of Kaolack," received Libyan aid when still in Senegal. After fleeing the country, he ended up in Libya, where Qadhdhafi gave him funds to build a Senegalese military force to invade Senegal, overthrow the government, and set up an Islamic republic. Soldiers for this force were recruited by promising jobs in Libya to Senegalese, then compelling them to serve in Niasse's militia. In July 1980, Senegal broke relations with Libya over this issue, relying on information made available by French and U.S. intelligence.

In return for Saudi munificence, said to reach $400 million, President Siad Barre expelled Soviet advisors from Somalia, abrogated a friendship treaty with the Soviet Union in 1977, de-emphasized Marxist socialism, and made gestures in favor of Islam. Although it did not activate Shar'i regulations, the government treated things Islamic with a new tolerance. To help the Somali autonomist struggle with Ethiopia, in 1978 the Saudis contributed $200 million to pay for arms.

Saudi aid to the Muslim Brethren of Syria helped propel them into a position to threaten the regime of Hafiz al-Asad. Although the Saudis provided his government with about $1 billion annually for many years, they had opposed many of Asad's policies, especially his alliance with the Soviet Union. Funds to fundamentalist Muslims arrived in various ways: the Muslim Brethren in Jordan, Saudi-sponsored Islamic institutions such as the Muslim World League, and the Saudi ambassador in Beirut. Syrian military leaders serving in Lebanon who were displeased with their government's reliance on the Soviet

Union apparently formed a group called the Organization of Muslim Officers; besides money, they received false papers from the Saudi embassy in Beirut which they passed on to the Muslim Brethren within Syria for use against the regime. When the Syrians antagonized Saudi leaders by having the state-controlled press declare that the film "Death of a Princess" was less anti-Islam than the Saudis claimed, Riyadh withdrew its ambassador from Damascus in protest and, presumably, increased its aid to the Muslim dissidents.

The Muslim Brethren (or, more properly, the Movement for the Renewal of Islam) in Tunisia was reported to receive funds from both Saudi Arabia and Libya.

Both the secular government of Turkey and the country's leading fundamentalist party, the National Salvation Party (NSP), came under the influence of oil money. Saudi Arabia gave the government grants with the intent of "orienting the country toward Islam and preparing it for solidarity with the Muslim nations."[73] Libyan money went clandestinely to the NSP; its subsequent orientation toward Libya had "nothing to do with al-Qadhdhafi's path toward social revolution but [followed] from Libya's economic involvement in Turkey."[74] After the imposition of martial law in 1980, fundamentalists, fascists, and Marxists were all jailed; but while the latter two remained in prison for months, fundamentalists were set free pending a court decision, "apparently because of strong pressures from some Arab nations."[75]

Through the 1970s, Saudi influence carried great weight in both Yemens, North and South, dampening their radicalism and pushing them in the direction of Islam. Saudi policies had dramatic success in North Yemen, which became virtually an economic ward of Saudi Arabia, receiving about $200 million annually. Fundamentalists secured twenty-five of the fifty seats in the newly-created Permanent Committee of the Popular Congress in August 1982, thanks in large part to Saudi funds. Even the Communist government in South Yemen was influenced slightly by Saudi money, as the two countries normalized relations in 1976 and the authorities in Aden eased restrictions on Islam.

MOIETIES

Muslim autonomists in Chad were perhaps the first non-Arabs to receive massive Libyan support, starting in 1971. Qadhdhafi's arms, money, and diplomatic pressure on the central government of Chad were critical to the Muslims having won control of the entire country by the late 1970s.

In addition to aiding the Somali forces in the Ogaden desert, Saudi Arabia also supported the most Islamic-oriented of the four Eritrean movements seeking independence from Ethiopia; Saudi pressure induced three of the organizations to unite in January 1983. Qadhdhafi also backed the Eritreans until a pro-Soviet government took power in Ethiopia, when he switched to its support. On occasions, Libya tried to bring peace between the two sides, for example by proposing talks in Tripoli, for Qadhdhafi had sympathies with both the Muslim autonomists in Eritrea and the revolutionaries ruling in Addis Ababa.

Both Libya and Saudi Arabia supported the National Front in the Lebanese civil war. The radical tone of this alliance made it far more appealing to Qadhdhafi, however, than to the House of Sa'ud: he urged it to fight till victory, while the Saudis arranged a peace settlement which reduced the fighting.

Some of Malaysia's most intolerant Muslim missionaries and preachers received salaries from Libya, others received training in Libya, and Libyans went to Malaysia intent on instilling desert customs in the jungle, haranguing local girls "to abandon the Malay sarong as well as Western dress and adopt the Arab veil and caftan."[76] A Libyan grant of $10 million helped fund the twenty-three-story building which housed PERKIM, the government's Islamic missionary agency. Anwar Ibrahim, head of a leading fundamentalist group, ABIM, visited Qadhdhafi in Libya in 1973 and his organization received money from Libya.

In a similar manner, the Saudis offered support to the missionaries, PERKIM, and ABIM. In addition, when Prince Muhammad al-Faysal of Saudi Arabia visited Malaysia in December 1980, he offered $100 million for an interest-free finance corporation. Not surprisingly, the Malaysian finance minister responded by announcing that the government would study the possibility of establishing an "Islamic economic system."[77] Two years later, the Saudis helped finance the government-sponsored Bank Islam Malaysia. These actions led some cynics to argue "that the expanded interest in Islam among Malaysian politicians reflects a desire to obtain economic aid from the Arabs or to guarantee continued oil during future embargoes."[78]

Circumstantial evidence points to Libyan involvement in the Yen Izala riots in Kano in December 1980. A report of the Nigerian secret services issued just before the riots broke out revealed the existence of a wide network of Libyan accomplices in Nigeria and concluded that armed intervention was imminent. The government claimed that Libyan money had backed the Yen Izala group, and political observers in the capital, Lagos, were convinced that Libya had instigated the violence.

The Saudis encouraged, and perhaps funded, the alliance of fundamentalists in the Sudan in 1972, called the National Front, which included as-Sadiq al-Mahdi of the Ansar, ash-Sharif al-Hindi of the National Unity Party, and Hasan at-Turabi of the Islamic Charter Front (the Muslim Brethren in the Sudan). Aid from Qadhdhafi followed, and, before long, most of the National Front was based in Libya. From there, they made more than one attempt at a coup d'etat (for instance, in November 1975), but it was the effort in July 1976 that came close to succeeding. Qadhdhafi's backing was revealed when a Libyan military plane was spotted circling the skies over Khartoum, carrying the coup's leaders, who tried to direct their forces on the ground from the plane, but without much success. So many participants in the coup received military training in Libya and carried arms acquired from there that Numayri called it "the Libyan invasion."[79]

This event apparently convinced both Numayri and the National Front of the need to end their hostilities; with active Saudi encouragement, they signed an agreement of National Reconciliation in July 1977. For Numayri to allow the fundamentalist leaders a role in his government, as he promised to do, was so striking a change in policy that many observers concluded he did so only to please his Saudi patrons. But if the Saudis brought old enemies together, Qadhdhafi encouraged them to stay apart. After Mahdi returned to the Sudan in September 1977, Hindi stayed in Libya with 7,000 or so Sudanese refugees, causing a split in the National Front. Relations between Libya and the Sudan subsequently warmed to the point that Qadhdhafi agreed in September 1978 to close all remaining National Front camps in his country, but then, as Numayri supported Sadat's peace initiative toward Israel, Qadhdhafi showed his anger by delaying implementation of this agreement until May 1979. Relations remained cool thereafter as Qadhdhafi fomented unrest by beaming radio broadcasts to border areas of the Sudan beyond the reach of the domestic radio transmission and spreading threats of assassination teams stalking Numayri. In the days after Sadat's assassination, Libyan planes bombed several Sudanese villages. By the end of 1981, Numayri had developed, in the words of a senior British diplomat, "a tendency to see the hand of Libya and Moscow everywhere"[80]—not wholly without reason.

MINORITIES

Reports circulated in 1978 that the Rohingya Patriotic Front, the autonomist organization of Muslims in Burma, received Arab funds. By widely publicizing the plight of the Rohingyas, Saudi Arabia and Libya protected them slightly from the wrath of the Burmese authorities. Their efforts may have also embued the Rohingyas with an overconfidence—characterized by a cabinet member in Bangladesh as "adventurism"—which provoked some of the increased problems with the government in Rangoon.[81]

The Saudis aided construction projects and education in Cameroon, while Libya intrigued in the military and among the students. The efforts of both encouraged Islamic autonomism.

Neither the Saudis nor Qadhdhafi could directly affect developments in China but both did successfully convince the government to improve conditions for the Muslims. Peking's receptivity to these pressures reflected the importance it attached to maintaining good relations with the oil-exporting giants. Restrictions on Islamic rituals were eased, new editions of the Qur'an were published, and pilgrims were once again, in 1979, allowed to go on the voyage to Mecca. Not surprisingly, the first Muslim delegation to leave the country after the Cultural Revolution went to Libya and Saudi Arabia. In Raphael Israeli's view, the combination of a "pro-Arab ambiance in the world, which by necessity generates a universal reluctance to antagonize Muslims" and a post-Mao trend toward liberalization could foster a "Muslim awakening" in China.[82]

Soon after independence in 1947, India's leaders adopted a pro-Arab policy as a way to offset the Arab's natural sympathy for Pakistan; then, during the initial days of non-alignment, Nehru and Abdul Nasser cooperated closely, furthering these ties. As Arab states gained vastly more influence in the late 1970s, the Indian government, fearing an oil embargo, a trade boycott, or the expulsion of Indian migrant workers from the Persian Gulf, carefully maintained this stance, despite the fact that most of the Hindu population had no sympathy for the Arabs. Widespread suspicion of Arab intent emerged with every Hindu-Muslim problem of the late 1970s, especially the communal riots, the Kashmir question, and the conversion of untouchables to Islam.

Many Indians suspected that money from the Arab oil states earmarked for mosques and Islamic schools really went to rabble-rousers. Riots in Aligarh, Jamshedpur, Allahabad, and Moradabad were linked to Arab funds and, in some cases, to specific educational institutions which received Arab money.[83] Many politicians, including cabinet members, suggested that a "foreign hand" had instigated the riots;[84] one of them was the home minister, Zail Singh, later elected to the presidency of the republic. So pervasive was the talk about outside money that the Saudi embassy in New Delhi felt compelled to issue a denial. Frustrated by the endless suspicions, one Arab ambassador, the Moroccan, retaliated by publicly accusing a "hidden hand" of planning "to accomplish the extermination of our brother Muslims in India," and set off a diplomatic flurry.[85] Although partially retracted, his statement testified both to the Arabs' new concern for India's Muslims and to the Hindus' acute sensitivity about the pressures the Arabs could exert.

When anti-Indian riots broke out for the first time ever in Kashmir, leading to two days of clashes with the police, the Arab-sponsored Jama'at-i Islami came in for most of the blame. The chief minister of Kashmir pointed to Arab funding of this organization and its youth wing, Jama'at-i Tulba, as the problem. One source claimed that Jama'at-i Islami received money from seven

Muslim countries and another estimated that it received about $150 million from abroad.[86]

The mass conversion of Untouchables in the south Indian village of Meenakshipuram prompted more concern about foreign money. The Islamic Cultural Centre in London issued a press release linking the conversion of fifty Untouchables to the building of an agricultural project worth $50,000; picked up by the *Arab Times* of Kuwait, this story provoked outrage in India. One official noted, "It is obvious that money power was the main motivating factor [behind the conversions]", and Prime Minister Indira Gandhi expressed the same thought more delicately: "Enormous amounts of Arab money are coming in. And they [the Arabs] made it a conscious effort to convert the very poor, mostly Harijans [Untouchables]." Some leaders called for laws banning conversions in the light of "foreign money and influences . . . at work . . . to weaken India's social fabric." Balasaheb Deoras, leader of the extremist Hindu organization, Rashtriya Sewak Sangh, went so far as to warn Indians of a global strategy to use Muslim petrodollars to win converts to Islam.[87]

Qadhdhafi decried any sign of acceptance of Israel's existence, adopting a position far more extreme than any other Arab state's. On one occasion, he expelled the P.L.O. from Libya on the grounds that it was too accommodating; in September 1982, Libya was the one Arab state to stay away from the Arab League meeting in Fez and refusing to sign a proposal implicitly recognizing Israel. Qadhdhafi engaged in the most virulent hostility against Israel, such as trying to sink the Queen Elizabeth II in 1972 as the ship carried passengers to Israel for the country's twenty-fifth anniversary celebrations; or giving a hero's funeral to the terrorists who killed the Israeli athletes at the Olympic Games in Munich. He supplied anti-Israel forces in Lebanon with money, sophisticated arms (SAM 9s), and Libyan soldiers.

The Saudis also played a key role in the conflict with Israel after 1967, providing billions of dollars in subsidies every year to the Arab states bordering on Israel and hundreds of millions of dollars to the P.L.O. It was the Saudi government which initiated the Arab oil embargo in 1973 and which set up a lobby in Washington challenging that of Israel's.

Members of the Northern Frontier District Liberation Front in Kenya sought help for their autonomist campaign in Saudi Arabia and other Arab states. Kenyan officials called on the Arabs to turn down the rebels' requests.

The Moro revolt in the southern Philippines would probably have been crushed soon after its inception in late 1972 were it not for Arab support. Aid to the rebels combined with pressure on the government in Manila kept the revolt alive—without making likely its ultimate success. Qadhdhafi was the first Muslim leader in the Middle East to take note of the Moros, rallying verbally to their side in October 1971 and offering to send "money, arms and volunteers" in June 1972.[88] Although "volunteers" probably never arrived, money and arms in profusion reached the Moros via the nearby Malaysian province of Sabah. Not long after, the Moro National Liberation Front (MNLF) set up its headquarters in Tripoli. Qadhdhafi was instrumental in getting both sides in the conflict to sign a peace treaty agreement in Tripoli in December 1976; indeed, he virtually directed the MNLF as to the terms to accept. One indication of his continuing influence was the fact that a subsequent MNLF demand was that Arabic be the language of an autonomous Muslim region in the Philippines—a language hardly anyone there speaks, but the one actively promoted by Qadhdhafi. When peace discussions collapsed in the spring of 1977, President Ferdinand Marcos of the Philippines tried unsuccessfully to talk with Qadhdhafi by telephone, then sent his wife Imelda to Libya to intervene in person. Qadhdhafi subsequently supplied the rebels with money and arms, including Soviet and East European weapons. In late September 1978, Marcos accused Libya of having contributed $100 million to the Muslim rebellion in his country.

The Saudis sponsored the Bangsa Moro Liberation Organization, a more respectable organization which could lobby in places where Libyan-backed organizations did not dare to tread, such as the United States Congress, where they urged a reduction in American military assistance to the Philippine government. When Libyan support for the MNLF cooled in late 1979, Saudi support increased and the MNLF moved its headquarters to Saudi Arabia. As in Afghanistan, Eritrea, and the Sudan, the Saudis urged rival Moro organizations to unite, but with less success in this case. The government in Manila paid close attention to Saudi wishes for obvious economic reasons: in 1982, 40 percent of the Philippines' oil imports came from Saudi Arabia and 150,000 of its workers were employed there. Thus, when the Saudi state-owned petroleum company, Petromin, sent a cable in December 1980 announcing its intent not to renew existing oil contracts, the government in Manila, responding with alarm, offered the Saudis assurances of a new flexibility on the Moro question. Delivery was quickly resumed. President Marcos spent three days in Saudi Arabia in March 1982 attempting to smooth his relations with the kingdom; in return for concessions on the Moro question, Marcos received—at a time when the banks were reluctant to lend more to his government—a critical $500 million loan. The Saudis also reportedly offered the Manila government up to $400 million in aid once the problem in the south was resolved to Saudi satisfaction.

The Islamic Conference became involved with the Moro problem when Qadhdhafi raised the issue in March 1973. He convinced the Muslim leaders to censure the Manila government and had a committee appointed to go to the Philippines and investigate the situation there at first hand. Despite the committee's clear sympathy for the rebels (it included, among others, the Saudi and Libyan foreign ministers), Marcos invited it into the country for fear that his refusal to do so would provoke an oil embargo, a loss of Arab loans and grants, Muslim enmity in the United Nations and other international forums, and increased assistance to the rebels. Marcos later regretted his decision to permit the Islamic Conference a role in the Moro problem, calling its mission "an act of intervention in our domestic affairs."[89] But it was too late. Led by Libya, the conference became an autonomous actor in the Philippines conflict, exerting pressure on Manila, funding the MNLF, and promoting its own peace plans. The importance of the conference was shown in early 1979 when concern about its decisions prompted Marcos to send his wife to Morocco to talk with King Hasan in advance of a meeting he was soon to host. A year later, an upsurge in Moro guerrilla activity was tied to efforts to win back the conference's flagging attention.

The Rumanian authorities reversed their decades-long policy of persecuting Muslims in the mid-1970s, a direct result of the Arab oil states' new power. Alexandre Popovic wrote in an article published in 1982:

The international situation pushed the Rumanian government to grant a number of concessions to the country's Muslim community, even if limited ones, in order to improve the image of the regime in some of the Arab and Muslim nations, especially among the Muslim producers of petroleum. . . . One can logically expect that the global oil crisis would convince the Rumanian authorities to make more concessions of this sort in coming years.[90]

Arab oil exporters pressured the Soviet Union to improve the conditions of its Muslim population. As in China, this brought more freedom to practice the Islamic rituals, more Qur'ans, and more pilgrims to Mecca. But the Soviets resisted Arab pressure to make further concessions, as shown by an exchange which reportedly took place during Qadhdhafi's visit to Moscow in 1977. The Soviet leader, Leonid Brezhnev, suggested opening a Soviet consulate in Benghazi, to which Qadhdhafi responded by requesting permission to open a consulate in Tashkent in Central Asia. When Brezhnev asked why in Tashkent, Qadhdhafi replied, "Because I understand there are a lot of Muslims in that part of Russia and I would like to take care of them." The topic of additional consulates was not brought up again.[91]

Libyan aid to the Muslim rebels in Thailand apparently began in 1974 and peaked in 1978 with grants of $18 million annually, military training courses, and arms. The arrest of a Libyan in southern Thailand on terrorist charges may have indicated a direct involvement as well. When Qadhdhafi's interest in Thailand faltered, the rebels staged spectacular attacks, such as the bombing of the Haadyai Railroad Station in February 1980. Libya put pressure on the rival groups to merge, but without success. Saudi Arabia hosted the Pattani United Liberation Organization (PULO), the biggest of these groups, gave it offices in Mecca, and permitted it to recruit new members from among Thai pilgrims making the hajj. The Muslim World League, a Saudi-dominated body, pressured the Thai government to provide better education to the Muslims and to raise their standard of living. Financial aid from the Middle East was so great that PULO, like the P.L.O., could invest abroad, for example, acquiring part ownership of a hotel in Hamburg.[92]

The Arab states had a crucial role in convincing Idi Amin of Uganda to shift from his pro-Israel policy to an Islamic orientation. Saudi Arabia provided money, and Qadhdhafi provided money and soldiers (for which, in return, the army's crack corps was named after him). Two thousand Libyan soldiers stood by Amin during his last days as ruler with the stated purpose "to save Islam in Uganda."[93] As Tanzanian troops closed in on Amin, the Libyans flew him out of the country on a Libyan Mystère jet. To win Arab support, "Idi Amin put on the garb of a Muslim head of state," writes Nehemia Levtzion. "Muslims in Uganda, however, represented no more than ten percent of the population, and in order to broaden the base of public support, Idi Amin led an official campaign, aided by Arab funds, for conversion to Islam."[94] A senior French official understood that Qadhdhafi "went to Uganda because Idi Amin was Muslim; he went there in the name of Muslim solidarity."[95]

The Saudis continued to support Amin even after his fall, funding his soldiers through an organization called the National Front for the Survival of Uganda. In the view of a subsequent foreign minister of Uganda, they did so "because the Saudis believe the current government to be anti-Muslim."[96] After his fall from power, Amin took refuge first in Libya and then in Saudi Arabia, where he adopted the demeanor of an intensely devout Muslim. Qadhdhafi eventually normalized relations with the post-Amin authorities and continued to finance such projects as the Islamic Cultural Centre at Jinja.

Riyadh gave $10 million to spread Islam in the United States in 1979-81. Libya reportedly gave millions of dollars to the presidential campaign of Sangoule Lamizana, the Muslim candidate in Upper Volta's 1973 elections; in return, Lamizana promised to apply the Shari'a on attaining power, although he later reneged.

The Yugoslav government was concerned to please Arab opinion already in the 1950s, when Egypt was one of the critical states in the nonaligned movement. The 1956 decision, for example, to recognize Islam as one of the Yugoslav nationalities was undertaken with this purpose in mind. Then, for reasons connected with oil, Saudi Arabia and Libya took Egypt's place in the 1970s. More Yugoslavs—ten thousand of them—went to work in Libya than in all other non-European countries combined. Maintaining good relations with the Arab states remained a high priority; so their pressure on Belgrade to improve the conditions of the Muslim citizens led to tangible results. Saudi Arabia gave $250,000 to found an Islamic seminary in Sarajevo, a most unusual action both for a Muslim government that normally had no transactions with Communist countries, and for a Communist government that normally did not accept foreign donations for religious institutions. In the aftermath of Tito's statement about the need for "severe measures" against signs of Islamic activism in Yugoslavia, it was the spokesman of the *foreign* ministry who tried to soften the president's remarks. Like so many other non-Muslim states, Yugoslavia faced a dilemma trying to balance strict control of Muslim citizens at home with the good will of Muslim states abroad.

The Islamic revival that began with the changed psychology of the oil boom received wide backing from Saudi Arabia and Libya. In some places they initiated an Islamic consciousness, elsewhere they furthered embryonic movements, and in yet other places they boosted already powerful Islamic currents. Then, at the end of the decade, a third major development occurred: the rise of Imam Khomeini in Iran.

Iran: Disruption and Inspiration

By unsettling the economies of oil importers and exporters alike, the oil boom created environments favorable to Islamic action. On the paying end, problems associated with the increase in energy costs exacerbated local tensions in Turkey and contributed to strife between Sunnis and Shi'is. Similar difficulties furthered the rise of fundamentalist movements in Egypt and Pakistan.

But it was those countries selling oil which were the most unsettled by the changes which accompanied the oil boom. The influx of fast and easy money impaired social relations and created an atmosphere of greed and self-interest. New wealth from oil money disrupted normal life in several ways. First, it turned people's heads, leading them to forget their values and causing them to lose "their personalities or their identity," as an Indonesian watching the changes in his country explained:

[They] cannot distinguish between right and wrong any more. Why? In their loss of identity they have lost all values except those associated with power. . . . It's not yet become a jungle, but we could get there. There are millions of people who are morally good, but they are powerless to enforce the good. There are thousands—and this is important—who are powerful but are not willing to enforce the good. So you feel adrift. . . . Where does all the money come from, that's encouraging all of this? It comes from oil.[97]

Similarly in Nigeria, corruption and profiteering proliferated as a direct consequence of the country's soaring oil wealth. "There is unprecedented indiscipline in Nigeria these days," a Nigerian political analyst observed. "There is smuggling, there is corruption, money permeates society."[98] In revulsion, many persons turned to fundamentalist Islam, the one ideology that seemed to provide direction in a disturbed time and structure in the face of rampant amorality.

Second, oil-exporting countries were unsettled by the predominant economic role of their governments; especially in the sheikhdoms, oil sales contributed well over 90 percent of the national wealth, so that the entire population lived off state spending, making the distribution of state funds critical to every person in the country. Anxieties about money imbued political life in the oil-rich states with a desperate edge, and again caused many Muslims to seek solace in Islam.

Third, oil production attracted great numbers of foreign workers to serve in every capacity from technical specialist to water carrier and they contributed to the Islamic revival in diverse ways. The largest concentrations of foreign workers appeared in the sheikhdoms, where they typically exceeded the native population in size, but they also had an important role in other countries. In Nigeria, foreign workers sparked the country's worst outbreak of fundamentalist violence, the Yen Izala revolt of December 1980; its leader came from Cameroon, and of the roughly thousand persons arrested, nearly one-quarter came from other countries, such as Niger, Chad, Cameroon, Mali, and Upper Volta,[99] lured to Nigeria by the oil boom. Islamic activism was a major reason for the expulsion of illegal foreign workers from Nigeria in January–February 1983. Tens of thousands of Americans in Iran constituted a presence which disturbed many Iranians, especially when those Americans received special legal rights.

New money, financial dependence on the state, and foreign workers created problems in countries such as Nigeria and Indonesia, as well as many others (Libya, Syria, Iraq, Bahrain, and Malaysia, for example). But Iran experienced disruption from oil most cataclysmically and with much the most importance for the Islamic revival. Were it not for oil wealth, Khomeini would never have overthrown the shah and there would have been no experiment with Islamic theocracy. New money in Iran raised the general standard of living enormously during the 1970s, making some Iranians fabulously rich and leaving many others dissatisfied with their inability to cash in on the affluence. As riches flowed in, expectations rose too fast. Income from oil sales leaped from $4.4 billion in 1972–73 to $9.6 billion in 1973–74 and then to $20.6 billion the next year. But then it remained virtually constant until the fall of the shah. The sudden quadrupling of prices led to extravagant planning, yet the plateau that followed meant that the shah's ambitions could not be carried out. Too much money came in after 1973 for life to remain as it had been, but not enough came in to satisfy the Iranians' growing expectations. As frustrations multiplied, virtually all sectors of the Iranian population, including students, merchants, day laborers, oil workers, and even religious officials, felt the pinch and turned against the government. Oil revenues made it possible for the government to initiate massive industrialization programs which undermined much of traditional agriculture, emptied the countryside, and filled the cities with deracinated peasants. Inflation, rapidly changing patterns of life, and shifting power created anxieties and stresses that undid the benefits of the wealth.

Oil wealth also had unfortunate effects on the government. The oil boom made it possible, for the first time in history, for the rulers not to tax their own citizens, freeing them from financial dependence on their people. The shah, Mohammed Reza Pahlavi, whose despotic tendencies had long been evident, succumbed to the temptation of ignoring the aspirations of his populace and lost all touch with them. Carried away by soaring ambitions and a euphoric sense of power, he blithely ignored the increasing dissatisfaction with his regime during the 1970s. He apparently did not realize how his grandiose self-celebration in 1971 for two and a half thousand years of alleged monarchy[100] aroused scorn, not awe. He seemed unaware or unconcerned that by 1976 the people had grown so hostile to his regime's actions that they refused to adopt the daylight savings time instituted by the government.

In combination, widespread economic tensions and the shah's misguided plans, both made possible by oil revenues, precipitated a revolt by nearly the entire population of Iran. Iran and the Islamic revival entered a new era in 1978 with the emergence of Ayatollah Ruhollah Khomeini as the country's leader. Khomeini personified Islamic activism, both legalist and autonomist: his Shar'i goals were possibly the most uncompromising of any leader's in modern times, his modest personal habits, manifest piety, utter determination, honesty, high religious standing, and advanced age made him the embodiment of fundamentalism. Indeed, after attaining power, he consistently carried out the fundamentalist vision, scorning economic concerns, Western influences, or any other obstacles in the way of living by the Shari'a. No less important, Khomeini also stood for Islamic autonomism. By portraying the shah as a puppet of the United States and his government as a vehicle for American control over Iran, Khomeini justified passionate hatred of the regime, giving the opposition religious sanction and embuing the anti-shah cause with an autonomist purpose which made it easier to mobilize Iranians.

Khomeini's ascent to power had enormous appeal to Muslims far beyond Iran's borders. Without armaments, oil revenues, or official position, but only with Muslim determination and "stirring arrogance,"[101] he faced and defeated the shah, whose ostentation, power, and international support were of no avail when confronted with Islam. Long a voice in the wilderness, Khomeini had spent fifteen years in exile; Iranians turned increasingly to him in 1978 until millions acclaimed his name as they marched in the streets of Iran; elation surged as victory approached by the end of the year; and finally, frenzy swept Iran on his return to the country in February 1979. To some, calling him imam even had eschatological overtones, implying the imminent end of the world. The drama of this episode resonated among discontent Muslims everywhere, particularly as it recalled the Prophet Muhammad's own rise to power; if Khomeini could do so well, other Muslims were inspired to believe that they could too. The divine favor Khomeini seemed to enjoy (how else does one explain his toppling so powerful a regime?) gave heart to all those who wanted to force the pace of change; and it influenced them to approach politics in a more Islamic manner.

It was oil that enabled Muslims outside Iran to hear of Khomeini and to follow his progress, for oil made Iran newsworthy. Events there attracted attention in the West because Iran was the second largest oil exporter and because it served as a buffer between the Soviet Union and the world's primary oil reserves in the Persian Gulf. Also, oil made Iran critical to the world economy and a source of profits and jobs in the West. With such critical Western interests at stake, the Islamic revolution received consistent front-page coverage in Europe and America, and it was this *Western* attention that brought news of Khomeini to Muslims outside Iran, who depended on American, British, and French news agencies for most of their international coverage. What the West chose to report reverberated back to Islamdom, shaping the information Muslims received about each other and influencing their perceptions of current events. By way of contrast to Iran, the Western news media ignored Islamic agitation against Zulfikar Ali Bhutto in 1977 so that events in Pakistan had virtually no repercussions beyond the country's borders. Oil made Khomeini important to the West which in turn made information about him available to Muslims outside Iran and increased his impact on Islamdom. (Concern with oil also generated increased international coverage of the Muslim Brethren in Egypt and Syria; it gained attention for Qadhdhafi, the Meccan mosque seizure, and other developments, thus augmenting the sense of a worldwide movement toward Islam and prompting the spread of Islamic action.)

Khomeini furthered the Islamic revival outside Iran in two principal ways: by inspiring Muslims and by direct intervention. The former had the greater importance, while the latter resembled, on a smaller scale, the activities of Saudi Arabia and Libya.

INSPIRATION

So great was Khomeini's effect throughout Islamdom that in several cases, governments tried to restrict news coming from Iran to temper the excitement of his sympathizers. An Egyptian official gathered the editors of Cairo newspapers and informed them of President Sadat's "profound displeasure . . . concerning the manner in which the press has covered events in Iran, making Khomeini into a hero."[102] An Iranian emissary to Bahrain accused the government there of trying to "throw a cordon" around the Iranian Revolution by censuring reports from Iran.[103] Malaysians who visited Iran and Pakistan complained that their state-controlled press did not properly report the Islamic developments in those countries "in order to diminish the strength of the traditional Islamic forces in Malaysia."[104]

Another sign of Khomeini's impact was the emergence in Islamdom of locally prominent fundamentalists who became known by his name: Ahmed Khalifa Niasse of Senegal was the "Ayatollah of Kaolack," an "Ayatollah of Malaysia" distributed extremist leaflets titled "Letter from the Sky," and the governor of Jakarta, Indonesia, became known as "Mr. Khomeini No. 2" when he closed down nighttime amusement houses.[105] When Khomeini made the improbable, even paranoiac accusation against the United States, that it had instigated the Meccan mosque seizure, Muslims responded in six countries by attacking American embassies and consulates.

Where Muslims constituted majorities, Khomeini encouraged the fundamentalists. In Algeria, revolutionary Iran was held up as a model by Ahmed Ben Bella, the formerly pro-Soviet president of the country. Calling Khomeini's rise to power "the greatest event to affect the Muslim world in centuries," he saw it as proof that Islam can work. "A brilliant light appeared in Iran which illuminated the whole Muslim world, putting immense hope in the hearts of a great majority of Muslims."[106] In Bangladesh, the student organization Islami Chatra Shibir considered Iran the only true Islamic state and derived hope from Khomeini's rise. The Muslim Brethren held a rally in Cairo in February 1979 to celebrate Khomeini's accession to power and the imposition of Shar'i law in Pakistan. At the meeting, their leader, 'Umar at-Talmasani, urged his members to follow the path marked out by Khomeini. Fundamentalist elation resulting from events in Iran was understood to have kept Sadat from challenging their growing influence in 1980. After Sadat's assassination, Husni Mubarak explained that Sadat's killers were "trying to imitate something like what happened in Iran. . . . They planned to assassinate the President, maybe the whole leadership, at the celebration of the sixth of October, and then to declare something like the so-called Islamic revolution";[107] their goal was to establish an Islamic republic like Khomeini's, he later elucidated. Egyptian police found a summary of Khomeini's book on Islamic government among the assassins' possessions. A year later, 302 fundamentalists were put on trial and charged with conspiring to establish an Islamic Republic along Iranian lines.

According to Rémy Lèveau, "the events in Iran precipitated . . . a reawakening of fundamentalism in Morocco"; many people shared the view of 'Abd as-Salim Yasin, editor of *Al-Jam'a,* that the whole umma should follow Iran's example: "A new vision of Islam appeared among the Iranian people, a vision of leaders with faith which, God willing, will illuminate the way for all Muslims."[108] Responding to fundamentalist pressures aroused by events in Iran, the Saudi authorities tightened restrictions on women working alongside men, banned mixed swimming in hotel pools, forbade table soccer, and took other measures. The Sunni Muslim Brethren of Syria used slogans from the Iranian Revolution, but their own government's Shi'i character and its good relations with Iran reduced Khomeini's appeal. *Al-Mujtama'a,* a voicepiece of fundamentalists in Tunisia, promoted the Iranian Revolution as a suitable model for Tunisia. The revolution also served as evidence to the fundamentalists that they could challenge the Tunisian government: "The example of Iran is our proof. It is time to wake up and fight against lethargy and drift."[109] Fundamentalist enthusiasm for Khomeini worried secularists in Turkey and contributed to the coup of September 1980 carried out by the military leadership.

Khomeini had a similar impact in the moieties. Fundamentalists in Malaysia exploited the news coming from Iran and Pakistan "to excite their membership, attract new adherents, and force the government to consider more carefully their cause."[110] Anwar Ibrahim, leader of ABIM, traveled to Iran and met with Khomeini shortly after the revolution, greatly adding to his stature back in Malaysia. The Lord President of the Federal Court of Malaysia, Tun Mohamed Suffian, facing increased legalist pressures, warned that "recent events in Iran give encouragement to Muslim extremists in Malaysia who desire the enforcement of Muslim law."[111] In Nigeria, fundamentalists saw Khomeini's Iran, in the words of a diplomat, as a place "where Islam has returned to its true values and where the heresies have been swept away."[112] In March 1979, thousands of students marched through the streets of Khartoum, Sudan, chanting their support for Khomeini and warning Numayri that he would soon go the way of the shah. As-Sadiq al-Mahdi of the Ansar, the Sudan's foremost fundamentalist party, visited Khomeini and other Iranian leaders in late 1979 and was seen to be radicalized by developments in Iran.

Finally, in minority situations, Khomeini's progress emboldened autonomists. The appearance of a new and more aggressive Muslim attitude in India, and especially the readiness to take on the police, was widely attributed to the Khomeini effect. In Kashmir, a conference for fundamentalist youth was canceled by the government because of fears that it would plan an "Iranian-type Muslim revolution."[113] Khomeini's success influenced the Palestinians in several ways. The P.L.O.'s brief alliance with Khomeini was rich with symbolism (Yasir Arafat was the first foreign leader to visit Khomeini in Tehran, the two embraced publicly, the P.L.O. took over former Israeli buildings) and added to the Islamic tone of the P.L.O.'s conflict with Israel. Arafat's battle cry, "Today Teheran, tomorrow Tel-Aviv," made an explicit connection between the two movements.[114] On the West Bank, a leaflet distributed in January 1979 in Nablus urged believers to "join the Great Islamic Revolution that has been taking place in other lands of Islam."[115] A group of West Bank youths made an attempt to dash across the Allenby Bridge that links the West Bank with Jordan, carrying placards declaring solidarity with Iran and calling on Imam Khomeini to liberate Jerusalem. In Gaza, rioters gutted a liquor shop, a cinema, and a restaurant while chanting "Long live Khomeini";[116] that same slogan was scrawled in big black letters on the walls of the city, while Muslims at a Jewish-Arab soccer game shouted "Khomeini" and "Down with Zionism." A Gazan carpenter who named his shop "Khomeini" explained that the name was fashionable and appealing to Muslims.[117] The emergence of a fundamentalist group among the Arabs living in Israel proper, the Family of Jihad, was widely viewed as a consequence of events in Iran.

Rebels in the Philippines took heart from Khomeini's revolution and looked to him for support. Nur Misuari, head of the MNLF, visited Iran and met with Khomeini and other leaders in June 1979. Muslims in Singapore were arrested in September 1979 on charges of fomenting an Iranian-style Islamic revolution. Even Yugoslavia felt reverberations from Iran; when some Muslims asserted their identity with talk of a "pan-Islamic brotherhood," the government accused the Mufti of Belgrade and other Islamic figures of spreading "Khomeini ideology." Marxist analysts then went to great lengths to prove that the Iranian model had no bearing on Yugoslavia. In April 1983, when eleven Muslims arrested in Sarajevo for "Muslim nationalism" were accused "of being linked with reactionary circles abroad," Iran was understood to be the source of government concern.[118]

For a year or two after the revolution, fundamentalists exploited fear of the Iranian example as a way to get their way. The Muslim Brethren leader in the Sudan, who was also the country's attorney general, proposed a law gradually to introduce the Shari'a; at the same time, he pointed out that not to apply the Shari'a meant denying a "strong, popular Islamic sentiment which, if ignored, will grow and burst into an Islamic revolution."[119] In many countries, fundamentalists were eager to point out the similarity of their rulers to the shah and of themselves to the Iranian fundamentalists, while rulers were just as quick to deny these parallels. "Do not fear that we shall be having a Khomeini here," Sadat told journalists less than a month before his death at the hands of fundamentalists. Similarly, President Chadli Bendjedid of Algeria felt compelled to assert that "Algeria is not Iran and I am not the shah."[120] To a great extent, Islamic activism became associated with Khomeini and his ascent to power.

INTERVENTION

Khomeini's determination to spread his ideology was spelled out in the Iranian constitution promulgated shortly after his return to the country. It called for "trying to perpetuate [the Islamic] revolution both at home and abroad."[121] But as his government became embroiled in domestic difficulties—the breakdown of the coalition that overthrew the shah, economic degeneration, revolt in the provinces, and war with Iraq—Iran lost its attraction as a model for fundamentalists and autonomists. Ironically, as internal problems increased, and the resources to devote to foreign causes diminished, the more Tehran was compelled to back its ideology with money. The Bahraini information minister observed that

the Iranian revolution is no longer a model for anybody. Three years ago [in 1979], when it just began, of course, it looked nice. But now . . . the export of the revolution from Iran is really no longer a problem, that is the export of ideals. But the export of subversion, yes, that is a problem.[122]

Subversion took many forms. On occasion, it involved nothing more than Khomeini attempting to duplicate his success in Iran by calling for the overthrow of a regime at its most vulnerable moment. Thus did he appeal to the "disinherited" to assert their rights in Saudi Arabia at the time of the Meccan mosque takeover. Three days after President Sadat's assassination, he called on the Egyptian people to destroy their government and set up an Islamic republic.

But without backing from Tehran, such appeals had little effect and the Iranians became actively engaged in helping Islamic causes much as the Saudis and Qadhdhafi before them. Even more than Qadhdhafi, they were by temperament drawn to anti-establishment causes. Egyptian authorities announced that they had unmasked a plot to set fire to and bomb Egyptian cities organized by Iranian agents. An Iranian was among the thirty-three arrested by the Turkish government in March 1983 and charged with plotting to establish an Islamic state. That same month, the Kuwaiti government expelled a Shi'i religious leader on the grounds that he supported Islamic revolution. North Yemen expelled an Iranian chargé d'affaires after catching him distribute anti-government leaflets. Iranian money went to autonomist groups in Ethiopia. Reports circulated that Iran, Libya, and the P.L.O. had agreed to cooperate to help the Moros win their independence from the Philippines and that the 4,000 Iranians studying in the Philippines had been directed by their government to assist this cause; a visiting Iranian ayatollah complained in Manila that the students were discriminated against and harassed by the police. According to the Philippine defense minister, Iran sent $1 million to the Moro rebels in 1980. Malaysian security forces uncovered links to Iran among some of the *dakwah* groups and political parties. They learned that a special unit in Tehran to encourage an Islamic revolution in Malaysia worked with Parti Islam.

The Iranian "oil weapon" amounted to not much more than cutting off oil exports to two governments fighting Muslims, the Philippines and Israel. Iranian military aid also had minimal impact. A handful of Iranian volunteers reached southern Lebanon in December 1979 to fight Israel, but they caused more trouble to Lebanon and Syria than to Israel. A second contingent of Iranians dispatched to Lebanon in June 1982 again had a neglible military role. Instead, they became intensely involved in Lebanese domestic politics and tried to set up an Islamic republic, at least in the area under their control near Baalbek. Khomeini termed the Soviet invasion of Afghanistan a "hostile act against Iran and all Muslims,"[123] but his government sent little humanitarian or military aid to the Afghans. Resentment of Iran grew so strong among the Afghan mujahidin that by early 1983 even the fundamentalists among them were willing to accept Iranian help only as a last resort.

Like the Saudis and Libyans, the Khomeinists established international Islamic organizations to further their influence. Such institutions as the Permanent Committee on the Hajj, the World Congress of Friday Imams, and the Islamic Propaganda Office competed directly with their Saudi-sponsored counterparts. In addition, the Iranians endeavored to dominate existing international organizations, such as the Non-Aligned Movement.

Events in Iran had special significance for Shi'is. In part this was because the Shi'i rulers of Iran wanted to assist their co-sectarians, in part because Shi'is so often filled the ranks of the "disinherited" to whom Khomeini directed his appeal. Inspiration from Iran encouraged Shi'is in many countries to demand more rights and aid from Iran increased their effectiveness. Events in Iran lay behind the Shi'i riots on Bahrain in September 1979; later, Iran funded and trained members of a Shi'i fundamentalist group, the Islamic Front for the Liberation of Bahrain, which it hoped would replace Bahrain's easy-going Sunni monarchy with an Islamic republic along Iranian lines. Of the seventy-three persons arrested in connection with this conspiracy, fifty-eight were Bahrainis, thirteen Saudis, one Omani, and one Kuwaiti—but all were Shi'is who had spent time in Iran. Responding to this threat, the Bahraini government tightened its application of the Shari'a.

The Shi'is of Turkey were increasingly willing to stand up for themselves, and this resulted in increased communal fighting with Sunnis. Shi'is in Pakistan, "emboldened by the moral and political support from the neighboring *Shia* Iran," demanded a special status.[124] Sectarian clashes in Karachi were widely ascribed to Iranian influence. Weapons, money, and organizational assistance to Shi'is in Lebanon and Iraq made the Amal and Mujahidin movements powerful. Shi'i riots occurred in eastern Saudi Arabia in November 1979; later, clandestine organizations came to light when the Saudi authorities arrested thirteen Shi'is on charges of plotting to overthrow the government.

Having concluded that less direct methods produced too few results, the Iranians resorted in 1982 to terrorism as a way to influence events beyond their borders. They were thought to have had a role behind explosions in France and Pakistan. In Lebanon an organization known as Islamic Jihad—reportedly associated with Islamic Amal, the breakaway Shi'i militia attempting to set up an Islamic republic in Lebanon—claimed responsibility for car-bomb explosions at the French and American embassies.

The oil boom was, for these many reasons, the single most critical factor leading to the Islamic revival of the 1970s. The ties that existed between oil deposits and Islam did much to change the mood among Muslims, they bestowed political importance on Saudi Arabia and Libya, and they lay behind the Iranian Revolution. Despite ideological differences, these three countries effectively cooperated. In the words of an observer in Bangladesh, "The Saudis are at work on the right, the Libyans on the left, and the Iranians wherever they can have an impact." As the faith and civilization of Islam won new luster, Muslims had new reasons to turn to Islam.[125]

Conclusion:
The Revival and
Future Choices

However imposing the
"Islamization" movement may
appear, . . . it ultimately rests on
oil—which is to say, on sand.
—*Duran Khalid*

TO THE EXTENT that the Islamic revival is based on the oil boom, it is a
mirage. Legalist and autonomist impulses strengthened and proliferated during the 1970s in large part because some activist Muslim regimes had huge
amounts of discretionary revenues and others were able to exploit oil's disruptive effects to agitate for power; but neither of these can endure for long.

The ability of Saudi Arabia and Libya to further Islamic causes was as much
a function of low consumption as it was one of high revenues. Because both
countries received incomes far in excess of their immediate needs, they could
exert economic pressure, they could fund institutions, and they could acquire
sizable arsenals. With time, however, the amounts available for such expenditures are diminishing and will eventually disappear. In part this is because expectations increase and governments of oil-exporting countries must spend
more and more to keep up with consumer demands. Having tasted the good
life, citizens of the sheikdoms want more.

To make matters worse, the sheikdoms will have less income in the coming years. This might result from a breakthrough in alternate energy sources, a consumer counter-cartel, or a military cataclysm in the Persian Gulf, but it is more likely to follow from quiet and inexorable economic forces. The high price of oil prods consumers to conserve energy through more efficient cars, insulated housing, better designed factories, and so forth; it also induces them to substitute for Middle East oil with natural gas, coal, nuclear fission, non-Middle East oil, and so forth. High prices reduce the demand for OPEC oil, which is the energy of last resort; as sales diminish, so do revenues. Nothing the OPEC states do can avert this. Should they raise prices to compensate for smaller volume, they earn more in the short term but then lose still more of their market through yet greater conservation and substitution. If, to the contrary, they lower prices to increase volume, they face quotas or import fees imposed by the importing countries which will keep down their revenues. In brief, the higher the price, the shorter the bonanza and the sooner the sheikhdoms' discretionary funds dry up.

As OPEC's surpluses level off and then diminish, the result will be financial over-extension, revenue shortages, borrowing, and even bankruptcy. Domestic investments will probably not generate any income, for nearly all the industrial, agricultural, and other projects initiated during the boom years consume more money than they produce. Except in Kuwait, dividends from foreign investments amount to only a small fraction of current expenditures; Kuwait alone has invested enough abroad so that its whole citizenry could conceivably live off the interest payments.

As the financial circumstance of the sheikhdoms decline, Islamic hopes in many countries will suffer. The excitement of the early boom years will sour, signaling the end of an era. The confidence that played so large a role in leading Muslims to experiment with fundamentalist and autonomist solutions will be destroyed. The power of Saudi Arabia and Libya will fade as their disposable funds diminish and the two countries return to their former inconsequential isolation.[1]

Iran's moral influence is fated to end as surely as the sheikhdom's financial power. Thirteen and a half centuries of Islamic history make it clear that the fundamentalist ambition to implement Shar'i precepts *in toto* must fail, and this is even more so in the modern era. The effort to wrench Iran back to a standard that no one has ever been able to live by is doomed; as the Khomeinist regime falls, non- or anti-Islamic forces seem likely to take its place. Having found the fundamentalists' vision impractical, harsh, and unstable, Iranians will probably reject any role for Islam in politics and return to a program which approximates that of the shah's (though in less ambitious form), to develop the country along Westernizing lines. No people's modern experience will have harmed Islam so much as the Iranians', whose experiment with theocratic government will surely be consigned to what Imam Khomeini calls the "refuse bin of history."[2]

Diminishing surpluses and the collapse of Khomeini's government can be expected to have jolting consequences. The Islamic alternative, once so full of promise, will lose its appeal and many Muslims will again regard their religion as an obstacle to progress. As Muslim wealth and power vanish as rapidly as they appeared, hopes generated during the boom years will fade. The events of 1973 will be seen as a false signal which set back Muslim efforts to modernize by at least a decade. Fundamentalist movements will be discredited as the Islamic option appears less credible. Muslims who turned to fundamentalism in the 1970s to cope with modernization will try other, Western-oriented routes in the next decades—liberal, Communist, or some combination of the two. It is difficult to foresee which variant of Western ideologies will prevail, but every one of the Western approaches implies rejecting the Islamic path in politics. In all likelihood, Nasserism will again appeal to Egyptian and Arab youth, Atatürk's legacy will be reinvigorated in Turkey, Pakistan will rediscover its British heritage, and so forth.

Autonomist movements too will lose morale and falter, but not so badly as legalist causes. Strife in Chad, Ethiopia, Cyprus, Lebanon, Afghanistan, Thailand, and the Philippines should continue, even if the Muslim forces weaken as a result of losing money, arms, and diplomatic support from the sheikhdoms. Minorities in Yugoslavia, the Soviet Union, Uganda, and India will be bereft of foreign patrons, giving them less room to maneuver. Prospects for the most visible autonomist cause, the Arab struggle against Israel, look especially dim, for the Arab states and the P.L.O. grew unduly dependent on the sheikhdoms during the 1970s. Saudi Arabia, Libya, Kuwait, and the U.A.E. used their financial resources and political clout to win friendly gestures from governments and businesses, they got access to the most advanced weaponries, and their funds made the P.L.O., with a budget of about $1 billion annually,[3] the richest revolutionary movement in history. Syria, Jordan, and Egypt at times all received substantial annual subventions from the Gulf, and Iraq added whatever it could to the effort. As the sheikhdoms consume more and receive less, the advantages from the era of easy money will disappear. The Arabs will find themselves face-to-face with Israel, without external help, and Israel can be expected to emerge from the crucible of the oil boom much strengthened.

In retrospect, the revival will appear as a curious aberration. Just as the power of a commodity price-setting organization (OPEC) defied long-term trends, so the concomitant resurgence of Islam was fortuitous and transient. Islam's revival was inappropriate because it resulted in such large part from freak circumstances, not Muslim achievements; the unearned nature of the oil wealth cannot be ignored. Buoyed by unexpected good fortune, Muslims allowed themselves to imagine that they had solved their basic problem, the inability to come to terms with the West. As the deluge of free wealth improved the umma's economic and political position without requiring it to deal with this problem, fundamentalists sounded increasingly convincing; it did appear that the umma could modernize without confronting its reluctance to Westernize. When some of the most primitive and observant Muslims flourished without effort, seemingly through strength of faith alone, false hopes were raised, giving many Muslims the unrealistic expectation that God's bounty might allow them to retreat into faith, to glorify their heritage, and to reject Western ways. Wilfred Cantwell Smith observes that "the new Islamic upsurge is a force not to solve problems but to intoxicate those who cannot abide the failure to solve them."[4]

As oil revenues subside, the umma will be left with expectations which exceed its skills and resources; the process of readjusting to earned income will destroy the illusion that success can be attained on Islamicate terms. At that point, Muslims will have to chose between adaptation to realities and coming to terms with Westernization, or accepting an increase in apologetics, introversion, and poverty. The revival will have served some good if its bitter aftermath spurs the umma fully to confront the challenges of Western ways. In turn, this will require Muslims to deal with Islam's principal legacies from premodern times: the imperatives of the sacred law, Islamicate patterns in public life, the expectation of divine rewards, and hostility toward the Christian West.

Muslims can either struggle to implement the fundamentalist vision, or they can adapt to Westernization. While reformist and secularist approaches will eventually prevail, this might not happen for some time. The Jewish experience sheds light on this: it took about 200 years, from the mid-eighteenth to the mid-twentieth century, for Jews to resolve their dispute over the sacred law. Long as this took, the process was accelerated by the destruction of traditional Jewish life during World War II and by the fact that Jews, unlike Muslims, were not in competition with Christendom and therefore had fewer inhibitions about accepting Western ways. In the Muslim case, intensive contact with the West has gone on for only 100 to 150 years; if the Jewish case is any indication, the umma still faces many decades of conflict over questions of faith, the law, ethics, and the social order.

The legalist impulse in general and fundamentalism in particular present great difficulties to Muslims trying to modernize, but the Islamicate legacy presents no less of an impediment. Muslims need to confront the assumption of success in worldly affairs, then they must try to eliminate it. The destruction of the Temple in 586 B.C. created a dilemma which parallels that of the Muslims today; what Ezekiel and Second Isaiah did to disengage faith from mundane matters must be imitated by Muslims, for God's will is inscrutable to humans and misfortune may serve His intent. Islamicate expectations of nearly fourteen centuries cannot be undone instantly, but progress in this direction is essential if the umma is to modernize.

Another obstacle to modernization is the Islamicate heritage of hostile relations with Europe. Although the Christians were primarily to blame for this in the past, changes are slowly taking place in the West as some influential persons make efforts to treat Islam more fairly; if Muslims respond with equal introspection and candor, this relationship could make significant progress. There are no shortcuts: Muslims must confront the problems concerning the Shari'a and Islamicate civilization and reluctance to do so means prolonging the era of their despondency.

While John Obert Voll may read too much into recent events when he writes that Islamdom at the beginning of the fifteenth century hijra (which started in November 1980) is "in the midst of major transformations in all dimensions of its experience,"[5] the Islamic revival has altered the umma by providing it with new temptations and new opportunities.

Appendix:
Muslim Populations
by Country

The following lists, which give the numbers of Muslims according to their proportion of the total population, parallel the organization of chapter 9.

Figures for total populations derive mostly from the 1982 edition of *The World Factbook*. Because almost all statistics on the oil-rich countries of the Persian Gulf (Bahrain, Kuwait, Qatar, Saudi Arabia, the United Arab Emirates) usually include foreign laborers in their populations, I have provided my own, much lower, estimates of the numbers of citizens.

Figures of Muslim percentages derive from *The World Factbook;* Richard V. Weekes, ed., *Muslim Peoples: A World Ethnographic Survey* (Westport, Conn.: Greenwood, 1978), Appendix; and a great variety of specialized studies on individual countries.

According to the figures supplied here, 68.8 percent of Muslims live in countries where they make up the dominant majority of the population; only 9.9 percent live in moieties; while 21.3 percent live as small minorities.

Dividing the umma geographically, 14 percent of Muslims live in Sub-Saharan Africa, 26.4 percent in North Africa and the Middle East, 10.7 percent in Communist countries from Yugoslavia to China, 30.1 percent in South Asia, 18.6 percent in Southeast Asia, and .2 percent in other countries.

TABLE A.1
Muslim Population by Countries
(in thousands)

	Total Population	Percentage of Muslims	Muslim Population
Dominant Majorities (more than 85 percent Muslim)			
Afghanistan	15,328	99	15,174
Algeria	20,030	97	19,827
Bahrain	150	91	136
Bangladesh	93,040	85	79,084
Djibouti	306	94	287
Egypt	44,740	91	40,667
Gambia	635	86	546
Guinea	5,278	85	4,486
Indonesia	157,595	90	141,835
Iran	41,203	96	39,554
Iraq	14,034	95	13,332
Jordan	3,246	93	3,018
Kuwait	500	96	480
Libya	2,620	98	2,567
Maldive Islands	163	99	161
Mali	7,615	90	6,853
Mauritania	1,561	96	1,498
Morocco	22,230	95	21,118
Niger	5,833	85	4,958
Oman	948	99	938
Pakistan	93,106	97	90,312
Qatar	60	99	59
Saudi Arabia	5,000	99	4,950
Senegal	5,991	86	5,152
Somalia	6,142	99	6,080
Syria	9,423	87	8,198
Tunisia	6,842	98	6,705
Turkey	48,105	98	47,142
United Arab Emirates	200	92	184
Western Sahara	86	99	85
Yemen (North)	5,490	99	5,435
Yemen (South)	2,022	99	1,999
Subtotal	619,522	92.5	572,820
Moieties (between 85 and 25 percent Muslim)			
Albania	2,792	70	1,953
Brunei	252	70	176
Chad	4,852	50	2,426
Comoro Islands	442	80	353
Ethiopia	30,569	48	14,673
Guinea-Bissau	823	30	246
Lebanon	3,177	49	1,556
Malaysia	14,661	47	6,890
Nigeria	82,396	47	38,726
Sierre Leone	3,535	30	1,060
Sudan	19,868	72	14,304
Subtotal	163,367	50.4	82,363

	Total Population	Percentage of Muslims	Muslim Population
Small Minorities (less than 25 percent Muslim)			
Australia	15,011	.6	90
Benin	3,636	12	436
Bulgaria	8,940	10	894
Burma	36,166	4	1,446
Burundi	4,438	1	48
Cambodia	5,882	1	60
Cameroon	9,049	17	1,538
Central Africa	2,471	5	123
China			
(People's Republic of)	1,008,175	2	20,007
Congo	1,641	1	22
Cyprus	642	18	115
Fiji	654	8	52
France	54,174	1	620
Gabon	662	1	8
Ghana	12,943	12	1,553
Greece	9,743	2	194
Guyana	870	9	82
India	723,762	10.5	75,995
Israel	3,916	8	313
Ivory Coast	8,569	22	1,885
Kenya	17,832	9	1,604
Liberia	2,024	15	303
Madagascar	8,992	7	629
Malawi	6,410	15	961
Mauritius	990	17	168
Mongolia	1,759	4	70
Mozambique	12,695	10	1,269
Nepal	15,715	5	785
Philippines	51,574	5	2,558
Rumania	22,510	.2	45
Rwanda	5,451	1	54
Singapore	2,472	17	420
South Africa	30,021	.6	180
Soviet Union	269,876	17	45,878
Sri Lanka	15,398	8	1,231
Suriname	356	20	71
Tanzania	19,868	24	4,768
Thailand	49,823	4	1,992
Togo	2,783	7	194
Trinidad and Tobago	1,203	6	72
Uganda	13,651	6	819
United Kingdom	56,095	.2	112
United States	232,195	.4	928
Upper Volta	6,208	22	1,365
Yugoslavia	22,689	19	4,310
Zaire	30,289	2	605
Zambia	6,222	1	62
Subtotal	2,816,445	6.3	176,934
Total	3,599,334		832,117

Glossary

Ahl al-Kitab: People of the Book; adherents of tolerated religions, especially Jews and Christians.

Allah: Arabic for God; ordinarily not used in this book because it implies that the God of Islam differs from the God of Judaism and Christianity.

Autonomism: The drive, deriving from Islamic principles, of Muslims to control land.

Caliph (from Arabic, *khalifa*): Political successor of Muhammad as leader of the umma.

Caliphate: The office of the caliph.

Dar al-Harb: Territory ruled by non-Muslims.

Dar al-Islam: Territory ruled by Muslims.

Da'wa (*dakwah* in Malay): The call to Islam.

Dhimmi: One of the Ahl al-Kitab (especially a Jew or Christian) living in Dar al-Islam.

Faqih: An expert in Islamic jurisprudence.

Fiqh: Islamic jurisprudence.

Fitna: Civil disorder, fighting between Muslims.

Franks: In Muslim usage, the Christians of West Europe.

Fundamentalist Islam: Radical legalism. In modern times, a response to the West which holds that Islam holds all the answers.

Hadd: The penal laws of the Shari'a.

Hadith Report: An account concerning the sayings or deeds of the Prophet Muhammad.

Hajj: The pilgrimage to Mecca at a designated time of the Islamic year.

Halakha: Jewish sacred law.

Harbi: A non-Muslim living in Dar al-Harb.

Imam: (1) Caliph; (2) Prayer leader.

Islam: Faith in one God and in the Qur'an as the literal word of God.

Islamdom: The lands where Muslim communities are present.

Islamic: Pertaining to the religion of Islam.

Islamicate: Pertaining to the civilization of Islam.

Jihad: War by Muslims which accords with the Shari'a; in general, war against non-Muslims.

Kafir: A non-Muslim.

Khariji (adj. or noun): The branch of Islam that developed in the seventh century from the conviction that the most capable Muslim should become caliph.

Legalism: The drive to apply the Shari'a.

Madhhab: A legal rite of the Shari'a.

Mahdi: The messianic figure of Islam who, in the last days, will either (1) fully implement the Shari'a or (2) create a new order in which Muslims may ignore the law.

Maks: A tax not allowed by the Shari'a.

Marabout (from Arabic, *murabit*): A Sufi leader in Africa.

Mazalim: A non-Shar'i court sponsored by the government.

Medieval Synthesis: Acceptance of the virtual impossibility of implementing the Shari'a in its entirety and the working out of the implications of this fact.

Modern (as a definition of time): The period when Europe dominates the life of a non-Western people; (as a personal attribute): Those qualities conducive to running a factory.

Mujahid (pl. *mujahidin*): A fighter of jihad.

Glossary

Mullah: One of the 'ulama in Iran.

Muslim (noun): An adherent of Islam; (adj.): Pertaining to Muslims.

Non-fundamentalist: In modern times, a traditionalist, a reformist, or a secularist.

Pan-Arabism: The drive to unify Arabic-speaking peoples; failing that, to foster cooperation between them.

Pan-Islam: The drive to unify Muslims; in modern times, to foster cooperation between them.

Premodern: Time periods before Europe dominated the life of a non-Western people.

Ramadan: The ninth month of the Islamic year, when Muslims are normally required to abstain from food, drink, and sexual activity during the daylight hours.

Qadi: The judge in a Shar'i court.

Qur'an: The Word of God, made available to humans by Muhammad.

Reformist Islam: The view that, if properly understood, Islam and Western ideologies are compatible.

Secularist Islam: The view that Muslims can respond successfully to modern life only by withdrawing Islam from public affairs.

Shar'i (adj.): Pertaining to the sacred law of Islam.

Shari'a (noun): The sacred law of Islam. Based on the precepts found in the Qur'an and the *Hadith* Reports, it was elaborated by the jurists over a period of centuries.

Sharif (or *Sayyid*): A descendant of Muhammad.

Sheikhdom: Literally, the domain ruled by a sheikh; here used as a shorthand for the oil exporters with the smallest populations and the largest per capita incomes.

Shi'i (adj. or noun): The branch of Islam that developed from the conviction that 'Ali ibn Abi Talib was the rightful successor as caliph to the Prophet Muhammad.

Sufi (adj. or noun): The Islamic form of mysticism; devotees organized into orders which carried great political weight by the eighteenth century.

Sunni (adj. or noun): The branch of Islam that accepted as legitimate the reigning caliphs who did actually follow the Prophet Muhammad.

Traditionalist Islam: An acceptance of the medieval synthesis; the prevalent form of Islam among Muslims who have not yet encountered the full force of modernity.

'Ulama (sing. 'alim): Men learned in the Islamic tradition, especially its laws; comparable to the rabbis of Judaism.

Umma: The community of all Muslims.

'Ushr: A tithe on agricultural produce.

Waqf: Mortmain or trusts; perpetual ownership of real estate.

Westernization: Adoption of European or American customs not necessary for economic development.

Zakat: An annual tax on property paid by Muslims for charity purposes or to pay for government expenses.

Zina: Fornication as judged by the Shari'a.

Notes

Chapter 1

1. John B. Kelly, *Arabia, the Gulf and the West* (New York: Basic Books, 1980), p. 494.

2. Ernest Krausz, "Religion and Secularization: A Matter of Definitions," *Social Compass* 18 (1971–72): 212. He defines religion as "an institutional aspect of society based on beliefs in a super-human or supernatural realm" (p. 211).

3. Bernard Lewis, "The Return of Islam," in *Religion and Politics in the Middle East,* ed. Michael Curtis (Boulder, Colo.: Westview, 1981), pp. 10–11.

4. John Olbert Voll, *Islam: Continuity and Change in the Modern World* (Boulder, Colo.: Westview, 1982), p. 2.

5. In the words of a veteran Indian administrator, writing in 1901: "All Mussulmans in particular are assumed to have fanaticism, as if it were some separate mental peculiarity, belonging to the Mahomedan faith, which accounted for everything, and especially for any very marked impulse." Meredith Townsend, "Asia and Europe," *Westminster,* 1901; quoted by Norman Daniel, *Islam, Europe and Empire* (Edinburgh: At the University Press, 1966), p. 468.

6. Boulder, Colo.: Westview.

7. Wilfred Cantwell Smith, *On Understanding Islam* (The Hague: Mouton: 1981), p. 252.

8. J. Harris Proctor, ed., *Islam and International Relations* (London: Pall Mall, 1965), pp. 61, vii. In the same book, however, H. A. R. Gibb wrote the following prescient passage:

> The traditional linking of Islam to social and political activity persists, and will continue. I am not prophesying the revival of an overtly militant Islam, but among the unknown range of possibilities now being produced by contemporary stresses in every continent, one that the West would be wise not to discount is the re-emergence of a revived and reconstructed Islam as a world factor (p. 23).

9. Lewis, "Return of Islam," p. 11.

10. Martin Kramer, *Political Islam,* The Washington Papers, no. 73. (Beverly Hills: Sage, 1980), p. 15.

11. Edward Mortimer, "Islam and the Western Journalist," *Middle East Journal* 35 (1981):502.

12. For an argument making this point, see my article, "A Border Adrift: Origins of the Conflict," in *The Iran-Iraq War: New Weapons, Old Conflicts,* ed. Shirin Tahir-Kheli and Shaheen Ayubi (New York: Praeger, 1983), pp. 3–25.

13. William L. Richter, "The Political Dynamics of Islamic Resurgence in Pakistan," *Asian Survey* 19 (1979): 554–55.

14. This raises the intriguing thought: What would the Arabs have done had the Zionists made Arabic, instead of Hebrew, their national language?

15. For example, note the opening sentence of Mangol Bayat's article, "Islam in Pahlavi and Post-Pahlavi Iran: A Cultural Revolution?": "The 1978–79 Iranian revolution is too often perceived by the superficial observer, the uninformed media representative as well as the religiously inclined Iranian himself, as symbolizing the rise of Islam and the Muslims against its enemies from within and without." In *Islam and Development: Religion and Sociopolitical Change,* ed. John L. Esposito (Syracuse, N.Y.: Syracuse University Press, 1980), p. 87.

16. Michael C. Hudson, *Arab Politics: The Search for Legitimacy* (New Haven, Conn.: Yale University Press, 1977), p. 17.

17. Thomas W. Lippman, *Understanding Islam, an Introduction to the Moslem World* (New York: New American Library, 1982), pp. 182–83; Edward Mortimer, *Faith and Power: The Politics of Islam* (New York: Random House, 1982), p. 406. I am grateful to John Voll for pointing out both these statements.

18. *New York Times,* 6 January 1980.

19. Ibid. 2 January 1978.

20. *Far Eastern Economic Review,* 25 November 1972.

21. Morroe Berger, *The Arab World Today* (Garden City, N.Y.: Anchor, 1964), p. xiv.

22. Who was the father of Kim Philby, the Soviet double agent, a man who turned even more radically against his own society.

23. Smith, *On Understanding Islam,* pp. 43–44.

24. Admirable exceptions include: Clifford Geertz, *Islam Observed: Religious Development in Morocco and Indonesia* (New Haven, Conn.: Yale University Press, 1968); Xavier de Planhol, *Les Fondaments géographiques de l'histoire de l'Islam* (Paris: Flammarion, 1968); and Voll, *Islam.* Almost every other work which deals with more than one region is written by many authors.

25. My article, "Understanding the Middle East: A Guide to Common Terms," *International Insight,* July/August 1981, pp. 33–36, explains usage of Middle East, Arab, Semite, and Islam.

26. *The New Roget's Thesaurus,* ed. Norman Lewis (Garden City, N.Y.: Garden City Books, 1961), p. 399.

27. Marshall G. S. Hodgson, *The Venture of Islam* (Chicago: University of Chicago Press, 1974), 1:56–60.

28. Outside the Arabic-speaking countries, however, "Allah" often acquires a specifically Islamic tone. For example, in late 1981 the Malaysian government banned a Bible translated by Christian missionaries into the Malay language because "some Muslims complained that it translated God as Allah rather than using the generic Malay word for God, which is *tuhan.* Allah, they said, was the name only for the Muslim God" (*Far Eastern Economic Review,* 2 April 1982).

29. H. A. R. Gibb, "Social Change in the Near East," in *The Near East: Problems and Prospects,* ed. Phillip W. Ireland (Chicago: University of Chicago Press, 1942), p. 60.

30. Gustave E. von Grunebaum, *Islam: Essays in the Nature and Growth of a Cultural Tradition,* 2d ed. (London: Routledge & Kegan Paul, 1961), p. 185.

Chapter 2

1. Ernest Gellner, *Muslim Society* (Cambridge: Cambridge University Press, 1981), p. 99.

2. *G. Bergsträsser's Grundzüge des islamischen Rechts,* reworked and edited by Joseph Schacht (Berlin and Leipzig: W. de Gruyter, 1935), p. 1; Christiaan Snouck Hurgronje, *Oeuvres Choisies,* ed. G.-H. Bousquet and J. Schacht, (Leiden: E. J. Brill, 1957), p. 48.

3. Biblical references are to *The New English Bible,* ed. Samuel Sandmel (New York: Oxford University Press, 1976). The Qur'an is numbered in slightly variant ways; I have used the edition of A. Yusuf Ali, *The Holy Qur'an* (n.p., 1946), which has the virtue of providing both the Arabic original and an English translation.

4. This is echoed in Qur'an 16.114.

5. The recent "Jews for Jesus" movement, which so dramatically defies the normal religious divisions, thus has ancient roots.

6. See pp. 108–109.

7. Erwin I. J. Rosenthal, *Islam in the Modern National State* (Cambridge: At the University Press, 1965), p. 10.

8. Wilfred Cantwell Smith, *On Understanding Islam* (The Hague: Mouton, 1981), p. 32.

9. Howard L. Nixon, "The Development of Judaic and Islamic Law—A Comparison," *Islam and the Modern Age* 5, no. 2 (May 1974): 15.

10. Marshall G. S. Hodgson, *The Venture of Islam* (Chicago: University of Chicago Press, 1974), 1:317.

11. Snouck Hurgronje, *Oeuvres Choisies,* p. 49.

12. S. D. Goitein, *Jews and Arabs: Their Contacts Through the Ages* (New York: Schocken, 1964), p. 60. These connections, presumably of key importance, have gone almost unstudied and should become a major area of future research.

13. Rosenthal, *Judaism and Islam* (London: Th. Yoseloff, 1961), p. 29. For reasons of brevity, the following account ignores the four legal rites (madhhabs) of Sunni Islam as well as the differences between them and Shi'i or Khariji rites.

14. Reuben Levy, *The Social Structure of Islam* (Cambridge: At the University Press, 1971), p. 126.

15. For further similarities, see my "Jewish-Muslim Connections: Traditional Ways of Life," *Present Tense,* Autumn 1981, pp. 40–42.

16. Joseph Schacht, "Islamic Religious Law," in *The Legacy of Islam,* 2d ed., ed. Joseph Schacht and C. E. Bosworth (Oxford: Oxford University Press, 1974), p. 392.

17. Gustave E. von Grunebaum, *Modern Islam* (New York: Vintage, 1962). p. 24; V. S. Naipaul, *Among the Believers: An Islamic Journey* (New York: Alfred A. Knopf, 1981), p. 106.

18. Wilfred Cantwell Smith, *Islam in Modern History* (Princeton, N.J.: Princeton University Press, 1957), p. 43.

19. S. Abdul Hasan Ali Nadwi, *Calamity of Linguistic and Cultural Chauvinism* (Lucknow, India: Academy of Islamic Research and Publications, 1972), p. 21.

20. Gopal Krishna, "Piety and Politics in Indian Islam," *Contributions to Indian Sociology,* n.s. 6 (1972): 144.

21. Grunebaum, *Modern Islam,* p. 10.

22. Ibid., p. 92.

23. Naipaul, *Among the Believers,* pp. 367–68.

24. Public life corresponds roughly to the Islamic categories of *mu'amalat* (human relations) and *'uqubat* (sanctions); private life corresponds to *'ibadiyat* (ritual observances) and *imaniyat* (beliefs). It must be noted, however, that Islam makes no distinction between public and private precepts.

25. Deut. 17:14–20; 20:1–20; 23:9–14; 24.5. Exod. 30:12–13. Also Ezek. 45–48.

26. Max Weber, *Economy and Society,* transl. and ed. Guenther Roth and Claus Wittich, 2 vols., (Berkeley and Los Angeles: University of California Press, 1978), p. 625.

27. Rosenthal, *Islam in the Modern National State,* p. 8.

28. Shi'is require a direct descendant of Muhammad's; Sunnis accept someone descended from Muhammad's tribe; and Kharijis (who have nearly disappeared except in Oman and in North Africa) choose the best man available without regard to lineage.

29. Jihad has three other meanings in Islam. The first concerns personal righteousness; the second and third involve doing one's best in speech and deed to create a society which lives according to Islam's laws.

30. Rudolph Peters, *Jihad in Mediaeval and Modern Islam* (Leiden: E. J. Brill, 1977), p. 3.

31. Ulrich Haarmann, "Islamic Duties in History," *Muslim World* 68 (1978): 9.

32. John Obert Voll, *Islam: Continuity and Change in the Modern World* (Boulder, Colo.: Westview, 1982), p. 8.

33. According to *The Shorter Oxford English Dictionary,* legalism originally meant: "Adherence to the Law as opposed to the Gospel, the doctrine of justification by works, or teaching which savours of it." Only later did it come to mean, "A disposition to exalt the importance of law or formulated rule" (ibid.). Still later did it take on the meaning of legalistic, or "strict, literal adherence to law" *(The American Heritage Dictionary of the English Language).*

34. More technically, legalism and autonomism correspond to the different meanings of jihad (see note 29).

Chapter 3

1. Patricia Crone and Michael Cook, *Hagarism: The Making of the Islamic World* (Cambridge: Cambridge University Press, 1977), p. 147.

2. Joseph Schacht, *An Introduction to Islamic Law* (Oxford: At the Clarendon Press, 1964), p. 76.

3. Halil İnalcik, "The Ottomans and the Caliphate," in *The Cambridge History of Islam*, ed. P. M. Holt et al. (Cambridge: At the University Press, 1970), 1:320.

4. Claude Cahen, "The Body Politic," in *Unity and Variety in Muslim Civilization*, ed. Gustave E. von Grunebaum (Chicago: University of Chicago Press, 1955), p. 155.

5. Ibid.

6. Ulrich Haarmann, "Islamic Duties in History," *Muslim World* 68 (1978): 12.

7. Ibid.

8. Ibid., pp. 12–13.

9. Noel J. Coulson, *Conflict and Tension in Islamic Jurisprudence* (Chicago: University of Chicago Press, 1969), p. 65. The difficulty of fulfilling the requirements for evidence in adultery cases led a chief justice of the Federal Shariah Court in Pakistan to observe: "This is not punishment for adultery. This is punishment for doing it in public." (*Washington Post*, 6 December 1982.)

10. Schacht, *Introduction to Islamic Law*, p. 195.

11. Coulson, *Conflict and Tension*, pp. 63–64.

12. Marshall G. S. Hodgson, *The Venture of Islam* (Chicago: University of Chicago Press, 1974), 1:339.

13. Coulson, *Conflict and Tension*, p. 71.

14. Schacht, *Introduction to Islamic Law*, pp. 54–55.

15. Ibid., p. 56.

16. M. Jamil Hanifi, *Islam and the Transformation of Culture* (New York: Asia Publishing, 1974), p. 92.

17. H. A. R. Gibb, *Modern Trends in Islam* (Chicago: University of Chicago Press, 1947), p. 89.

18. C. Snouck Hurgronje, *Mekka in the Latter Part of the 19th Century*, trans. J. H. Monahan (Leiden: E. J. Brill, 1931), pp. 189–90.

19. Clive S. Kessler, "Islam, Society and Political Behaviour: Some Comparative Implications of the Malay Case," *British Journal of Sociology* 23 (1972): 40.

20. V. S. Naipaul, *Among the Believers: An Islamic Journey* (New York: Alfred A. Knopf, 1981), p. 178.

21. Gibb, *Modern Trends in Islam*, p. 117.

22. Elie Kedourie, *Islam in the Modern World* (New York: Holt, Rinehart and Winston, 1981), pp. 44–45; Charles Issawi, *An Economic History of the Middle East and North Africa* (New York: Columbia University Press, 1982), p. 173.

23. Bernard Lewis, "Politics and War," in *The Legacy of Islam*, 2d ed., ed. Joseph Schacht and C. E. Bosworth (Oxford: Oxford University Press, 1974), p. 163.

24. Christiaan Snouck Hurgronje, *Oeuvres Choisies*, ed. G.-H. Bousquest and J. Schacht (Leiden: E. J. Brill, 1957), p. 290.

25. Snouck Hurgronje, *Mekka*, p. 190; Snouck Hurgronje, *Oeuvres Choisies*, p. 266.

26. Only Muslims coming from beyond the pale of organized rule regularly participated in politics, so they became the rulers almost everywhere in Islamdom. For an explanation, see my *Slave Soldiers and Islam: The Genesis of a Military System* (New Haven, Conn.: Yale University Press, 1981), pp. 75–86.

27. Hamilton A. R. Gibb, "Religion and Politics in Christianity and Islam," in *Islam and International Relations*, ed. J. Harris Proctor (London: Pall Mall, 1965), p. 10.

28. Cahen, "The Body Politic," p. 133.

29. Gibb, "Religion and Politics," p. 17.

30. Hanifi, *Islam,* p. 67.

31. Claude Cahen, "Mouvements populaires et autonomisme urbain dans l'Asie musulmane du moyen âge, II," *Arabica* 6 (1959): 26.

32. Crone and Cook, *Hagarism,* p. 114: Ira M. Lapidus, "Muslim Cities and Islamic Societies," in *Middle Eastern Cities,* ed. Ira M. Lapidus (Berkeley and Los Angeles: University of California Press, 1969), p. 60.

33. Maxime Rodinson, *The Arabs,* trans. Arthur Goldhammer (Chicago: University of Chicago Press, 1981), p. 155.

34. John Obert Voll, *Islam: Continuity and Change in the Modern World* (Boulder, Colo.: Westview, 1982), p. 15.

35. Gibb, *Modern Trends in Islam,* p. 111.

36. Wilfred Cantwell Smith, *On Understanding Islam* (The Hague: Mouton, 1981), p. 202.

37. Kessler, "Islam, Society and Political Behaviour," p. 37.

38. Georg W. F. Hegel, *Philosophy of History,* transl. J. Sibree (New York: Dover, 1956), p. 358. More recently, V. S. Naipaul referred to "the thuggish life of the Muslim polity" (*Among the Believers,* p. 99).

39. Gustave E. von Grunebaum, *Modern Islam* (New York: Vintage, 1962), pp. 184–85.

40. Gustave E. von Grunebaum, *Islam: Essays in the Nature and Growth of a Cultural Tradition,* 2d ed. (London: Routledge & Kegan Paul, 1961), p. 26.

41. Erwin I. J. Rosenthal, *Islam in the Modern National State* (Cambridge: At the University Press, 1965), p. 10.

42. Kessler, "Islam, Society and Political Behaviour," p. 38.

43. Gibb, "Religion and Politics," p. 12.

44. What I refer to as fundamentalism others sometimes call "neo-orthodoxy" or (in French) "intégralisme." Fundamentalism was a conservative American Protestant movement dating from the turn of this century which developed in reaction to the liberal and modernist interpretations prevalent at that time. The modernists engaged in "higher criticism" (studying the Bible using textual analysis), supported the theory of evolution, and de-emphasized the divinity of Jesus; in contrast, Fundamentalists stressed the literal truth of the Bible. Rather than espouse new doctrines, they upheld what they believed to be the accepted truths of Christianity. In this, they resemble Muslim fundamentalists who also respond to new ideas by re-emphasizing old truths. In both religions, fundamentalists insist on a more rigid interpretation of religion than did traditional believers. They differ mainly in that Christians stress theology and Muslims stress laws.

Neo-orthodoxy, also a Protestant movement, began after World War II in response to the crises of war, totalitarianism, and the decline of Christian faith. Several leading theologians, including Karl Barth, Reinhold Niebuhr, H. Richard Niebuhr, Rudolf Bultmann, Nikolai Berdyaev, and Paul Tillich, used the traditional language of the Christian Church to express radical new theological themes about man's responsibility to himself and to God. Neo-orthodox is less satisfactory than fundamentalist to describe radical Muslim legalists, for the Neo-Orthodox thinkers tried to develop new ideas rather than imitate the ways of their ancestors. *Intégralisme,* a term widely used in French discussions of Islam, refers to result more than intent and is therefore less descriptive. Fundamentalism stresses a concern to apply the law; its effect is to make Islam integral.

45. Gibb, "Religion and Politics," p. 10.

46. Raphael Israeli, "Muslim Minorities under Non-Islamic Rule," *Current History,* 78, no. 456 (April 1980): 159–60.

47. The combination of (1) a withdrawal from politics in normal times, (2) hyperactivity in moments of legalist or autonomist involvement, and (3) waves of fundamentalism in the eighteenth century help account for the otherwise inexplicably contradictory European image of Muslims as both fatalistic and fanatical. Muslim political inactivity was occasionally interrupted by intense commitment.

Chapter 4

1. William H. McNeill, *The Rise of the West* (Chicago: University of Chicago Press, 1963), p. 163.

2. *Apologeticus,* 50

3. Wilfred Cantwell Smith, *Islam in Modern History* (Princeton, N.J.: Princeton University Press, 1957), p. 31.

4. R. Brunschvig, "Problème de la décadence," in *Classicisme et déclin culturel dans l'histoire de l'Islam,* ed. R. Brunschvig and G. E. von Grunebaum. (Paris: G. P. Maisonneuve et Larose, 1977), p. 34.

5. Smith, *Islam in Modern History,* p. 29.

6. J. H. Parry, *The Establishment of the European Hegemony, 1415–1715* (New York: Harper & Row, 1966), p. 8.

7. McNeill, *The Rise of the West,* p. 485.

8. Smith, *Islam in Modern History,* p. 31.

9. Ibid., p. 32.

10. Monotheisms that followed Islam are viewed in another light entirely, for they defy the Islamic claim to being the perfected and therefore the final revelation. This explains the intense Muslim hostility to Baha'ism, the offshoot of Twelver Shi'i Islam that emerged in nineteenth-century Iran.

11. Smith, *Islam in Modern History,* p. 104, n. 11.

12. Qur'an 4.157.

13. Ibid. 43.59.

14. Ibid. 9.30.

15. Ibid. 9.31.

16. Ibid. 112.3.

17. Henri Michaud, *Jésus selon le Coran* (Neuchatel: Editions Delachaux et Niestlé, 1960), p. 12.

18. Al-Mas'udi, *Kitab at-Tanbih wa'l-Ashraf,* ed. M. J. de Goeje (Leiden: E. J. Brill, 1894), pp. 23–24.

19. Ibn Sa'id, *Kitab Tabaqat al-Umam,* ed. Louis Cheikho (Beirut: Imprimerie Catholique, 1912), pp. 8–9.

20. Bernard Lewis, *The Muslim Discovery of Europe* (New York: W. W. Norton, 1982), p. 89.

21. Usama b. Munqidh, *Kitab al-I'tibar,* ed. P. K. Hitti (Princeton, N.J.: Princeton University Press, 1930), p. 134.

22. Ibn Khaldun, *al-Muqaddima,* ed. E. Quatremère (Paris: Académie des Inscriptions et Belles-Lettres, 1858; reprinted in Beirut: Maktabat Lubnan, 1970), 3:93.

23. Lewis, *The Muslim Discovery,* p. 51.

24. Marshall G. S. Hodgson, *The Venture of Islam* (Chicago: University of Chicago Press, 1974), 3:3.

25. Lewis, *The Muslim Discovery,* p. 168.

26. Hodgson, *Venture of Islam,* 3:136.

27. Elaine Sanceau, *Portugal in Quest of Prester John* (London: Hutchinson, 1943), p. 84. In 1541, three hundred and fifty Portuguese soldiers and 200 natives held off 15,000 bowmen, 1,500 horsemen, and 200 Turkish arquebusiers led by the Muslin conqueror, Ahmad Gran. For details, see Sanceau, *Portugal in Quest of Prester John,* part II.

28. Norman Daniel, *Islam and the West: The Making of an Image* (Edinburgh: The University Press, 1958), p. 109.

29. Sir William Muir writing in the *Calcutta Review* in 1845, quoted by Norman Daniel, *Islam, Europe and Empire* (Edinburgh: At the University Press, 1966), p. 32.

30. Smith, *Islam in Modern History,* pp. 105–06.

31. *Doctrina Jacubi nuper baptizati,* ed. N. Bonwetsch (Abhandlungen der Königlichen Gesell-

schaft der Wissenschaften zu Göttingen, Philologisch-historiche Klasse, N.F. Bd. 12, Nr. 3 [1910]), pp. 86–87; cited by Walter Emil Kaegi, Jr., "Initial Byzantine Reactions to the Arab Conquest," *Church History* 38 (1969), pp. 3–4.

32. Sophronius, "Weihnachtspredigt des Sophronos," ed. H. Usener, *Rheinisches Museum für Philologie*, N. F. 41 (1886): 514; cited in ibid., p. 2.

33. Daniel, *Islam and the West*, p. 107.

34. *Oxford English Dictionary*, s.v. "Mahomet" and "Mahometry."

35. Daniel, *Islam, Europe and Empire*, p. 6; R. W. Southern, *Western Views of Islam in the Middle Ages* (Cambridge, Mass.: Harvard University Press, 1962), p. 28.

36. Edward Gibbon, *The History of the Decline and Fall of the Roman Empire*, ed. J. B. Bury (New York: Fred de Fau, 1907), 9:254.

37. Donald F. Lach, *Asia in the Making of Europe* vol. 1, book 1, (Chicago: University of Chicago Press, 1965), p. 22.

38. John Meyendorff, "Byzantine Views of Islam," *Dumbarton Oaks Papers* 18 (1964): 131–32.

39. Roger Bacon, *Baconiis Operis Maius Pars Septima seu Moralis Philosophia*, ed. Eugenia Massa (Turici: In aedibus Thesauri mundi, 1953), 3:122; cited in Southern, *Western Views on Islam*, p. 57.

40. Southern, *Western Views on Islam*, pp. 2–3.

41. K. G. Jayne, *Vasco da Gama and His Successors, 1460–1580* (London: Methuen, 1910), p. 33.

42. C. Raymond Beazley, "Prince Henry of Portugal and the African Crusade of the Fifteenth Century," *American Historical Review* 16 (1910–11): 12–13.

43. Abbas Hamdani, "Columbus and the Recovery of Jerusalem," *Journal of the American Oriental Society* 99 (1979):45.

44. Lewis, *The Muslim Discovery*, p. 34.

45. Daniel, *Islam, Europe and Empire*, p. 480.

46. Parry, *European Hegemony*, p. 84. Through no fault of their own, the American Indians had the misfortune of being associated by Cortes's and Pizarro's soldiers with Islam. Spaniards saw the Indians as kin to the Moors whom they had recently expelled from Iberia and called their temples *mezquitas*, Spanish for mosque. In the metaphorical language of Rafael G. Bazan, "the image of al-Andalus [Muslim-controlled Spain] engraved on the retina of the *reconquistador* [Christian soldiers fighting the Muslims] once again appeared in the eyes of the *conquistador* of the New World" ("Muslim Immigration to Spanish America," *Muslim World* 56 [1966]:173). This view of Indians probably contributed to the brutality they suffered at the Spaniards' hands.

47. My forthcoming article, tentatively entitled "Godless Saracens Threatening Destructions: Muslims in Western Eyes," deals with the topic of Christian hostility toward the umma at greater length.

Conclusion to Part I

1. George Marçais, *L'Art de l'Islam* (Paris: Larousse, 1946), p. 5.

2. Gustave E. von Grunebaum, *Medieval Islam*, 2d ed. (Chicago: University of Chicago Press, 1961), p. 324.

3. Marshall G. S. Hodgson, *The Venture of Islam* (Chicago: University of Chicago Press, 1974), 1:57, 59.

4. The terms "Muslim" and "Islamicate" differ in that Muslim refers to individual believers and Islamicate to the entirety of the civilization. A Muslim rug is made by or belongs to a believer; the Islamicate rug is that which embodies the features which make rugs made by Muslims distinctive. A Muslim regime is a specific government in which Muslims reign; an Islamicate regime is an abstract notion refering to those qualities common to Muslim rulers.

5. H. A. R. Gibb, *Modern Trends in Islam* (Chicago: University of Chicago Press, 1947), p. 89.

6. Xavier de Planhol, *The World of Islam* (Ithica, N.Y.: Cornell University Press, 1959), p. 59.

7. Ibid., p. 52.

8. Ibid., pp. 73, 64.

9. Ibid., p. 22.

10. Xavier de Planhol, *Les Fondements géographiques de l'histoire de l'Islam* (Paris: Flammarion, 1968), p. 35.

Chapter 5

1. What does one make of modernity being defined as "the process by which historically evolved institutions are adapted to the rapidly changing functions that reflect the unprecedented increase in man's knowledge, permitting control over his environment, that accompanied the scientific revolution"? C. E. Black, *The Dynamics of Modernization* (New York: Harper & Row, 1975), p. 7.

2. Marshall G. S. Hodgson, *The Venture of Islam* (Chicago: University of Chicago Press, 1974), 3:182.

3. Alex Inkeles and David H. Smith, *Becoming Modern: Individual Change in Six Developing Countries* (Cambridge, Mass.: Harvard University Press, 1974), p. 19, defines modern personal qualities as those likely to be inculcated by working in a factory and which help it to operate efficiently and effectively.

4. Only the very most extreme fundamentalists reject modernization as well as Westernization. They throw television sets into rivers, ban wrist watches, and reject the internal combustion engine. The impracticality of their program severely limits the appeal of such groups, however; and in several cases—such as the Yen Izala of Kano, Sadat's assassins, the Mecca mosque attackers, and some Malaysian *dakwah* groups—their defeats in violent encounters with the authorities caused them then to disappear with few traces.

5. Jews living among Muslims never experienced a comparable isolation. Sacred law cut Jews off from Christians but made them kindred to Muslims.

6. William H. McNeill, *The Rise of the West* (Chicago: University of Chicago Press, 1963), p. 588.

7. Hodgson, *Venture of Islam,* 3:237.

8. Erwin I. J. Rosenthal, *Islam in the Modern National State* (Cambridge: At the University Press, 1965), p. xi.

9. Hodgson, *Venture of Islam,* 1:349.

Chapter 6

1. Erwin I. J. Rosenthal, *Islam in the Modern National State* (Cambridge: At the University Press, 1965), p. 8.

2. H. A. R. Gibb, *Modern Trends in Islam* (Chicago: University of Chicago Press, 1947), p. 69.

3. For this reason, Goldziher and Schacht had probably more influence on the civilization of Islam than any other kafirs in the religion's history.

4. Sir Muhammad Iqbal, *The Reconstruction of Religious Thought in Islam* (London: Oxford University Press, 1934), p. 160.

5. Rosenthal, *Islam in the Modern National State,* p. 9.

6. Marshall G. S. Hodgson, *The Venture of Islam* (Chicago: University of Chicago Press, 1974), 3:389–90.

7. Gibb, *Modern Trends,* p. 76.

8. This sort of comparison between Islamic norm and Western reality pervades reformist thinking.

9. Ibid., p. 105.

10. Ibid., p. 95.

11. Ibid., p. 104.

12. Raymond Scupin, "Islamic Reformism in Thailand," *Journal of the Siam Society* 68 (1980): 2.

13. Mu'ammar al-Qadhdhafi, *As-Sijill al-Qawmi* (Tripoli: Matba'at ath-Thawra al-'Arabiya, 1978), pp. 1021, 1043–44; cited in Ann Elizabeth Mayer, "Islamic Resurgence or New Prophethood: The Role of Islam in Qadhdhafi's Ideology," in *Islamic Resurgence in the Arab World* ed., Ali E. Hillal Dessouki (New York: Praeger, 1982), p. 202.

14. D. H. Khalid, "Der 'moderne' Islam," in *Begegnung mit Türken, Begegnung mit dem Islam,* ed., Hans-Jürgen Brandt and Claus-Peter Haase (Hamburg: ebv, 1981), p. 21.

15. 'Ali 'Abd ar-Raziq, *Al-Islam wa Usul al-Hukm* (Cairo: Matba'at Misr, 1925).

16. *Jaysh ash-Sha'b,* 25 April 1967.

17. Richard P. Stevens, "Sudan's Republican Brothers and Islamic Reform," *Journal of Arab Affairs* 1 (1981): 135–44.

18. B. J. Boland, "Discussion on Islam in Indonesia Today," *Studies on Islam* (Amsterdam: North-Holland, 1974), p. 43.

19. Gopal Krishna, "Piety and Politics in Indian Islam," *Contributions to Indian Sociology* n.s. 6 (1972): 168.

20. Said Amir Arjomand, "The State and Khomeini's Islamic Order," *Iranian Studies* 13 (1980): 152–53.

21. David Menashri, "Shi'ite Leadership: In the Shadow of Conflicting Ideologies," *Iranian Studies* 13 (1980): 124.

22. Hodgson, *Venture of Islam,* 3:389.

23. Hamilton A. R. Gibb, "Religion and Politics in Christianity and Islam," in *Islam and International Relations,* ed. J. Harris Proctor (London: Pall Mall, 1965), p. 9.

24. Title of a book by Harold Lasswell.

25. Rosenthal, *Islam in the Modern National State,* p. xvii.

26. Qur'an 42.38, 17.26.

27. *The Criterion* [Karachi], January/February 1970; reprinted in D. H. Khalid, *Die politische Rolle des Islam im Vorderen Orient: Einführung und Dokumentation,* 2d ed. enlarged (Hamburg: Deutsches Orient-Institut, 1979), pp. 114–20. I make extensive use of Khalid's clippings in this study.

28. Clifford Geertz, *Islam Observed: Religious Development in Morocco and Indonesia* (New Haven, Conn.: Yale University Press, 1968), p. 103.

29. Boland, "Discussion on Islam in Indonesia Today," p. 44.

30. Lahore: Islamic Book Service, 1979, p. 7.

31. G. H. Jansen, *Militant Islam* (New York: Harper & Row, 1979), p. 17.

32. R. Stephen Humphreys, "Islam and Political Values in Saudi Arabia, Egypt, and Syria," in *Religion and Politics in the Middle East,* ed. Michael Curtis (Boulder, Colo.: Westview, 1981), p. 292.

33. Hodgson, *Venture of Islam,* 3:389.

34. *New York Times,* 28 March 1980.

35. Martin Kramer, *Political Islam,* The Washington Papers, no. 73 (Beverly Hills: Sage, 1980), p. 39.

36. Ibid., p. 37.

37. Ibid., pp. 38–39.

38. V. S. Naipaul, *Among the Believers: An Islamic Journey* (New York: Alfred A. Knopf, 1981), p. 107.

39. Ibid., p. 355.

40. Wilfred Cantwell Smith, *Islam in Modern History* (Princeton, N.J.: Princeton University Press, 1957), p. 235.

41. R. Stephen Humphreys, "The Contemporary Islamic Resurgence in the Context of Modern Islam," in *Islamic Resurgence in the Arab World,* ed. Ali E. Hillal Dessouki (New York: Praeger, 1982), p. 78.

42. Smith, *Islam in Modern History,* pp. 192, 240, 241. The same observations apply almost equally well to modern Jews and Christians.

43. Malcolm Yapp, "Contemporary Islamic Revivalism," *Asian Affairs* 11 (1980): 187.

44. S. D. Goitein, "Djuma," in *The Encyclopaedia of Islam,* new edition.

45. *Dawn,* 22 February 1977.

46. *Asia Record,* May 1980, p. 6; *Asiaweek,* 29 June 1979.

47. *Sudanow,* February 1980, p. 14.

48. *Impact International* [London], 12 June 1981.

49. Only a few extremists, referred to in note 4 of chapter 5, reject modernization too.

50. Mohamed Heikal, *Iran: The Untold Story* (New York: Pantheon, 1982), p. 136.

51. Oriana Fallaci, "An Interview with Khomeini," *New York Times Magazine,* 7 October 1979, p. 31.

52. Clive S. Kessler, "Islam, Society and Political Behaviour: Some Comparative Implications of the Malay Case," *British Journal of Sociology* 23 (1972):40.

53. *Chaab* [Nouakchott], 16 January 1983.

54. Gopal Krishna, "Piety and Politics in Indian Islam," *Contributions to Indian Sociology,* N.S. 6 (1972):161.

55. Naipaul, *Among the Believers,* pp. 91, 90, 376, 124.

56. Maxime Rodinson, *Islam and Capitalism,* trans. Brian Pearce (New York: Pantheon, 1974), p. 241.

57. Ibid., pp. 35–36.

58. Ibid., p. 43.

59. Spoken on the occasion of the Iranian new year's celebration, 21 March 1983, and broadcast by Iranian radio.

60. *Asiaweek,* 20 November 1981.

61. Gustave E. von Grunebaum, *Islam: Essays in the Nature and Growth of a Cultural Tradition,* 2d ed. (London: Routledge & Kegan Paul, 1961), p. 26.

62. Yapp, "Contemporary Islamic Revivalism," p. 183.

63. Ibid.

64. John Obert Voll, *Islam: Continuity and Change in the Modern World* (Boulder, Colo.: Westview, 1982), p. 155.

65. Yapp, "Contemporary Islamic Revivalism," p. 184.

66. Hodgson, *Venture of Islam,* 3:387.

Chapter 7

1. Wilfred Cantwell Smith, *Islam in Modern History* (Princeton, N.J.: Princeton University Press, 1957), p. 47.

2. V. S. Naipaul, *Among the Believers: An Islamic Journey* (New York: Alfred A. Knopf, 1981), p. 35.

3. *Kayhan,* 7 March 1982.

4. H. A. R. Gibb, *Modern Trends in Islam* (Chicago: University of Chicago, 1947), p. 117.

5. Ruhollah Khomeini, *Islam and Revolution: Writings and Declarations,* trans. and ed. Hamid Algar (Berkeley, Calif.: Mizan, 1981), p. 302.

6. G. H. Jansen, *Militant Islam* (New York: Harper & Row, 1979), p. 103.

7. John Obert Voll, *Islam: Continuity and Change in the Modern World* (Boulder, Colo.: Westview, 1982), p. 151.

8. Gustave E. von Grunebaum, *Modern Islam* (New York: Vintage, 1962), p. 310.

9. Sayyed Abulala Maudoodi, *Nationalism and India,* 2d ed. (Pathankot, Pb.: Maktaba-e-Jama'at-e-Islami, 1947), p. 40.

10. William H. McNeill, *The Rise of the West* (Chicago: University of Chicago Press, 1963), p. 773.

11. These classifications derive from Voll, *Islam,* pp. 156–57; the figures come from the population estimates provided in the appendix to this book, pp. 337–39.

12. Malcolm H. Kerr, *The Arab Cold War,* 3d ed. (London: Oxford University Press, 1971), p. 1.

13. Fouad Ajami, "The End of Pan-Arabism," *Foreign Affairs,* Winter 1978–79, p. 355. The internal quotes are from Bernard Lewis, *The Middle East and the West* (New York: Harper & Row, 1964), p. 94.

14. Jansen, *Militant Islam,* p. 96.

15. Clive S. Kessler, "Islam, Society and Political Behaviour: Some Comparative Implications of the Malay Case," *British Journal of Sociology* 23 (1972): 39.

16. *Washington Post,* 2 December 1981.

17. *International Impact,* 27 October 1978; *Jeune Afrique,* 20 February 1980; *Christian Science Monitor,* 1 July 1980.

18. *New York Times,* 13 July 1982.

19. A typical example of this distinction comes from the editorial page of *Dawn Overseas,* the Karachi weekly, 23 July 1982: one editorial is entitled "Time to call a halt," referring to the war between Iraq and Iran; another is "Solidarity with Palestinians," referring to their conflict with the Israelis in Beirut.

20. Fazil Karim Khan Durrani, *The Meaning of Pakistan* (Lahore: Sh. M. Ashraf, 1944), p. xii.

21. Nantawan Haemindra, "The Problem of the Thai-Muslims in the Four Southern Provinces of Thailand," *Journal of Southeast Asian Studies* 8 (1977): 104.

22. Raphael Israeli, "The Muslim Minority in the People's Republic of China," *Asian Survey* 21 (1981): 915.

23. Martin Kramer, *Political Islam,* The Washington Papers, no. 73 (Beverly Hills: Sage, 1980), p. 33.

Chapter 8

1. This account derives from T. J. S. George, *Revolt in Mindanao: The Rise of Islam in Philippine Politics* (Kuala Lumpur, Malaysia: Oxford University Press, 1980).

2. G. H. Jansen, *Militant Islam* (New York: Harper & Row, 1979), p. 51.

3. Norman Daniel, *Islam, Europe and Empire* (Edinburgh: At the University Press, 1966), p. 482.

4. Ibid.

5. Ibid., p. 480.

6. Ibid., p. 67.

7. Ibid., pp. 482–83.

8. Norman Daniel, *Islam and the West: The Making of an Image* (Edinburgh: The University Press, 1958), p. 278.

9. Linda Blandford, *Superwealth: The Secret Lives of the Oil Sheikhs* (New York: William Morrow, 1977). For a recent fictional example of traditional Western beliefs, see Richard Grenier, *The Marrakesh One-Two* (Boston: Houghton Mifflin, 1983).

10. The following account derives largely from the extraordinary study by Fatima Mernissi, *Beyond the Veil: Male-Female Dynamics in a Modern Muslim Society* (Cambridge, Mass.: Schenkman, 1975).

11. Abu'l-Hamid al-Ghazali, *Ihya' 'Ulum ad-Din* (Cairo: al-Maktaba at-Tijariya al-Kubra, n.d.), p. 27; cited in Mernissi, *Beyond the Veil*, pp. 2–3.

12. Ibid., pp. 5, 62.

13. Ibid., p. 62.

14. Ibid., pp. 4, 11.

15. Ibid., p. 12.

16. Ibid., p. 14.

17. Ibid., p. xvi.

18. Ibid., p. 51.

19. Ibid., p. 85.

20. Ibid., p. 62.

21. Ibid., p. xvi.

22. Ibid., p. 41.

23. George Peter Murdock, *Social Structure* (New York: Macmillan, 1949), p. 273.

24. Ibid., pp. 273–74.

25. Ibid.

26. Mernissi, *Beyond the Veil*, p. 41.

27. Quoted in Mernissi, *Beyond the Veil*, p. 57; *Asiaweek*, 12 February 1982.

28. Louis Gardet, *La Cité Musulmane: vie sociale et politique* (Paris: Librarie Philosophique J. Vrin, 1954), p. 37.

29. Elie Kedourie, *Islam in the Modern World* (New York: Holt, Rinehart and Winston, 1981), p. 3.

30. Wilfred Cantwell Smith, *Islam in Modern History* (Princeton, N.J.: Princeton University Press, 1957), p. 263.

31. Ibid., p. 41.

32. *Impact International*, 14 November 1980; Donald K. Emmerson, "Islam in Modern Indonesia: Political Impasse, Cultural Opportunity," in *Change and the Muslim World*, ed. Philip H. Stoddard et al. (Syracuse, N.Y.: Syracuse University Press, 1981), p. 161.

33. Ruhollah Khomeini, *Islam and Revolution: Writings and Declarations*, trans. and ed. Hamid Algar (Berkeley, Calif.: Mizan, 1981), pp. 139, 128, 136.

34. "Constitution of the Islamic Republic of Iran," *Middle East Journal* 34 (1980): 184, 190.

35. *New York Times*, 6 January 1980.

36. Gustave E. von Grunebaum, "An Analysis of Islamic Civilization and Cultural Anthropology," in *Actes du Colloque sur la Sociologie musulmane* (Brussels: Centre pour l'Etude des Problèmes du Monde Musulman Contemporain, [1962]), p. 39.

37. Stimulated by the Muslim need to calculate shares of inheritance.

38. Ali E. Hillal Dessouki, "The Islamic Resurgence: Sources, Dynamics, and Implications," in *Islamic Resurgence in the Arab World*, ed. Ali E. Hillal Dessouki, (New York: Praeger, 1982), p. 17.

39. H. A. R. Gibb, *Modern Trends in Islam* (Chicago: University of Chicago Press, 1947), p. 100.

40. Smith, *Islam in Modern History* p. 192.

41. Ibid., pp. 111, 85.

42. Gustave E. von Grunebaum, *Islam: Essays in the Nature and Growth of a Cultural Tradition*, 2d ed. (London: Routledge & Kegan Paul, 1961), p. 186.

43. Grunebaum, "Analysis," p. 33.

44. Grunebaum, *Islam*, p. 185.

45. Gustave E. von Grunebaum, *Modern Islam* (New York: Vintage, 1962), p. 257.

46. Gibb, *Modern Trends in Islam*, p. 69.

47. Some non-Muslims raised in Islamdom have achieved international renown, including Khalil Jibran of Lebanon (a Christian) and Albert Camus of Algeria. Acclaimed Muslims living in the West include the film maker Güney, the actor Omar Sharif, the poet Zülfü Livaneli, and the scientist Farouk El-Baz. Abdus Salam, a Qadiyani Ahmadi, shared the Nobel Prize for physics in 1979.

48. Maxime Rodinson, *Islam and Capitalism,* trans. Brian Pearce, (New York: Pantheon, 1974), p. 117.

Conclusion to Part II

1. V. S. Naipaul, *Among the Believers: An Islamic Journey* (New York: Alfred A. Knopf, 1981), p. 168.

2. Ibid., p. 117.

3. R. Stephen Humphreys, "The Contemporary Islamic Resurgence in the Context of Modern Islam," in *Islamic Resurgence in the Arab World,* ed. Ali E. Hillal Dessouki, (New York: Praeger, 1982). p. 110.

4. M. Jamil Hanifi, *Islam and the Transformation of Culture* (New York: Asia Publishing House, 1974), p. 90.

5. Hamilton A. R. Gibb, *Studies on the Civilization of Islam,* ed. Stanford J. Shaw and William R. Polk (Boston: Beacon, 1962), pp. 200–201.

Chapter 9

1. *Christian Science Monitor,* 30 January 1980.

2. *Impact International,* 8 May 1981.

3. Jamil M. Abun-Nasr, "Islam und die algerische Nationalidentität," *Welt des Islam* n.s. 18 (1978): 178.

4. *El Moudjahid,* 4 November 1982.

5. For background on Bangladesh, see the sections on India and Pakistan in this chapter.

6. Cited in Joseph T. O'Connell, "Dilemmas of Secularism in Bangladesh," *Journal of Asian and African Studies* 11 (1976): 65–66.

7. *Impact International,* 22 June 1979.

8. Cited in Peter J. Bertocci, "Bangladesh: Composite Cultural Identity and Modernization in a Muslim-Majority State," in *Change and the Muslim World,* ed. Philip H. Stoddard et al. (Syracuse, N.Y.: Syracuse University Press, 1981), p. 78.

9. O'Connell, "Dilemmas of Secularism," p. 81; *New Nation* [Dhaka], 15 January 1983.

10. *Al-Ahram,* 15 May 1978.

11. *Christian Science Monitor,* 3 March 1980.

12. *New York Times,* 6 September 1981.

13. *Jeune Afrique,* 13 December 1981.

14. Harold Crouch, "Indonesia," in *The Politics of Islamic Reassertion,* ed. Mohammed Ayoob, (New York: St. Martin's, 1981), p. 205.

15. Khaidir Anwar, "Islam in Indonesia Today," *Islamic Quarterly* 23 (1979):102; Sidney R. Jones, " 'It Can't Happen Here': A Post-Khomeini Look at Indonesian Islam," *Asian Survey* 20 (1980):317.

16. *Economist,* 7 November 1981.

17. *Impact International,* 16 April 1979.

18. Donald K. Emmerson, "Islam in Modern Indonesia: Political Impasse, Cultural Opportunity," in *Change and the Muslim World,* ed. Philip H. Stoddard et al., (Syracuse, N.Y.: Syracuse University Press, 1981), p. 167.

19. Shi'is also accommodated to the existing power, by turning inward and dissimulating. In Ernest Gellner's words, they were "not so much for giving Caesar that which is his as for telling him what he wishes to hear, whilst keeping one's own counsel." *Muslim Society* (Cambridge: Cambridge University Press, 1981), p. 2.

20. Ruhollah Khomeini, *al-Hukuma al-Islamiya* (Beirut: n.p., 1970), pp. 41, 26–27.

21. Ibid., p. 46.

22. "Constitution of the Islamic Republic of Iran," *Middle East Journal* 34 (1980): 184–204.

23. M. Jamil Hanifi, *Islam and the Transformation of Culture* (New York: Asia Publishing, 1974), p. 71.

24. Claude Cahen, "The Body Politic," in *Unity and Variety in Muslim Civilization*, ed. Gustave E. von Grunebaum, (Chicago: University of Chicago Press, 1955), p. 139.

25. D. Khalid, "Der 'moderne' Islam," *Begegnung mit Türken, Begegnung mit dem Islam* eds., Hans-Jurgen Brandt and Claus-Peter Haase, (Hamburg: ebv, 1981), p. 18.

26. Hanna Batatu, "Iraq's Underground Shi'a Movements: Characteristics, Causes and Prospects," *Middle East Journal* 35 (1981): 591.

27. [Gideon Gera, in] *The Islamic Factor in Arab Politics* (Tel Aviv: Shiloah Center, 1979), p. 66.

28. Ann Elizabeth Mayer, "Islamic Law and Islamic Revival in Libya," in *Islam in the Contemporary World*, ed., Cyriac K. Pullapilly, (Notre Dame, Ind.: Cross Roads, 1980), p. 298.

29. Ibid., pp. 299–300.

30. *Jeune Afrique*, 22 November 1978; Oriana Fallaci, " 'Iranians are Our Brothers': An Interview with Col. Muammar el-Qaddafi of Libya," *New York Times Magazine*, 16 December 1979.

31. *Events*, 12 January 1979.

32. Mayer, "Islamic Law," p. 304.

33. *Events*, 12 January 1979.

34. *Majallat Rabitat al-'Alam al-Islami*, December 1980.

35. Mayer, "Islamic Law," p. 304.

36. *Le Monde*, 20 June 1978; *Chaab*, 16 January 1983.

37. *Jeune Afrique*, 26 December 1979.

38. *Financial Times*, 21 May 1979; *Al-'Alam*, 17 May 1979.

39. Jean-Claude Vatin, "Revival in the Maghreb: Islam as an Alternative Political Language," in *Islamic Resurgence in the Arab World* ed., Ali E. Hillal Dessouki, (New York: Praeger, 1982), p. 232.

40. Jean-Louis Triaud, "L'Islam et l'Etat en République du Niger (1974–1981)," in *L'Islam et l'Etat dans le monde d'aujourd'hui*, ed., Olivier Carré (Paris: Presses Universitaires de France, 1982), p. 248.

41. Aziz Ahmad, *Islamic Modernism in India and Pakistan, 1857–1964* (London: Oxford University Press, 1967), p. 243.

42. William L. Richter, "The Political Dynamics of Islamic Resurgence in Pakistan," *Asian Survey* 19 (1979): 550.

43. *Observer*, 9 December 1979.

44. *Introduction of Islamic Laws: Address to the Nation by President General Mohammad Zia-ul-Haq* (Islamabad: Ministry of Information and Broadcasting, 1979), p. 3.

45. *Dawn Overseas*, 16 November 1979.

46. Marshall G. S. Hodgson, *The Venture of Islam* (Chicago: University of Chicago Press, 1974), 3:160.

47. *New York Times*, 25 February 1980.

48. David Holden and Richard Johns, *The House of Saud* (New York: Holt, Rinehart and Winston, 1981), p. 515 (from a chapter written by James Buchan).

49. Christian Coulon, "Les marabouts Sénégalais et l'Etat," *Revue Française d'Etudes Politiques Africaines* 158 (February 1978), pp. 27–28, 29.

50. *Foreign Report*, 5 December 1979.

51. *Jeune Afrique*, 23 May 1979.

52. *Arab Report*, 18 July 1979.

53. Abbas R. Kelidar, "Religion and State in Syria," in *The Syrian Arab Republic*, ed. Anne Sinai and Allan Pollack, (New York: American Academic Association for Peace in the Middle East, 1976), p. 52.

54. *Baltimore Sun,* 24 August 1980.

55. Mark A. Tessler, "Political Change and the Islamic Revival in Tunisia," *The Maghreb Review,* 5 (1980), p. 10.

56. *Al-Majalla,* 19 September 1981.

57. Souhayr Belhassen, "Femmes tunisiennes islamistes," *L'Annuaire de l'Afrique du Nord,* 1979, p. 77.

58. *Le Monde,* 1 September 1977.

59. *Impact International,* 22 May 1981.

60. *Middle East Economic Digest,* 29 February 1980.

61. *Jeune Afrique,* 26 December 1979.

62. *Impact International,* 24 April 1981.

63. *Milliyet,* 26 November 1979. Ağca was not alone in this interpretation; *Milli Gazete,* the official publication of the NSP, saw the purpose of the visit "to set a strategy against the Muslim world." The Pope's subsequent visit to northern Nigeria prompted similar concerns. An Iranian magazine discussed these in an article entitled "The Pope's Suspicious Visit to the Islamic Countries," *Al-Wahda al-Islamiya,* June 1982, p. 47.

64. *Newsweek,* 25 May 1981.

65. Ibid., and *New York Times,* 23 May 1981.

66. Peter R. Prifti, *Socialist Albania since 1944: Domestic and Foreign Developments* (Cambridge, Mass.: MIT Press, 1978), p. 150.

67. Ibid., p. 164.

68. Robert Buijtenhuijs, "Notes sur l'évolution du Front de libération nationale du Tchad," *Revue Française d'Etudes Politiques Africaines* 138–39 (June/July 1977): 124.

69. Guy Nicolas, "Islam et 'constructions nationales' au sud du sahara," ibid., 165–66 (September/October 1979): 98.

70. *Wall Street Journal,* 18 June 1982.

71. I suggest one alternative in "Lebanon: The Real Problem," *Foreign Policy,* no. 51 (Summer 1983), pp. 139–591.

72. Cited in Mohamad Abu Bakar, "Islamic Revivalism and the Political Process in Malaysia," *Asian Survey* 21 (1981): 1051.

73. *Far Eastern Economic Review,* 24 March 1978.

74. *Asiaweek,* 1 August 1980.

75. *Far Eastern Economic Review,* 29 September 1978; *Asiaweek,* 1 August 1980.

76. Abu Bakar, "Islamic Revivalism," pp. 1050, 1052–53, 1055.

77. *Africa,* October 1979.

78. John Voll, "Islam: Its Future in the Sudan," *Muslim World,* 63 (1973): 294–95.

79. *Impact International,* 11 January 1980.

80. Donald E. MacInnis, *Religious Policy and Practice in Communist China: A Documentary History* (New York: Macmillan, 1972), p. 292.

81. Wilfred Cantwell Smith, *Islam in Modern History* (Princeton, N.J.: Princeton University Press, 1957), pp. 286, 288. Italics in the original.

82. *India Today,* 1 September 1980.

83. *India Today,* 1 September 1981.

84. *India Today,* 15 October 1981.

85. *Caravan,* April 1981, p. 22.

86. *Southeast Asia Record,* 31 January 1980; *Asia Record,* May 1980, p. 9.

87. *Impact International,* 23 November 1979.

88. *Far Eastern Economic Review,* 22 January 1982.

89. Alexandre Bennigsen, "Muslim Conservative Opposition to the Soviet Regime: The Sufi Brotherhoods in the North Caucasus," in *Soviet Nationality Policies and Practices,* ed. Jeremy R. Azrael (New York: Praeger, 1978), p. 341.

90. Alexandre Bennigsen and Chantal Lemercier-Quelquejay, "Muslim Religious Conservatism and Dissent in the USSR," *Religion in Communist Lands* 6 (1978): 158.

91. Bennigsen, "Muslim Conservative Opposition," pp. 342, 344, 345.

92. Geoffrey Wheeler, "Islam and the Soviet Union," *Asian Affairs* 10 (1979): 250.

93. Alexandre Bennigsen, quoted in the *Christian Science Monitor*, 25 June 1980.

94. Alexandre K. Bennigsen, "Islam in the Soviet Union," in *Change and the Muslim World*, ed. Philip H. Stoddard et al. (Syracuse, N.Y.: Syracuse University Press, 1981), p. 124.

95. *Far Eastern Economic Review*, 5 June 1980.

96. *Dawn Overseas*, 27 August 1982.

97. Astri Suhrke, "The Thai Muslims: Some Aspects of Minority Integration," *Pacific Affairs* 43 (1970): 537.

98. *Impact International*, 28 April 1978; *Far Eastern Economic Review*, 20 June 1980.

99. Colin Legum, ed., *Africa Contemporary Record, 1977–78* (New York: Africana, 1979), p. B442.

100. Jon Kraus, "Islamic Affinities and International Politics in Sub-Saharan Africa," *Current History* 78, no. 456 (April 1980): 158.

101. *Impact International*, 24 October 1980.

102. Ibid.

103. *New York Times*, 8 February 1981.

104. Most of my information comes from Zafar Ishaq Ansari, "Aspects of Black Muslim Theology," *Studia Islamica* 53 (1981): 137–76.

105. *New York Times*, 17 June 1975.

106. *Foreign Report*, 17 October 1979.

107. *Borba*, 26 November 1979.

108. *Politika*, 12 and 17 April 1983.

109. Pedro Ramet, "Problems of Albanian Nationalism in Yugoslavia," *Orbis* 25 (1981): 371.

110. *Le Nouvel Observateur*, 12 March 1979, p. 56.

111. Voll, "Islam: Its Future in the Sudan," p. 290.

Chapter 10

1. Thomas W. Lippman, *Islam: Politics and Religion in the Muslim World* (New York: Foreign Policy Association, 1982), pp. 11–12.

2. Ali A. Mazrui, "Changing the Guards from Hindus to Muslims: Collective Third World Security in a Cultural Perspective," *International Affairs* 57 (1980–81): 12.

3. V. S. Naipaul, *Among the Believers: An Islamic Journey* (New York: Alfred A. Knopf, 1981), p. 23.

4. R. Hrair Dekmejian, "The Anatomy of Islamic Revival: Legitimacy Crisis, Ethnic Conflict, and the Search for Islamic Alternatives," in *Religion and Politics in the Middle East*, ed. Michael Curtis, (Boulder, Colo.: Westview, 1981), p. 39.

5. Hamid Enayat, "The Resurgence of Islam: The Background," *History Today*, February 1980, pp. 18–19.

6. *The Middle East and North Africa, 1979–80*, 26th ed. (London: Europa, 1979), p. 166.

7. Yvonne Haddad, "The Arab-Israeli Wars, Nasserism, and the Affirmation of Islamic Identity," in *Islam and Development: Religion and Sociopolitical Change*, ed. John L. Esposito (Syracuse, N.Y.: Syracuse University Press, 1980), p. 120.

8. Fadwa El Guindi, "Religious Revival and Islamic Survival in Egypt," *International Insight*, May/June 1980, pp. 7–8.

9. Martin Kramer, *Political Islam*, The Washington Papers, no. 73 (Beverly Hills: Sage, 1980), p. 18.

10. Raphael Israeli, "The New Wave of Islam," *International Journal* 34 (1979): 370.

11. William H. McNeill, *The Rise of the West* (Chicago: University of Chicago Press, 1963), p. 566.

12. OPEC is not listed among the factors leading to the oil market's turnabout for it had almost no role in this. OPEC did, however, lead to oil prices going higher than they would have in a free market.

13. Steven Emerson, "The Petrodollar Connection, I," *The New Republic,* 17 February 1982, p. 25.

14. On this, see my "Politics of Muslim Anti-Semitism," *Commentary,* August 1981, pp. 39–45.

15. John B. Kelly, *Arabia, the Gulf and the West* (New York: Basic Books, 1980), p. 261.

16. Ibid. p. 423. It is inaccurate, however, to refer to a racial component in this relationship.

17. Ibid. p. 379.

18. *Newsweek,* 21 April 1980.

19. *8 Days,* 31 May 1980.

20. *New York Times,* 24 April 1980.

21. *New York Times,* 8 May 1980.

22. *International Impact,* 11 January 1980.

23. *Asiaweek,* 26 December 1980.

24. *Economist,* 22 April 1980.

25. Haddad, "The Arab-Israeli Wars," p. 107.

26. Nehemia Levtzion, *International Islamic Solidarity and its Limitations,* Jerusalem Papers on Peace Problems, no. 29 (Jerusalem: Magnes, 1979), p. 50.

27. Naipaul, *Among the Believers,* p. 374.

28. Levtzion, *International Islamic Solidarity,* p. 41; Lilian Craig Harris, "China's Islamic Connection," *Asian Affairs* 8 (1980–81): 299–300.

29. Udo Steinbach, "Saudi Arabiens neue Rolle im Nahen Osten," *Aussenpolitik* 25 (1974): 210. One analyst agrees on the importance of oil wealth for the Islamic revival but for exactly opposite reasons from mine. M. Ali Fekrat points to a pattern of "pervasive underdevelopment side by side with extreme and highly concentrated wealth" which resulted from the oil boom. Such a disparity between rich and poor is, in his view, "diametrically opposed to the fundamental precepts of Islam," and thus leads to a "widening gap between the Islamic socioeconomic ideals on the one hand and the actual state of economic affairs on the other." This causes the umma to find itself "on the threshold of a new but stress-filled area." M. Ali Fekrat, "Stress in the Islamic World," *Journal of South Asian and Middle Eastern Studies* 4 (1981): 7.

Those are two problems with Fekrat's argument. First, Islam does not prescribe a proper way to distribute wealth and there is nothing wrong with riches so long as a small proportion of it is given away—which the sheikhdoms do. Second, he argues that non-implementation of Shar'i precepts spurs Muslims to action, whereas the record shows just the opposite; on its own, non-implementation causes Muslims to withdraw from public life. It was Muslim optimism about God's favor and the feasibility of living up to Shar'i standards that stimulated Islamic political activism in the 1970s. Fekrat's misconceptions—that Islam entails an ideology and that Muslims once lived by the Shari'a—are depressingly typical.

30. *Jeune Afrique,* 11 February 1981.

31. Bruce Borthwick, *Christian Science Monitor,* 25 September 1981; *Frankfurt Allgemeine Zeitung,* 29 November 1982.

32. Hamadi Essid, *Le Monde,* 20 March 1979.

33. Mu'ammar al-Qadhdhafi, *Thus Spoke Colonel Moammar Kazzafi* (Beirut: Dar-al-Adwa, 1974), p. 12; cited in Lisa S. Anderson, "Religion and Politics in Libya," *Journal of Arab Affairs* 1 (1981): 71.

34. On this, see Sami G. Hajjar, "The Jamahiriya Experiment in Libya: Qadhafi and Rousseau," *Journal of Modern African Studies* 18 (1980): 181–200.

35. *Jeune Afrique,* 28 March 1979.

36. *Asiaweek,* October 1980.

37. Levtzion, *International Islamic Solidarity,* p. 27.

38. *Jeune Afrique,* 20 September 1978.

39. *Fortune,* 31 July 1978.

40. J. Law, *Arab Aid: Who Gets It, For What, and How* (New York: Chase Manhattan Bank, 1978), Appendix 4; *Middle East Economic Digest,* 24 September 1976; *Al-Ba'th,* 8 January 1978, cited in Adeed I. Dawisha, "Internal Values and External Threats: the Making of Saudi Foreign Policy," *Orbis* 23 (1979): 139.

41. Henry Kissinger, *Years of Upheaval* (Boston: Little, Brown, 1982), pp. 658–59.

42. Martin S. Kramer, *An Introduction to World Islamic Conferences* (Tel Aviv: Shiloah Center, 1978), p. 25.

43. Ibid., p. 24.

44. D. Khalid, "Der 'moderne' Islam," in *Begegnung mit Türken, Begegnung mit dem Islam,* ed. Hans-Jürgen Brandt and Claus-Peter Haase, (Hamburg: ebv, 1981), p. 23.

45. D. H. Khalid, "Das Phänomen der Re-Islamisierung," *Aussenpolitik* 29 (1978), p. 446.

46. Haddad, "The Arab-Israeli Wars," p. 107.

47. *Die Katholische Missionen,* November/December 1977.

48. *Washington Post,* 16 August 1980.

49. *Jeune Afrique,* March 1981.

50. *Jeune Afrique,* 9 September 1981.

51. *Jeune Afrique,* March 1981.

52. *New York Times,* 6 January 1980.

53. *Christian Science Monitor,* 31 January 1980.

54. *New York Times,* 26 January 1982.

55. Khalid, "Re-Islamisierung," p. 441.

56. *Afrique-Asie,* 15 March 1979.

57. John Waterbury, "Egypt: Islam and Social Change," in *Change and the Muslim World,* ed. Philip H. Stoddard et al. (Syracuse, N.Y.: Syracuse University Press, 1981), p. 56.

58. John Alden Williams, "Veiling in Egypt as a Political and Social Phenomenon," in *Islam and Development,* ed. John L. Esposito, (Syracuse, N.Y.: Syracuse University Press, 1980), p. 81.

59. Ibid., p. 80.

60. Zehra Önder, *Saudi-Arabien: Zwischen islamischer Ideologie und westlicher Ökonomie* (Stuttgart: Klett-Cotta, 1980), p. 216.

61. *Jeune Afrique,* 16 December 1981.

62. *Far Eastern Economic Review,* 22 September 1978.

63. Michael C. Hudson, *Arab Politics: The Search for Legitimacy* (New Haven, Conn.: Yale University Press, 1977), p. 51.

64. *New York Times,* 29 October 1980.

65. *Majallat Rabitat al-'Alam al-Islami,* December 1980.

66. *Le Monde,* 20 June 1978; *Majallat Rabitat al-'Alam al-Islami,* October/November 1978.

67. John L. Esposito, "Pakistan: Quest for Islamic Identity," in *Islam and Development,* ed. John L. Esposito, (Syracuse, N.Y.: Syracuse University Press, 1980), p. 151.

68. Önder, *Saudi-Arabien,* p. 219.

69. *Los Angeles Times,* 26 December 1978.

70. Kramer, *Political Islam,* pp. 27–28.

71. *Newsweek,* 24 December 1979.

72. *Wall Street Journal,* 24 August 1981.

73. Önder, *Saudi-Arabien,* p. 214.

74. D. H. Khalid, *Die politische Rolle des Islam im Vorderen Orient: Einführung und Dokumentation,* 2d ed. enlarged (Hamburg: Deutsches Orient-Institut, 1979), p. 97.

75. *New York Times,* 28 December 1981.

76. *Far Eastern Economic Review,* 24 February 1978; quoted from a letter to the editor.

77. *Impact International,* 9 January 1981.

78. Fred R. von der Mehden, "Islamic Resurgence in Malaysia," in *Islam and Development,* ed. John L. Esposito, (Syracuse, N.Y.: Syracuse University Press, 1980), p. 168.

79. *Middle East Contemporary Survey* 1 (1976–77), pp. 587, 597.

80. *Christian Science Monitor,* 31 December 1981.

81. *Impact International,* 14 December 1979.

82. Raphael Israeli, "The Muslim Minority in the People's Republic of China," *Asian Survey* 21 (1981): 918.

83. *India Today,* 1 September 1980; *Caravan,* April 1981.

84. *Impact International,* 12 September 1980.

85. *Majallat Rabitat al-'Alam al-Islami,* November 1980; *Onlooker,* 16 June 1979.

86. *8 Days,* 16 August 1980; *Caravan,* April 1981.

87. *India Today,* 16 July 1981; *New York Times,* 1 August 1982; *Far Eastern Economic Review,* 29 October 1982; *Times of India,* 17 January 1983.

88. Peter G. Gowing, "Muslim Filipinos Between Integration and Secession," *South East Asia Journal of Theology* 14 (1973): 71.

89. *Far Eastern Economic Review,* 25 November 1977.

90. Alexandre Popovic, "Islam et l'Etat dans les pays du Sud-Est européen," in *Islam et l'Etat dans le monde aujourd'hui,* ed. Olivier Carré, (Paris: Presses Universitaires de France, 1982), pp. 125–26.

91. *Arab Report,* 20 June 1979.

92. *Far Eastern Economic Review,* 20 June 1980.

93. *Jeune Afrique,* 11 April 1979.

94. Levtzion, *International Islamic Solidarity,* pp. 36–37.

95. *Jeune Afrique,* 11 February 1981.

96. *Jeune Afrique,* 22 October 1980.

97. Naipaul, *Among the Believers,* pp. 358–59.

98. *New York Times,* 29 April 1982.

99. *Impact International,* 13 February 1981.

100. Nothing of note occurred in 529 B.C. Also, after long periods of domination from outside Iran (for example, under Alexander the Great and his successors, as well as under the Arabians and the Mongols), the modern monarchy was established less than five hundred years ago, in 1501.

101. Kramer, *Political Islam,* p. 20.

102. *Afrique-Asie,* 15 March 1979.

103. *The Middle East,* October 1979.

104. Mehden, "Islamic Resurgence in Malaysia," p. 170.

105. *Jeune Afrique,* 16 July 1980; *Asia Record,* May 1980; *Asiaweek,* 30 January 1981.

106. *Jeune Afrique,* 11 June 1980.

107. *New York Times,* 20 October 1981.

108. Rémy Lèveau, "Réaction de l'Islam officiel au renouveau islamique au Maroc," *L'Annuaire de l'Afrique du Nord,* 1979, pp. 210–11.

109. Mark A. Tessler, "Political Change and the Islamic Revival in Tunisia," *The Maghreb Review* 5 (1980): 13.

110. Mehden, "Islamic Resurgence in Malaysia," p. 170.

111. *Far Eastern Economic Review,* 25 November 1979.

112. *New York Times,* 29 April 1982.

113. *Christian Science Monitor,* 25 August 1980.

114. Raphael Israeli, "Muslim Minorities under Non-Islamic Rule," *Current History* 78, no. 456, (April 1980): 162.

115. Ibid., p. 163.

116. *Christian Science Monitor,* 16 January 1980.

117. Shalom Cohen, "Khomeinism in Gaza," *New Outlook,* March 1980, p. 8; *New York Times,* 21 January 1980.

118. *Christian Science Monitor,* 28 December 1979; *Tanjug,* 8 April 1983.

119. *Sudanow,* February 1980, p. 13.

120. *Washington Post,* 10 September 1981; *Ad-Dustur,* 10 January 1983.

121. "Constitution of the Islamic Republic of Iran," *Middle East Journal* 34 (1980): 185.

122. *Washington Post,* 31 March 1982.

123. *New York Times,* 5 February 1980.

124. Mumtaz Ahmad, "Islamic Revival in Pakistan," in *Islam in the Contemporary World,* ed. Cyriac K. Pullapilly, (Notre Dame, Ind.: Cross Roads, 1980), p. 268.

125. Some authors strongly dispute the idea that oil had anything to do with the Islamic revival. Jean-Francois Clément writes: "Let us ignore the thesis that the revival is due to a plot in which the maestro is supposed to be the owner of petrodollars, yesterday the leaders of Saudi Arabia and Libya, today [1980] those of Irán." ("Pour une compréhension des mouvements islamistes," *Esprit,* January 1980, p. 46.) Ernest Gellner believes "it would be quite wrong to explain" the recent success of fundamentalism "in terms of whatever oil-financed subsidy it may receive." (*Muslim Society* [Cambridge: Cambridge University Press, 1981], p. 67.) Oil may not be the key to the revival, but neither Clément nor Gellner offers a satisfactory alternative.

Conclusion to Part III

1. On the sheikhdoms' prospects, see my article, "The Curse of Oil Wealth," *The Atlantic Monthly,* July 1982, pp. 19–25.

2. *New York Times,* 10 April 1980.

3. *Time,* 18 July 1977; *Christian Science Monitor,* 1 October 1981. P.L.O. dependence on the Arab states is the topic of my article, "How Important is the PLO?" *Commentary,* April 1983, pp. 17–25.

4. Wilfred Cantwell Smith, *On Understanding Islam* (The Hague: Mouton, 1981), p. 159.

5. John Obert Voll, *Islam: Continuity and Change in the Modern World* (Boulder, Colo.: Westview, 1982), p. 347.

Index